CHRISTIAN MORAL THEOLOGY IN THE EMERGING TECHNOCULTURE

We are living in an emerging technoculture. Machines and gadgets not only weave the fabric of daily life, but more importantly embody philosophical and religious values which shape the contemporary moral vision—a vision that is often at odds with Christian convictions.

This book critically examines those values, and offers a framework for how Christian moral theology should be formed and lived-out within the emerging technoculture. Brent Waters argues that technology represents the principal cultural background against which contemporary Christian moral life is formed. Addressing contemporary ethical and religious issues, this book will be of particular interest to students and scholars exploring the ideas of Heidegger, Nietzsche, Grant, Arendt, and Borgmann.

Ashgate Science and Religion Series

Series Editors:

Roger Trigg, *Emeritus Professor, University of Warwick, and Academic Director of the Centre for the Study of Religion in Public Life, Kellogg College, Oxford*

J. Wentzel van Huyssteen, *Princeton Theological Seminary, USA*

Science and religion have often been thought to be at loggerheads but much contemporary work in this flourishing interdisciplinary field suggests this is far from the case. The *Ashgate Science and Religion Series* presents exciting new work to advance interdisciplinary study, research and debate across key themes in science and religion, exploring the philosophical relations between the physical and social sciences on the one hand and religious belief on the other. Contemporary issues in philosophy and theology are debated, as are prevailing cultural assumptions arising from the 'post-modernist' distaste for many forms of reasoning. The series enables leading international authors from a range of different disciplinary perspectives to apply the insights of the various sciences, theology and philosophy and look at the relations between the different disciplines and the rational connections that can be made between them. These accessible, stimulating new contributions to key topics across science and religion will appeal particularly to individual academics and researchers, graduates, postgraduates and upper-undergraduate students.

Other titles in the series:

God and the Scientist
Exploring the Work of John Polkinghorne
Edited by Fraser Watts and Christopher C. Knight
978-1-4094-4569-2 (hbk)

Cyborg Selves
A Theological Anthropology of the Posthuman
Jeanine Thweatt-Bates
978-1-4094-2141-2 (hbk)

The Cognitive Science of Religion
James A. Van Slyke
978-1-4094-2123-8 (hbk)

Christian Moral Theology in the Emerging Technoculture
From Posthuman Back to Human

BRENT WATERS
Garrett-Evangelical Theological Seminary, USA

LONDON AND NEW YORK

Frist published 2014 by Ashgate Publishing

Published 2016 by Taylor & Francis
2 Park Square, Milton Park, Abingdon, Oxon OX14 4RN
711 Third Avenue, New York, NY 10017, USA

Routledge is an imprint of the Taylor & Francis Group, an informa business

Copyright © 2014 Brent Waters.

Brent Waters has asserted his right under the Copyright, Designs and Patents Act, 1988, to be identified as the author of this work.

All rights reserved. No part of this book may be reprinted or reproduced or utilised in any form or by any electronic, mechanical, or other means, now known or hereafter invented, including photocopying and recording, or in any information storage or retri eval system, without permission in writing from the publishers.

Notice:
Product or corporate names may be trademarks or registered trademarks, and are used only for identification and explanation without intent to infringe.

British Library Cataloguing in Publication Data
A catalogue record for this book is available from the British Library.

The Library of Congress has cataloged the printed edition as follows:
Waters, Brent.
  Christian moral theology in the emerging technoculture : from posthuman back to human / by Brent Waters.
      pages cm.—(Ashgate science and religion series)
  Includes bibliographical references and index.
  ISBN 978-0-7546-6691-2 (hardcover) 1. Christian ethics. 2. Theological anthropology—Christianity. 3. Technology—Religious aspects—Christianity. I. Title.
  BJ1241.W38 2014
  241—dc23
                                                                                            2013020871

ISBN 9780754666912 (hbk)

To David Hogue and Stephen Ray

Contents

Acknowledgments		ix
Introduction		1
Part I	**Philosophical Description and Critique**	
1	The Philosophical Background of the Emerging Technoculture	7
2	George Grant: Illuminating the Darkness as Darkness	35
3	Hannah Arendt: Mortality and Natality	57
4	Albert Borgmann: Devices and Desires	81
Part II	**Theological Construction**	
	Philosophical Critique and Theological Construction	105
5	Confession: Admitting the Darkness as Darkness	109
6	Repentance: The Renewing Possibilities of Second Births	131
7	Amendment of Life: Desiring the Good	159
Part III	**Moral Engagement**	
	Theological Construction and Moral Engagement	187
8	The Translucent Self In an Age of Transparency: Parasitic Self-Fulfillment	191
9	Creation into Nothing: Nihilistic Power	207
10	Dissembling the Other: Consuming Predation	227
Bibliography		245
Index		253

Acknowledgments

Writing incurs debts, and I cannot fully acknowledge, much less repay, all my debtors. At Garrett-Evangelical I am blessed with students who patiently endure my attempts at teaching. I am also blessed with colleagues who, most of the time, tolerate my eccentricities with grace and good humor. I am particularly grateful for President Philip Amerson's and Dean Lallene Rector's keen abilities to structure the odious chores of faculty governance in ways that allow time for reading, thinking, and writing. Ron Anderson, Timothy Gaines, David Ahn, William Novak, and Bernard Wong have read parts or the entire manuscript, and I very much appreciate their helpful comments and criticisms. As will be apparent in the following pages, I remain indebted to Oliver O'Donovan for some key theological concepts employed throughout the book, and for Joan O'Donovan's guidance in trying to come to some understanding of George Grant. Once again, Sarah Lloyd and her colleagues at Ashgate were a pleasure to work with, and I am especially thankful for their patience in awaiting my delivery of a long overdue manuscript. As always, my wife, Diana, and daughter, Erin, were constant sources of strength and support. They also serve as checks against my false and pretentious disordering of priorities, reminding me that love and the mundane sharing of daily life is of far greater significance than anything I might read, think, or write. Finally, this book is dedicated to David Hogue and Stephen Ray. They are trusted faculty colleagues who have helped me think through many ideas and steered me away from some bad ones. They are also trustworthy friends who never fail to fill my day with joy and good-hearted laughter. And I give God thanks and praise that they exemplify the pursuit of three key practices enabling friendship: namely, good conversation, fine dining, and savoring excellent single-malt whisky.

Introduction

There is a growing body of literature that greets the prospect of a posthuman future with either anticipation[1] or apprehension.[2] With advances in computer science, nanotechnology, neuroscience, and biotechnology, optimists foresee a golden age of individuals enjoying greatly extended longevity along with enhanced physical and cognitive capabilities, while pessimists worry that human dignity will be lost as the world slides into a new dark age of technology run amok. The tone of the authors in each of the respective camps runs from strident to subdued: will a posthuman future prove heavenly or hellish, utopian or dystopian, neither or both?

I place myself in the company of the latter group. As part of the Ashgate Science and Religion series, I wrote *From Human to Posthuman* in which I argued that posthuman discourse is driven by largely inarticulate religious beliefs regarding human nature and destiny, and that a counter-theological discourse is needed to expose it as a false and dangerous collection of beliefs.[3] Although I continue to assert the veracity of this thesis, I made two crucial mistakes regarding its development and exposition. First, I granted posthuman discourse a futuristic, rather than descriptive, orientation, and this emphasis serves to occlude the principal issues at stake, for attention becomes fixated on speculative technological development. Posthuman discourse, however, is predominantly a hyperbolic description and apology of our present circumstances. Portraying a titillating and tantalizing future is to add a rhetorical flourish to what we have already become, albeit to a much less exciting degree. This fixation on a glamorous future serves to misdirect attention away from the demanding and crucial task of critically examining the moral formation and pattern of daily, mundane life, which is precisely where technology, for both good and ill, works its greatest formative influence. Consequently, a more sustained critique of this influence is needed—one stripped of utopian dreams. In

---

[1] See, e.g., James Hughes, *Citizen Cyborg: Why Democratic Societies Must Respond to the Redesigned Human of the Future* (Cambridge, MA: Westview, 2004); and Julian Savulescu and Nick Bostrom, eds., *Human Enhancement* (Oxford and New York: Oxford University Press, 2009).

[2] See, e.g., Francis Fukuyama, *Our Posthuman Future: Consequences of the Biotechnology Revolution* (New York: Farrar, Straus and Giroux, 2002); and Leon R. Kass, *Life, Liberty and the Defense of Dignity: The Challenge for Bioethics* (San Francisco, CA: Encounter Books, 2002).

[3] See Brent Waters, *From Human to Posthuman: Christian Theology and Technology in a Postmodern World* (Aldershot, UK, and Burlington, VT: Ashgate, 2006).

this respect, critics of posthumanism who remain fixated on dystopian nightmares also do little good in redirecting attention toward the ordinary and contemporary.

Second, although I argued that a counter-theological account is needed to expose the latent and false religious beliefs underlying posthuman discourse, I devoted insufficient attention to ascribing the shape and content of the moral life this account might inspire.[4] In short, I did not offer a constructive proposal for what difference Christian theological discourse might make in respect to moral formation and practice. Yet, if technology's greatest influence takes place in shaping the mundane patterns of daily life, this is a serious shortcoming that needs to be corrected. Criticism alone cannot sufficiently address technology's formative (and malformative) role in shaping the patterns of late modern life unless such criticism is accompanied by constructive engagement.

In this book I try to correct these two mistakes.[5] Part I redirects attention away from futuristic proposals and technological feasibility, and toward the patterns of daily life. This reorientation is achieved through a critical description of late modern culture or, better, the emerging technoculture. Chapter 1 initiates this task by examining selected themes in the works of Friedrich Nietzsche and Martin Heidegger, arguably the most prescient philosophical interpreters of late modernity and its emerging technoculture. Both have been appropriated by the more vociferous advocates and critics of a posthuman future. For instance, Nietzsche's emphasis on the will to power and his portrayal of the *Übermensch* (Overman) and Heidegger's account of technology as modernity's ontology have been used to justify the prospect of transforming humans into a superior species. Critics, however, have seized upon Nietzsche's last men and nihilists, and Heidegger's despair of late modernity's technological enframement, to expose the inevitable evil consequences of posthuman proposals. Yet many proponents and critics often fail to note the sense of loss and lament that accompany Nietzsche's and Heidegger's bold declarations. This failure helps to account, in part, for some of the more extravagant proposals that are made regarding a posthuman future, as well as for its most anxious criticisms. In order to restore this balance between loss and promise, much of the chapter is devoted to examining selected themes in Heidegger's lectures on Nietzsche.

The following chapters assess these themes by surveying selected arguments in the works of George Grant, Hannah Arendt, and Albert Borgmann. These philosophers were chosen because each has, either explicitly or implicitly, engaged with these themes in a sustained, critical, and constructive manner. In each instance a principal criticism and constructive proposal is identified and examined. Grant laments late modernity's loss of reverence which he blames on a

---

[4] I am indebted to Alan Jiggins for bringing this insufficiency to my attention in his review of my book *From Human to Posthuman*. See Allan Jiggins, "Book Review: From Human to Posthuman," *Science and Christian Belief*, 19/2, p. 208.

[5] I do not assume that the reader has read *From Human to Posthuman*, but if you have not, it would make my publisher happy if you would purchase a copy.

prevalent historicism that promotes nihilistic mastery of nature and human nature. In reaction, he proposes a recovery of the philosophical and religious languages of ancient Athens and Jerusalem in order to illumine the present darkness *as* darkness. Arendt argues that the crucial work of political construction is impoverished because of the late modern fixation on mortality that is reflected in relentless technological mastery. She proposes natality—the possibility of renewal—as an alternative metaphor in ordering the construction of institutions and structures that enable a "second birth" into the political realm of equality, cooperation, and forgiveness. Borgmann decries the loss of sociality and civility endemic to the late modern world and identifies the "device paradigm" and its distorting influence on the fabric of daily living as the primary culprit. In reaction, he proposes the reform of technology through a series of focal things and practices that reorients human values and thereby the development and use of various technologies.

Part II expands the criticisms and proposals examined in Part I in developing an alternative moral discourse drawn from selected theological and doctrinal themes. In response to Grant's indictment of late modernity's historicism and nihilism, Chapter 5 offers an account of *confession*: the present darkness must first be confessed before any fitting engagement with the emerging technoculture can be undertaken. Confession therefore entails both judgment upon present cultural circumstances and receptiveness to divine grace to illumine them. Consequently, *Christology* is the primary doctrinal theme developed.

In response to Arendt's argument regarding the impoverishment of late modern political construction, Chapter 6 provides an account of *repentance*: the shift away from mortality to natality requires a second birth, yet not into the *polis* but into the body of Christ. It is within and through the work of the church that the social structures for equality, cooperation, and forgiveness find their formative metaphor in the natality of the Incarnation. Consequently, *ecclesiology* is the principal theological theme developed.

In response to Borgmann's charge of late modernity's loss of sociality and civility, Chapter 7 offers an account of *amendment of life*: following confession and repentance, individuals and communities may change their lives in ways that counter the distorting influence of the device paradigm. Building upon Borgmann's notion of focal things and practices, Christians may form their lives in remembrance of, and obedience to, Jesus Christ. Sabbath and the sacraments, as focal things and practices, provide a model for such a formation that is characterized as remembrance and expectation. Consequently, *eschatology* is the primary doctrinal theme developed.

Part III applies the philosophical and theological themes developed previously to engage with the emerging technoculture in both a critical and constructive manner. I argue that the nomadic inhabitants of the emerging technoculture privilege the notions of *space, information,* and *exchange* in order to fully implement their autonomy and mobility. Although each of these notions is necessary, they are not sufficient to pursue and sustain a good life. In response, I contend that the contrasting priorities of *place, narration,* and *communication* need to be maintained in ordering human life toward its good. These contrasts are drawn out by examining the focal practices of *baptism*, *Eucharist*, and *Sabbath*, and their corresponding virtues of *faith*, *hope*, and *love*. The basic contours of the engagement that these practices and virtues inspire are sketched out in the three chapters focusing, respectively, on the individual, political, and economic spheres of life. In each instance I argue that individuals require physical space as opposed to space; that politics requires narration ordered to speech and not merely information-serving exercises in coercive power; and, finally, that human flourishing cannot be sustained by exchange alone but should serve the greater purpose of enabling human associations to communicate the goods of creation. Consequently, the emerging technoculture should be reoriented away from its nomadic life in favor of what Christians characterize as pilgrimage.

This book is not an anti-technology manifesto or a plea to return to a simpler time. I am not Luddite, and I have no quarrel with the many machines and gadgets that I encounter daily. Rather, my concern is what technology often hides: namely, what its development and use discloses about the culture in which it originates and in turn reinforces. I find that culture both alluring and troubling, and the following pages mark my attempt to clarify, critique, and engage with their sources. In the process I also hope to clarify the good that humans should be pursuing and assess the extent to which the emerging technoculture assists or hinders that pursuit.

PART I
Philosophical Description and Critique

Chapter 1
The Philosophical Background of the Emerging Technoculture

To say that we live in an emerging technoculture is to state the obvious. The late modern world is dominated and shaped by ubiquitous gadgets and artifacts of human design and ingenuity. It is a world of sprawling cities, elaborate transportation infrastructures, instantaneous communication and information networks, and global markets. Many of the earth's inhabitants now live, and move, and have their being within artifices that have become their "natural" habitat. Late moderns are most at home in environments of their own making. Consequently, they construct, deconstruct, and reconstruct themselves in order to take full advantage of a world they are creating in an image of what they will it and themselves to be and to become. This is to refer not merely to the constant fabrication of so-called unique lifestyles, but to advances in medicine, biotechnology, and bionics that have extended longevity and enhanced physical and cognitive capabilities. Late moderns literally embody the project of collapsing the natural and artificial into a singular act of will enacted pre-eminently through technological development and mastery. Moreover, this emerging technoculture is inescapable. Even those who do not benefit directly from the mobility, material goods, and healthcare it offers are nonetheless affected by global markets; the livelihood of nomadic herders in Mongolia, for instance, depends on consumers of cashmere in Paris and Los Angeles.[1]

To speak meaningfully of an emerging technoculture, however, requires critical inquiry into what is being designated by the neologism. What is being referred to in a word joining technology (*techne*) and culture (*ethos*)? To say that we are living in a global culture that is being shaped by technology is true, but it is a partial, and thereby misleading, truth. The truism implies that technological development is somehow prior to, and independent of, the culture that forms the interests of the developers and consumers. New technologies magically appear, reflecting the popular notion that their development is a novel creation preceding and precipitating cultural change; people must adapt their daily lives in response to the newest product. The personal computer, for example, has forced people to adjust their work and leisure in order to create, store, and access information.

Asserting technological priority is misleading, for it grants an unwarranted autonomy to a so-called technological system. Various technologies are developed within a self-contained structure that is somehow outside or unaffected by the

---

[1] See Gordon Fairclough, "The Global Downturn Lands with a Zud on Mongolia's Nomads," *Wall Street Journal*, April 20, 2009, p. A1.

culture in which they are introduced and used. Technological development is incessant, inevitable, and irresistible, and is not subject to any moral controls, for it is driven by its own inherent rationality. Technology creates the values of late moderns and not vice versa. Social and political ordering is thereby reduced to an organizational task of simultaneously promoting technological development and fashioning receptive consumers who come to expect continuous innovation. The masses did not need the personal computer; it was a novelty foisted upon them, and they have been forced to adopt appropriate values regarding this new necessity to manage information.

Yet the prominence of technology as a formative force betrays the veracity of the preceding portrayal. If a particular technology was ever genuinely novel, it would never be widely adopted. It is not so much the case that technology creates new values as that it satisfies prior desires in often unanticipated ways. The development of a new technology is emblematic of a reformulation of values that have already occurred. Once the introduction of a technology is widely accepted, a new round of value reformulation is initiated in response to unanticipated applications that are opened with its use. The computer fulfilled a desire for a more efficient means of creating, storing, and accessing information, and the subsequent development of personal computers and the Internet, especially in conjunction with mobile telephony, embodied the values of the speed and ubiquity of transmitting information. Had there not been an initial need or desire for readily available data, it is doubtful whether the information technologies that are now taken for granted would have gained widespread acceptance.

This does not imply, however, that technology is a dutiful servant. The perception of technology as a collection of neutral instruments subject to absolute human control is equally misleading. Proponents of this view reassure consumers that various technologies are simply tools that individuals may use in whatever ways they choose. Any problems associated with a particular technology, or any lifestyle changes resulting from its use, is the consequence of the independent values and choices of the users. To paraphrase George Grant, technology does not impose on its users the ways in which it should be used.[2] The fact that a computer can be used by a doctor to make a more accurate diagnosis or that it can be used by a thief to steal identities does not make it an inherently good or evil instrument.

Yet technology does impose the ways it should be used on its users; otherwise, it could not be used at all. Using a technology requires users to adjust their actions and lives accordingly. This is especially the case in respect to time and place. To use the Internet, for instance, one must be in a particular place where it can be accessed at a particular time. Moreover, the use of a technology prompts changes in what the user values. An individual may prefer to peruse bloggers rather than read a newspaper. Moreover, using a computer requires that information must be created, stored, and accessed in prescribed ways. Although an email resembles a

---

[2] See George Grant, *Technology and Justice* (Notre Dame, IN: University of Notre Dame Press 1986), pp. 28–29.

letter, the two are not identical. Admittedly, most technologies are subject to the control of their users, which in turn enables those users to exert greater command over how they live their lives or, more accurately, how they allocate their time in particular places. This control, however, is not as extensive as it first appears. To devote time to an activity provided by a technology means that time cannot be devoted to some other pursuit. The greater control gained by the use of a technology comes with the price of also having one's time and attention controlled by its use; the time spent networking on Facebook® is time that cannot be devoted to face-to-face conversing.

These seemingly contradictory tendencies of technological determinism and neutrality do not pose an either/or dilemma. Rather, both are operative and mutually reinforcing. A particular technology is developed to satisfy certain desires. As the technology becomes more widely used, its own inherent potential unfolds, leading to further refinements and improvements. If the users are to take full advantage of the proffered benefits they must adjust their lives accordingly. These adjustments prompt another round of new desires and values in response to this unfolding potential, spurring another spate of technological innovation. Within this cyclical pattern the users encounter technology as both a determinative force over and against them *and* as neutral instruments under their control. In effect they are subjected to simultaneous and paradoxical episodes of greater and diminished control, increased dependency and greater autonomy, enriched sociality and greater isolation.

To return to the example of the computer—a machine that was designed initially to process data more efficiently—has become the foundation for a globally integrated network of information and communication technologies that is altering the patterns of daily activities, particularly in respect to work and commerce. More and more time, for instance, must be devoted to managing the burgeoning volume of information that is instantaneously available and exchanged. As this network becomes more enmeshed in the fabric of daily life there are also accompanying changes in what is valued and desired. A higher premium is placed on the reliability, malleability, and confidentiality of information that is needed to accomplish various tasks and transactions, prompting a corresponding desire for speedier, easier, and more secure access to information. Yet there is also the need not only to protect data, but also to protect users from becoming overwhelmed by irrelevant and unwanted information, prompting further refinements that simultaneously enlarge and restrict the scope of available information. With each round of refinements, the tension between these determinative and neutral tendencies becomes more pronounced. Information technology has improved productivity, but it also dictates the structure of work and the design of the workplace.

The paradoxical effect of this tension is amplified in that there is greater control over how information is created, disseminated, and accessed but less control over regulation and use. A computer connected to the Internet grants me more efficiency in regard to my work and financial transactions, but I cannot control how other individuals might access and use information that is compiled about me. The dispersed structure and accompanying safeguards of information networks enhance individual autonomy. With each advance in information technology I am freer and better able to construct my lifestyle. The ubiquity of information technology allows me to create and access information that cannot be easily subjected to centralized control and monitoring, and an array of safety devices protect my privacy. My enhanced autonomy, however, depends on networks that are entirely beyond my control in terms not only of maintaining the various technical components, but also of trusting strangers who are in a position to override the safeguards employed to protect my privacy. The proliferation of information technology also expands my range of social interactions. Through the Internet I can communicate instantly with individuals across the globe. Yet, ironically as remote communication becomes easier, individuals grow increasingly isolated. The more time I spend emailing the less attentive I can be to those in close physical proximity.

It is due to this tension between these determinative and instrumental tendencies that we may speak of a techno*culture*. It is through various cultural channels that the respective centripetal and centrifugal forces are mediated. Within this tension the individuals and associations comprising a culture evaluate, reform, and align their values, affirming some while discarding, reconstructing, and inventing others. On the basis of these changing valuations, new patterns of social and political ordering emerge while others fade or are redirected. These patterns in turn promote the construction, renovation, reform, and dismantling of the economic, social, and political institutions comprising the civil community. Mediating this tension is fraught with conflict. Which values should be embraced and which should be shunned? What patterns of social and political ordering are best suited for actualizing the values that are embraced, and what are the patterns that should be avoided? What kinds of economic, social, and political institutions are best suited to promoting the welfare of civil community, and what kinds are inimical? The contentious nature of trying to answer these questions reflects both the vitality and uncertainty of what the emerging technoculture is and what it might and should endeavor to become. The operative word is "emerging," for it is far from clear whether a technoculture will be primarily the product of a determinative force beyond human control or an artifact of human inventiveness afforded by technology's instrumental neutrality.

The contentious issues accompanying the emerging technoculture often stem from these conflicting determinative and instrumental presuppositions, and they are most often disputed and resolved in political terms. Should telecommunication, for example, be subjected to more or less regulation? It could be argued that the telecommunication industry should be deregulated because such a policy is better aligned to take advantage of inevitable technological development—a progressive trajectory that should not be restrained. Or, conversely, it could be argued that the telecommunication industry should be tightly regulated to protect the public interest—caution is warranted to protect consumers. But what is not at issue in this dispute is technology *per se*. There is virtual unanimity that improved telecommunication is a good goal to pursue, but where the disputants differ is over the means of achieving it.

In this respect, it is *not* the machines and devices that should capture attention, but the underlying values and rationality of the emerging technoculture that they signify. Following Oliver O'Donovan, the issue at stake is not the "technical *achievements* of the age, but the mutation of *practical reasoning* into 'technique'."[3] The effects of this mutated practical reasoning is disclosed in the values and language that are permitted, forbidden, and privileged in the political and public moral discourse of the emerging technoculture. Much of the deeper, underlying rationality in which this discourse is embedded, however, is hidden. Consequently, moral and theological inquiry into the emerging technoculture must not only subject what is revealed in this discourse to critical scrutiny, but also dig deeply into its roots to expose its principal ideological, philosophical, and religious convictions. Such excavation reveals that the emerging technoculture represents a concerted effort to master time and place within a more extensive endeavor of mastering nature and human nature. But this is to anticipate, and the remainder of this chapter initiates a critical examination of this discourse and, more importantly, an inquiry into its roots.

Nihilism and historicism

Time and place are two closely related features that play prominent roles in defining and delineating the human condition. Every person must be in a particular place at a particular time, and no one can be in two places at the same time. These limitations constrain where one can be and what one can do. If one is here, then one cannot be there; if one is doing this, then one cannot be doing that. If, for example, I am in a classroom delivering a lecture, I cannot be home reading a murder mystery.

The constraints of time and place are epitomized in embodiment. Through their bodies, humans encounter the world and each other. They are sensual beings who see, hear, taste, smell, and touch. All physical, mental, and emotional characteristics that define what being human means depend on sensual input. The richest life of the mind or most saintly spiritual life cannot be pursued in the absence of the body. Dualistic imagery separating mind from brain or body from soul is deceptive, for it implies that humans are only accidently or derivatively related to their bodies. This bifurcation is untenable, for such immaterial things as mind, soul, and will are embedded in, and dependent on, the material brain which in turn is integrated within a particular body. In this respect, even the term "embodiment" is deceptive, for it still suggests that the body is a host for an immaterial guest. Humans are not so much embodied creatures as they are, to use an inelegant term, "bodied." There

---

[3] Oliver O'Donovan, *The Desire of the Nations: Rediscovering the Roots of Political Theology* (Cambridge, UK: Cambridge University Press, 1996), p. 274 (emphasis in original).

can be no geniuses or saints without bodies that see, hear, taste, smell, and touch. It is as a bodied person that I deliver a lecture or read a murder mystery.

It is also the constraints of the body, and therefore time and place as well, that shape and limit one's desires and aspirations. The body imposes distinct constraints on what a person can do, accomplish, and hope to achieve within a given locale and period of time. Daily activities are ordered around the necessity for work, rest, shelter, and sustenance. Desires and aspirations are influenced by physical factors. Some bodily characteristics such as strength or agility, for instance, better equip some individuals over others for a particular occupation—not just anyone can be a Tiger Woods. Sedentary pursuits, such as thinking, are to a large extent prescribed by the capacities of particular brains and their interaction with various environments—not just anyone can be an Albert Einstein. These limitations in turn dictate, to a large extent, the places in which time is spent. Since I have the abilities to be a teacher instead of a golfer, I must spend my time in classrooms and libraries rather than on golf courses.

In addition, the constraints of time, place, and body structure forms of human association. Cooperation is needed to meet basic bodily needs in a manner that frees time to satisfy more complex wants. In the absence of specialized labor and trade, culture could only exist in a highly diminished form, for time would be largely allotted to satisfying such natural necessities as food, shelter, and rest. In this respect, humans are social creatures that require one another's assistance if they are to thrive both as individuals and as a species. As Johannes Althusius observed, man cannot "provide by his own energies all the requirements of life. The energies and industry of many men are expended to procure and supply these things."[4] I cannot be a teacher without students, administrators, and support staff, and I cannot read murder mysteries in the absence of authors, publishers, and distributors.

May we not say that, at least to some extent, technological development is motivated by a desire to overcome bodily limitations, particularly in respect to reconfiguring the constraints of time and place? Transportation technologies, for instance, have eased the limits of geographical location. If one is restricted to how far one can walk (or run) within a period of time, opportunities for social interactions, commercial transactions, participating in public events and the like are also constricted accordingly. Domesticating animals, such as horses and oxen, expands the range of these opportunities by increasing traveling speed. Individuals can accomplish tasks more quickly while decreasing the time expended for each journey. Although traveling by horse or carriage improves one's mobility, the constraints of time and place are merely eased a bit rather than significantly surmounted. I still spend a considerable amount of time walking or riding a horse to campus to deliver a lecture, or to the bookstore to buy a murder mystery.

It is with the advent of mechanized transportation that the constraints of time and place are more substantially relaxed. Trains, boats, cars, and airplanes provide relatively convenient, speedy, and comfortable travel to virtually any destination

---

[4] Johannes Althusius, *Politica* (Indianapolis, IN: Liberty Fund, 1995), p. 18.

in the world. Opportunities for social, commercial, and cultural interaction are now global and, for many people, readily available. As the time to travel from this point to that may be said to "shrink," the number of activities that may be undertaken within a period of time is increased dramatically. I can travel to remote locations to deliver lectures, and read a murder mystery while traveling in an airplane.

Concomitantly, enhanced mobility promotes increased travel, trade, and production of goods and services. Each transportation technology requires supportive and interconnected infrastructures. Industries and other commercial interests use these infrastructures to produce and distribute goods and services in various markets. A factory in Tokyo, for instance, builds televisions that are shipped to a port in Los Angeles where they are then transported to a railroad station in Chicago where they are placed on trucks that distribute them to stores and homes throughout the Midwest. In addition, this infrastructure enables extensive urbanization and highly mobile patterns of work. Some workers live many miles away from their workplace, using trains, buses, or cars to commute, while others travel extensively throughout the week, meeting with clients and spending little, if any, time in an office.

Although the increased mobility afforded by transportation technologies ease the constraints of time and place, the effect remains highly inefficient in isolation from communication technologies. Trade and commerce cannot be conducted efficiently in the absence of information concerning demand, availability, and delivery of goods and services. Freighters, for instance, do not arrive unexpectedly at Los Angeles and inquire if there are any takers for its cargo of televisions manufactured in Japan. Production and delivery schedules must be carefully coordinated. Furthermore, this communication is conducted by exchanging information between remote locations. The television manufacturer in Tokyo and the distributor in Los Angeles do not need to be constantly flying back and forth across the Pacific to coordinate their respective tasks. In the absence of distant communication, traveling becomes a haphazard enterprise, effectively wasting time rather than ameliorating its constraints. I waste my time if I travel from campus to campus inquiring if anyone would like to hear me lecture.

The speed of communicating is also a significant factor in mitigating the limits of time and place. Exchanging written communiqués often proves slow and cumbersome, delaying the production and distribution of goods and services. Various technological advances improve the speed of communicating. Railroads, boats, trucks, and airplanes move documents back and forth more quickly than a courier on foot or on horseback, and the telegraph cut response time to minutes rather than days or weeks. Each of those innovations, however, cannot provide "real-time" communication. It is telephony that makes instant, two-way (or more) communication among remote locations possible.

The benefit of providing real-time communication, however, is also accompanied by three liabilities. First, there is the problem of time itself. If the locations in question are in widely divergent time zones, finding a convenient hour to talk may prove difficult. The problem is exacerbated if the parties are also highly mobile, frequently shifting between time zones. An answering machine mitigates, but does not eliminate, the problems of coordination and time-lag. Reviewing a voice message does not have the advantage of communicating in real time. When a message is reviewed, circumstances may have changed, resulting in unwanted consequences. A student, for example, has a brilliant idea for a chapter in her thesis. Knowing that I am attending a conference in Hong Kong, she leaves a message on my voicemail. Many hours pass before I am able to review the message and ring her back to warn her that her idea is silly and should be avoided, only to discover that she has already wasted a great deal of time writing the chapter. Or there is a message from my favorite book dealer that he has a rare first edition of a murder mystery written by my favorite author. I need to ring him back within an hour, however, or he will sell it to a less favored customer. By the time I review the message the hour, alas, has elapsed.

Second, the telephone is not designed to transmit copious amounts of information. Listening to a detailed document being read, either in real time or as a message, is not an adequate substitute for a copy, especially if accuracy is a paramount concern. A fax machine mitigates, but does not eliminate, this problem. Although a great volume of data can be transmitted, the recipient must be in a particular location to receive the document. The problem is further compounded if one or both parties are mobile for they must coordinate the time of transmission and reception. Late Friday afternoon I learn that my student's examination of her thesis has been rescheduled for the following Monday. I need to read and confer with her before she faces this ordeal. I will be leaving shortly to travel to a cottage I have rented for the weekend in the hinterlands of Michigan's Upper Peninsula, so I tell her that I will locate a fax machine and she can send me her thesis. Upon my arrival I discover, much to my dismay, that the closest fax machine is not available during the weekend. To add to my frustration, my favorite book dealer has obtained another rare first edition of the murder mystery I want. However, he is selling it as part of a Saturday "silent auction" promotion, and bids can only be submitted in person or by fax.

Third, the range and types of transactions that can be conducted over a telephone are restricted. Not only is the telephone not equipped to deal with an extensive amount of data, it is also unable to perform multiple tasks. Telephony is effective only within a narrow range of parameters which, for practical purposes, amplifies the constraints of time and place. I can discuss my student's thesis over the telephone if we both have printed copies, and I could participate in her examination through a conference call. But it would be beyond human endurance if she were to read her thesis over the phone (especially the lengthy footnotes discussing arcane details of obscure texts). I would save time if, rather than driving from bookstore to bookstore in search of that cherished first edition murder mystery, I rang them instead. But I would not be able to do any extensive browsing; if I were to ask the sales representative to step over to the murder mystery section and tell me over the telephone all the authors and titles on the shelves, I assume my request would not be cheerfully received.

When telephony is integrated with other communication and information technologies the effectual parameters are greatly expanded. Large volumes of data, including images, and audio and video recordings, can be quickly transmitted, stored, and accessed as dictated by the needs and the convenience of the users. Moreover, these technologies permit users to transmit and access information in combinations of real and virtual time which are largely configured in accordance to purposes assigned by the users. This ability to reconfigure real and virtual time enables the implementation of two important and interrelated strategies for overcoming many of the constraints of time and place. On the one hand, it allows individuals to interact with various locations, either sequentially or simultaneously, without the necessity of physically traveling anywhere. One need not travel from point A to point B to accomplish a particular goal. On the other hand, it enables individuals, using a combination of real and virtual time, to simultaneously engage in a wider range of activities that would otherwise be impossible. One cannot be in two places at once, but one can be engaged with a number of remote locations at the same time. In the comfort of my favorite room at home, I am talking on the phone with my student about her thesis, referring to it as needed by means of a document stored in my computer. I mention that she will need to consult an obscure text, and as we continue to talk she uses her computer to access the library's catalog and submit her lender's request. Since the book is hardly ever used, it is stored at an offsite location, but within a few seconds a robotic arm is retrieving the book, and it will be available the next morning. At the same time my computer is transmitting one of my video-recorded lectures to a class in Cape Town, and I am visiting the websites of various book dealers still in search of that elusive first edition. Occasionally, a small window on my computer opens, alerting me of a breaking news story. All the while the television is on so I can occasionally glance at my favorite episode of *Inspector Morse* or the smaller screen-in-screen with its hypnotic scrolling stock-ticker.

The point of this scenario is not to demonstrate my multi-tasking skill (which is meager), but to illustrate how these technologies render the constraints of time and place less rigid and more permeable and malleable. I am talking to my student in real time about a document that is simultaneously present in two different locations. She accesses the catalog of a library at a time when it is "closed," triggering the retrieval of a book at a location at which she is not physically present. My computer is transmitting a lecture to students I will probably never meet. I am shopping at online bookstores that never close, and eventually someone will send me the books I purchase from a variety of distant locations, or download them if they are e-books. I am watching a video that I can pause, rewind, and fast forward as needed, and although the news alerts and stock-ticker are delayed, they nonetheless provide timely information.

These technologies complement, supplement, and amplify the benefit of the increased mobility resulting from the transportation technologies and infrastructures discussed previously. The same technologies that allow people to travel great distances are also used to deliver goods and services around the world in a timely manner. The integration of transportation, communication, and information technologies enables individuals to extend their physical reach, so to speak, in, over, and through time. The relation between time and place becomes more fluid, giving individuals greater freedom in allotting their time by enlarging the range of options for how they structure the patterns of daily living. I can talk with a student face-to-face or on the telephone. She can deliver her thesis to me in person or send it as an email attachment. I can deliver a lecture in a classroom or over the Internet. I can travel to the quirky little bookstore in Missoula that has the first-edition murder mystery I want, or have it shipped to me. Moreover, the combination of technologies that makes these options possible also makes time and place increasingly, though certainly not entirely, irrelevant. What we do is often not dictated by where we are and when we do it. In the scenarios described above, for instance, it does not matter whether I am at home, in my office, or in a hotel room, nor does it matter if my student is in her apartment, a cafe, or wherever else graduate students congregate.

The development and deployment of various technologies, however, should not be regarded as merely attempts to ease the inconvenience resulting from the constraints of time and place. The convergence of transportation, communication, and information technologies enable humans to accomplish more in a shorter period of time. Yet these technologies ultimately cannot overcome absolute limits imposed by time and place. No matter how mobile and connected a person might be, she is still confined to a particular locale at any given time and no matter how efficiently time may be used, it remains limited in quantity. Can we not say, therefore, that technology is also used to address a deeper, underlying anxiety regarding finitude and mortality? This anxiety brings us back to the bodied character of human life in which finite and mortal limits are encountered with an exacting urgency. The body imposes distinct limitations that often frustrate a person's desires and aspirations. Moreover, these limitations become more pronounced and frustrating as people grow older, and eventually bodied creatures run out of time and die. Consequently, technological advances that ameliorate the constraints of time and place should not be viewed in isolation from technological developments designed to both increase longevity and preserve and enhance physical and cognitive capabilities. Together, they may be seen as related strategies in waging a war against finitude and mortality. The most extreme effort in this regard is the posthuman project.[5] Utilizing recent and anticipated advances in information technology, particularly computational speed, an ongoing attempt is being made to collapse real and virtual times and realities into a singular time and reality, effectively transcending the

---

[5] For a more extensive critique of posthumanism, see Brent Waters, *From Human to Posthuman: Christian Theology and Technology in a Postmodern World* (Aldershot, UK and Burlington, VT: Ashgate, 2006); see also Waters, *This Mortal Flesh: Incarnation and Bioethics* (Grand Rapids, MI: Brazos, 2009).

finite constraints of bodied existence.⁶ In addition, recent and anticipated advances in biotechnology, bionics, nanotechnology, artificial intelligence, and robotics are being employed to greatly extend longevity, perhaps even to the point of achieving virtual immortality, effectively negating the mortal limits that constrain the lives of bodied beings.⁷ Together, these attempts to overcome finite and mortal limits require that humans, both individually and collectively, transform themselves into a superior, posthuman species.

These prognostications of a posthuman future populated by infinite and immortal beings are admittedly highly speculative, if not whimsical, based largely on unproven technological capabilities. Yet the principal issue at stake is not about the future. Indeed, debates over the technological feasibility of a posthuman future serve to occlude the more immediate concern of what kind of world late moderns are currently constructing and how they are refashioning themselves to inhabit this world. In the construction of such a world technology is simultaneously *the formative instrument and operative ontology*. Technology is instrumental in that it enables individuals to satisfy an expanding range of desires despite the constraints of time and place. Technology is also the premier mode of being in late modernity in that it represents the continuous effort to master time and place. Consequently, the natural necessity of time and place that is inherent, but indifferent, to the life of bodied beings is gradually overcome in constructing a fabricated world that is designed to promote human flourishing. This flourishing is further supported by extending longevity and enhancing physical and cognitive capabilities so that humans may take better advantage of the world they are constructing. The instrumental value of intervening more extensively into human biology is that it again enables individuals to satisfy (and create) a more expansive range of desires as finite and mortal boundaries are redrawn. Moreover, reconfiguring human biology in line with what humans will themselves to be amplifies the ontological status of technology as representing the ongoing struggle against finitude and mortality. The natural necessity of finite and mortal limits which are inherent and inimical to bodied beings is surmounted through the mastery of nature and human nature.

Technology alone, however, cannot bear the intellectual and moral weight assigned to it in the preceding paragraph. Artifacts cannot, on their own, both perform the instrumental tasks of fabricating a world and its inhabitants and provide the content of what is desired in such fabrication. Rather, we must turn our attention to the underlying values that drive technological development in accordance with certain desires and aspirations stemming from those values. Admittedly, technology may be regarded as an efficient tool and formative symbol

---

⁶ See, e.g., Ray Kurzweil, *The Singularity is Near: When Humans Transcend Biology* (New York and London: Penguin Books, 2005).

⁷ See, e.g., Hans Moravec, *Mind Children: The Future of Robot and Human Intelligence* (Cambridge, MA, and London: Harvard University Press, 1988); and Moravec, *Robot: Mere Machines to Transcendent Mind* (Oxford and New York: Oxford University Press, 1999).

that both confirms these desires and aspirations, as well as opening up new possibilities for creating new values, but its very efficiency and formational power depend on an initial set of convictions, desires, and aspirations in reaction to finite and mortal limits, and are in turn enacted through projects designed to master time and place by mastering nature and human nature. In this respect, posthuman rhetoric may be understood as hyperbolic commentary on the two principal and related modes of late modern ontology—namely, *nihilism* and *historicism*. In short, posthuman discourse is a description and prescription of our late modern circumstances.[8] The future tense of posthuman verbiage is thereby misleading, for it effectively redirects attention away from assessing the ideological grounding of its own discourse that it is purportedly attempting to supersede.

The deceptive nature of posthuman rhetoric can be seen, for example, in the assertion that *Homo sapiens* is an evolutionary work in process, and to date the work is not progressing well. If humans are to achieve their full potential, both as individuals and as a species, they must use their technology to both create a world and refashion its inhabitants in ways that more directly promote this latent potential. To achieve this objective, purposeful selection must displace natural selection as the principal evolutionary trajectory. A posthuman future is propounded in which finite and mortal limits have been transcended, along with policy proposals promoting requisite technological development. This rhetorical tactic portrays a dramatic, if not titillating, vision of the future in which attention is fixated on technological feasibility in conjunction with adequate policy formulation, and dismissing any opposition as the product of irrational fears or religious superstitions that leave humans enslaved to their finitude and mortality.

The rhetoric, however, not only deflects criticism of the propounded vision, but also masks a failure on the part of posthumanists to assess the adequacy of their project. They presume that finite and mortal limits are inimical to human flourishing, but they do not offer an argument why a life free of these constraints would necessarily be a good one. What is being proposed is world in which posthumans can do whatever humans might want to do, but on a much grander scale since time and place are no longer delimiting factors. Yet if the posthuman world is merely a highly amplified version of the late modern world, is it not incumbent to subject the ontological presuppositions of the latter to greater critical scrutiny? In short, posthumanists are either unwilling or unable to assess the endemic late modern nihilistic and historicist foundations of their project. In this respect, the futuristic trajectory of posthuman rhetoric is a distraction that diverts attention away from the more immediate questions of moral, social, and political ordering, and how technology, as a formative instrument and ontological foundation, shapes theses processes. More importantly, the dramatic character of posthuman rhetoric

---

[8] See N. Katherine Hayles, *How We Became Posthuman: Virtual Bodies in Cybernetics, Literature, and Informatics* (Chicago, IL, and London: University of Chicago Press, 1999).

dismisses as irrelevancies the mundane characteristics of late modern life even though it is here where technology exerts its greatest formative influence.[9]

To shift the tone of this inquiry to the present tense requires an examination of the nihilistic and historicist character of the late modern world. Nihilism and historicism shape the instrumental and ontological values that drive the emerging technoculture. Although a more precise and in-depth explication of nihilism and historicism is developed in the following chapters, a brief and provisional observation may be offered at this juncture. *Nihilism* denotes a continuous process of valuation, devaluation, and revaluation. Since late moderns believe there is no objective good that can be discovered, they must, over time, create, negate, and recreate values. Consequently, the tasks of moral, social, and political ordering do not consist of attempts to align these endeavors in accordance with any inherent or given good, but to construct provisional structures and institutions in response to what emerges in the process of valuing, devaluing, and revaluing—a process characterized by conflict, thin consensus, and impermanence. *Historicism* refers to the mode of being in the fabricated world resulting from the continuous destruction and construction of values. History is not merely the investigation and narration of prior events, but the enactment and disclosure of what it means to be human in a world that is largely what humans make of it. The historicist mode of being provides a modicum of stability by instantiating the expectations of change, impermanence, and ceaseless becoming as the norms of the human condition.

Technology is the principal late modern, and therefore historicist, instrument for enacting the process of valuation, devaluation, and revaluation within the world of the late moderns' own making, and is thereby also the premier symbol of the power of humans to make reality into what they will it to be and to become. Technology is both the instrument and symbol of what it means for humans to assert their mastery over time and place, and correlatively over nature and human nature. We may return to the preceding discussion to illustrate these instrumental and symbolic roles. The initial development of transportation and communication technologies was prompted, in part, by the value of mobility in overcoming the constraints of time and place. The value of mobility becomes more pronounced with further technological advances which not only enable the physical movement of people and products, but also provide instantaneous communication and exchange of information to remote and multiple locations. In this respect, technology enables, exacerbates, and confirms the requisite valuing, devaluing, and revaluing required in enacting greater mobility. The relatively static, familial, and cyclical character of agrarian life, for instance, must be destroyed in order to adopt the more dynamic, anonymous, and linear qualities of urban life. The city skyline and mobile smart phone become the symbols of what it means for late moderns to live in a world of their own making. Moreover, no normative judgments can be made regarding the process of negating and creating values, for there is no good

---

[9] See Albert Borgmann, *Technology and the Character of Contemporary Life: A Philosophical Inquiry* (Chicago, IL, and London: University of Chicago Press, 1984).

against which they may be measured. No one is in a position to say that small towns are good and large cities are bad; that horses and buggies are better than automobiles; that printed books are superior to their electronic counterparts. For late moderns these are matters of personal taste and preference, and either option can survive only for so long as there is sufficient value assigned to one or the other, and both may be negated in the future by the emergence of unforeseen options. Consequently, there is no inherent reason why existing values should be protected in response to the creation of new ones, for historicist construction is predicated on nihilistic destruction. This is why posthumanists can advocate, without any apparent sense of irony, that humans should will their own extinction in order to become a superior species.

The preceding comments are admittedly little more than caricatures. A more careful inquiry into late modern nihilism and historicism is required before any theological and moral assessment of the emerging technoculture can be conducted. We may begin such an inquiry by examining the works of two of the most prescient interpreters of late modernity.

Nietzsche and Heidegger; Heidegger and Nietzsche

Friedrich Nietzsche and Martin Heidegger are arguably two of late modernity's premier interpreters. Joan O'Donovan describes Nietzsche as late modernity's seer and conscience,[10] and George Grant asserts that "Nietzsche's words raise to an intensely full light of explicitness what it is to live in this era."[11] In coming to terms with late modernity and the technoculture it is producing there is no avoiding these two philosophers. A comprehensive survey, comparison, and critique of their respective works are beyond the scope of this section. Large tomes would be required to give these tasks their due. Some selected themes, however, may suffice for conducting this inquiry into the nihilistic and historicist context of the late modern world.

Heidegger's lectures on Nietzsche offer a promising avenue for investigating these selected themes by providing a substantial yet manageable corpus of material. In his four-year lecture sequence, Heidegger engaged with a wide range of Nietzsche's works while never straying too far from his principal purpose of portraying him as the last Western metaphysician. The end of metaphysics is also the beginning of the end of modernity whose demise late moderns fail to recognize because they cannot acknowledge their own nihilism as part of a long succession of unsuccessful attempts at overcoming human finitude and mortality. In and through Nietzsche, Heidegger exposes a deep anxiety and simmering rage of an

---

[10] See Joan E. O'Donovan, *George Grant and the Twilight of Justice* (Toronto and London: University of Toronto Press, 1984), pp. 119–125.

[11] George Grant, *Time as History* (Toronto and London: University of Toronto Press, 1995), p. 34.

era that is intellectually and morally estranged from what it perceives vaguely as an indifferent, if not inimical, world, for it fails to understand that its "desire to *overcome* nihilism exhibits a craving for *results* in history, a craving that itself has a history that is none other than the history of nihilism."[12] Late moderns are both repulsed and seduced by a world that they are unable to recognize, and thereby embrace, as the handiwork of their own nihilistic and historicist efforts.

The period during which these lectures were delivered, 1936–1940, should also be kept in mind. Little more than half a century separate these two philosophers. Nietzsche's works still retain a fresh and crisp narration, while sufficient time has elapsed to begin drawing out some of the moral, social, and political implications of his work, especially against the backdrop of unfolding events in Europe in general and Germany in particular. Moreover, it is also a trying time for Heidegger in coming to terms with his failed rectorship at the University of Freiburg and his troubled relationship with the Nazis—he claimed, for instance, that his lectures were a thinly veiled critique of National Socialism.[13] Heidegger's philosophical gaze, then, is not merely fixed upon Nietzsche as a figure from the past, but also directed toward the present and future. Ideas emerge concerning the fate of late modernity, particularly in respect to technology, which he develops over the next three decades. Consequently, there are moments when it is not clear whether Heidegger is explicating Nietzsche, or whether he is using Nietzsche to propound his own thinking. It is precisely this ambiguity that guides our inquiry, for the purpose of this section is not to assess whether or not Heidegger's account of Nietzsche is accurate. Rather, it is both through Heidegger's reading of Nietzsche, and Heidegger being read by Nietzsche, that we may begin to disclose, with an admittedly ambiguous clarity, the nihilistic and historicist contours of the emerging technoculture.

Heidegger's lectures are based on the premise that any philosopher who seeks an understanding of what it means to be human cannot avoid confronting Nietzsche, for he is an "essential thinker" who embodies both the history and culmination of Western philosophy. As an essential thinker, he also "thinks ahead," disclosing a modern world that, despite its ascendant facade, is already in decline.[14] In this disclosure he also reveals modernity's destiny and what it means to live in its present, decaying trajectory. This keen ability to think ahead assures his legacy, for even "when Nietzsche is no longer known by name, what his thinking had to think will rule."[15]

Nietzsche's great insight is that metaphysics, and philosophy more generally, does not entail a search for "truth,"[16] but is a process of assigning value. Some

---

[12] David Farrell Krell, "Introduction to the Paperback Edition," in Martin Heidegger, *Nietzsche*, 4 vols. (San Francisco, CA: HarperCollins, 1991), p. xvii (emphasis in original).

[13] See ibid., pp. ix–xii.

[14] See Heidegger, *Nietzsche*, III, pp. 3–9; see also I, pp. 3–4.

[15] Ibid., III, p. 8.

[16] According to Heidegger, Nietzsche's definition of "truth" is that which is taken or believed to be true. See ibid., III, pp. 22–31, 53–56.

ranking of relatively higher and lower values is required, for this is not a static condition but an ongoing process of negation and revaluation, nor are there any natural or eternal standards that determine how value should be assigned. These nihilistic acts of destruction and aspiration are not peculiarly modern phenomena. Rather, the history of Western thought is the history of the evolution of nihilism. Nihilism is therefore driven by strife and violence for its evolving character over time requires the annihilation of all values and goals in which the "uppermost values devalue themselves" and "all estimates of values collide against one another."[17] It is through such conflict that excellence emerges, not as the exemplar of an abstract "good" but in those who excel in the struggle among competing values.[18] Moreover, nihilists who excel in this struggle participate in the negation of "anything grounded on tradition, authority, or any other definitive value."[19] Nihilism is the "truth" of perpetual becoming over being since there is no end to be fulfilled. Consequently, all prior notions of ontology and teleology are invalidated, in turn liberating humans to devaluate and revaluate as they will.

It must be reiterated that nihilism *per se* is not uniquely modern, but "points to a historical movement that extends far behind us and reaches forward far beyond us."[20] Nihilism does not have a history; nihilism *is* history. What is peculiarly modern is the growth of public atheism in its explicit, implicit, or practical forms. In what is perhaps his most famous aphorism, Nietzsche proclaims that "God is dead."[21] In this respect, the death of God is a watershed event in the history of Western thought. The God Nietzsche refers to is the God of traditional or conventional morality. Humans have murdered this God by dragging him down to their level and stripping him of any grandeur and power. Nietzsche, however, is not like other modern atheists who replaced the God of morality with the god of progress. The only gods that are needed are those that humans may choose to create and valuate. The world, therefore, effectively becomes God. This divination is a consequence of encountering the perpetual becoming of human existence. Since there is nothing of permanent value, such as God, humans must necessarily believe in their own value. This necessity is expressed through a "capacity" and "concern" for humankind's "self-assertion."[22] Humans assert themselves through a historicist construction of a world oriented toward their self valuation. Such construction is predicated on and enacts values that are little more than "constructs of domination."[23] The nihilist knows, however, that such a world, as well as any other so-called objective "truth," is merely a fabrication stemming from a

---

[17] See ibid., I, pp.156–157.
[18] See ibid., I, pp. 157–158; see also III, pp. 201–208.
[19] Ibid., IV, p. 3.
[20] Ibid., IV, p. 57.
[21] See Friedrich Nietzsche, *The Gay Science* (New York: Vintage Books, 1974), p. 167.
[22] See Heidegger, *Nietzsche*, IV, pp. 33–34.
[23] See ibid., IV, pp. 47–51.

desire to assert oneself and dominate others in fulfilling the psychological need of self-valuation. In the end, all the nihilist has created is an appearance of a world which, like its creators, is of no lasting, much less permanent, value. The so-called historical reality that moderns prize is little more than an imagined stage upon which humans present themselves as they wish to appear in fabricating the appearance of a world. "Image" is modernity's dominant "reality," and "truth" is little more than imaging.[24]

The only conclusion the nihilist can draw is that ontology is the study of nothing, for "being" and "nothing" are synonymous terms. In this respect, Heidegger portrays Nietzsche as the first consummate nihilist, for, unlike other philosophers, he does not merely think about nihilism but lives it out to its end.[25] He knows firsthand that nihilism *is* the Being of human beings, but it is a sobering knowledge for "the essence of nihilism is the history in which there is nothing to Being itself."[26] Moderns may take solace in their feverish attempts at fabricating their world and its history, but it provides comfort through delusion and deception.

Although Nietzsche is the consummate nihilist, this does not mean that he commends nihilism. Heidegger is aware that description and explication do not imply endorsement. Nietzsche lives a life he cannot commend, insisting that the purpose of his work as a philosopher is to partake deeply of nihilism in order to overcome it. How does he propose to accomplish this task? The first step is to frankly admit that the end of nihilism is the annihilation of Being; that "being as a whole is nothing."[27] The fabrication of the world and fabricating oneself within it are nothing more than temporary appearances of no permanent value and devoid of any real being. It is admitting that there is no core to life, that any "center of gravity is missing,"[28] an admission corresponding and amplifying the death of God. The void exposed in this death is particularly acute in the modern world, because the "essence of modernity is fulfilled in an age of consummate meaninglessness."[29] Instead of falling into despair in acknowledging the nothingness of being, however, Nietzsche contends that nihilism can be overcome by loving this meaningless fate. This love does not attempt to fill the void at the center of life as disclosed in God's death. Such efforts to fill this void, as seen in modern science and ideologies, are simply more fabricated appearances that are ultimately futile because they fail to embrace the fate of their own futility and therefore succumb to the nihilism they purportedly were deployed to surmount. Loving our meaningless fate, however, does not merely entail consenting to the nothingness of being, for this is merely and meekly surrendering to nihilism as the negation of being. Rather, we must will

---

[24] See ibid., III, pp. 28–31. It should be noted that Nietzsche (or perhaps Heidegger via Nietzsche) draws upon Heraclitus rather than Kant in his analysis of appearance.
[25] See ibid., II, pp. 173–174.
[26] Ibid., IV, p. 201.
[27] Ibid., II, p. 173.
[28] See ibid., II, p. 159.
[29] Ibid., III, p. 178.

the will to will nothing, for it is the prerequisite step toward the self-mastery that can overcome nihilism. What is entailed in this self-mastery, how is it achieved, and what does it accomplish? To answer this question we must attend to two of Nietzsche's central and closely related doctrines: the will to power and the eternal recurrence.

The will to power "names what constitutes the basic character of all beings."[30] The Being of beings is a perpetual becoming, and becoming requires willing, and willing in turn requires power if it is to be effective. The will, then, is in essence the will to power. The will to power can be further distilled to the "will to will," and the will is also self-willing.[31] Consequently, "will" and "power" are virtually synonymous, or at the very least they cannot be thought through in isolation from each other. Since willing is always self-referential it necessarily entails asserting the self so that the will to power is a "willing to be more," a "willing to be more power."[32] At its most essential level the will to power is the will to be, for it "designates the basic character of beings; any being which is, insofar as it is, is will to power."[33] Since beings will to be, the will to power necessarily entails the will to mastery. In order to gain the self-mastery which can overcome nihilism, humans also master and order their natural and historical circumstances.

In attempting to achieve such mastery, however, humans encounter the futility of their efforts, for there is no single act that can achieve a final or permanent mastery. The futility of these efforts discloses the eternal recurrence of the same. Such recurrence is not merely cyclical repetition for this would imply an underlying order or purpose to the world that does not exist. Rather, the eternal recurrence is a conceptual device for acknowledging and confronting the stark priority of becoming over being. The world is perpetually chaotic, devoid of any natural order. In its "*permanent* becoming" the world turns back upon itself in a fluctuating and unstable process that does not stop "whenever its finite possibilities are exhausted," for the process repeats itself "an infinite number of times. And as permanent becoming it will continue to repeat itself in the future."[34] It is within such an unstable world that humans strive to be through their own becoming. Consequently, acknowledging the eternal recurrence of the same brings us back to the will to power. As Heidegger reiterates on a number of occasions, the eternal recurrence and will to power are synonymous concepts.[35] Both emphasize the impermanent character of the world and therefore the impermanent character of what it means to be human in such a world.

Again, Nietzsche does not counsel despair in reaction to this world. As was the case with his meditations on the will to power he urges that once again humans

---

[30] Ibid., I, p. 3.
[31] See ibid., I, pp. 37–43.
[32] See ibid., I, pp. 59–66.
[33] Ibid., I, p. 18.
[34] See ibid., II, pp. 109–110 (emphasis in original); see also II, pp. 121–132.
[35] See, e.g., ibid., I, p. 19 and II, pp. 202–203.

must love this fate of the eternal recurrence; indeed, more strongly, that they must will it.[36] In coming to love and will this fate humans are liberated to assert the will to power by asserting their mastery over a chaotic world. It is a mastery, however, which is acknowledged to be temporary and impermanent, for all attempts to master are themselves part of a process of perpetual becoming. This acknowledgement simultaneously affirms and negates modernity as an "age of consummate meaninglessness,"[37] for in rejecting any modern notion of inevitable progress humans are nonetheless freed to impose their order on the world however provisional and ultimately meaningless it will inevitably prove to be. In short, loving the fate entailed in the eternal recurrence of the same both liberates and compels humans to impose their values—their will to power—on the world, for its chaos makes the "humanization" of the world both possible and necessary.[38]

How is this will to power and mastery asserted over a chaotic world? The starting point is a recovery of passion. Moderns believe that reason, especially science, can be employed to bring about a lasting, if not permanent, ordering of the world. The belief is mistaken, however, for the appearance of order proffered is precisely that: an apparition of their own projected construction. Modernity has fallen into the trap of believing that the appearance it has concocted of an orderly world disclosed through reason is an objective reality in its own right. Moderns therefore fail to recognize that the task at hand is not to tame and domesticate the world, but to deconstruct and reconstruct it in line with the values they impose on it. Consequently, art, instead of science, is the point of origin for the will to power. Art is the "nucleus" of the will to power because art exemplifies that what is good is what pleases the beholder, thereby displacing any objective ground for determining good art from bad in any other terms than the values assigned to the artwork.[39] Art and the artist are, for Nietzsche, emblematic of the will to power. The artist is a creator who brings something into being that did not previously exist, and in such creative expression the artist brings himself or herself into being as an artist. More expansively, "art is the basic occurrence of all beings; to the extent that they are, beings are self-creating, created."[40] Artists are well positioned to love the meaningless fate of the eternal recurrence because they recognize that reality itself is nothing but a semblance. Since artistic work is the creation of semblances, artistic expression entails the fabrication of what, for the time being, is real. Such creativity, however, requires severing any relation between art and "truth," for art becomes a lie if it claims there is any "truth" to capture and portray. When the artist embraces this severance art becomes the "supreme configuration of will to power."[41]

---

[36] See ibid., II, pp. 206–207.
[37] See ibid., III, pp. 175–180.
[38] See ibid., II, pp. 91–92.
[39] See ibid., I, pp. 67–76, and pp. 124–150.
[40] Ibid. I, p. 72.
[41] See ibid., I, pp. 217–218.

Understanding the work of the artist discloses the source of creativity more broadly, for "will to power, as self-assertion, is a constant creating."[42] As was discussed above, the world is not naturally hospitable to humans, but must be humanized by being reshaped and mastered through the forceful imposition of human values. Such human mastery of the world is also the prerequisite of human self-mastery. Modern technology is an example of how this twofold mastery is pursued. According to Heidegger, the *technē* of classical Greek thought was never an art or craft that was isolated from, and dependent on, theoretical forms of knowledge. Rather, it always incorporated its own inherent knowledge regarding the manipulation and fabrication of material objects; knowing and making have always been conjoined.[43] Modern technology is an outgrowth of this ancient *technē* rather than a derivative of modern science; it is more akin to artistic creativity than scientific application. In this respect, knowledge *is* power, but it is aligned with the will to the mastery of nature and human nature and not a dispassionate reason. Science and technology are related activities, particularly in the modern world, but the former is the servant of the latter.

For Nietzsche, according to Heidegger, technology encapsulates both the modern, and therefore historicist, mode of being as becoming and its eventual fate. History is not an account of the past, but a human artifact through and in which humans create themselves as appearances that in turn create and encounter a world as the semblance of past and aspirational semblances. History is the manifestation of humankind's "self-representing representation."[44] For moderns, this self-representation is asserted most directly through the mastery of nature that entails the construction of horizons as objects of human desire and striving. Since these horizons are historicist constructs they too are semblances, yet necessary if humans are to project their will to power into the future. They are necessary because willing entails striving for something not yet obtained. Technology is a useful instrument in this regard, for it enables such striving by asserting greater mastery over nature and human nature. Technology, however, has more than instrumental value, for it also shapes the values and desires that are projected in the historicist creation of horizons and therefore indicates the fate entailed in such striving. The historical trajectory toward greater "technological organization"[45] is inescapable because the "completion of modernity history" is a capitulation to "historiology, which is of the same essential stamp of technology."[46] Stated more tersely, technology signifies what a culture is and thereby what it is also striving to become.

Admittedly, technology assists moderns in asserting their will to power by providing greater mastery over nature in a historicist construction of a world

---

[42] Ibid., I, p. 139.
[43] See ibid., I, pp. 77–79.
[44] See ibid., IV, pp. 173–177.
[45] See ibid., II, pp. 16–17.
[46] See ibid., III, p. 180.

striving after horizons of its own creation. Yet historicism allied with technological development is insufficient to overcome nihilism because once again we encounter the eternal recurrence. There is no final horizon to be reached, so the striving that instantiates the will to power and mastery is itself ceaseless and perpetually unfulfilled. The absence of any permanent fulfillment inherent in this perpetual striving produces a simmering frustration and resentment for those ill-prepared to undertake this endless journey, a condition that characterizes the vast majority of moderns. The technological power which is now in the hands of the petty last men and angry nihilists who populate the modern world is perilous, for it exacerbates and amplifies their lust for violence and insatiable appetite for vengeance.

An additional step is required for overcoming nihilism, one that is fully cognizant of the late modern circumstances bequeathed by the sheer technological power that humans now possess. According to Heidegger, there is a "mysterious law of history" which dictates that humankind shall reach a point when it "no longer measures up to the metaphysics that arose from its own history." Nietzsche knew that point had been reached with the advent of "modern 'machine economy,' the machine-based reckoning of all activity and planning," and in turn demands a "new kind of man who surpasses man as he has been hitherto." Simply mastering technology itself will not do for it cannot be treated "as if it were something neutral, beyond benefit and harm, creation and destruction, to be used by anybody at all for any ends at all."[47] Heidegger baldly declares that:

> What is needed is a form of mankind that is from top to bottom equal to the unique fundamental essence of modern technology and its metaphysical truth; that is to say, that lets itself be entirely dominated by the essence of technology precisely in order to steer and deploy individual technological processes and possibilities.[48]

Nietzsche's Overman (*Übermensch*) is the new form of humankind that fulfills this need. The Overman truly loves the meaningless fate of the will to power and eternal recurrence, and is therefore genuinely and happily free to assert his being of perpetual becoming as manifested in the historicist construction of a world endlessly pursuing its fabricated horizons. Consequently, the Overman discards a lust for violence and thirst for vengeance.[49] The Overman is not a superhuman or new species, but a superior human being that overcomes and displaces the inferior last men, yet in such displacement he negates all previous forms of being human. The Overman will need to become "the master of the last men" to insure their disappearance over time,[50] but in asserting this mastery the Overman also takes the decisive step in overcoming nihilism—namely, the step of self-mastery.

---

[47] See ibid., IV, pp. 116–117.
[48] Ibid., IV, p. 117.
[49] See ibid., II, pp. 215–220.
[50] See ibid., II, pp. 127–128.

Does Nietzsche overcome nihilism? According to Heidegger, he does not. Rather, he becomes more deeply entangled, remaining the consummate nihilist. Nietzsche purportedly wants to overcome nihilism by assaulting its Platonic and Christian roots, but he merely reinforces them with his emphasis on the human will. In eliminating God there is no stopping humans from making themselves into an inadequate substitute; the Overman cannot fill the void created by God's death. In brief, Heidegger contends that Nietzsche's argument ends in an insurmountable impasse. Nietzsche believes that his "extreme nihilism" dissipates into a metaphysics that is no longer nihilistic—a nihilism cleansed by its own self-inflicted purgation.[51] Nietzsche asserts that this purging originates in value-thinking in which all previous values are devalued. In this total devaluation humans can assert the will to power, leading to a self mastery which overcomes nihilism. This step is seen most clearly in the assertion that even the essence of Being as becoming is nothing more than a value. This contention, however, reduces value-thinking to a principle of devaluation which thereby loses its purgative power. All Nietzsche really has to offer is the tautological claim that what should be valued is the recognition that Being as becoming *is* Being as becoming. Ironically, Nietzsche's account of nihilism is of little, if any, philosophical value because if nihilism is fulfilled in this tautology, then we have effectively shut ourselves off "from the possibility of ever being able to think and to know the essence of nihilism."[52] Consequently, if the essence of nihilism cannot be thought, then it is invulnerable to critique. "This implies not only that Nietzsche's nihilism does not overcome nihilism but also that it can never overcome it"; hence his "ultimate entanglement in nihilism."[53]

If Heidegger is correct, then Nietzsche's hopeless entanglement may help to explain, in part, why he attracts such bad company. The Nazis, for instance, invoked an eviscerated understanding of will to power to justify their senseless violence, brutality, and racial hatred, and the posthuman is proffered as the Overman in which a vain and quixotic quest for immortality appeals to a shallow rendering of self-mastery. Arguably, Nietzsche would find both movements to be bemusing if not appalling.

More tellingly, Nietzsche's entanglement with nihilism can be seen in his prescient but insufficient account of technology. In this respect, we must turn our attention to Heidegger's later work for in his musings on technology in which he elaborates themes that are introduced in his critique of Nietzsche. A comprehensive analysis of Heidegger's account of technology is again beyond the scope of this book, but a few exemplary themes will again suffice and are examined below. These themes expose in greater detail the failure of Nietzsche's nihilistic attempt to overcome nihilism. A related question, however, also needs to be kept in mind: to what extent has Heidegger disentangled himself from Nietzsche? This is not

---

[51] See ibid., IV, p. 202.
[52] Ibid., IV, p. 203.
[53] Ibid.

merely a clever rhetorical question, for if Heidegger remains entangled with Nietzsche, then he also remains trapped within the very nihilism that cannot be known, critiqued, and overcome. This is especially important given Heidegger's prognosis that late modernity is embracing a technological destiny leading to annihilation. His proffered solution for avoiding this grim fate lies solely in readying ourselves for a "god who can save us."[54] Yet if this is another god that can be murdered when convenient, then Heidegger, like Nietzsche, offers nothing of any real value, particularly in assessing the emerging technoculture.

Critical and constructive philosophical assessments

In Heidegger's subsequent reflections on technology, he attempts, albeit more implicitly than explicitly, to further demonstrate Nietzsche's failure to disentangle himself from nihilism, while at the same time building on and distancing himself from Nietzsche in his own efforts at overcoming nihilism. Technology is especially pertinent in this regard for it simultaneously encapsulates the ontology and destiny of late modernity. Moderns establish their Being through their historicist construction of the world. Heidegger draws a distinction between ancient *technē* and modern technology. The former revealed what was thought to be good and true about the world, whereas the latter is used to dominate and master nature. Such mastery entails a destiny of purportedly greater power and control but at the price of an anxious nomadic mobility and isolation. In Heidegger's stark words: "Homelessness is coming to be the destiny of the world."[55]

Heidegger is troubled by the prospect of such an itinerant world, for it destroys the fabric of civil community. The modern scientific and technological nihilism originating in the Enlightenment is replacing the *Volk* (the people) with a collection of autonomous individuals who are reduced to little more than ravenous consumers. The *Volk* must be restored and invigorated to prevent the final decline of the West, a process already underway in twentieth-century Europe in general and Germany in particular. In this respect, Heidegger is attracted initially to Nazism as an antidote to the equally cancerous options of capitalism and communism, for he shares with Hitler an organic understanding of political order and social stability.

Why is modern technology a leading culprit in this demise? The domination of nature leads inevitably to the end of philosophy, and the end of philosophy means a world predicated on technological power. Late moderns have become so deeply entrenched within the world of their own making that they fail to recognize that technology discloses the essence of modern Being: namely, its essence of no essence. The sheer ubiquitous, ordinary, and banal presence of modern technology disguises its deeply seductive and formative power. Late moderns are simply

---

[54] Martin Heidegger, "Only a God Can Save Us: Der Spiegel's Interview with Martin Heidegger," *Philosophy Today*, 20/4 (Winter 1976), p. 277.

[55] Martin Heidegger, *Basic Writings* (San Francisco, CA: HarperCollins, 1993), p. 243.

unaware that they are nothing more than nihilists marching onward toward the destiny of their own obliteration.

To help further unfold Heidegger's construal and assessment of modern technology, we may draw upon Michael Zimmerman's interpretative framework of technology's "three interrelated meanings." The first meaning has to do with the "techniques, devices, systems, and production processes usually associated with *industrialism*."[56] At a basic level, technology is a human activity entailing the manufacturing of goods and services. Heidegger admits that this simple observation is correct but incomplete. Although technology enables work, the increased productivity resulting from *modern* industrialization exhibits the will to power in a concrete manner. Modern machines and factories, for instance, are highly visible signs of humans attempting to master and control nature. Technology, however, not only enables this mastery, but also dictates its meaning and how society should be organized in its execution. The more humans employ sophisticated machinery the more their lives become reshaped in the image of technology. The "mass society" of late modernity is creating a "technological man" that "can be kept reliably on call only by gathering and ordering all his plans and activities in a way that corresponds to technology."[57] One symptom of this reshaping of human life is seen in a fascination with gadgets and banal spectacles that are endemic to late modernity. Yet at a deeper level modern technology instantiates, often in subtle ways, a cybernetic orientation that is also dedicated to the mastery, and therefore reshaping, of human nature. Heidegger's "technological man" is moving toward manufacturing himself, for asserting the will to power now entails the cybernetic task of the will willing itself to will.

To oppose the nihilistic trajectory of industrialism, work should be transformed into art. This is no easy task, however, for technology negates beauty because it is deeply embedded in the second interrelated meaning of the "rationalist, scientific, commercialist, utilitarian, anthropocentric, secular worldview usually associated with *modernity*."[58] Since technology is a basic human activity, it is also a means to an end. Heidegger admits that this instrumental understanding of technology is largely correct, but it is nonetheless deceptive. This deception is seen in the relation between science and technology. With the advent of modern science, nature no longer refers to an inherent essence of reality but to a mode in which location and motion are determined as exhibited through universal, uniform, and numerical measurement.[59] Consequently, nature is effectively reduced to a series of coherent forces that can be harnessed, providing in turn a treasure-trove of resources to be

---

[56] Michael E. Zimmerman, *Heidegger's Confrontation with Modernity: Technology, Politics, and Art* (Bloomington and Indianapolis, IN: Indiana University Press, 1990), p. xiii (emphasis in original).

[57] Heidegger, *Basic Writings*, p. 255.

[58] Zimmerman, *Heidegger's Confrontation with Modernity*, p. xiii (emphasis in original).

[59] See Heidegger, *Basic Writings*, pp. 288–293.

exploited. The deceptive quality of this relationship stems from the modern belief that science is prior to technology, so that the latter is based on the reason and rationality of the former. Heidegger insists this is simply not the case, for although science precedes technology, chronologically the two have always been intimately related and mutually reinforcing; science itself embodies a technological vision and *telos*.[60] Since *technē* is a mode of knowledge in its own right, it orders the means and ends of scientific research that serve technological development. More pointedly, Heidegger insists that "we still seem afraid of facing the exciting fact that today's sciences belong in the realm of the essence of modern technology, and no where else."[61] Moreover, there is no prospect of reversing the order of priority between technology and science, for both "will soon be determined and regulated" by a pervasive cybernetics—a mode of understanding and mastery that reduces everything to information that is infinitely malleable.[62] In short, the late modern world is both a realm and artifact of cybernetic control and manipulation.

Recognizing the priority of technology over science would presumably ease the task of transforming work into art. The creation of artifacts is, after all, more akin to artistic expression than theoretical thought. The problem, however, is late modernity's failed recognition—or worse, self-deception—for the third meaning of technology involves the "contemporary *mode of understanding* or *disclosing things* which makes possible both industrial production processes and the modernist worldview."[63] According to Zimmerman, Heidegger placed the greatest significance on this third meaning.[64] Technology always entails a "bringing-forth", a simultaneous "unconcealment" and disclosure.[65] To unconceal something is to also disclose it for what it is and thereby to reveal its truth. Modern technology reveals the truth of modernity's incessant attempts at mastering nature and human nature. It is through historicist acts that humans construct their Being within a temporal and finite world. The Being of late moderns is therefore "enframed" within modern technology which both reveals their essence while plotting a trajectory toward a particular destiny.[66] Late modernity is encased in this technological enframing which in turn delimits what being human means, particularly in respect to freedom. The principal problem at stake with technological enframement is that it hides its own act of disclosure. Consequently, late moderns never encounter the essence of modern Being as having no essence and are thereby oblivious to the nihilistic destiny toward which they are headed. Late moderns are simply unaware

---

[60] See Martin Heidegger, *The Question Concerning Technology and Other Essays* (New York: Harper and Row, 1977), p. 22.
[61] Heidegger, *Basic Writings*, pp. 378–379.
[62] See ibid., p. 434.
[63] Zimmerman, *Heidegger's Confrontation with Modernity*, p. xiii (emphasis in original).
[64] See ibid.
[65] See Heidegger, *The Question Concerning Technology*, pp. 11–13.
[66] See ibid., pp. 20–21, 24–25.

of the futility of their own acts to construct their own Being whose essence is literally nothing. They have deceived themselves into believing that they have gained greater freedom through exerting greater mastery over nature and human nature, yet the means employed to exert this mastery has in fact enslaved them to the pervasive cybernetic control on which modern technology is predicated.

In order to encounter the truth which technology discloses, we must first think its language. By immersing ourselves in its own modes of thought "we shall be able to experience the technological within its own bounds" and "respond to its essence."[67] And in responding to its essence of Being as no Being, we may also know and embrace the horror of modern technological nihilism both as a historical phenomenon and, more importantly, as the destiny toward which we are heading. The destructive character of late modernity's future is captured in Heidegger's contention that "homelessness" is its destiny.[68] Ironically, in trying to construct a more hospitable home by humanizing the world, humans are in fact fabricating an inhospitable habitat; they grow increasingly alienated from the world of their own making. Late moderns have no place to dwell, for they have transformed the world into a machine rather than a place suitable for human dwelling. Like a machine, late moderns are in constant motion; they have constructed a world populated by autonomous nomads. Moreover, when there is no place to dwell there are also no stories to tell. Herein lies the danger: if late moderns have no place to dwell and no stories to tell, then they also have no alternative destiny to technological nihilism to narrate. And in the absence of an alternative narration the sheer destructive capability of technology becomes a grave threat, for if the world that humans have created for themselves is not fit for human dwelling, then nothing of value would be lost in its annihilation.

Heidegger's proffered solution is to turn to art as a means resisting and reforming late modernity's technological ontology. In this scheme "art" is broadly conceived as a series of practices that shape the production of various artifacts, thereby reducing technology's formative influence while increasing its instrumental value that is subject to human control. Heidegger's goal is not to overcome technology but to restructure its enframement in less nihilistic ways, which opens the possibility of conceiving alternative destinies. In this respect, technology is not dangerous *per se*. Rather, the danger lies in the naive and false promise of salvific power that late moderns have foisted upon technology.[69] Although Heidegger's proposal is more extensively examined and assessed in the following chapters, an initial observation may be offered as this juncture: Heidegger invokes art as the basis of an alternative narration that can reconfigure late modernity's technological enframement and thereby redirect its destiny. Yet what sustains the appeal of this alternative narrative? Is it ultimately an attempt

---

[67] See ibid., pp. 3–4.
[68] Heidegger, *Basic Writings*, p. 243.
[69] For an overview and assessment of Heidegger's proposal, see Zimmerman, *Heidegger's Confrontation with Modernity*, pp. 222–247.

to revalue technology so that a thinly disguised nihilistic strategy is deployed to contain and redirect the late modern will to power? Can nihilism be used to domesticate the nihilistic essence of modern technology? Or, in thinking through modern technology, do we arrive at Heidegger's invocation of desperate hope in a god that purportedly can save us, even though we are never certain if it, too, will prove to be but one more recurring apparition that humans are constantly constructing, deconstructing, and reconstructing? Since Heidegger has adopted the Nietzschean strategy of partaking so deeply of modern technology that he can transcend its enframement, it is fair to ask the question he posed to Nietzsche: has Heidegger escaped the modern technological enframement or does he remain hopelessly entangled within it?

In conducting this examination and assessment of Heidegger's solution we turn our attention in the following chapters to three philosophers: George Grant, Hannah Arendt, and Albert Borgmann. Each philosopher was chosen for two reasons. First, each engages, sometimes directly while in other instances obliquely, with selected aspects of Heidegger's account of modern technology. Grant largely accepts Heidegger's prognosis of late modernity's dark destiny stemming from its unacknowledged technological enframement. Consequently, Heidegger helps to illumine late modernity's darkness *as* darkness. Grant, however, contends that although Heidegger illumines late modernity's present circumstances, his assessment is not illuminating because he remains too entangled with Nietzsche and therefore cannot overcome the nihilism and historicism he decries. Arendt uses a Heideggerian structure to argue that late modern technology represents another phase in the perennial attempt to overcome finite and mortal limits through a quest for immortality. Although Heidegger dismisses this current phase as another nihilistic and historicist project that will end in failure, he cannot move beyond the will to power and eternal recurrence as the bases for human thought and action. Consequently, such thought and action are fixated on finitude and mortality, and this fixation in turn is manifested in a destructive politics predicated on death and violence. Borgmann shares Heidegger's premise that the problem at hand is not technology *per se* but its false salvific promise. Late modern technology does not need to be discarded but reformed in ways that promote genuine human flourishing by recovering and preserving the world as a suitable dwelling place. Although Borgmann believes that a reformation of technology is possible, he recognizes that it cannot be achieved on Heidegger's terms, for he shares Nietzsche's disdain and loathing of the ordinary and common patterns of daily life where the needed reforms have their greatest influence in recapturing the world as a suitable dwelling place. Heidegger and Nietzsche have simply failed to read late modernity's future correctly: the destiny to be avoided is not apocalyptic but one of boredom and banality.

Second, each of these philosophers suggests themes that, with further development, set the stage for theological and moral engagement with the emerging technoculture. Grant uses the eternal as the world's destiny to bracket human finitude and mortality, thereby offering a more illuminating account of the present darkness as darkness. In doing so he suggests the necessity of confession as the first step in negating late modernity's pervasive nihilism and historicism. Arendt contends that the deadly and recurring violence stemming from a futile quest for immortality can be broken through the recognition that new and renewing possibilities can occur within the finite and temporal ordering of human life. Her emphasis on natality as the primary metaphor for political ordering suggests the need for repentance, forgiveness, and promising if the deadly consequences of late modernity's fixation on mortality are to be avoided. Borgmann proposes that technology can be fruitfully reformed through a series of focal things and practices that cumulatively redirect patterns and trajectories of daily life. His proposal suggests the possibility of amendment of life in response to prior acts of confession, repentance, and forgiveness.

Chapter 2
George Grant: Illuminating the Darkness as Darkness

George Grant believed he was living in the twilight of Western civilization. The lengthening shadows are seen in the philosophical, moral, and political questions being raised that cannot be addressed by conventional modes of thought. This failure stems from late modernity's belief in progress. This belief has supplanted the Christian doctrine of providence: humans, not God, dictate the course of history and its eventual destiny. Consequently, late moderns place their hope in science and technology as the means of their salvation. Grant insists, however, that it is a false salvific promise. Invoking the Spanish proverb, "Take what you want, said God—take it and pay for it,"[1] late moderns do not understand what they are taking by placing their hope in technology, or the price being exacted. Why are they so heedless? Because they continue to place their faith in technological progress, but this is a decrepit religion being crushed by the heavy debt accumulated by its fraudulent assurance of salvation. For Grant, the seemingly limitless power that late moderns project onto technology is a sure sign of inexorable demise. Appealing to Hegel's adage that the "owl of Minerva only takes flight at twilight" as a sign that an era is drawing to an end,[2] he is certain that the owl is already soaring above the terrain of late modernity and that the ensuing shadows can only lengthen and darken.

The principal philosophical task at hand is to illumine this darkness *as* darkness. The darkness in which late moderns reside is a consequence of their rejection of any lingering objective semblance of the good, true, and beautiful required by their embrace of the pre-eminence of the human will. In brief, the purported freedom gained in utilizing technology to assert the will actually enslaves its users within the meaninglessness entailed in such assertion—the price humans pay for taking their fate into their own hands. Although late moderns may be troubled by occasional questions or issues that their faith in progress cannot resolve, they fail to see their enslavement because as shadow-dwellers they have grown accustomed to the darkness. In order to illumine this darkness as darkness, philosophy must assess the truth of late modernity's inadequacy.[3]

---

[1] George Parkin Grant, *Technology and Justice* (Notre Dame, IN: Notre Dame University Press, 1986), p. 9.

[2] See George Grant, *Philosophy in the Mass Age* (Toronto: University of Toronto Press, 1995), p. 7.

[3] In this respect, Grant believes that philosophy should be used to subvert modernity in order to free people to be receptive to the truth of Christianity. See Ted Heaven, "George

Grant undertakes this task by turning to Nietzsche and Heidegger. He turns to them for two reasons. First, he rejects a Hegelian account of a progressive history. Although his early writings were deeply influenced by Hegel, Grant eventually condemned Hegel's philosophy of history as a Gnostic corruption of the Christian doctrine of providence that served as a thin justification for liberal progressivism and its accompanying technological mastery of nature and human nature. Hegel is of little use in assessing late modernity because he is nothing more than its most articulate apologist.[4] Second, for Grant, the issue at stake is not the wholesale rejection of late modernity but coming to terms with it. Late modernity, after all, can only be assessed by late moderns.[5] Consequently, there is no compelling reason not to turn to Nietzsche and Heidegger as late modernity's two greatest expositors and critics.

Grant finds in Nietzsche a voice that exemplifies what it means to live in the late modern era.[6] His "words raise to an intensely full light of explicitness what it is to live in this era."[7] Although Nietzsche did not invent late modernity, he is without peer in unfolding it and coming to terms with the fate of late moderns. There is simply "no escape from reading Nietzsche if one would understand modernity."[8] To think Nietzsche's thoughts is to think how late moderns think, for he is the first philosopher to comprehend and articulate the finitude and temporality enfolding late moderns, along with an exacting clarity of the anxiety and restiveness accompanying this realization. Through him the layers of late modern life are

---

Grant on Socrates and Christ," in Ian Angus, Ron Dart, and Randy Peg Peters, eds., *Athens and Jerusalem: George Grant's Theology, Philosophy, and Politics* (Toronto and London: University of Toronto Press, 2006), p. 309.

[4] Grant's initial interest in Hegel is due to his friend and colleague, James Doull, who Grant credits with teaching him about Hegel; see Grant's letter to Joan O'Donovan in William Christian, ed., *George Grant: Selected Letters* (Toronto and London: University of Toronto Press, 1996), p. 315. Although Hegel's influence is apparent in Grant's first book, *Philosophy in the Mass Age*, published in 1959, there are also some inklings of unease, and his "Introduction" to the 1966 edition reiterates the decisive break that came with the publication of *Lament for a Nation* in 1965. Grant credits his repudiation of Hegel to his reading of Leo Strauss. Although Grant wrote extensively about Strauss's influence on his thinking, toward the end of his life he contends in a 1986 letter to David Bovenizer that Eric Voegelin is the "profounder of the two," and in a 1988 letter to David Dodds admits that he is "fundamentally more in Voegelin's ambience than Strauss's" (see Christian, ed., *George Grant: Selected Letters*, pp. 359, 380).

[5] See "Conversation," in Larry Schmidt, ed., *George Grant in Process: Essays and Conversations* (Toronto: Anansi, 1978), pp. 141–145.

[6] For a more extensive discussion of Grant's critique of Nietzsche, see Brent Waters, *From Human to Posthuman: Christian Theology and Technology in a Postmodern World* (Aldershot, UK, and Burlington, VT: Ashgate, 2006), pp. 21–31.

[7] George Grant, *Time as History* (Toronto and London: University of Toronto Press, 1995), p. 34.

[8] Grant, *Technology and Justice*, p. 89.

stripped away, revealing the nihilistic void at its core and in turn exposing a world populated by frenetic nomads, for "homelessness is the particular mark of modern nihilism."[9] Such homelessness is the inevitable consequence of modern science which has stripped away any sense of permanence in the world, thereby reinforcing the disquieting acceptance of the "finality of becoming."[10] In accepting this finality, moderns assume that a Hegelian-like philosophy of history could compensate for the death of God to give humankind a sense of meaning, but Nietzsche destroys this assumption by demonstrating that historicism can provide no such horizon. All horizons purporting to offer a sense of meaning are merely fabrications expressing the "values which our tortured instincts will to create."[11] Once this acknowledgement is made, there is no turning back, for the power of any meaning-bearing horizon is shattered. The issue at hand is how to live in a world in which its various horizons disclose nothing that is real or true, much less permanent.

The late modern world is populated by last men and nihilists, neither of whom is adept at coping with their homelessness and meaninglessness. The last men have embraced a defective concept of happiness that is incapable of inspiring any sense of nobility. This diminished conception of happiness and nobility promotes a leveling effect in which only those things that can be attained by all are permitted. The last men are clever, self-critically unaware, and cannot rise above an inordinately low bar of expectations, for all they require is comfort and entertainment. Although the last men believe they have liberated themselves from Christian precepts, they are in reality little more than the "products of Christianity in its secularized from."[12] Nihilists know that they are little more than their wills. They also know that since all values are relative there is no good to be willed. It is better, therefore, to will nothing since there is nothing noble to will. Consequently, they are "resolute in their will to mastery, but they cannot know what that mastery is for."[13] And such unyielding mastery results inevitably in appalling violence. The last men want revenge against any semblance of nobility, while the nihilists seek revenge against a world in which the pursuit of anything noble is forbidden; thus the recurring drive for revenge and mastery.

Grant identifies Nietzsche's last men with late liberals who value the goods and services afforded by technology to preserve their freedom. The leveling effect Nietzsche decried is seen in voracious consumerism is proffered as both liberating and progressive. The progress of late liberalism, as an expression of secularized Christianity, thereby places its hope in technological development, but it is a vain hope for progress *per se* cannot be found in either nature or human nature. Eventually late liberalism must degenerate into nihilistic despair, because

---

[9] George Grant, *Technology and Empire: Perspectives on North America* (Toronto: Anansi, 1969), p. 17.

[10] See Grant, *Time as History*, pp. 36–39.

[11] See ibid., pp. 40–41.

[12] Ibid., p. 45.

[13] Ibid., p. 46.

"its manifold contradictions testifies [*sic*] to the debased, banal, petty view of happiness it propounds."[14] Late liberalism and its accompanying progress must ultimately fail, for freedom is debased into the tautological will to will.

Nietzsche's solution to this conceptual impasse, according to Grant, is that loving the fate of the eternal recurrence creates the possibility of the Overman. Since the Overman is necessarily predicated on the will to power it should be directed by art rather than science. Grant, however, contends that this solution is inadequate. Drawing upon Strauss's and Heidegger's critique of Nietzsche,[15] Grant contends that loving a meaningless fate is equivalent to seeking redemption from the futility of the eternal recurrence. Yet there can be no true love of fate in the absence of the eternal, which Nietzsche has replaced with endless time. This substitution is simply not sufficient. Although Grant does not necessarily disagree that art plays an important role in overcoming the banality of late liberalism and its nihilistic violence, he asserts that what Nietzsche offers is a highly distorted, if not false, rendering of what art discloses. For Nietzsche, art and any so-called "truth" are opposed. If the former discloses anything about the latter, it is its ugliness; art discloses that truth is ugly rather than beautiful. For Grant, however, art is inherently ordered to beauty, and what is beautiful is also true. Any so-called "art" which ultimately can only reveal an ugly truth is, by definition, not art but a projection of the artist's will. Rather than overcoming nihilism such "art" confirms and escalates its ill effects.

One such effect is the loss of reverence and obedience. Since there is no eternal good, truth, and beauty to be acknowledged, affirmed, and honored, then there is correspondingly nothing inherent in nature or human nature to be acknowledged, affirmed, and honored. Rather, nature and human nature are materials to be manipulated in asserting the will to mastery and self-mastery, and there are no moral constraints that can be appealed to in limiting the extent of this manipulation other than the power of a counter-will to mastery and self-mastery. Grant does not dispute the accuracy of Nietzsche's depiction of late modern nihilism. He instead quarrels with reducing the will to the will to power and mastery.[16] According to Grant, Nietzsche does not demonstrate conclusively that the good, the true,

---

[14] Joan E. O'Donovan, *George Grant and the Twilight of Justice* (Toronto and London: University of Toronto Press, 1984), p. 122. Similarly I have argued that Nietzsche's last men and nihilists are not two different classes of human beings, but extreme ends of a common spectrum. The most comfortable last man (or late liberal) is a frustrated nihilist, while the ardent nihilist is at heart a deeply resentful liberal. See Waters, *From Human to Posthuman*, pp. 29–30.

[15] See Ronald Beiner, "George Grant, Nietzsche, and the Problem of Post-Christian Theism," in Arthur Davis, ed., *George Grant and the Subversion of Modernity: Art, Philosophy, Politics, Religion, and Education* (Toronto: University of Toronto Press, 1996).

[16] In this respect, Nietzsche personifies the corruption of the will to the will to power. See George Grant, "The Triumph of the Will," in William Christian and Sheila Grant, eds., *The George Grant Reader* (Toronto and London: University of Toronto Press, 1998).

and the beautiful do not exist—they are more akin to inconvenient realities to be ignored. This inattention prevents him from consenting to human finitude and mortality which is the prerequisite for preparing oneself for "genuine life rather than a prelude into nothingness."[17] Consequently, he offers no necessary or even compelling reason why the will cannot, in obedience, be aligned with dictates and constraints imposed by these transcendentals.

In rejecting Nietzsche's solution, Grant does not refute him but refuses him.[18] His refusal is based primarily on Nietzsche's glib account of *amor fati* as the proffered means of overcoming nihilism. Genuine love is not grounded in the realm of necessity, but originates in the eternal and is manifested in human suffering. Any account of love that attempts to ignore or evade suffering by consigning it to a consequence of necessity or incessant revenge is stripped of any substantive content and can offer only a counterfeit salvation. Again, it must be stressed that Grant's refusal of Nietzsche does not entail a wholesale refutation. Grant never denies the acuity of his interlocutor's description of modern nihilism.[19] Rather, his refusal requires a counter-narration, one based on the centrality of love as opposed to the will to power in order to resist nihilism. One important source in fashioning the conceptual schema of this counter-narrative is Heidegger's critique of Nietzsche.

Following his prolonged encounter with Nietzsche, Grant turned increasingly to Heidegger as his philosopher of choice for coming to terms with late modernity. Grant makes this turn for several reasons. Most importantly, it intensified and clarified his perception of late modernity in general and Nietzsche in particular. Grant refers to Heidegger's published lectures on Nietzsche as a "great but terrible read"[20] that enabled him to "understand more deeply than ever before what is so frightening in the roots of modernity. It really has shown me new things about Nietzsche that I had never seen in my own studies of that thinker."[21] Secondarily, Grant's turn to Heidegger confirms his earlier break with Hegel. Hegel is the supreme representative figure in Western philosophy's failed metaphysical quest for being, and part of the collateral damage of that failure is an eviscerated Protestantism that accommodated itself to the modern project. Grant is also attracted

---

[17] See Harris Athanasiadis, *George Grant and the Theology of the Cross: The Christian Foundations of his Thought* (Toronto and London: University of Toronto Press, 2001), pp. 191–192.

[18] See O'Donovan, *George Grant and the Twilight of Justice*, pp. 166–167, and Laurence Lampert, "The Uses of Philosophy in George Grant," in Schmidt, ed., *George Grant in Process*, p. 189.

[19] Grant's appreciation of Nietzsche's discursive skills, however, does not retard his reaction, as noted by William Christian, of "limitless repugnance"; see "Editor's Introduction," in Grant, *Time as History*, p. xxxi.

[20] Letter to David Dodds in Christian, ed., *George Grant: Selected Letters*, p. 381.

[21] Letter to David Bovenizer in ibid., p. 380.

to Heidegger because of his critique of Plato.[22] In his devastating dismantling of ancient wisdom, Heidegger personifies modern knowledge as power, complete with its nihilistic and historicist accouterments. Grant came to believe that if one is to understand late modernity, as well as recover Platonism and Christianity as the bases for a counter-narrative, there is no evading its greatest philosopher. In engaging Heidegger, Grant was forced to sharpen the critical tools he needed for his enucleation[23] of late modernity, particularly in respect to technology as its most striking formative and expressive symbol.

Grant accepts as a given Heidegger's observation that "technique" has become the "metaphysic" of the present age.[24] More broadly, technology serves as the ontology of late modernity. In and through technology late moderns express who they are and what they are aspiring to become. What late moderns value is inexplicable in the absence of technological capability. Three instances may suffice to illustrate how Grant engages and expands upon these Heideggerian inspired premises. First, modern science and technology are organized around cybernetics. What Heidegger means by "cybernetics" is the reduction of animate and inanimate matter to underlying information that can be manipulated and reformulated into differing patterns.[25] Such cybernetic organization and control spurs technological development which is dedicated not only to mastering nature but also, and more troubling, human nature. Grant identifies behavior modification, genetic engineering, and abortion as examples of prevalent attempts at mastering human nature.[26] Grant argues that it is far from certain if late liberalism can preserve its commitment to freedom and rights as it becomes increasingly dependent on the mastery afforded by technology, because the assumptions underlying the simultaneous exultation of freedom and dependence on cybernetic control remain largely unexamined. Grant feared that liberal safeguards, particularly in respect to justice, would be overwhelmed in the inexorable technocratic impulse toward a global homogenization of cultures and accompanying universal tyranny. Cybernetic principles simply provided a thin "scientific" rationale for the historicist

---

[22] Grant contends that Heidegger's *Nietzsche* is in "some ways ... more his *magnum opus* than *Sein und Zeit* because in it his criticism of Plato is laid bare": letter to David Dodds in Christian, ed., *George Grant: Selected Letters*, p. 381. Grant also intended to write a refutation of this criticism but never completed the project.

[23] Grant is rather fond of this word and its derivations: "To enucleate means to extract the kernel of a nut, the seed of a tree" (Grant, *Time as History*, p. 13).

[24] See George Grant, *Lament for a Nation: The Defeat of Canadian Nationalism* (Montreal and Kingston: McGill-Queen's University Press, 2000), p. 11.

[25] See Martin Heidegger, *Basic Writings* (San Francisco, CA: HarperCollins, 1993), p. 434. Heidegger asserts: "No prophecy is necessary to recognize that the sciences now establishing themselves will soon be determined and regulated by the new fundamental science that is called cybernetics" (p. 434).

[26] See George Grant, *English-Speaking Justice* (Notre Dame, IN: University of Notre Dame Press, 1985), pp. 9–10.

project of creating the Hegelian universal and homogenous state that, following Strauss, is inherently tyrannous.[27]

What Grant finds in Heidegger is a voice that simultaneously describes late modernity's historicism with great clarity while also being fully aware of the correlate dangers.[28] Although it is only late moderns that can assess late modernity, they remain too deeply enframed within late modern technology to gain much perspective on the culture they are presumably assessing. The truth of their present circumstances which technology should be disclosing thereby remains concealed. Social and political goods are diminished to technical goods.[29] Consequently, to assess late modernity on late modern terms is ineffectual because its destiny of tyranny is not recognized for what it is.

Grant's essay, "Thinking About Technology,"[30] provides a convenient synopsis for how technology can be coaxed into performing its revelatory function, for it represents Grant's most sustained meditation on Heidegger. Grant begins with the striking observation: "In each lived moment of our waking and sleeping, we are technological civilisation."[31] Technology consists of the "whole apparatus of instruments" constructed by humans which they in turn use in pursuing their various interests and purposes.[32] Moreover, the very neologism, "technology," which combines "art" and "systematic study" discloses the novelty of late modern circumstances in which the once discrete acts of knowing and making are collapsed into a single act of the willful mastery of nature and human nature.[33] Modern technology, therefore, bears little, if any, resemblance to ancient *technē*, for it is organized around and driven by cybernetics. Consequently, technology is the ontology of late modernity, for it is the "pervasive mode of being in our

---

[27] Grant's disenchantment with Hegel begins with his reading of Strauss, particularly his debate with Alexandre Kojève. See Leo Strauss, *On Tyranny* (Chicago, IL, and London: University of Chicago Press, 2000).

[28] Although Grant admired Heidegger's clarity of thought, he was also deeply ambivalent about its value. As Hugh Donald Forbes relates, "Students who knew Grant well have told me that he kept a small framed photograph of Heidegger on the mantel over the fireplace in his study. On days when he was well disposed towards his thought, the photograph was turned to face the room. On those days when Grant was feeling his antagonism to Heidegger ... the photograph was turned to the wall." Forbes, *George Grant: A Guide to His Thought* (Toronto and London: University of Toronto Press, 2007), p. 220.

[29] See Robert Song, *Christianity and Liberal Society* (Oxford: Clarendon Press, 1997), pp. 92–93.

[30] See Grant, *Technology and Justice*, pp. 11–34.

[31] Ibid., p. 11.

[32] See ibid., p. 19; cf. Jacques Ellul, *The Technological Society* (New York: Vintage Books, 1964), p. xxvii.

[33] See Grant, *Technology and Justice*, pp. 11–12. Grant believes that the novel circumstances of late modernity are most pronounced in North America; see his essay "In Defence of North America," in Grant, *Technology and Empire*, pp. 15–40.

social and political lives,"[34] and cybernetics is the corresponding science of late modernity's destiny.

According to Grant, the question of destiny is largely ignored when late moderns think about technology. This ignorance stems from their mistaken belief that technology is merely a neutral set of instruments that humans may use in fashioning whatever future they might choose. Grant admits that the idea of technological neutrality appears to be self-evidently true, but it nonetheless hides the novelty of modern technology that is presumably being assessed. The reassuring adage of a computer scientist that the "computer does not impose on us the ways it should be used" illustrates this perceptual mistake and its troubling implications.[35] The statement assumes that a computer is a manufactured artifact that does not incorporate any intended purpose. It is the users that determine how a computer is used. The computer, however, is unintelligible when removed from the purposes it is designed to fulfill. Or, in Grant's terminology, the computer carries with it a particular destiny and, like all destinies, it imposes its ways on its users, and the users in turn are enfolded within this destiny.[36] Ignoring this destiny prevents the computer from performing its revelatory function. The presumption of neutrality, for instance, hides the fact that the computer invariably promotes greater homogenization. Using a computer requires that data be collected, processed, stored, and distributed in certain ways, which also precludes alternative ways, and these homogenizing and exclusionary requirements are amplified by these particular applications. Consequently, computers are "not neutral instruments, but instruments which exclude certain forms of community and permit others."[37]

Grant's principal concern, however, is not to assess the computer *per se*, but to argue that the account of reason that produces modern technology is the same that produces modern accounts of justice based on prevailing political ideologies. Modern technology's underlying rationality is inseparable from late modernity's political rationality. How computers, for example, are made and used cannot be separated from prevailing concepts of justice that rationalize and validate the need for their production and subsequent usage. Consequently, technology discloses the deep chasm separating ancient and modern accounts of justice: for the ancients, the claim of the Good is the claim of justice, whereas for moderns the idea of multiple goods is diminished to subjective values as captured in the slogan "quality

---

[34] Grant, *Technology and Justice*, p. 17.

[35] See ibid., pp. 19–20. Grant's discussion regarding the computer and its uses is a distillation of a previous article "The Computer Does Not Impose on Us How It Should Be Used," in Arthur Davis and Henry Roper, eds., *Collected Works of George Grant: Vol. 4, 1970–1988* (Toronto and London: University of Toronto Press).

[36] Grant is quick to add that describing a destiny is not synonymous with judging it; see Grant, *Technology and Justice*, p. 22.

[37] Ibid., p. 26.

of life"[38]—the modern understanding of goodness as that which satisfies one's desires or values. As a consequence, nature stands before humans as raw material to be exploited in constructing whatever late moderns believe is good as a result of their own creativity. With and through technology, humans are progressively liberating themselves from the random dictates of natural necessity.

Although only late moderns can assess late modernity, they are ill-equipped to undertake this task because they are deeply enframed within its technological metaphysic and ontology. To assess technology is inseparable from the demanding, and too often deceptive, task of self-assessment. It is at this point that Grant invokes his most breathtaking rhetoric, and it is worth quoting him at length:

> The result of this is that when we are deliberating in any practical situation our judgment acts rather like a mirror which throws back the very metaphysic of the technology which we are supposed to be deliberating about in detail. The outcome is almost inevitably a decision for further technological development.[39]

The assessment of technology is little more than self-affirming mirror-gazing because it encapsulates the ontology of modernity, and it is virtually impossible for late moderns to transcend, much less escape, their mode of being. This difficulty can be seen by returning to the misleading perception of neutrality:

> When we represent technology to ourselves as an array of neutral instruments invented by human beings and under human control, we are expressing a kind of common sense, but it is a common sense from within the very technology we are attempting to represent.[40]

This inability to gain some distance in evaluating technology also occludes the destiny enfolding late modernity, as exemplified in the mistaken notion that the users of technology determine its purposes and how it is used:

> To put the matter crudely: when we represent technology to ourselves through its own common sense we think of ourselves as picking and choosing in a supermarket, rather than within the analogy of the package deal. We have bought a package deal of far more fundamental novelty than simply a set of instruments under our control. It is a destiny which enfolds us in its own conceptions of instrumentality, neutrality and purposiveness.[41]

Since late modern technology is analogous to a package deal, Grant believes that subjective values will completely supplant any lingering notion of the Good,

---

[38] See ibid., p. 30.
[39] Grant, *Technology and Justice*, p. 33.
[40] Ibid., p. 32.
[41] Ibid.

as exemplified in the eviscerated concept of late liberal justice as the satiation of desire.[42] Late moderns have simply not come to terms with their novel set of circumstances, because they are unable to perceive a cybernetic destiny requiring the devaluation and revaluation of all values:

> The coming to be of technology has required changes in what we think is good, what we think good is, how we conceive sanity and madness, justice and injustice, rationality and irrationality, beauty and ugliness.[43]

So long as late moderns continue to evade a destiny predicated on the effective negation of the Good they are ill-equipped to assess late modernity, for they remain fixated on fabricating a world they cannot understand yet nonetheless delude themselves into believing that its eventual destiny is subject to their control. They "are called to understand technological civilisation just when its very realisation has radically put into question the possibility that there could be any such understanding."[44] The fate of late modernity may, after all, prove to be an inevitable, inescapable, and recurring nihilism.

Grant is at his bleakest is this essay, but he avoids falling into despair by rejecting Heidegger's solution. According to Grant, Heidegger overcomes Nietzsche's nihilism but not late modernity's, for he continues to assert that humans are ultimately what they will themselves to be.[45] Heidegger remains too deeply entangled in late modern historicism, thereby lacking the necessary perspective to assess its adequacy. He can describe the poisonous influence of nihilism with great precision, but he has no effective antidote to offer because he cannot conceive an alternative narrative and destiny. At the end of the day, Heidegger is not so much a critic of late modernity as he is its ambivalent apologist. His thoroughgoing historicism is seen in what Grant credits as a brilliant but nonetheless distorted interpretation of Plato: since there is no Good beyond the realm of necessity he cannot perceive evil as the absence of good. He thereby grants evil an existence in its own right, leading to his failure to understand what justice consists of and what it requires. Heidegger knows that in murdering God late moderns have also discarded any natural equality as the foundation of justice and freedom —hence his diffident appeal to a feeble god proffering an untrustworthy salvation.[46]

---

[42] For a sustained explication and critique of late liberal justice, see Grant, *English-Speaking Justice*.

[43] Grant, *Technology and Justice*, p. 32.

[44] Ibid., p. 34.

[45] See O'Donovan, *George Grant and the Twilight of Justice*, pp. 118–119.

[46] Grant suggests that Heidegger may have been trying to recover a Greek-inspired polytheism. See George Grant, "Interview on Martin Heidegger," in William Christian and Sheila Grant, eds., *The George Grant Reader*, p. 301; cf. H. Richard Niebuhr's account of modern polytheistic faith in *Radical Monotheism and Western Culture* (New York: Harper and Row, 1970).

Grant insists, however, that Heidegger and Nietzsche—and he increasingly cannot think of one without conjuring the other—remain indispensible interlocutors for both coming to terms with late modernity and offering a counter-narrative. Together they are perceptive teachers that need not be approved by their students. Consequently, they also present the crucial challenge of how modern knowledge might be affirmed without forsaking ancient wisdom.[47] Grant accepts this challenge by affirming, in contrast to Nietzsche and Heidegger, the love of the eternal God and how that love also affirms human finitude and mortality. To use this affirmation as the basis of a counter-narrative to that of nihilism and historicism, however, requires a defense of Platonism and Christianity against Heidegger's and Nietzsche's attacks. The first step in mounting this defense, as well as setting the stage for an alternative Platonic–Christian narrative, is to illumine the darkness of late modernity in a way that does not negate it. Nietzsche and Heidegger may be said to expose the darkness of late modernity, but they do not illumine it as such because the former remains entangled in its nihilism while the latter is trapped in its historicism. Grant builds upon their critiques to illumine the darkness *as* darkness, and in doing so discloses it as an evil that should be resisted. The basic gist of this critique is captured in Grant's account of late modern historicism and technological mastery.

Grant defines historicism as the "doctrine that all thought (particularly the highest) depends, even in its very essence, upon a particular set of existing experienced circumstances—which in the modern world we call 'history'."[48] Late moderns believe that they create their own history. This belief stems from rejecting the ancient construal of time and history as spheres in which the Good and the necessary are played out as bracketed by the eternal. For moderns, there is no eternity or eternal Good, so time and history have significance only in dealing with the finite and mortal constraints imposed by necessity. Consequently, history is the principal mode through which late moderns know the world and know themselves within that world. Such historicism, however, does not look to the past but is oriented toward the future. When late moderns are purportedly appraising their past and present circumstances they are in fact calculating how to construct a more desirable future. History is thereby ordered to human self-fulfillment. Liberalism is the political manifestation of this drive toward self-fulfillment. Nothing should restrict the freedom of humans to create the kind of world they desire. The paramount political task, then, is to overcome, or at least ameliorate to the fullest extent possible, the constraints of natural necessity.

---

[47] See Arthur Davis, "Justice and Freedom: George Grant's Encounter with Martin Heidegger," in Davis, ed., *George Grant and the Subversion of Modernity*, p. 139.

[48] Grant, *Technology and Justice*, pp. 83–84. Elsewhere he asserts: "Historicism is the belief that all profound thought arises from and is dependent on a particular dynamic context in human life, and to understand the thought one must understand that particular dynamic context" (David Cayley, *George Grant in Conversation* (Concord, ONT: Anansi, 1995), p. 89.

Yet Grant contends that undertaking this task is self-defeating, for historicism corrodes the foundational principles of liberalism. Late liberalism is heading toward the destiny of the universal and homogenous state. As was noted above, this state is populated by last men and nihilists. Such a state is ordered toward providing material goods that are consumed by individuals in a voracious quest for self-fulfillment. However, since there are no eternal or objective standards for determining what the true self is and therefore what goods should be desired in fulfilling the self, the quest is endless and unsatisfying, often deteriorating into a nihilistic orgy of destructive self-indulgence and violent self-assertion. Late liberals are not free but have exchanged their enslavement to natural necessity to that of historical necessity. It is in this exchange that the menace of late modernity is most pronounced, for again, in the absence of any eternal and binding standards of justice, it is corrupted into whatever means is needed to assert the will to power. And this usually results in the powerful asserting a violent mastery over the weak, for nothing should stand in the way of constructing the universal and homogenous state as dictated by historical necessity. Consequently, "modern history-making must be viewed as a form of idolatry,"[49] for to worship history is to effectively worship violence.[50] When history is allowed to be the judge of human acts it is little more than a thin rationalization of force as the final arbiter in assessing the justice of those acts. In what may be the most chilling sentences penned by Grant: "The screams of the tortured child can be justified by the achievements of history. How pleasant for the achievers, but how meaningless for the child."[51]

For Grant, late liberal historicism is inextricably entwined with asserting mastery over nature and human nature. Although the quest for human self-fulfillment is insatiable, it is nonetheless pursued voraciously, requiring nature and human nature to be reshaped in whatever configurations that are provisionally valued. Technology is the dominant means employed by late moderns in asserting their mastery. To worship the idol of history-making is to worship an equally idolatrous technology. Technological mastery, then, is not merely a means that is external to human being, but encapsulates what being human is coming to mean. In Grant's words:

> Technology is not something over against ontology; it is the ontology of the age. It is for us an almost inescapable destiny. The great question is not then "the race between technology and ontology," but what is the ontology which is declared in technology?[52]

---

[49] See Larry Schmidt, "George Grant and the Problem of History," in Schmidt, ed., *George Grant in Process*, p. 138.

[50] See Sheila Grant, "George Grant and the Theology of the Cross," in Davis, ed., *George Grant and the Subversion of Modernity*, pp. 252–253; see also Grant, *Lament for a Nation*.

[51] Grant, *Lament for a Nation*, p. 100.

[52] George Grant, "The Computer Does Not Impose on Us," p. 431.

In answering this question, Grant defines technology as the "endeavor which summons forth everything (both human and non-human) to give its reasons and, through the summoning forth of those reasons, turns the world into potential raw material at the disposal of our 'creative' wills."[53] The ontology declared in technology is one of willful mastery, for Western civilization is coming to dominate the world and homogenize its inhabitants through the universality of technological development and applications.

Liberalism has emerged as the most prominent political philosophy of late modernity because it is predominantly discourse on mastery. With its emphasis on personal freedom it is an ideology well suited for liberating individuals from the constraints of natural necessity. The close relationship between modern liberalism and technology is not coincidental because the essence of one is reflected in the other. Moreover, liberalism can avoid exchanging natural necessity for an equally enslaving historical necessity through its legal protection of individual rights and liberties. Since the liberal state is an artifact of the corporate will, individual citizens must exercise self-mastery through willful self-restraint in order to preserve the order of the political associations they have created. Grant points to what he calls the "American Empire" as *the* exemplar of a modern liberal state dedicated to such freedom-enabling mastery.[54]

Grant contends that late liberalism is deceptive because it degrades freedom into the pursuit of individual interests rather than the common good. Consequently, liberalism masks the homogenizing and universalizing tendencies of technology which undermine the individual rights and liberties that a liberal regime is purportedly dedicated to uphold. Liberalism's proffered freedom is a simulacrum because it fails to recognize that it has not liberated humans from the dictates of natural necessity and its historical counterpart, but has merely exchanged them for those of technological necessity, and this necessity is no less demanding than those it has replaced. Late liberals deceive themselves by fixating on the "freedom" of picking and choosing among an expanding range of goods and services provided by technology, while remaining blind to the enslaving destiny of its package deal in which their picking and choosing are enfolded. At a superficial level the emergence of the modern mass society was initially liberating, but it is a limited freedom that is purchased at the price of indentured servitude to subtle, yet pervasive, bureaucratic control and manipulation.

In more provocative terms, late liberals fail to recognize that the trajectory of technological necessity is drawn inexorably toward the destiny of the

---

[53] Grant, *English-Speaking Justice*, p. 82. Elsewhere, Grant virtually equates modernity with technology: "I mean by modernity the society that has come to be in the western world and which has arisen since western people have concentrated on what is best called 'technology'" (Grant, "Conversation," in Schmidt, ed., *George Grant in Process*, p. 141).

[54] See, e.g., Grant, *Lament for a Nation*, pp. 9–10; *Technology and Empire*, pp. 23–24; "The Great Society," in Christian and Grant, eds., *The George Grant Reader*, pp. 97–98.

universal and homogenous state. And such a state, both in its provisional and final manifestations, is one populated by last men who are susceptible to nihilistic despair and rage when their quest of petty desires remains unfulfilled. Consequently, a liberalism oriented to cybernetic control is self-defeating.[55] The thin veneer of a progressive liberation of humankind proclaimed by the alliance between liberalism and technology cloaks an underlying necessity to control the masses, for the mediocre desires they pursue can only debase rather than fulfill their humanity, thereby promoting nihilistic despair.[56] This threat, in turn, necessitates ever greater reliance on techniques of control, which is inherently illiberal given their cybernetic orientation.

The corrosive influence of technological necessity is exemplified in late liberalism's distorted understanding and practice of justice. Following John Rawls, justice consists of a fair allocation of material resources and equality of opportunity among the members of a civil community.[57] Within this scheme natural and social inequalities are not merely inconvenient, but are unjust circumstances that should be rectified by the state, because otherwise the affected individuals are unfairly disadvantaged in pursuing their respective interests. These circumstances are addressed by creating and enforcing applicable rights that are often enacted with the aid of technological interventions. Reproductive rights, for instance, may be exercised with the aid of contraception, abortion, or assisted reproduction, or the right to die with dignity may be exercised through recourse to euthanasia or assisted suicide. Moreover, these technologies are also liberating by creating a greater range of options: individuals are free to decide whether or not to have children, and when and how they will die. Yet once these technologies become widely employed they promote an expanded range of uses that were not initially intended or anticipated: technologies designed to assist reproduction are used to exert greater quality control over reproductive outcomes, or technologies assisting the death of dying patients may also be employed by individuals who are not dying but whose quality of life is greatly diminished. More troubling, the expanding range of technological interventions morphs the rights they were designed to assist into subtle duties: parents should prevent the birth of severely disabled babies, and old people or persons with greatly diminished lives should not strain scarce medical resources by needlessly prolonging their lives.

Grant's complaint with late liberalism's construal of justice is that it is effectively stripped of any *normative* content. Since justice does not embody

---

[55] William Christian claims that Grant was not opposed to a kind of general liberalism that all good people can affirm. The liberalism that Grant opposes is a later species "oriented by cybernetics"; see William Christian, "George and the Terrifying Darkness," in Schmidt, ed., *George Grant in Process*, p. 174.

[56] See George Grant, "An Ethic of Community," in Christian and Grant, eds., *The George Grant Reader*, p. 61.

[57] See Grant, *English-Speaking Justice*, pp. 13–47.

an eternal good or truth, the resulting moral and political ordering is oriented toward asserting greater mastery over nature and human nature. And, he asks, in "imposing" the human will to mastery over an "accidental world, does not 'justice' take on a new content?"[58] In failing to address this question, late liberals have allowed justice to become a means of asserting the will to power while also failing to recognize the influence technological necessity exerts on the formation of the humans asserting that will. As the natural events of birth and death become artifacts of the human will, social, political, and intergenerational relationships, and what constitutes their just ordering, are transformed in subtle, yet profoundly troubling ways. How else, Grant wonders, can we account for the exclusion of fetuses and other non-persons, in the name of justice, from the full regard and protection of the moral and political communities?[59] When justice is ripped away from the good and the true and is attached to the will to mastery, it is reduced to little more than a thin rationale justifying a nihilistic will to power. The unborn, weak, and dying are placed at the mercy of the healthy, strong, and powerful.

Late liberals simply fail to recognize that, in adopting technology as the principal means of enacting their freedom, they have bought a package deal and its attendant destiny. The resulting moral myopia prevents them from seeing the horizon of the universal and homogenous state toward which they are heading. Should they arrive at this destination they will not find there a perfected freedom but its tyrannous purgation, both for the sake of negating its underlying nihilism and in the name of technological efficiency and necessity. In the name of freedom and justice late liberals are creating a world and destiny in which they cannot exist in any objective or enduring manner. In Grant's sobering words, "as our liberal horizons fade in the winter of nihilism, and as the dominating amongst us see themselves within no horizon except their own creating of the world, the pure will to technology (whether personal or public) more and more gives sole content to that creating."[60] Moreover, it is a horizon that casts a long and dark shadow, preventing late moderns from seeing their world as it is.

To a large extent, Grant's account of historicism and mastery reiterates themes explicated by Nietzsche and Heidegger. Yet they can only expose but not illumine the darkness of late modernity since they cannot call the darkness dark, for both remain too deeply entangled in its nihilism and historicism. Grant, however, is able to illumine the darkness *as* darkness for he utilizes a light emanating from an alternative source. In order to understand why the darkness of late modernity is dark, we must direct our attention toward this other horizon. Grant came to believe that the principal philosophical task at hand is not to condemn late modernity but to comprehend it for what it is, and he is therefore self-convicting.[61] Attention should

---

[58] See ibid., pp. 79–80.
[59] See ibid., pp. 69–89; see also Grant, *Technology and Justice*, pp. 103–130.
[60] Grant, *Technology and Empire*, p. 40.
[61] See Lampert, "The Uses of Philosophy in George Grant," pp. 193–194.

be shifted away from describing what is wrong with late modernity and toward disclosing the truth that is absent.[62] Revealing this absence requires a recovery and defense of Platonic Christianity. Grant adopts this strategy in response to his reading of Simone Weil.[63]

Through Weil, Grant adopts a Platonic philosophical framework that enables him to move his assessment of late modernity beyond critique. This move is seen in his discussion of the relation between the necessary and the good. The fundamental flaw at the core of late modernity is its refusal to bracket the temporal within the eternal, and the corresponding late liberal move of collapsing the eternal into the temporal—hence the herculean historicist efforts to transform the necessary into the good. These efforts, however, are self-defeating, for they amount to little more than vain and inept attempts at asserting the will to power as compensation for the loss of the eternal. Historicism, then, does not enable humans to overcome the constraints of natural necessity but, rather, promotes its exchange for a technological necessity as a way of domesticating the nihilism that inevitably plagues all assertions of the will to power. Late moderns cannot consent to their own finitude and mortality because they presume that since the eternal is not readily apparent in the temporal, it must therefore not exist. This is a false presumption because it stems from the mistaken belief that knowledge originates in the temporal will to power. Following Plato via Weil, Grant refuses this belief and offers the alternative conviction that knowledge originates in eternal love, and out of love the eternal has absented itself from the temporal. It is in and through love that creation is brought into being, and because of love that the eternal removes itself from creation in order that it might be other than its creator which can in turn be loved and love in return. Correspondingly, the realm of necessity can never be a realm of goodness, for the good originates in the eternal and not the temporal. All attempts at constructing the good within the realm of necessity are doomed to fail because humans are cut off from the true source of the good, and the chasm separating the temporal from the eternal cannot be bridged by any historicist or technological projects.

In refusing late modernity's historicism, Grant is offering in its stead a purposeful history. But it is not an account of history derived from a theological doctrine of providence as a series of divine interventions that can be easily

---

[62] In Grant's words: "I want to think less about what is wrong with the modern and more about the truth of what is not present in the modern" (Cayley, *George Grant in Conversation*, p. 187).

[63] For discussions of Weil's influence on Grant, see Athanasiadis, *George Grant and the Theology of the Cross* (esp. ch. 3); Edwin B. Heaven and David R. Heaven, "Some Influences of Simone Weil on George Grant's Silence," in Schmidt, ed., *George Grant in Process*, and Lawrence Schmidt, "George Grant on Simone Weil as Saint and Thinker," in Davis, ed., *George Grant and the Subversion of Modernity*. Grant's most sustained meditation on Weil is contained in his essay "Faith and the Multiversity," in Grant, *Technology and Justice*, pp. 35–77.

debased into a liberal belief in progress.⁶⁴ Rather, he invokes an understanding of providence in terms of God's loving absence from the world: history is an account of God's waiting for the world. The late modern world cannot truly love its fate because it cannot embrace a genuine love as absence as opposed to a presence that can be manipulated, and the derivative principle that such love is expressed in the surrender rather than assertion of mastery. Providence, as divine waiting, is always inscrutable and never subject to human manipulation, and true love as the trajectory of the world's history thereby entails the renunciation of force and control. The moral challenge is to recover love as the foundation of knowledge. This love as absence is disclosed most pointedly and poignantly in suffering and affliction, and any philosophical account attempting to dismiss or evade this fundamental experience is pursuing a fraudulent knowledge.

This foundational love, however, cannot be narrated in late modern terms for it is rendered inexplicable. Affliction is an unwanted by-product of natural or historical necessity that must be ameliorated or prevented by employing, more often than not, technological remedies. Yet this recourse to technology merely amplifies the priority of a manipulative power over a suffering love. What is needed to narrate the primacy of love is an alternative language, and Grant turns to Athens and Jerusalem to supply the requisite vocabulary and concepts. These two ancient cities symbolize, respectively, Platonism and Christianity, or, broadly, philosophy and theology. Although Grant acknowledges that there are inevitable tensions between the Platonic philosophical and Christian theological traditions, he nonetheless insists that they are inseparable, for he commends Weil's assertion that "[f]aith is the experience that the intelligence is enlightened by love."⁶⁵ Contrary to the values rhetoric of late modernity, Athens and Jerusalem enables discourse on good and evil. Admittedly, those appropriating this ancient discourse remove themselves from the public arena of progressive politics,⁶⁶ but it is this peripheral position that grants the ensuing narrative its discursive and moral appeal. The language of good and evil requires a differing set of initial questions from those of values rhetoric, in turn opening the possibility of recovering a normative understanding of justice—one based ultimately on love rather than power.

This shift to the periphery is seen in Grant's account of the theology of the cross as the centerpiece in his recovery of the language of Athens and Jerusalem.⁶⁷ The

---

⁶⁴ This is Grant's principal complaint against Oman in his D.Phil thesis; see "The Concept of Nature and Supernature in the Theology of John Oman," in Arthur Davis and Peter Emberley, eds., *Collected Works of George Grant: Volume 1, 1933–50* (Toronto: University of Toronto Press, 2000), pp. 157–419.

⁶⁵ Grant, *Technology and Justice*, p. 38.

⁶⁶ See Grant, *Technology and Empire*, pp. 43–44.

⁶⁷ Although the language of Grant's published works is predominantly Athenian, it is the faith of Jerusalem that provides the background against which his refusal is formulated. In many respects, it is Grant's theological convictions that provide the conceptual content of his philosophical critique of late modernity. If these theological convictions are ignored

crucifixion of Jesus reveals God's absence in a striking and decisive manner. In striking contrast to Socrates, who dies peacefully in the company of friends, Jesus suffers an agonizing death, alone and abandoned. Yet God's absence at Golgotha should be seen as a gift of grace and truth. God's absence is a work of love that allows the world to be the world; and the world thereby cannot overcome the necessities imposed by its temporality and finitude. It is in this absence, then, that God's presence through God's waiting is revealed. In Christ crucified the Good and the necessary are mediated, for in this act the will to power and mastery are renounced in favor of a self-emptying love. In the crucifixion, the necessary and the good are separated by "an infinite distance."[68] Justice appears to be entirely absent in this event, but it is an expression of eternal justice, entailing suffering and affliction, which cannot be chosen by any temporal being because it can only be undertaken by the just. In his crucifixion Christ consents to necessity in order to be its mediator with the Good. Intimations of this mediation are seen more expansively in the world's suffering and affliction. When seen in this light, the cross itself discloses the reality of the world which is grounded in what is eternally good, true, and beautiful, and it is this grounding in turn that enables humans to love the world and its fate.

According to Grant, the theology of the cross enables humans to know and engage in the world as it is. The dark reality of the late modern world is captured most distinctly in its attendant technological civilization. As a civilization embodying the nihilistic will to mastery, it is destined for the universal and homogenous state, complete with its inherent tyranny and denial of justice. Grant attributes the dark destiny of technological civilization to its underlying theology of glory. The theology of glory stems from an account of providence that is derived from God's will rather than God's waiting. Consequently, more emphasis is placed on the assertion, rather than renunciation, of power. As Christianity grew more secular following the Enlightenment, this notion of divine power was distorted into the nihilistic will to power, and in this respect Protestantism bears a heavy responsibility for unwittingly underwriting the modern liberal belief in progress.[69] For Grant, the chief weakness of the theology of glory is that it fails to see the world as it is. It therefore cannot inspire a true love of the world and its fate because it attempts to refashion God as an accomplice of humans pursuing any purposes

---

or casually dismissed, Grant can easily be dismissed as an eccentric antiquarian. For a detailed inquiry into Grant's theological convictions see Athanasiadis, *George Grant and the Theology of the Cross*; for a concise overview see Harris Athanasiadis, "Waiting at the Foot of the Cross: The Spirituality of George Grant," in Ian Angus *et al.*, eds., *Athens and Jerusalem: George Grant's Theology, Philosophy, and Politics* (Toronto and London: University of Toronto Press, 2006); cf. Sheila Grant, "George Grant and the Theology of the Cross.".

[68] See George Grant, "St Augustine," in Arthur Davis, ed., *Collected Works of George Grant, Volume 2: 1951–1959* (Toronto: University of Toronto Press, 2002), p. 483.

[69] See Grant, *Technology and Empire*, pp. 15–40.

and goals they might will or desire. As a result, suffering can be easily justified as a casualty of necessity. This justification, however, corrupts justice because evil is called good, and good evil. In short, the darkness of late modernity is its ignorance of the good and true, and therefore of its corresponding denial of justice.

If, as Grant insists, the cross illumines late modernity's darkness *as* darkness, then the proper response is one of consent, obedience, and reverence. These acts provide the rough lineaments of the alternative narration inspired by Athens and Jerusalem. Since Christ consented to necessity, so too should humans, albeit in an attenuated way. Responding to Christ's cross requires consenting to the finitude and mortality delineating the human condition, rather than trying to overcome them as inimical constraints against the will. Here again, there is a strong anticipatory, as opposed to immediate, element, for to "consent to death and finitude ... is preparation for genuine life rather than a prelude into nothingness."[70] Moreover, such consent is an act is an act of obedience, again emulating Christ's obedience to God.[71] It is not, however, obedience based on compulsion or blind devotion, but a joyful response to the eternal source of love which brackets the temporal world or, in more theological terms, God's love as the origin and destiny of the world. Such obedience promotes a knowledge of the world as it is—namely, a work of God's love—and therefore it is a knowledge accompanied by reverence as opposed to mastery. For Grant, reverence entails rejoining the true and the beautiful which late modernity has torn apart. In this rejoining, the world may be seen for what it is: an other to be respected and loved as an other; a whole which in its own right is true and beautiful, rather than raw material to be exploited and mastered. Or in Grant's words: "The key difficulty in receiving the beauty of the world is that such teaching is rooted in the act of looking at the world as it is, while the dominant science is rooted in the desire to change it."[72]

The import of such consent, obedience, and reverence is that they instantiate practices that make the recovery of Athens' and Jerusalem's language of good and evil explicable, and therefore make the recovery of normative justice plausible. For justice is not a human invention assisting the assertive will to power, but part and parcel of a world that is an other and not an artifact of the human will. And this world is a whole with a given order, derived from the reality of its truth and beauty. Consequently, what is "given in our knowledge of the whole" is a "knowledge of good" which we "do not measure and define, but by which we [are] measured and defined."[73] Justice serves to both constrain the will and orient the trajectory of moral deliberation and action in line with what is required by the true and the good. It is in consenting to the necessity of the world as it is that humans may reverently partake of its reality in and toward which they obediently conform their will.

---

[70] Athanasiadis, *George Grant and the Theology of the Cross*, p. 192.
[71] According to Athanasiadis, consent and obedience are the chief concepts of Grant's spirituality; see Athanasiadis, "Waiting at the Foot of the Cross," pp. 265–266.
[72] Grant, *Technology and Justice*, p. 50.
[73] See ibid., pp. 58–59; cf. Grant, *English-Speaking Justice*, pp. 74–75.

Grant, however, adds a cautionary note that the counter-narration ensuing from recovering the language of Athens and Jerusalem is not narrated in late modern terms. Otherwise it simply becomes one more value among the many from which late moderns can pick and choose—a commodity to be consumed by shoppers who happen to fancy it. Rather, in narrating the truth, beauty, and goodness that are absent from the technological civilization entails the refusal of late modernity's description of what is real. The questions of technological civilization are simply not the questions of Athens and Jerusalem. Grant is well aware of the moral and political consequence of this simultaneous recovery and refusal: namely, a muted voice along the fringe which, if late moderns hear at all, they greet with bewilderment or hostility, for what is offered in response to an endlessly recurring will to will is a patient waiting for a waiting God. A severe conceptual and political tension rests at the heart of Grant's Platonic–Christian counter narrative, a tension elegantly captured by Yusuf Umar and worth quoting at some length:

> To be a Christian … is to accept the eventuality of salvation. To be Platonic is to accept the attainability of the truth by the few only. To be a Platonist and Christian is to believe in the necessity of reason and revelation, as the proper domains of the few and of the multitude, respectively. But this belief not only cannot be popularized or made the basis for a meaningful public life, but also seems to the rest of liberal and democratic society to be antiquarian lunacy or undemocratic elitism.[74]

For the sake of justice, Grant is willing to endure the affliction of being charged as a lunatic or elitist, though pleading, like Socrates and Jesus, his innocence.

Does Grant's counter-narration succeed in revealing late modernity's darkness *as* darkness? To a large extent it does, but there is inadequate explication of what is or should be entailed in waiting for a waiting God in light of this darkness. This inadequacy stems largely from Grant's failure to develop a more extensive and robust theological foundation underlying both his critique of technology and constructive account of justice. In short, he spends a little too much time in Athens and not enough in Jerusalem. Although this need for further theological development is examined in greater detail in Chapter 5, the more prominent themes may be noted briefly at this juncture in bringing this inquiry into Grant's thought to a close.

Grant believes that he can employ Platonic philosophy to subvert late modernity in order to prepare late moderns to receive the truth of Christianity. Yet, in undertaking this task, he finds himself in the difficult position of trying to serve two masters equally. He is not altogether successful in striking the right balance, for, as Ted Heaven has observed, "Grant's Platonism pared down his Christianity to the bare essentials."[75] Grant pays a heavy price for his dependence on minimalist Christian convictions,

---

[74] Yusuf K. Umar, "The Philosophical Context of George Grant's Political Thought," in Yusuf K. Umar, ed., *George Grant and the Future of Canada* (Calgary: University of Calgary Press, 1992), p. 3.

[75] Heaven, "George Grant on Socrates and Christ," p. 316.

for it creates unresolved tensions, unanswered questions, and insufficient doctrinal exposition that weaken both the intellectual and spiritual groundwork on which to build the counter-narrative he envisions and wishes to espouse. As suggested by Umar, Grant is aware of the tension between Athens' elitism and Jerusalem's egalitarianism, but he makes no attempt to reconcile them.[76] The resulting responses of bewilderment and hostility are, therefore, not entirely unwarranted, consigning his Platonic–Christian narrative to a more marginalized status than need be. More broadly, Grant leaves unanswered the question of how people come to know the eternal truth, good, and beauty he is proclaiming. Following Weil, for instance, he suggests, rather enigmatically, that Christ's cross reveals most profoundly that in "God's absence is God's *secret* presence."[77] Grant cannot or will not tell us how we might come to know this secret, for within his minimalist Christianity there are Gnostic strands that skew his doctrinal emphases and their exposition.[78]

This skewing is seen most prominently in Grant's soteriology. In response to naming the darkness *as* darkness, the best hope Grant has to offer, following Joan O'Donovan,[79] is a irresolute "perhaps": maybe late moderns can recover the necessary love and reverence to think morally again, but this will require that they undertake the task of remembering ancient wisdom in order to discover the good and the true. Consequently, philosophy must think within and speak out of the neglected traditions of Plato and the Bible. But he says little about thinking within and speaking out from the Christian biblical and theological traditions, and what he does say is both eccentric and condensed. He is right, for example, in insisting that Christ's cross should play a prominent role in Christian thought and practice, but he comes perilously close to reducing salvation to the crucifixion, and consequently assigning a redemptive significance to suffering and affliction that they are ill-equipped to bear. Grant says little, if anything, about Christ's resurrection, exaltation, and *parousia*, presumably because of their implicit triumphalism which he associates with the theology of glory. Sequestering the crucifixion from these subsequent events and expectations, however, effectively strips his theology of the cross of its teleological orientation toward the eternal. Christ is not merely the foundation of a tradition within the realm of necessity, but also the eschatological end toward which the world is being drawn. The cross is a sign of judgment and redemption, but the latter is a vague afterthought. In stripping away this eschatological anticipation, Grant effectively reduces his soteriology to the recurrence of suffering and affliction;[80] the crucifixion must be repeated in every generation.

---

[76] See also Grant Havers, "Leo Strauss's Influence on George Grant," in Angus *et al.*, eds., *Athens and Jerusalem*, pp. 129–130.

[77] Pam McCarroll, "The Whole as Love," in Angus *et al.*, eds., *Athens and Jerusalem*, p. 278 (emphasis added).

[78] See Song, *Christianity and Liberal Society*, p. 121.

[79] See O'Donovan, *George Grant and the Twilight of Justice*, pp. 128–129.

[80] Grant alludes to the Eucharist as the grounding of a morality which relates joy to suffering, but he does not develop this idea further; see Grant, *Philosophy in the Mass*

This diminished soteriology in turn creates what may be characterized as two crucial voids in Grant's counter-narrative. First, although Grant has much to say about the mastery of nature, he remarkably has no operative doctrine of creation. This is due, in part, to a virtual absence of any eschatology. Grant wishes to speak about a "natural law"[81] inherent in the world as a whole against which humans are measured and defined. Yet it is never clear what end this law serves, and therefore the *telos* of its subsequent measurement and definition is rendered equally vague. If nothing substantively can be said about a created order vindicated in Christ's resurrection, reoriented toward Christ's return, and the world ordered (that is, measured and defined) accordingly in the meantime, then it is difficult to imagine how reverence and obedience can embody the kind of counter-narration Grant envisions. Second, although Grant fears late modernity's fate of the universal and homogenous state, he has no ecclesiology on which to base an alternative. He cannot invoke the rich imagery of a corporate body comprised of its many parts, or a universal community that does not negate the particularity of its constituents' gifts and talents. His weak ecclesiology is again due, in part, to the unwarranted salvific significance he places on suffering and affliction. The church should honor its martyrs, but they cannot be honored in the absence of an enduring community that remembers them, and recurring suffering and affliction alone cannot sustain the church over time; the cross is incomplete without the accompanying signs of an empty tomb, ascension, and promise of return. The church bears witness not only to its crucified Lord, but also to a resurrected, exalted, and returning Lord who is present through the Holy Spirit in the meantime. What Grant fails to acknowledge is that the church's witness is eschatological as well as providential, and its universality is therefore predicated on the love of the other which he wishes to acclaim rather than on the homogenizing power that he despises. Consequently, it is the glorification of the crucified Christ that commands the reverence and obedience that Grant affirms but which, at best, he can only reluctantly embrace.

The most unsatisfying aspect of Grant's otherwise masterful exposure of late modernity's darkness *as* darkness is his ambivalent response of "perhaps." The response is, maybe, inevitable for he remains too fascinated with Heidegger. Grant uses Heidegger to describe the nihilistic and historicist narrative of late modernity against which the counter-narrative of Athens and Jerusalem is ascribed. Yet in undertaking this ascriptive task, Grant does not discard Heidegger but continues to use him in fashioning the structure of his counter-narrative. Consequently, in purportedly refusing Heidegger, and therefore Nietzsche as well, Grant still allows them to frame the argument. As will be argued in Chapter 5, however, with further theological development, particularly in respect to eschatology, the darkness that Grant so brilliantly unveils does not elicit the ambivalent response of "perhaps" but one of confession and repentance.

Age, pp. 102–103.

[81] See ibid., pp. 26–37.

Chapter 3
Hannah Arendt: Mortality and Natality

According to Hannah Arendt, both Nietzsche and Heidegger fail in their respective attempts to overcome nihilism. Nietzsche's failure stems, in part, from his mistaken perception of what he is endeavoring to surmount. He believes that he can overcome nihilism by becoming the foremost nihilistic thinker. Yet thinking itself cannot prevail over what is thought, for the thinker remains entrapped in the categories of thought that one is attempting to transcend. In Arendt's words, "[t]here are no dangerous thoughts; thinking itself is dangerous, but nihilism is not its product. Nihilism is but the other side of conventionalism; its creed consists of negations of the current so-called positive values, to which it remains bound."[1] In attempting to reverse Plato, for instance, Nietzsche is seemingly unaware that his thinking remains Platonic, and, as a consequence, he cannot recognize that "inversion and reversal can occur only within a set of givens that must first be accepted as such."[2] In fixating on nihilism as a way of thinking that can be thought through and ultimately transcended, Nietzsche effectively eviscerates the potency of his account of the will to power. He contends that willing is not synonymous with desiring or wanting but is grounded in the power to command. Freedom is thereby the power both to command and to refuse a command. In and through such willing humans can overcome the world, and in turn become the Overman who can save the world from its nihilism. The world, however, does not need to be saved from a nihilism that is thought but from nihilistic acts that are willed. The issue at stake is not to "overcome the nihilism inherent ... in the notions of the thinkers, but in the reality of modern life."[3] In focusing on thinking the thoughts of nihilists, Nietzsche's will to power is ineffectual in dealing with this modern reality, for since nihilism is but the flip-side of conventionalism the nihilistic principle that anything is possible because everything is permitted is negated as nonsense by the finite and mortal limitations that constrain and shape the realities of the modern world. The will to power is actually little more than the will to live—a common survival instinct ingrained in every living creature that defines and delimits how the freedom to command and refuse a command is exercised. Consequently, Nietzsche's claim of being a moralist rings hollow because life itself cannot be the highest value. Freedom, justice, or the *polis*, for instance, may

---

[1] Hannah Arendt, *The Life of the Mind, Vol. 1: Thinking* (San Diego, CA, and London: Harcourt, 1978), p. 176.
[2] Hannah Arendt, *The Promise of Politics* (New York: Schocken Books, 2005), p. 71.
[3] Hannah Arendt, *Between Past and Future: Eight Exercises in Political Thought* (New York and London: Penguin Books, 2006), p. 30.

serve as alternatives that at times may require denying the will to survive for the sake of preserving such values. Ultimately, Nietzsche's Overman looks more like a last man emboldened by false bravado than a savior of the world.

Arendt's criticism of Heidegger, albeit oblique, is that he too fails to overcome nihilism because he is fixated on the wrong question. For Heidegger, the will (following Nietzsche) is the key concept for understanding modern nihilism. The will is asserted primarily through technologies that are deployed to master nature and human nature. Such mastery, however, will prove to be ultimately destructive, if not fatal, because the will being asserted remains so deeply enframed by modern technology that it cannot see that what it is willing is its own eventual demise. Contrary to Nietzsche, no Overman can arise to save humans from this fate, for such a creature would simply be an artifact of the nihilistic will to power. Only that which transcends the technological enframement—a god—can save the world from this self-destructive fate, yet it too will likely prove to be little more than a figment of late modernity's nihilistic imagination. In response to the question of what can save the world from modern nihilism, the only realistic answer to be gleaned from Heidegger is nothing. Consequently, death is *the* constitutive element of late modern ontology; being is always headed toward death.[4]

In many respects, Arendt shares Heidegger's sobering account. She agrees that the will, particularly the will to will, is the centerpiece of late modernity's ontology. Furthermore, she agrees that technology is enabling a nihilistic assertion of the will that is driving the world toward a potentially fatal end. She does not dispute that the attempt to master nature and human nature (which has always been an underlying feature of Western metaphysical thought) results in a pervasive alienation and loss of freedom; the ubiquity of late modern technology has instrumentalized the world and its inhabitants. She offers no rebuttal to the portrayal of late modernity as a barren wasteland of banal desire, trivial pursuits, and narcissistic self-indulgence. Heidegger's account is flawed, however, because he tells only half the story. Death is certainly *a* constitutive element of late modern ontology, but it is not the only or even necessarily definitive element. Heidegger simply fails to mention the other crucial element that defines and delimits the human condition—namely, birth—and in that failure he cannot entertain the possibility that something new might emerge that can redirect the world's fatal course. Late modernity need not remain fixated on mortality and its resulting anxiety and despair, but it can also be oriented toward natality and the hope it inspires. The fate of the world is not a unidirectional and recurring drift toward death, but a bidirectional orientation toward both death and birth. In consenting to, rather than attempting to overcome, mortality, humans are enabled to embrace natality and thereby the new and renewing possibilities it embodies.

To correct Heidegger's flawed account, Arendt knows she must offer an alternative narrative and, like Grant, she too turns to Athens and Jerusalem in undertaking this task. But, unlike Grant, her objective is not to refuse Heidegger's

---

[4] See Patricia Bowen-Moore, *Hannah Arendt's Philosophy of Natality* (London: Macmillan, 1989), p. 4.

account and the late modern world he describes, but to complete and thicken his narration. Her objective is not to illumine the darkness *as* darkness, but to tell the full, and thereby more illuminating, story. Consequently, she need not choose sides in the "quarrel between the ancients and the moderns" over discovery or mastery,[5] for Athens and Jerusalem are not cities to be resettled but selectively plundered.[6] Such plundering enables Arendt to revisit the crucial question of the will with a more precise interpretive lens than that afforded by Heidegger. The will is crucial not because of its relation to power, but because the question of the will is also the question of freedom, and there is more freedom in willing than in thinking. According to Arendt, the origin of the will in Western thought lies in Christian theology rather than in Greek philosophy.[7] Consequently, the will is not inevitably directed by and toward death, and accordingly nihilism cannot be overcome through thinking alone but must be joined with action.

For Arendt the will is always and necessarily split (hence the underlying potential for bidirectional orientation) and, to explicate why this is the case, she turns to her "old friend" St Augustine. The Augustinian question—I have become a question to myself—can never be answered fully. Humans lack the self-transcendence that is required, and philosophical attempts to do so somewhat resemble "jumping over our own shadows."[8] Only God can answer this question, and since humans can never know the mind of God with any degree of certainty, all they can do is employ a clumsy theological vocabulary to speak about what they think they know about God. Although the essence of human ontology is enigmatic, Augustine appeals to a notion of friendship drawn from the equally enigmatic doctrine of the Trinity to at least gain some suggestive analogies for coming to terms with this unanswerable question. Ultimately, he takes solace in the belief that the divided will is overcome by being transformed in and by God's love. Given his Platonic and Neo-Platonic sensibilities, Augustine must explain how this transformative love originating in the eternal can enter and participate in the temporal. The Incarnation is the lynchpin of his explanation: the Word becomes flesh and dwells among mortal creatures. In offering this theological explanation, however, Augustine also sews some modern (or proto-modern) seeds that later take root. Although Augustine maintains a cyclical view of history, it is uniquely interrupted by the Incarnation and will only be consummated when God brings history to an end.[9] Yet, in introducing the idea that the novel intervention

---

[5] See Arendt, *The Life of the Mind*, I, pp. 53–54.

[6] In contrast to Grant, Arendt prefers Aristotle over Plato (or Socrates), and draws upon Jesus as a teacher rather than a suffering savior.

[7] Again, in contrast to Grant, Athens and Jerusalem do not represent reason and faith respectively, but the origins of thinking and willing.

[8] See Hannah Arendt, *The Human Condition* (Chicago, IL, and London: University of Chicago Press, 1998), pp. 10–11.

[9] In this respect, Augustine rejects the notion that the cyclical repetition of history is endless or eternal.

of the Incarnation can disrupt the world's cyclical history and joining it with the eventual end of that history, he also introduces a secular space between disruption and consummation. It is within this space that modernity emerges, and once God has been killed, Augustine's enigmatic solution of the divided will is rendered untenable. It is the will to will that eventually fills the void, but, rather than repairing the divided will, the resulting nihilism exacerbates the problem, for late moderns fall into the deceptive trap of believing that what the will asserts and projects constitutes reality. In short, late moderns have come to believe that the shadows they are jumping over constitute what is real.

Although Augustine's appeal to divine love fails to bring together the divided will, Arendt deploys an essentially Augustinian framework for joining thinking and action. The two categories simultaneously correct and reinforce each other. What is most significant in this symbiotic process is the direction or orientation of simultaneous critique and construction. Yet if divine love is unable to heal the divided will, what can Arendt offer as an efficacious substitute? Natality—humans may organize themselves to be oriented and open to the prospect that, through their mutually critical and constructive thought and action, new and renewing possibilities might emerge within their shared public life. In short, they may discover and will the priority of natality over mortality as the fundamental ontological principle. The remainder of this chapter inquires into what natality means and how Arendt proposes to reorient human, especially political, life toward it, and also assesses the extent to which she achieves her objective. Moreover, the following analysis employs an Arendtian style in which construction is never far removed from criticism and vice versa.

We may begin with the relationship between mortality and immortality. The ancients, according to Arendt, were obsessed with, and perplexed by, their mortality. Death was a brute fact that brought to an end one's hopes and aspirations; an obliteration and cessation of all that one holds near and dear. In death, humans face the "only reliable law of life" that inevitably consigns "everything human to ruin and destruction."[10] This reliable law, however, rendered humans as unnatural creatures within the immortal world they inhabited; hence their equally obsessive and perplexing fascination with immortality:

> The Greeks' concern with immortality grew out of their experience of an immortal nature and immortal gods which together surrounded the individual lives of mortal men. Imbedded in a cosmos where everything was immortal, mortality became the hallmark of human existence. Men are "the mortals," the only mortal things in existence, because unlike animals they do not exist only as members of a species.[11]

Humans were trapped within a realm of necessity in which their very existence was predicated on birth and death—a beginning and an end. The "reality and

---

[10] Arendt, *The Human Condition*, p. 246.
[11] Ibid., p. 18.

reliability" of the world extended from the sheer impermanence of human lives and their activities.[12] Although the Greeks admired individuals who asserted a heroic indifference to the constraints of necessity, such an apathetic stance was incapable of sustaining a worthwhile public life. If humans were to truly inhabit an immortal world, they must somehow overcome their mortality.

It is in pursuing immortality, Arendt contends, that the Greeks made a fateful division between thought and action. The *vita contemplativa* focused on eternal matters that transcended, and were unconstrained by, the realm of necessity. The eternal is a timeless, divine domain, unaffected by the temporality and finitude of the material world. To contemplate the eternal, then, is to stand outside the arena of human affairs, for no acts performed by mere mortals can be associated with the eternal. Immortality is achieved in death which frees the soul from the body, thereby fixating philosophy upon eternity as the principal object of contemplation. In contrast, the *vita activa* fixes its gaze squarely on the realm of necessity. In this realm immortality is understood as enduring within and over time and is achieved through corporate and intergenerational action. To overcome necessity, humans must strive to perform immortal deeds, an endeavor encapsulated in the *polis*. In the supreme political act of building and maintaining a city over time, a people live on beyond the death of its individual members. It is through the *polis* that humans overcome the mortal constraints of necessity, for as long as an immortal world exists, the work of political construction continues.

There is, however, an inherent contradiction in this scheme that the Greeks could never resolve. On the one hand, death offers no real solution for the philosopher, because contemplation of the eternal must necessarily come to an end when the contemplator inevitably dies. Contemplating eternity relieves the anxiety of mortality for a period of time, but does not negate it. On the other hand, a generic *polis* may be part of an immortal world, but particular cities regularly come and go, stripping political action of any pretension to performing an immortal deed; when a particular *polis* dies, so too do the generations of people who built it. In the end, neither the philosopher nor the politician can escape their mortal fate. The Romans relieved this tension somewhat by shifting the focus of philosophical reflection on the task of political construction, effectively privileging the *vita activa* over the *vita contemplativa* by transforming philosophy into the practical application of theory. It was through politics, therefore, that humans could come closest to attaining the divine, immortal life. Consequently, it was the life of the commonwealth, as opposed to the life of the mind, which held realistic potential for achieving a semblance of immortality. Despite its imperial pretensions, however, Rome was aware that achieving this potential was slim at best, which only heightened its underlying fear of death.

According to Arendt, this underlying fear provided a fertile field for Christianity. Following Augustine, anxiety is a natural reaction to mortality. Since all persons to want to live, life is therefore a good to be cherished. Love is also a craving,

---

[12] See ibid., pp. 95–96.

and every craving has an object to be desired. Since humans should love life, they should also desire to live forever. Yet such a healthy love can easily turn to fear because its craving remains unsatisfied. In fearing death, humans inevitably come to fear life as well. "Thus the future in which man lives is always the expected future, fully determined by his present longing or fears."[13] Only a present without a future is unthreatening. Through its promise of eternal life, Christianity offered such an unthreatening future. But this offer was no mere reprise of previous Greek and Roman solutions in a Christian tune, for what was being offered was neither a fixation on an ethereal eternity nor the construction of an enduring *polis*, but the immortal soul of every individual believer. Faith, not contemplation or politics, could satisfy the human craving stemming from the love of life. Although Christians rightly shared some sympathy with a philosophical contemplation of the eternal, it is a doomed strategy for even the greatest mind is so disfigured by sin that the eternal cannot be known correctly or fully. The eternal can only be received in faith as a gift of grace given by God. More pointedly, Christians had little patience with the notion of an immortal *polis*, for "[n]othing could be more alien to Christian thought than this concept of an earthly immortality of mankind."[14] No work undertaken by mortal and finite beings can endure in a material world that is destined to come to an end. Not even the *Civitas Dei* is immortal, for the church itself ultimately has no future when time is fulfilled in God's eternity. It is neither contemplation nor politics that can bind humans together over time, but faith in the promise of eternal life. Consequently, the Greek and Roman solutions for overcoming mortality are stillborn because they are fixated on the wrong problem. The issue at hand is not overcoming a mortal state that all humans share, but to consent to it as a fate that has been redeemed by God. It is precisely the mortality that is feared which should be embraced as the chief ingredient that binds individuals together as a people and directs their corporate action:

> The individual is not alone in this world. He has companions-in-fate (*consortes*), not merely in this situation or that, but for a lifetime. His entire life is regarded as a distinct fateful situation, the situation of mortality. Therein lies the kinship of all people and at the same time their fellowship (*societas*).[15]

With the rise of Christianity came the ensuing task of cobbling together a society of mortals that ordered and oriented them as individuals toward an eternity beyond their shared fate. It was this stress on the fate of individuals that captured consequent intellectual attention, and in turn unwittingly sowed the seeds of a subsequent fixation on self-interest. If the fate of one's soul was of paramount concern, then social bonds were effectively reduced to a secondary consideration

---

[13] Hannah Arendt, *Love and Saint Augustine* (Chicago, IL, and London: University of Chicago Press, 1996), p. 13.
[14] Arendt, *Between Past and Future*, p. 68.
[15] Arendt, *Love and Saint Augustine*, p. 100.

or, worse, a distraction. A corresponding denigration of political thought was an inevitable outcome. With the concurrent rise of modern thought and decline of Christianity, however, the need to provide a substitute underpinning for a stable social order revived an interest in political philosophy. But this effort was not directed toward a political vision of ordering the common good of the *polis*, but of crafting structures to protect and promote the peace of civil communities comprising self-interested individuals. Hence, the challenge of modern politics to somehow reconcile interests which were often irreconcilable. In confronting this challenge, modern political thought made a fateful turn, for contemplation, action, and faith were rejected in favor of the will. The will became crucial when it was widely believed that humans had the sole responsibility for dictating their own destiny. Yet assuming this responsibility effectively transformed politics into the deliberate assertion or constraint of power. Two dominant schools of thought emerged for prescribing how such willful power should be exercised. The liberal prescription entailed a state that asserted whatever minimal power was required to preserve peaceful associations and structures in and through which individuals could pursue their respective interests. In contrast, the communitarian remedy entailed a state that constrained and redirected the interests of individuals toward more common goals and pursuits. At their best, both schools produced relatively stable regimes based on constitutional principles establishing varying degrees of the power of the state and varying guarantees of individual rights and liberties. At their worst, liberalism degenerates into a mindless and decadent consumerism,[16] and communitarianism mutates into brutal totalitarianism.[17]

It must be stressed, however, that the modern revival of political thought does not mark the victory of the *vita activa* over its ancient counterparts of the *vita contemplativa* or Christian faith. For moderns, the *polis* is not the end of their work, but the means. Politics is merely a useful tool for undertaking the larger work of constructing whatever history and destiny that humans might will. For moderns, history is no longer an account of human deeds but an artificial process of being in the world. In short, humans *make* their own history: hence the progressivism pervading both modern liberalism and communitarianism, culminating in the aspirations of autonomous individuals or the universal and homogenous state respectively. It is not surprising that such seemingly desperate goals would share a common belief in progress, for it "not only explains the past without breaking up the time continuum but it can serve as a guide for acting into the future."[18] Yet when progress, however it is defined, is the template for constructing history and destiny as an artifact of the human will, then the ancient fear of mortality and quest for immortality return with a vengeance, for the latter

---

[16] See Arendt, *The Human Condition*, pp. 22–78.

[17] See Hannah Arendt, *The Origins of Totalitarianism* (San Diego, CA: Harvest Book, 1968), part 3.

[18] Hannah Arendt, *Crises of the Republic* (San Diego, CA, and London: Harcourt Brace, 1972), p. 129.

is not confined to contemplation or the *polis*, but entails the very refashioning of the world into what humans will it to be and to become.[19] Consequently, if death is to be conquered through the work of an immortal human history, the constraints of natural necessity must be broken and refashioned in compliance with the human will. And in breaking the chain of necessity and constructing their immortal work, moderns turned increasingly to technology as the "ground" on which the "two realms of history and nature have met and interpenetrated each other."[20]

In order to come to terms with the extent of this interpenetration, we must first come to see how moderns collapsed nature and history into a singular act or, better, work of the will. Drawing on classical Greek thought, Arendt draws a fundamental distinction between labor and work. Labor entails physical effort to provide objects—such as food, shelter, and tools—which sustain human life. Labor is a response to the dictates of natural necessity. Work, however, is a human artifact that endures over an extended period of time beyond the lifetime of the worker and thereby transcends, or at least ameliorates, constraints of natural necessity. A genuine work, then, is an artificial construct that is intergenerational in character. Printing and binding a book is labor, whereas writing it is work; the printer is a laborer, while the author is a worker.

The Greeks disdained labor and cherished work. The craftsman and shepherd, for instance, were held in contempt because they were "enslaved by necessity" and relegated to lowly "occupations that served the needs for the maintenance of life," and it was precisely due to the "slavish nature" of these chores that they were often performed by slaves.[21] Work could only be undertaken by those free from the burdens of necessity and was thereby pursued by a small and elite cadre that was, by nature, capable of bearing the weight of its freedom. Labor was associated with the *oikos* whereas work was pursued in the *polis*. The *oikos* was where the needs of necessity were met and was thereby necessarily a private and hierarchical realm. Heads of households—superior husbands-fathers-masters—ruled over and ordered the laboring of inferior wives, children, and slaves. And given its enslavement to the cruel and crushing dictates of necessity, the private and "prepolitical" *oikos* was often a realm of violence.[22] Since heads of households were free of the burden of necessity, they alone were the citizens who were permitted entrance into the *polis*. Here, they entered a public realm of freedom, for, unlike the inequality of the *oikos*, the *polis* was predicated on equality. Here, one was surrounded by peers who together pursued the work of non-violent political speech. It was their words uttered in public that would endure beyond their deaths. Consequently, the *polis*

---

[19] See Arendt, *Between Past and Future*, pp. 74–75.

[20] See ibid., pp. 61–62.

[21] See Arendt, *The Human Condition*, pp. 82–84. Arendt contends that the Greeks justified slavery not on the basis of cheap labor and increased profit, but on the basis that free men (and here there is no reason to pretend to be inclusive, given classical Greek anthropology) should be spared the degradation of being enslaved to necessity.

[22] See ibid., p. 31.

was, for the ancient Greek, *the* supreme work, and although the *oikos* was inhabited by humans, it was only the fortunate few who could experience a "second birth"[23] into the *polis* where, to use Arendt's terms, they became men.

Modern political thought, however, reversed the priority by privileging labor over work. It was the production and consumption of goods and services that best promoted the interests of self-interested individuals, an endemic condition that more communitarian experiments could not eliminate and, ironically, in some instances unwittingly promoted.[24] Modern political thought assumed that autonomous agents have no substantive need of each other, as demonstrated in modernity's politics and morality. One fateful consequence of this reversal was the invention of "society." For Arendt, modern society is a vast wasteland of mindless consumption and purposeless activity. Labor is deployed to produce goods that can be readily and voraciously consumed. Late moderns are either laboring or playing, and anything not connected with "making a living" are hobbies or leisure pursuits requiring still more items to be produced and consumed.[25] Occupations are therefore valued only in terms of their utility in respect to production and consumption.[26] A grave consequence of late modern society is that there can be no public space, but only a series of private acts done publicly, or what Arendt identifies as the emergence of "what is euphemistically called mass culture" comprising happy and greedy consumers.[27]

Ironically, the modern *work* of creating human history and destiny is rendered absolutely dependent on labor. This dependency is seen most acutely in the development and deployment of modern technology. Technology does not solely make the production and delivery of goods and services more efficient; it is not merely an instrumental means of assisting labor. Rather, technology represents the far more ambitious enterprise of overcoming, if not negating, the dictates of natural necessity. With increasing ease, humans continue to labor in order to survive, but in overcoming necessity they are enabled to work harder at making themselves at home in a world they are in the process of making. Labor, which is grounded in natural necessity, is now devoted to preserving and enhancing human artifice. Yet, as Arendt insists, this reordering of labor and work is deceptive. "Tools and instruments ease pain and effort and thereby change the modes in which the urgent necessity inherent in labor was manifest to all. They do not change the necessity

---

[23] See ibid., pp. 175–181; see also Patricia Bowen-Moore, *Hannah Arendt's Philosophy of Natality,* pp. 40–41.

[24] According to Arendt, Marxism was one of the principal forces driving this reversal. See Arendt, *Between Past and Future*, pp. 21–24.

[25] See Arendt, *The Human Condition*, pp. 126–135.

[26] Arendt notes in passing that this is why modern intellectuals tried to portray their work as labor. See ibid., pp. 92–93.

[27] See ibid., pp. 133–134; cf. George Grant, *Philosophy in the Mass Age* (Toronto: University of Toronto Press, 1995).

itself; they only serve to hide it from our senses."[28] One result is that nature becomes objectified, thereby effectively removing human life, or at least creating the perception of its removal, from its necessary constraints. Concurrently, the purported "elimination of necessity ... only blurs the distinguishing line between freedom and necessity."[29] Ironically, in reordering labor to overcome necessity, humans have enslaved themselves to superimposing their work over a nature on which they remain ultimately dependent, despite the concealed ease of their labor.

More troubling, this reordering occludes the formative influence that technology exerts over the fabrication of the world as a human work. Although tools are admittedly instruments, they have more than an instrumental quality. The line separating humans from their tools is becoming increasingly blurred. The act of making, rather than the finished product of physical effort, is what now drives laboring. Humans literally live in a world that has been reduced to a process of their own perpetual fabrication. Consequently, the design and application of technology requires that humans adapt their lives to constant innovation. The resulting "need" for innovation displaces the natural rhythms of the body as machines replace physical labor. Technology, then, begins to appear less artificial and more like a biological process that takes on a life of its own.[30] The work of creating a human history and destiny is little more than a fool's errand, for a technological world is meaningless because meaning must have permanence, a condition that is anathema to the late modern reversal of labor over work. In attempting to overcome necessity, humans have forsaken any possibility of genuine labor and work, and thereby any meaningful life. As Arendt contends, contrary to popular perception, technology was never intended to promote or improve the quality of life:

> The question therefore is not so much whether we are the masters or the slaves of our machines, but whether machines still serve the world and its things, or if, on the contrary, they and the automatic motion of their processes have begun to rule and even destroy world and things.[31]

To use Heidegger's concepts, technology serves as the ontology of a late modernity that it has enframed within itself.

Why is Arendt disturbed by this reordering of work and labor? Modernity transformed a differentiated society into an entirely laboring one, and its inhabitants are freeing themselves from the toil of labor at a time when they know nothing other than laboring. And since there is no recognized spiritual or political aristocracy that may guide this transition, what will laborers do when then there is no labor left? According to Arendt, when necessity has been domesticated humans are purportedly free to fix their gaze upon the beautiful that is expressed

---

[28] Arendt, *The Human Condition*, p. 125.
[29] Ibid., p. 71.
[30] See ibid., pp. 152–153; see also Arendt, *Between Past and Future*, pp. 59–60.
[31] Arendt, *The Human Condition*, p. 151.

through three modes of life: bodily pleasure in which beauty is consumed; politics in which excellence produces beautiful deeds; and philosophy that contemplates eternal things.[32] In pursuing these modes of life, however, late moderns ignored Aristotle and embraced Nietzsche. Eternity is rejected out of hand in favor of an endless time that cannot be contemplated because of its constant flux and change. Consumption and politics are eagerly pursued, but within a world that is ugly rather than beautiful. Hence the consumerism that Arendt decries as mindless, but it is late modern politics that she finds most distressing, if not threatening, because of its inherently violent character. She attributes this violence to the transference of the labor required to overcome necessity from the private (and violent) realm of the *oikos* into an ill-defined society, in turn redefining labor as the principal supportive means of pursuing the work of creating human history and destiny. Moderns have been attempting for quite some time to make their life artificial, reflecting the desire to reject the human condition that is grounded in nature. Following Hegel, late moderns have "succumbed to the strange illusion that man, in distinction from other things, has created himself."[33]

This desire, however, marks a fundamental rejection of the gifted quality of life. The decision to deploy technology as the primary means of severing the necessary ties with nature is, therefore, a political one. Nature is being reconfigured into patterns imposed on it by humans and has become an arena in which humans manufacture their artificial life. But, as Arendt warns, violence is always present in all acts of fabrication, and since all creative acts undertaken by finite and mortal creatures cannot be *ex nihilo*, they constitute a Promethean revolt against nature. Technology, in short, makes human action dangerous, particularly in respect to the political ordering that is required in its development and deployment. This pervading violence is seen opaquely in the subtle transformation of various forms of human associations and interactions,[34] and more extensively in the growing recourse to the seemingly endless political tasks of pursuing revolutionary upheaval, preparing for war, and developing the capabilities of destructive weapons on a global scale.[35]

This potential for violence is exacerbated by the contradictory and ultimately futile attempt by humans to manufacture their artificial life. They turn to technology to construct their immortal history, yet although technology provides a common present, it does so by destroying any and all links to a common past or

---

[32] See ibid., pp. 12–13.

[33] Arendt, *Life of the Mind*, I, p. 37.

[34] Arendt notes that technological research and development has transformed the university into a willing servant of the state in its creation of a violent world; see Arendt, *Crises of the Republic*, pp. 117–119; cf. Grant's meditation on the multiversity in *Technology and Justice* (Notre Dame, IN: University of Notre Dame Press, 1986), pp. 35–77.

[35] Arendt's most extended reflections on these violent political tasks are found in *The Promise of Politics*, *On Revolution* (New York: Viking Press, 1965), and *On Violence* (New York: Harcourt, Brace and World, 1970).

future. Consequently, the late modern quest for immortality only serves to both hide and amplify an anxious fixation on mortality, and its concomitant politics becomes oriented toward death and destruction. Arendt's solution is to recover the true nature of politics as persuasive speech. Following Karl Jaspers, she insists that "limitless communication" is the only unifying principle for the late modern world, not only as an antidote to technology but as a way of binding generations, and thereby past and future, together.[36] Recovering politics as persuasive speech, however, requires a reorientation away from mortality and toward natality.

In order to reorient politics as the premier human work, Arendt narrates natality as an alternative to that of mortality. Although she admits that mortality is the only certainty of human life, individuals are not born to die but to begin.[37] It is natality, then, that saves humankind from its mortality, for the possibility of new beginnings is what gives humans some hope which, in turn, at least potentially bestows meaning to their actions. Moreover, it is a hope most clearly expressed in the Christian account of the birth of Jesus in which a child as gift "has been born unto us."[38] The decisive fact of human life is natality, for every person enters the world through birth.[39] "Birth" and "child" serve as central metaphors in Arendt's alternative narration. According to Patricia Bowen-Moore, there are three principal notions of natality employed by Arendt: "factual natality—birth into the world; political natality—birth into the realm of action; and birth into the timelessness of thought."[40] Every person has, like the world, a beginning. Natality situates a person in a particular time and place, for every child is born into a particular nexus of relationships, in turn confirming the fact that humans are born into a world and communities not of their own choosing or making. It is the given nature of birth that enables the principle of natality as a worldly event that affirms a love for the world. The birth of every baby embodies the prospect of new and renewing possibilities that resist the deadening anxiety of mortality. Although history may appear deterministic, birth renews it on a daily basis.

It is the second birth into politics that concerns us. Natality enables a love for the world that is encapsulated in freedom, and in the continuity *and* disruption of human action over time. Freedom is pre-eminently the ability to act. Humans have "received the twofold gift of freedom and action" with which they can "establish a reality of their own."[41] Following St Augustine, freedom is not a possession but an ontological condition, for each person represents a new beginning, and this new beginning occurs within a world that pre-exists and continues after the death of an

---

[36] See Hannah Arendt, *Men in Dark Times* (San Diego, CA: Harcourt Brace, 1993), pp. 81, 94.

[37] See Arendt, *The Human Condition*, pp. 246–247.

[38] Ibid., p. 247.

[39] Coextensively, Arendt notes that mortality defines desire; see Arendt, *Love and Saint Augustine*, pp. 51–52.

[40] See Bowen-Moore, *Hannah Arendt's Philosophy of Natality*, p. 1.

[41] See Arendt, *Between Past and Future*, p. 169.

individual. "A characteristic of human action is that it always begins something new, and this does not mean that it is ever permitted to start *ab ovo*, to create *ex nihilo*."[42] The modern understanding of freedom, then, is derived from Christian teaching, particularly its insistence of removing freedom from citizenship and participation in the *polis*.[43] This removal, however, proved fateful, for it stripped the *vita activa* away from organizing structures that could simultaneously provide continuity and disruption of action over time. Freedom was thereby achieved by escaping, rather than participating in, the *polis*.

Yet such disdain for politics could not endure if history was to have any meaning, much less *telos*, a deficiency recognized by Augustine whose masterful account of history was narrated under the guiding metaphor of God's *city* in the world. On the one hand, politics is needed to provide continuity, enabling an explicable narration of human life over time. Individuals both embody and live by the stories they tell, and if the larger story of a people that both pre-exists the birth and continues on after the death of individuals is to be sustained, a requisite and enduring political community is required. The "reason why each human life tells its story and why history ultimately becomes the storybook of mankind, with many actors and speakers and yet without any tangible authors, is that both are the outcome of *action*."[44] And the supreme action Arendt has in mind is political. On the other hand, political ordering must allow for disruptive action if it is to encourage freedom. Even the realm of natural necessity incorporates the new and unexpected, for evolutionary advances in biological life in general, and human life in particular, occur in response to genuinely new events. Every "new beginning" is "seen and experienced from the standpoint of the processes it necessarily interrupts."[45] Particularly in regard to political action predicated on freedom, "something that was there before must be removed or destroyed, and things as they were before are changed."[46] Change is thereby a "constant" and "inherent" feature of the human condition, but its "velocity" is not, and politics is the work of proving relative stability within this chaotic turbulence.[47] Through political ordering the past drives history toward the future, while the future pushes it back toward the past; hence the need for both continuity *and* disruption.

Arendt does not decry the late modern project *per se* of creating its own world. Rather, she wishes to embed such work within a political order that provides continuity over time, but in a manner allowing for disruptions that strengthen the

---

[42] Arendt, *Crises of the Republic*, p. 5.

[43] As Arendt notes, "Only when the early Christians, and especially Paul, discovered a kind of freedom which had no relation to politics, could the concept of freedom enter the history of philosophy" (*Between Past and Future*, p. 156).

[44] Arendt, *The Human Condition*, p. 184 (emphasis added).

[45] See Arendt, *The Promise of Politics*, pp. 126–127. Arendt goes so far as to refer to these interruptions as miracles.

[46] Arendt, *Crises of the Republic*, p. 5.

[47] See ibid., pp. 78–80.

freedom to act. Natality provides the requisite formative metaphor by reorienting political action toward new and renewing possibilities instead of the certainty of death, concurrently reclaiming a politics of persuasive speech over that of violence. It is speech that makes humans political creatures, for the artificiality of the political realm creates an equality that displaces natural inequalities. The danger of late modern politics is that a technologically-oriented culture renders speech meaningless. Such a technological orientation is purportedly based on factual information that lends itself to vanquishing natural necessity,[48] but facts preclude debate, and debate is the essence of politics. So-called "factual truth," however, "is no more self-evident than opinion," and be easily interpreted by those in positions to manipulate public opinion.[49] More extensively, technology occludes the underlying reality of a world populated by particular men and women rather than abstract human beings. The resulting politics ignores the webs of given relationships and thereby fails to adequately address the endemic suffering of particular people. Yet no political action can be undertaken without suffering since such action is undertaken by finite women and men. In this respect, politics rightfully tries to ameliorate the burdens of natural necessity, but the task is not to vanquish necessity but to create a political space within it, and that action is properly predicated on speech rather than violence. In this space of freedom and equality a genuine politics may be pursued, for it is a space freed from coercion and domination since it entails discourse and action undertaken by equals. Consequently, politics is not about human beings but about the world constructed by particular men and women. It must be stressed in this regard that Arendt does not preclude the necessity to resort to coercive acts in preserving public order and protecting freedom, but she draws a sharp distinction between an appropriate and limited exertion of lawful force and a more pervasive violence.[50]

Within this space it is also acknowledged that political speech and action are not undertaken by autonomous individuals but by particular women and men who must cooperate in the work of constructing their world, and these men and women are plural in character. A politics predicated on speech must affirm and deal with the existence of different and differing people, for if all people were naturally the same there would be no need for the artificial work of politics. When too much similarity is presumed, differentiation and human nature are destroyed, for politics becomes distorted into a process of refashioning particular people into generic

---

[48] Arendt notes: "Necessity, not freedom, rules the life of society; and it is not by chance that the concept of necessity has come to dominate all modern philosophies of history, where modern thought has sought to find its philosophical orientation and self-understanding" (*The Promise of Politics*, p. 149).

[49] See Arendt, *Between Past and Future*, pp. 235–244; cf. Jacques Ellul, *The Humiliation of the Word* (Grand Rapids, MI: Eerdmans, 1985).

[50] See Arendt, *On Violence*. In this respect, Arendt also notes that, contrary to late modern political rhetoric, the principal purpose of the nation-state is to provide security rather than preserving freedom; see Arendt, *The Promise of Politics*, pp. 144–145.

human beings and a homogenous mass society. Again, technology is deployed as both the principal instrument and formative symbol for achieving these goals.

Arendt is aware, however, that in the absence of equality there can be no freedom, but it "does not require an egalitarian democracy in the modern sense, but rather a quite narrowly limited oligarchy or aristocracy, an arena in which at least a few or the best can interact with one another as equals among equals. This equality has, of course, nothing to do with justice."[51] In order to see how she resolves this dilemma between freedom and justice, we may turn to her two chief political acts of promising and forgiving. Arendt contends that human beings cannot undo deeds they have committed in the past. Action results in unanticipated consequences that inspire a sense of guilt, remorse, and responsibility. Humans, both individually and collectively, suffer the consequences of their deeds, leading them to be less free within the very realm of freedom (the *polis*) that they created through their action. Her political narration of natality, however, is stymied by the necessity to undo prior acts that cannot be undone. She proposes a twofold solution to this dilemma: forgiveness is the remedy for the irreversibility of past deeds, and making and keeping promises is the remedy for unanticipated consequences of present action. Although people are unable to undo what they have done or control all the outcomes of what they will do, they have the capability to ameliorate the ill-effects of the irreversible and unpredictable nature of what they do and fail to do.

Consequently, *forgiving* and *promising* are requisite and inseparable political concepts and practices. An inability to forgive and keep promises would prevent any meaningful political action because individuals and associations would be frozen by the anxiety of unintended consequences. Forgiveness and promise-keeping are thereby predicated on plurality: political association is not a static whole, but a dynamic amalgamation of different individuals and groups pursuing their respective interests. Forgiving and promising enable a political association to embrace a wide range of differences, contradicting the restrictive and exclusionary Platonic principles of rule, domination, and control. Keeping promises, however, is an unpredictable enterprise, because the intent and outcomes of deeds and particular circumstances cannot be known with exact precision; a promise is based on trust rather than certainty. When unwarranted certainty is attributed to promises they lose their binding power, diminishing in turn their capacity to serve as an antidote to rule, domination, and control. Civil community is bound together by its promises, and it is due to these mutual pledges that uncoerced political action is possible and effectual. The imprecision and uncertainty of promise keeping is the price that must be paid to preserve freedom.

The uncertainty of promise-keeping is the reason why it is linked with forgiveness and why together they provide the lynchpin of a good political order. Arendt contends that Jesus discovered the central role that forgiveness should play in human affairs. The religious foundation of his teaching, however, is irrelevant, because its secularized version already lies, albeit buried, within Western

---

[51] Arendt, *The Promise of Politics*, p. 118.

civilization.[52] In this respect, forgiveness is based on mutual respect instead of love, promoting a kind of civil friendship.[53] Most importantly, such respect is not predicated on admiration or esteem, but on a fundamental equality shared among friends. This equality is already latent in Jesus' teaching. Neighbors do not forgive each other because God has first forgiven them. Rather, individuals are commanded to forgive neighbors who have wronged them. It is in forgiving and being forgiven that political relationships are renewed, and in their renewal comes the possibility of more just political action, because the act of forgiving is the prerequisite for keeping promises and making new ones. Although forgiving and promising cannot undo past wrongs, they can ameliorate their paralyzing aftermath. The uncertainty of forgiving and promising is substituted for the certainty of an escalating cycle of vengeance. Consequently, forgiveness can, should, and must play a central role in political ordering, for it is the only action that frees civil community from a destructive fate.

It should not be assumed that Arendt is proposing a naive solution to an intractable problem. She is aware that there are other alternatives, often entailing force or capitulation, for breaking the cycle of vengeance. She admits, for instance, that punishment is the fundamental "alternative to forgiveness."[54] Forgiveness is, in fact, unintelligible in the absence of punishment, for what cannot be punished cannot be forgiven. Arendt favors forgiveness as an alternative to punishment because it represents a partial, yet often preferable, attempt to undo the wrong that has been done, thereby creating a greater range of renewing and novel possibilities for political action.[55] When a judgment is made that an individual has wronged other individuals, groups, or the civil community, assigning a fitting punishment is an appropriate political response. This should not be a wooden judicial process, however, for that would preclude the possibility of forgiveness as the preferred method of breaking the cycle of vengeance. Judgment and punishment would effectively be corrupted into a crude political instrument of exacting a "final revenge" for those in a position to assert their will over their adversaries. Rather, Arendt envisions a fluid relationship between judgment and forgiveness in which punishment is one, but not the only, method for attempting, albeit imperfectly, to

---

[52] Arendt notes: "But the three political experiences that lie outside the tradition, the experience of action as starting a new enterprise in pre-polis Greece, the experience of foundation in Rome, and the Christian experience of acting and forgiving as linked, that is, the knowledge that whoever acts must be ready to forgive and that whoever forgives actually acts, have a special significance because they remained relevant for our history even though they were bypassed by political thought" (ibid. p. 60).

[53] Chiba contends that Arendt maintains an element of disinterested love in her account of politics; see Shin Chiba, "Hannah Arendt on Love and the Political: Love, Friendship, and Citizenship," *Review of Politics*, 57/3 (1995): pp. 505–535.

[54] See Arendt, *The Human Condition*, p. 241.

[55] See Hannah Arendt, *Essays in Understanding, 1930–1954* (New York: Harcourt Brace, 1994), p. 308.

undo a wrong that has been done: "Every judgment is open to forgiveness, every act of judging can change into an act of forgiving; to judge and to forgive are but two sides of the same coin."[56] These two sides, however, follow different rules. Law demands that only acts, not persons, matter. In contrast, forgiveness is focused exclusively on persons. Somebody, not something, is forgiven; the thief is forgiven but not the act of thievery. Such forgiveness disrupts and thereby rejuvenates political ordering, for justice demands equality, while mercy is predicated on inequality, requiring a relation of inevitable tension among judgment, punishment, and forgiveness which, when properly maintained, resists being reduced to any standardized formulae.

What, however, might motivate a civil community to prefer forgiveness over punishment to break the cycle of vengeance? Compassion and pity suggest themselves as possible candidates. The plight of a wronged group, for example, may prompt a sympathetic reaction, triggering in turn political acts promoting forgiveness and reconciliation with groups estranged within or from the civil community. Arendt, however, does not regard compassion and pity as synonymous terms. Compassion denotes an interpersonal concept: I can, perhaps out of love, forgive another individual or small cadre of intimates that have wronged me, and I in turn can accept the forgiveness of another individual or intimates I have wronged. But a similar pattern cannot be replicated within or by the civil community, for it is not an interpersonal relationship writ large since it is an association that is based on justice rather than love. A civil community can be merciful in the pursuit and administration of justice but not compassionate. Indeed, political acts purportedly based on compassion mostly do not result in forgiveness but in violence. Arendt notes, for instance, that the French Revolution was presumably based on a compassion for the poor and exploited. The subsequent revolutionary acts, however, did not end in reconciliation but in exterminating the aristocracy in order to bring an end to their exploitation.[57] In Arendt's words:

> As a rule, it is not compassion which sets out to change worldly conditions in order to ease human suffering, but if it does, it will shun the drawn-out wearisome processes of persuasion, negotiation, and compromise, which are the processes of law and politics, and lend its voice to the suffering itself, which must claim for swift and direct action, that is, for action with the means of violence.[58]

Pity encapsulates a larger reaction. A large association, for example, may pity another that is suffering persecution or injustice and take action on its behalf. Yet again, pity does not promote political acts leading to forgiveness and reconciliation between victims and perpetrators. Rather, pity requires ongoing misery in order to

---

[56] Hannah Arendt, *Reflections on Literature and Culture* (Stanford, CA: Stanford University Press, 2007), p. 254.
[57] See Arendt, *Men in Dark Times*, pp. 14–15.
[58] Arendt, *On Revolution*, p. 82.

be effective, ultimately resulting in the raw assertion of power: "Pity, taken as the spring of virtue, has proved to possess a greater capacity for cruelty than cruelty itself."[59] Out of a general pity revolutionaries, for instance, grow oblivious to the plight of particular individuals. Moreover, pity tends to disregard the demands of law and justice, which is especially damaging to the poor and exploited for they suffer most directly the effects of the violence that is the only means of relieving their condition. In short, when pity is the principal motivation anything is permissible in pursuing revolutionary political change as the ultimate act of vengeance.

Arendt insists that forgiveness is needed to break the cycle of vengeance in order to restore the political trajectory of civil community along the more promising route of nativity. As we shall see, she grounds forgiveness in political duty and obligation as opposed to compassion or pity. Before examining and assessing the efficacy of duty and obligation as the basis for forgiveness, we must first turn our attention to what Arendt admits are two strong objections to her proposal. The first is that forgiveness is the denial of justice. Forgiving, rather than punishing, the members of a brutal regime, for instance, is an expedient ploy to enable an orderly transition of governments at the cost of denying victims their due. Second, forgiveness cannot be given or received for wrongs committed in the distant past, because the dead can neither forgive nor be forgiven. Who, for instance, is in a position to represent an ethnic community that has suffered generations of persecution?

We may note at this juncture Arendt's replies to these objections without evaluating the adequacy of her defense. In response to the objection that forgiveness is the denial of justice, Arendt argues that forgiving is not synonymous with forgetting or ignoring. Some kind of reconciliation or compensation between the wronged and perpetrators must be achieved, otherwise justice is denied. Moreover, the possibility of forgiveness is a predicate of justice, for in principle a wrong that cannot be forgiven can also not be adequately condemned.[60] In reply to the objection that forgiveness cannot correct wrongs originating in the distant past, Arendt concedes that the dead can neither forgive nor be forgiven. Nonetheless, some kind of arrangement between aggrieved groups and the civil community approximating forgiveness can be negotiated. Although there is no such thing as collective guilt, there is a collective responsibility for the past that must be addressed.[61] The civil community, for instance, must in some manner forgive groups that have committed acts of terror over an extended period of time in order to be reconciled, and similarly aggrieved groups must in some sense forgive the civil community for past persecution. Failing to forgive, however imperfectly, condemns civil community to a deadly fixation on the past rather than being

---

[59] Ibid., p. 85.

[60] See, e.g., Hannah Arendt, *Responsibility and Judgment* (New York: Schocken Books, 2003), pp. 75–97; *Eichmann in Jerusalem: A Report on the Banality of Evil* (New York: Penguin Books, 1992), pp. 260–261, 296–297; and *On Revolution*, pp. 85–87.

[61] See Arendt, *Responsibility and Judgment*, pp. 17–48, 147–158.

attentive to a future of new and renewing possibilities; a morbid fascination with mortality rather than being attentive to natality.

There is, however, a third, unacknowledged objection that is more telling and brings us back to Arendt's attempt to embed forgiveness in political duty and obligation. Arendt insists that citizens are obliged to forgive one another. Presumably, this means that the coercive power of the state can be used to enforce compliance, for an obligation implies a right: if I wrong a fellow citizen or the civil community I have a right to be forgiven, and conversely I have a duty to forgive fellow citizens and the civil community if they wrong me. Yet what exactly would be entailed in the state using its power to enforce the obligation to forgive and right to be forgiven? Could I, for instance, be sued or incarcerated if I refuse to forgive or accept forgiveness? The idea of compelling forgiveness is admittedly preposterous *except* under the circumstances of a totalitarian state that intrudes upon and subsumes all private and public associations into the affairs of the state. It would be ironic, to say the least, if Arendt's beloved forgiveness was operable only within the kind of regime she despises.

Arendt's difficulty stems from her allergic reaction to the idea of *society*. Arendt grounds her account of natality in the classical categories of the private *oikos* and public *polis*. Her complaint with the late modern world is that it is profoundly unpolitical, because people should be about the work of creating public, and therefore political, space that encases private spheres. Arendt has little use for a so-called society that mediates or carves out a space between the *oikos* and *polis* because it distorts a genuine public space. As Hanna Fenichel Pitkin has observed, "In the modern world, Arendt argues, the public and private realms have been blurred and largely supplanted by something she calls 'society' or 'the social,' a 'relatively new phenomenon whose origin coincides with the emergence of the modern age'."[62] This so-called society is not so much a space but a malignancy that simultaneously eviscerates the privacy of the *oikos* while eroding the public life of the *polis*. Consequently, the only means left to modern political ordering in preserving some semblance of public life beyond a superficial consumerism is through threat or recourse to the coercive power of the state.

Arendt's allergy is unfortunate, for her notion of forgiveness requires a non-coercive social space that mediates the *oikos* and *polis*. Her account of politics as a realm of speech is not sufficient to carry the weight she places on the necessity to forgive. Although she insists that the recourse to coercion, more often than not, represents the failure of politics rather than its fulfillment, she also admits that political ordering requires the power to compel in order to punish, prevent anarchy, or intervene in breaking the cycle of vengeance. Try as she might, Arendt cannot entirely divorce a political obligation to forgive and a right to be forgiven from the coercive power of the state, thereby jeopardizing the efficacy of the forgiveness she is propounding. What she fails to recognize is that the power of

---

[62] Hanna Fenichel Pitkin, "Justice: On Relating Private and Public," *Political Theory*, 9/3 (1981), p. 333.

forgiveness to break the cycle of vengeance does not reside in obligation and duty, but in permission and grace; people forgive one another not because they must, but because they may.

In dismissing society as a worthless public space, Arendt's only remaining option is the political sphere in which forgiveness may be embedded. Yet in doing so she unwittingly appeals to a politics of rule, domination, and control that she purportedly rejects. She in effect attempts to surgically remove Jesus' teaching from its religious framework and transplant it into a Kantian host emphasizing the centrality of the will. The surgery fails, however, because too much confidence is placed in the goodwill and wisdom of the *polis* to provide the authority of its self-governance. The transplanted forgiveness does not negate the necessity of rule but cloaks it in the will to forgive, thereby masking, but not eliminating, the will to dominate and control. In short, the political will to forgive cannot replace the divine command and permission to forgive, and consequently the defense she offers against the objections that forgiveness is the denial of justice and cannot address wrongs committed in the distant past is ineffectual.

If natality is to be effective in forming a politics of speech, then forgiveness must be an imaginative and empathetic act, creating the possibility of new understandings of the relationship between justice and freedom. Such imaginative and empathetic acts, however, grow increasingly difficult to enact in the late modern world due to the erosion of common moral convictions and precepts that can authorize acts of forgiveness without an implicit threat of coercion. There is insufficient moral or political authority to command such uncoerced consent, thereby either confining forgiveness to a small range of interpersonal relationships devoid of any public significance or imposing it on the civil community through the power of the state. In the absence of such authority, the assertion of raw political power has filled the void.

Arendt admits that "authority has vanished from the modern world."[63] Its disappearance stems from the decline of religion and tradition, creating a world in which there are no common experiences and shared aspirations. Moreover, the void resulting from the disappearance of authority has not remained empty but has been filled by an easy recourse to violence that is often disguised beneath an authoritarian mantle. In Arendt's words, "[s]ince authority always demands obedience, it is commonly mistaken for some form of power or violence. Yet authority precludes the use of external means of coercion; where force is used, authority itself has failed."[64] Although the threat of violence can compel obedience, that does not make it synonymous with authority because it confuses function with form; coercion is simply a bad substitute for authority. Such coercion is not confined to overt acts of violence but pervades the political structures of the late modern world, for an "element of violence is inevitably inherent in all activities of making, fabricating,

---

[63] Arendt, *Between Past and Future*, p. 91.
[64] Ibid., p. 92.

and producing"[65] in contrast to the peaceful nature of political speech. According to Arendt, "force" and "power," which were once separable, have become joined in late modern politics, creating a public space dominated by the self-perceived "brutal reality" of perpetual conflict generated by endless assertions of contending interests.[66] Political weakness is the inevitable result, because politics has been disfigured into a violent activity rather than persuasive speech. For Arendt, the clearest indications of the loss of authority are seen in the totalitarian states of the twentieth century and the stockpiling of weapons of mass destruction.

Arendt is eager to restore authority to the late modern world, for in its absence the possibility of promising and forgiveness is negated, and with it the birth of new and renewing possibilities. She is aware, however, that restoring even a semblance of authority is no easy task. By its nature authority is not compatible with arguments among equals, for it requires that some command while others obey. Authority, then, is seemingly unpalatable to the egalitarian taste of late moderns. Yet Arendt insists that authority can be vested and respected in an office or person so long as it is exercised in a manner that promotes and preserves freedom. Those in authority can command obedience so long as they acknowledge that the power of their office is derived from the consent of the governed, and thereby act in ways that serve their needs. Again in Arendt's words, "[t]o remain in authority requires respect for the person or office."[67]

Arendt also admits that authority without religion cannot be binding in terms of present practice or over time in respect to the past and future. Without common religious bonds forgiveness is again rendered ineffectual because there are no common convictions that can be appealed to in breaking the cycle of vengeance. This necessity of religion seemingly destroys any thread of hope for recovering authority in the late modern world which is increasingly characterized by public secularism and private religious diversity. Yet Arendt believes that Kant offers a workable alternative; the universality of Kantian ethics provides a viable substitute for universal religious faith. Although late moderns cannot believe together, they can still think together; if not life in the Spirit, then the life of the mind can be binding. Moreover, they can think together in ways that unite them with past and future generations.

Is Arendt's proposal for recovering authority on a philosophical, rather than religious, basis promising? The short answer is "no." We may see why this is the case by examining the prospect of forgiving wrongs originating in the distant past within the terms of her proposal. Suppose, for example, that generations of an ethnic minority have suffered persecution by the larger civil community. A consensus has emerged that such persecution is wrong and should be rectified. Accomplishing this goal entails promises to reform the laws and practices of the civil community, and presumably these promises are predicated on the persecuted

---

[65] Ibid., p. 111.
[66] See Arendt, *The Promise of Politics*, p. 147.
[67] Arendt, *On Violence*, p. 45.

group forgiving the civil community, and the civil community in turn receiving their forgiveness. It is difficult to imagine, however, how this giving and receiving of forgiveness might occur in practice. With regard to the persecuted group, who has the authority to speak on behalf of both its living and dead members? More importantly, since forgiveness stems from mercy, how can the persecuted be merciful to their persecutors? Is not mercy the prerogative of the strong and not the weak? Enacting such mercy would require an awkward reversal of roles. A civil community would need to pronounce a judgment upon itself for the persecution it has committed over time, and then assign a fitting punishment. Would not the wronged group then be required to exercise its duty to forgive the civil community that has promised to reform itself? More problematic, political leaders in virtue of their office seemingly have the authority to apologize for past wrongs that have been committed by the civil community. This presumed authority, however, assumes a continuity of governance that may not exist. Is a newly formed republic dedicated to protecting human rights, for instance, culpable for persecuting ethnic minorities that originated in, and was perpetuated by, preceding tyrannical regimes? Despite Arendt's insistence that a civil community can think together in ways that bind the living and dead, she provides little assistance on how this is accomplished as a political act.

For all her emphasis on plurality and particularity it is ironic that, in propounding forgiveness as a political duty and obligation, Arendt insists that the particular associations comprising the civil community must translate their respective narratives into a common Kantian dialect. This is presumably the price that must be paid if a civil community is to be able to think together. The cost is dear, however, for such translation has a homogenizing effect that erodes the particularity and plurality she wishes to affirm. This erosive effect can be seen in her attempt to strip away the religious foundations of Jesus' teaching on forgiveness. Arendt readily credits Jesus as the inventor of the forgiveness she is propounding. She is wrong, however, in assuming that the theological trappings of his teaching can be easily discarded. The strength and import of Jesus' instruction is not the pedagogy employed, but the Christological status of the instructor. Jesus' teaching on forgiveness is not only wise counsel, but also a command given by the Word made flesh. In the crucifixion, resurrection, and exaltation of Jesus Christ as the incarnate Word, judgment, punishment, and forgiveness have already been representatively enacted in both a retrospective and prospective direction. Consequently, Jesus' teaching on forgiveness contains both imperative and teleological elements that are lost in Arendt's excision.

Some implications of this loss can be seen by focusing on the exaltation. The exaltation of Jesus Christ signals that the nations of the world are subject to his authority. Consequently, the world is governed by the rule of Christ. Such a rule should prompt a response of joy, for in Christ the desire of the nations is fulfilled. The rule of Christ both affirms the created order that was vindicated in the resurrection and aligns creation's unfolding history with its *telos* in the *parousia*. Such a rule, then, should prompt a response of joyful obedience, for the Lord of the church is also the Lord of creation, and the Lord of its history and destiny. According to Christian belief, the exaltation of Christ initiates a new rule for the ordering of creation in this time between the times. Such a rule is retrospective in that it is based on the vindication of created order in Jesus' resurrection from the dead, and is prospective in its expectation of his *parousia*. In respect to political ordering, the civil community is responsible for exercising judgment and punishment not because it possesses the will and power to do so, but because it has been authorized by Christ to perform these functions in obedience to his rule. What Arendt fails to recognize is that some type of rule is inescapable—such as the rule of public Kantian narration—but rule *per se* needs no antidote for it does not lead inevitably to domination and control. Rather, the rule of Christ is oriented toward forgiveness and mercy, the very qualities she champions, and in the absence of this rule they cannot be genuinely enacted. It is only in Christ that the dead can forgive and be forgiven. In this respect, the *polis* provides a fitting image, but it is the City of God rather than the City of Man that should seize the imagination in seeking the new and renewing possibilities that stem from promising and forgiving.

What Arendt fails to acknowledge is that transition from believing together to thinking together is neither as easy nor as effective as she might wish, especially in respect to the plurality she wants to affirm as the imaginative and empathetic basis of the political promising and forgiving she envisions. The prospect of promising and forgiving among a people sharing a common faith is explicable, but this prospect fades dramatically within a civil community comprising a plurality of faiths. One is hard-pressed to find a concrete historical example of a regime in which religious communities have peaceably coexisted for any sustained period of time in the absence of the coercive power of the state, or imperial or dictatorial rule, none of which is hardly representative of the kind of imaginative and empathetic responses promoting forgiveness. Arendt may have had the miserable historical track record of particular religions in mind when she turns away from common belief to common thought. Yet religious convictions cannot be easily translated into common political speech, for much of the compelling depth of such convictions is lost in the very act of translation.

It may appear to the reader that we have wandered far away from an emerging technoculture which is purportedly the topic of this book. Yet encountering the prospect of promising and forgiving leads us back to the heart of the matter. As Arendt recognized, natality is needed as an antidote to late modernity's fixation on mortality cloaked in its technological quest for immortality, and the capacity of communities to practice promising and forgiving are crucial if they are to be reoriented toward the possibility of renewed life rather than the certainty of death and its accompanying anxiety. This recognition and subsequent critique of late modernity entails an oblique critique of Heidegger's (and Nietzsche's) account of modernity's emergence and future. Yet by encasing her normative account of the public exclusively within the political, Arendt cannot escape an underlying will that inevitably cannot be extricated from the pervading will to power she is attempting to overcome. Her quest for old wineskins in the end proves futile. In short, Arendt allows Heidegger to dictate the terms of her critique and constructive proposals, but in doing so remains mired in the same historicism and nihilism from which he could find no release or alternative.[68] Her envisioned natality simply has no purchase in a late modern political environment predicated on violence, for the processes of social, and even increasingly biological, reproduction are subjected to increasingly willful control and manipulation.[69] The world she wishes to create as a human work cannot exist within a technological enframement that is driven by a violent destruction of nature and consequent self-destruction. Promising and forgiving are thereby relegated to small private havens driven by the dictates of necessity and labor rather than public work.

Arendt in effect admits this confinement when she confesses that late modernity's "worldlessness," diagnosed correctly by Nietzsche (and Heidegger), is a desert, and that the "danger lies in becoming true inhabitants ... and feeling at home in it."[70] Technology, particularly that of the psyche—psychology or therapy, for instance—helps its inhabitants to survive the frequent sandstorms by diminishing their capacity to suffer and endure in favor of merely adapting. But to live properly in this desert, oases must be discovered and preserved. These oases are largely unpolitical for they are based on love and friendship—secluded spaces where promising and forgiving can be genuinely practiced. It would appear that Arendt, to use her categories, can only find her natality in private, rather than public, spaces; the only suitable dwelling she can find is outside the public arena. Her second birth, perhaps much to her surprise, is not into a public *polis* but into a secluded haven. She insists, however, that drawing sustenance from an oasis is not escapism or withdrawal. If this is true, then we may ask: can her oases flourish and expand to transform the surrounding desert into a more hospitable environment that forms desires in which the politics of natality can find more receptive inhabitants?

---

[68] See Dana R. Villa, *Arendt and Heidegger: The Fate of the Political* (Princeton, NJ, and Chichester, UK: Princeton University Press, 1996).

[69] In one of Arendt's rare excursions into drawing out the practical implications of her political thought, she offers an account of council democracy that has generally not been well received by the guild of political philosophers; see *On Revolution*, pp. 252–285. For a more appreciative reception, see John F. Sitton, "Hannah Arendt's Argument for Council Democracy," *Polity*, 20/1 (1987), pp. 80–100.

[70] See Arendt, *The Promise of Politics*, pp. 201–204.

Chapter 4
Albert Borgmann: Devices and Desires

Up to this point I have examined two critiques of late modernity. For Grant, late moderns are akin to cave-dwellers who are unaware that they live in darkness. The ensuing religious and moral task is to illumine this darkness *as* darkness by refusing late modern nihilism and historicism. In undertaking this task, Grant turns to the ancient traditions of Athens and Jerusalem to help late moderns see through the artificial horizons they have constructed, subsequently catching an illuminating glimpse of the true horizon of eternity. For Arendt, the task at hand is not one of refusal, but of reorientation. Late modernity is fixated on mortality, and the resulting anxiety promotes a politics based on violence as well as its concurrent vacuous society. Arendt wishes to reorient late moderns toward natality with its new and renewing possibilities, in turn promoting a politics predicated on speech, forgiveness, and promising.

Although Grant's and Arendt's critiques are incisive and are drawn upon extensively in Part II, neither is entirely successful because they cannot sufficiently overcome the pervasive historicism and nihilism they are attempting to either refuse or reorient. Grant's refusal is more like stubborn resignation, for the best he has to offer as an alternative to late modernity's comfortable darkness is an ambiguous "perhaps" of waiting for a waiting God. Arendt's plea on behalf of natality apparently falls on deaf ears, for she admits that one can only find some isolated oases in the vast late modern desert. Grant cannot rescue his cave-dwellers nor can Arendt save her desert denizens, and both are thereby reduced to finding small niches within a world they can neither abide nor change.

Borgmann offers a third alternative. Instead of refusing or reorienting Heidegger's and Nietzsche's account of late modernity he proposes an alternative interpretation of their analyses. His strategy is threefold: (1) to reform technology; and in order to achieve this objective, (2) to pen a richer and more normative public vocabulary than what is presently available for negotiating the current crossing of the postmodern divide; and in implementing this vocabulary in a concrete manner, (3) to enrich the public life of liberal-democratic regimes.

Borgmann has no quarrel with Heidegger's and Nietzsche's contention that technology has become late modernity's dominant interpretive paradigm, thereby representing the final stage of Western metaphysics. Technology, rather than nature or politics, has become the dominant feature of the world in which late moderns reside. The wilderness, for instance, is now a protected garden. The "pattern of technology is fundamental to the shape that the world has assumed over the last three or so centuries."[1] It is such a deeply ingrained pattern, however, that it is often difficult to recognize. Technology asserts its greatest formative influence on the mundane fabric of daily life. Critics of technology, such as Grant and Arendt, largely fail to recognize this commonplace feature, resulting in overdramatic, and thereby misleading, assessments. This oversight is seen most explicitly in what Borgmann identifies as the substantive approach that views technology as an uncontrollable force in its own right. Critics adopting this stance, such as Jacques Ellul,[2] offer a "comprehensive elucidation of our world by reducing its perplexing features and changes to one force or principle. That principle, technology, serves to explain everything, but it remains itself entirely unexplained and obscure."[3] When technology is used as a heuristic device to explain everything, the resulting inquiry ends up explicating little. Borgmann, however, is no less dismissive of instrumentalists who assume that technology is value-neutral and therefore particularly well suited to be used in promoting the values of liberal-democratic regimes. This approach fails to recognize that ends and means cannot be separated and that any "penetrating" criticism of technology must also entail an extensive social and political critique.[4] In short, technology shapes not only the mundane patterns of daily life, but also its attendant and supportive political institutions and structures. Borgmann also dismisses the "pluralist" variant that explains technology as an outcome of a "complex web of numerous countervailing forces" as theoretically interesting but devoid of any real or practical import.[5]

What these various criticisms fail to recognize is the fundamental contradiction on which the project being scrutinized is predicated. The dominant discourse of late modernity entails prediction and control. Yet such prognostic and manipulative power promotes a sense of helplessness rather than control; humans tend to be dominated by changing circumstances rather than dictate events. The attempt to gain predictive control is an objectifying process, but individuals assume, wrongly, that they can exempt themselves and other people from becoming objectified. The net result, however, is the effective loss of a first-person perspective. "We vacate our first-person place and presence in the world just when we mean to take responsibility for its destiny."[6] The late modern world is, curiously, a place of objects trying to organize objects with barely a hint about how the ensuing configuration should appear—a world of perpetual motion but little direction. The resulting futility is exemplified in liberal efforts to engineer society and conservative appeals to natural order, both of which prove unsuccessful since

---

[1] Albert Borgmann, *Technology and the Character of Contemporary Life: A Philosophical Inquiry* (Chicago, IL, and London: University of Chicago Press, 1984), p. 35.

[2] Borgmann would presumably place Grant in this substantive camp.

[3] Borgmann, *Technology and the Character of Contemporary Life*, p. 9.

[4] See ibid., pp. 10–11.

[5] Ibid., p. 11.

[6] Albert Borgmann, *Crossing the Postmodern Divide* (Chicago, IL, and London: University of Chicago Press, 1992), pp. 2–3.

neither can ascribe the good life they are pursuing in the absence of first-person discourse. Late moderns thereby "live in self-imposed exile from communal conversation and action," the consequences of which include a naked public square, soulless procedural politics, cancerous individualism, rampant narcissism, and incessant pursuit of loneliness.[7] Given this withering list, there should be little wonder that late moderns feel increasingly helpless and vulnerable as they exert greater predictive control.

This sense of helplessness, however, may prove to be a crucial motivation in reforming technology. In Borgmann's words, "[t]here is at least a drowsy and perhaps even a dawning sense in the contemporary culture that the paradigmatic blessings of technology are vacuous."[8] This drowsy, dawning sense stems from Heidegger's suggestion that there is a given quality of human life that technology occludes and diminishes.[9] To recover a pattern of life as it is meant to be lived requires, therefore, a reformation of technology by restraining its paradigmatic influence. Why does Borgmann believe that such reform is possible? Because modernity and its technology is a project and, as such, can be altered and changed as needed. This is where Borgmann differs from the substantive critics, for technology does not, despite appearances to the contrary, have a life of its own. The issue at stake is not an uncontrollable technology, but its servicing of values that corrupt the quality of human life, and these values can be changed. Yet Borgmann avoids the instrumentalist mistake of a value-free technology, recognizing that technologies do in fact form their users, a consideration that must be taken into account in how technologies are developed and used. Moreover, since modernity is a project, it can also be left behind. The modern project has pretty much run its course, and late moderns are taking their first tentative steps toward crossing what Borgmann characterizes as the "postmodern divide." This, of course, is not an original insight, but unlike many other so-called postmodernists, Borgmann does not see a radical discontinuity between the two sides of this divide. Rather, he sees modernity as one phase of a larger, but unfulfilled, Enlightenment project, one that he remains committed to and believes that emerging postmodern sensibilities have the potential to consummate.[10] The challenge, as we shall see below, is to construct a postmodern public discourse that assists in recovering the good life, and which in turn promotes a reform of technology that enables its pursuit. Or to state the goal in negative terms: to prevent the possibility afforded by postmodernity from becoming corrupted into hypermodernity.

The first step in reforming technology is to name what one is endeavoring to reform. For Borgmann, the "device paradigm" is what should seize attention.[11]

---

[7] See ibid., p. 3.
[8] Albert Borgmann, *Power Failure: Christianity in the Culture of Technology* (Grand Rapids, MI: Brazos, 2003), p. 22.
[9] See Borgmann, *Technology and the Character of Contemporary Life*, pp. 197–198.
[10] See Borgmann, *Crossing the Postmodern Divide*, p. 26.
[11] See Borgmann, *Technology and the Character of Contemporary Life*, ch. 9.

In many respects, "paradigm" carries the weight of this designation. Any social reality is a patterned reality, and a paradigm is the way in which this pattern is seen and understood. A technological paradigm, for instance, perceives and interprets reality in technological terms. Since technology has become the dominant mode of life for late moderns, the device paradigm discloses the shape or pattern of daily living. A device is a commodity that is easily produced and readily consumed, for it is designed to be owned, used, and enjoyed in the absence of any particular social or cultural context; hence the emphasis on mobility and standardization. A laptop computer, for instance, can perform its identical functions regardless of its location, and there is no such thing as a South American, as opposed to an African, computer. Devices also require little maintenance, are quickly obsolete, and easily disposable. Other than charging the battery, updating software, and an occasional cleaning, a laptop computer requires no maintenance,[12] but needs to be replaced every two or three years with an improved model, prompting the old one to be unceremoniously discarded or handed down to someone who can make do with an inferior product. Moreover, a device eases the constraints of time and place. So long as one has access to the web, it makes no difference whether a laptop computer is located in Halifax, Cairo, or Seoul for one to communicate, conduct business, or be entertained in real or virtual time.

As devices become more ubiquitous, they simultaneously grow more invisible and formative. Borgmann contrasts devices with "things" to explicate this ostensibly paradoxical influence. A thing, unlike a device, "calls forth skilled and active human engagement," in turn inviting accompanying practices rather than promoting consumption. A thing is indivisible from its social environment or context, is multifunctional, and requires upkeep. A hearth, for example, is inseparable from a particular house, requires such frequent chores or practices as cutting wood, stoking, and cleaning, and, in addition to providing heat (and perhaps cooking), offers a focal point where household members gather to talk, read, or play games. In contrast, central heating can be installed in virtually any structure, requires little maintenance, and is virtually invisible; household members normally do not spend an evening huddled together around a furnace. Central heating is emblematic of the formative power of the device paradigm through its virtual invisibility. At one level, this power is seen in the transformation of things into devices. A gas-burning or electric fireplace with artificial logs provides neither sufficient heat nor a focal point, but is an accessory.[13] Processed food and kitchen appliances, particularly the microwave oven, have transformed family meals into fast-food grazing. Digitized music is an entertainment device that is easily consumed, displacing musical instruments as things that must be practiced and mastered. At another level, people change the pattern of their daily lives to accommodate and take advantage of various devices. Members of a household, for

---

[12] Additionally, should a hardware or software malfunction occur, computers, like most devices, are too complex or difficult for most owners or users to repair.

[13] Video recordings of logs burning in a fireplace are also available.

instance, can conduct their affairs with little face-to-face contact, for as individuals they can eat whenever they choose and sequester themselves in various rooms to surf the net, watch television, or listen to music.

Why is Borgmann troubled by this transformation of the household? Admittedly, its members spend less time together than in the past, but this is not necessarily bad since the familial togetherness he champions was often more imposed than chosen and welcomed. Moreover, individuals are now freed from the drudgery of the hard labor associated with his practices, freeing them to pursue more creative activities. Is he not merely indulging a nostalgic and romanticized fantasy of a bygone and less hectic era? Borgmann might reply that the banality of the late modern household is itself disturbing, but he is more concerned that its transformation is symptomatic of a broader social and political breakdown. The device paradigm engenders an "inconspicuous pattern" that late moderns use to orient themselves in their world, a world in which devices and commodities have become their normal or natural habitat.[14] The subsequent public policies governing the technological development focus on the production of devices and commodities, but there is no normative judgment regarding whether or not the end of consumption is good. As a result, the "pervasive transformation of things into devices … is changing our commerce with reality from engagement to the disengagement of consumption and labor."[15] Such disengagement in turn necessarily promotes a preference for leisure over work, and such leisure entails the "unencumbered enjoyment of commodities whereas labor is devoted to the construction and maintenance of the machinery that produces the commodities."[16] Borgmann notes, similarly to Arendt, that the purpose of labor is to promote greater leisure rather than meeting the needs of natural necessity. This redirection of labor discloses the deceptive quality of the device paradigm, for rather than enhancing the freedom of individuals by enlarging the range of available goods and services, consumers are actually constrained by the choices imposed on them. Like Grant, Borgmann believes that the device paradigm restricts freedom by limiting choices to those contained within the package deal of voracious consumption. Herein lies the menace of the device paradigm, for when the overriding objective is to consume as many commodities as possible, the principal moral strategy is reduced to asserting raw power. And when this power is asserted by autonomous consumers, any semblance of a common social life grows increasingly faint.

The rate of this disappearance, Borgmann fears, may be increased as we cross the postmodern divide. As was noted above, Borgmann is hopeful that postmodernism may inspire a promising reform of technology, but he also worries that rather than leaving the modern project behind, it may merely morph into hypermodernism. To date, postmodernism has not solved the problem of individualism, and as a consequence it has largely failed to critique its undergirding consumerism.

---

[14] See Borgmann, *Technology and the Character of Contemporary Life*, pp. 104–105.
[15] Ibid., p. 61.
[16] Ibid., p. 114.

Consequently, it is an open question whether or not postmodernism will become something other than technology, given the latter's pervasive influence in the late modern world. In light of postmodernism's failure to adequately address the problems of individualism and consumerism, Borgmann identifies its troubling fascination with hyperreality, hyperactivity, and hyperintelligence.

Hyperreality is an outcome of information technologies that manipulate data in reconfiguring and creating alternative, usually virtual, realities.[17] Hyperreality is highly malleable and disposable, thereby making it the perfect commodity. Imagine, for example, that while exercising on a treadmill, instead of being in a gym filled with torpid air and grunting voices, you are in an environment "elevated to hyperreal perfection." You are surrounded by a panoramic mountain scene displayed on huge high-definition monitors. You run on a "surface that rises and banks in coordination with the view that is being displayed," along with "scented and temperature controlled blowers that simulate the air movement and fragrance according to the changes of shade, sunlight, and season; speakers that produce the sounds of rushing water, chirping birds, and whispering pines."[18] You have spent your time exercising in an artificial environment that in many respects is better, and certainly more convenient, than the real alternative.

Hyperactivity is closely related to hyperrreality. Since the latter makes time and place increasingly irrelevant, hyperactivity threatens to invade every aspect of daily life.[19] This invasive potential is most apparent in the growing ubiquity of mobile communication devices that enable interaction and data transfer at virtually any time or location. Late modern professionals are rarely out of touch with those to whom they need to be connected. Consequently, work can be performed at nearly any time, in any place, and nowhere in particular. Such hyperactivity apparently contradicts Borgmann's earlier claim that labor is now oriented toward producing commodities that are consumed by individuals engaged in their respective leisure pursuits. If late moderns prefer leisure over work, don't hyperactive workers need to stop and consume commodities in their leisure time? What this question fails to recognize is that devices blur, if not erase, any lines separating work from leisure. Imagine you are ensconced on your favorite beach. Rather than napping or watching the waves, you bring your favorite mobile communication devices. One moment you are messaging a client, the next you are gossiping with a friend; you peruse the website of a competing firm and then play some online games; you edit a spreadsheet and then write some poetry; you read a report and then the latest murder mystery by your favorite author. Are you working or relaxing? The answer is presumably both, and, with that reply, hyperactivity has overwhelmed and subsumed both into a common effort. Leisure is not rest in the sense of refraining

---

[17] For an extensive critique of information technology, see Albert Borgmann, *Holding On to Reality: The Nature of Information at the Turn of the Millennium* (Chicago, IL, and London: University of Chicago Press, 1999).

[18] See Borgmann, *Crossing the Postmodern Divide*, p. 87.

[19] See ibid., pp. 100–101.

from labor, but redirecting one's attention (temporarily) toward a chosen pursuit, but in an equally hyperactive mode.

According to Borgmann, shared knowledge and responsibility are the two chief characteristics for how early postmoderns will pursue their work and leisure.[20] Such cooperation is enabled by an infrastructure consisting of electronic networks for exchanging information. Since these networks are integrated in ways resembling the human brain, it is not unreasonable that a hyperintelligence will eventually emerge, exceeding human intelligence. This prospect presumably endangers individual freedom, given its centralizing tendency; human intelligence, after all, is the outcome of a hierarchically structured brain. This tendency, however, can be easily resisted by using information networks to create virtual communities that preserve the freedom of its individual members. An individual may, for instance: be part of a network of co-workers and another community of professional colleagues; join groups dedicated to such shared interests as poetry and murder mysteries; and participate in smaller, more intimate communities comprised of close friends and family. It should be noted, however, that these communities, unlike their predecessors, will not be based on such accidental factors as birth, geographical proximity, and disparate interests, but on choice, shared interests, and ongoing will to participate. Consequently, these virtual communities are provisional and tentative, and thereby subject to frequent construction, deconstruction, and reconstruction; they are, in many respects, commodities to be produced and consumed.

Borgmann is not sanguine about the prospect of an emerging technoculture dominated by hyperreality, hyperactivity, and hyperintelligence. Hyperreality is an alluring and stimulating commodity, but commodities cannot sustain a person over time because they offer no real and enduring context. Once a commodity is consumed its allure and stimulation also disappears. Running on a hyperreal treadmill along a mountain trail, for example, may result in the same cardiovascular benefit, but when the machine is turned off, no objective reality remains; nothing real has been encountered. In Borgmann's words, "[h]yperreality and reality may result in the same experience indifferently understood, but when the experience of hyperreality is oriented within its context, its force turns out to be disposable and discontinuous, that is, it turns out to have no real force at all."[21] Hyperactivity can make individuals more productive and enhance a sense of personal accomplishment, but these fleeting outcomes are obtained at an exacting price. Leisure is disfigured into an inferior form of work, and is thereby no longer satisfying or regenerative. Moreover, hyperactivity is inherently elitist and escapist, for hyperactive professionals leave the "wasteland of mindless labor to the less driven and less educated," preferring instead hyperrealities of their own creation. But this only serves to further alienate them from the "real world," making "reentry into reality especially harsh," and leaving them "sad and sullen."[22] Although the emergence of

---

[20] See ibid., p. 102.
[21] Ibid., pp. 95–96.
[22] See ibid., p. 101.

hyperintelligence may increase knowledge and the distribution of responsibility, the confidence that virtual communities can resist its encroachment on individual freedom is misplaced. Genuine community can and does preserve freedom, but the envisioned virtual communities will be ineffective guardians because they are counterfeit. Unlike communities based on such accidental factors as birth and geographical proximity, these so-called substitutes cannot endure over time since they are founded and dependent on the ongoing will of its individual members. As even proponents admit, virtual communities are designed to be impermanent, given the fickle interests of its members. As a consequence, no one is really present to another, given the lack of a particular, shared location. So-called communities are thereby effectively reduced to collections of "arbitrary desires" that serve to erode, rather than promote, genuine freedom.[23]

It may be objected that Borgmann is merely asserting personal complaints rather than describing more general, troubling tendencies. There is no reason to assume that the tendencies he decries will be universal or even widespread, and even if this proves to be the case, he has not demonstrated why the values he commends are necessarily superior to those he condemns. Borgmann may not like the world that is emerging on the other side of the postmodern divide, but that does not mean it will be an evil or wicked world, at least for many, if not most, of its inhabitants.

Borgmann could retort, however, that disturbing social and political consequences are already in play, which should give us some pause in readily embracing the hyperreality, hyperactivity, and hyperintelligence on offer. This consequence is a pervasive "sullenness" that is poisoning contemporary political discourse and social interaction.[24] This sullenness is seen most prominently in a politics of resentment in which "brooding displeasure" becomes "aggressive and dismissive," preventing "open and constructive action" in favor of "indirection and obstruction."[25] Consequently, there is widespread support for policies promoting economic inequality accompanied by jealousy for those perceived to be more successful, and censure of those perceived to be less successful. The appearance of responsibility, then, often disguises an underlying resentment and self-indulgence; ironically, responsibility is frequently invoked to disclaim any sense of obligation other than to oneself. Inevitably, this sullenness has a corrosive influence on civil community as seen in growing incivility, domination by economic, social, and political elites, and subordination of the less intelligent and skilled.[26]

The situation is not irredeemable, however, for Borgmann believes that crossing the postmodern divide also affords an opportunity for extensive economic, social, and political reform. Such reform hinges on supplanting sullenness with joy. His proposed strategy is twofold: first, to reform the *foreground* of the device

---

[23] See ibid., pp. 104–109.
[24] See ibid., pp. 6–12.
[25] See ibid., p. 8.
[26] See ibid', pp. 12–19.

paradigm; and, second, to reform the *background* of political policies and social practices governing the production and consumption of devices and commodities.

The foreground should be reformed through the recovery of *focal things and practices*. A focal thing is an objective reality which exerts a "commanding presence" and "continuity with the world," a, world, it should be stressed, that is not a manufactured artifact, device, or commodity.[27] Accompanying focal practices are activities that are required to maintain the focal thing, and they thereby necessitate in turn a reordering of the practitioner's time and attention in compliance with the needs and dictates of the focal thing in question. Focal practices are also formative of the practitioner's moral vision and character, in part because they are habituating but, more importantly, because they are embedded within the values of a moral tradition embodied in the practices. In Borgmann's words:

> Focal things and practices are the crucial counterforces to technology understood as a form of culture. They contrast with technology without denying it, and they provide a standpoint for a principled and fruitful reform of technology. Generally, a focal thing is concrete and of commanding presence. A focal practice is the decided, regular, and normally communal devotion to a focal thing.[28]

Moreover, focal things embody a deep "continuity with the world," for they are *not* "warrants" but "warrant themselves. To present them is never more than to recall them." The accompanying focal practices thereby form the values and moral vision of the practitioners over time, simultaneously affirming and supporting the good or normative status of the focal thing in question. Consequently, practitioners must in turn shape the habitual patterns of their daily lives accordingly.[29] Two examples may suffice to illustrate the formative influence of focal things and their attendant practices.

The first example is the wilderness. In the wilderness humans encounter a reality that is far greater than the devices and commodities that normally capture their attention. The wilderness is a given thing that cannot be controlled and must be accommodated, requiring the ordering of one's activities accordingly. In this contextual setting, a person is neither a consumer nor master of nature, thereby restoring a proper sense of time and place. In ordering one's practices in accordance with the dictates of the wilderness, the resulting experience is fundamentally different from that of consuming commodities or encountering a fabricated reality. While running in the mountains, for example, a runner negotiates varying and invariable grades and terrain, smells the scents of real plants and trees, deals with weather and temperatures that cannot be adjusted, and may actually come upon living, wild animals along the way as opposed to simulations in a high-tech gym. At the end of the run, the wilderness remains a commanding presence, whereas

---

[27] See ibid., pp. 119–120.
[28] Borgmann, *Power Failure*, p. 22.
[29] See Borgmann, *Crossing the Postmodern Divide*, pp. 119–120.

simulation fades away; a commodity has been engaged with rather than a commodity consumed.

The second example is a family meal as a focal practice that engages its participants. "The great meal of the day, be it at noon or in the evening, is a focal event par excellence. It gathers the scattered family around the table."[30] It presents a particular tradition, such as favored recipes on a holiday, and a proper a structure which must be honored. There are also virtues involved such as generosity and gratitude, and conversation is engendered around the table, especially when guests are present. "Thus eating in a focal setting differs sharply from the social and cultural anonymity of a fast-food outlet."[31] To participate in this focal practice requires members of a family to adjust their respective schedules to be present at a particular time and location, and to undertake cooperative tasks such as cooking, setting the table, conversing, and cleaning up. Most importantly the meal promotes social interaction rather than the mere consumption of food.

But why are such mundane activities crucial? They disclose the need to recover what Borgmann characterizes as "deictic discourse." Such discourse entails an "ultimate concern" that is evocative and enduring, providing a "source of guidance and solace and … delight," in turn promoting an "attitude … of enthusiasm, sympathy, and tolerance."[32] Such discourse is to a large extent normative, but it is ascriptive and interrogative in tone, as opposed to descriptive and imperative, thereby inviting conversation rather than confrontation. The underlying attitude of enthusiasm, sympathy, and tolerance promotes engagement as opposed to late modern indifference or postmodern sullenness. In this respect, deictic discourse exposes the moral and social emptiness of the device paradigm and the lifestyle it promotes, for in contrast to the predominate banality, shallowness, individualism, and consumerism that permeates late modernity, it offers an alternative account based on excellence, depth, community, and celebration.[33] Consequently, deictic discourse is necessarily engendered by focal concerns, as can be seen in the examples of the wilderness and family dining. The wilderness is not so much a space that must be protected from the encroachment of a technological society as it is a reality challenging the fallacy of technological mastery by reinforcing a "proper respect for the limits and fragility of the natural environment."[34] A family meal calls into question the assumption that eating is merely a random and individualistic consumption of food that can be accomplished virtually at any time or place as opposed to a communal and celebratory event. In both instances, deictic discourse reverses the context in which the values of the wilderness and eating are described and assessed.

---

[30] Borgmann, *Technology and the Character of Contemporary Life*, p. 204.
[31] Ibid., p. 205.
[32] See ibid., pp. 176–177.
[33] See Borgmann, *Power Failure*, p. 33.
[34] See Borgmann, *Technology and the Character of Contemporary Life*, p. 185.

The deictic discourse stemming from and reinforcing focal things and practices provides a stark contrast to that derived from the device paradigm, and in turn exposes its superficial character. It may be objected that Borgmann is simply propounding his personal preferences for a particular lifestyle, which he has every right to do. He is free to make a persuasive case for others to join him in adopting a simpler life; to establish a niche market where his commodities of respecting the wilderness and family dining may be consumed. This objection would be correct, to a large extent, if Borgmann confined his inquiry to the foreground, but he also devotes considerable attention to criticizing the background of the values, social mores, and political policies supporting and promoting the dominance of the device paradigm. This is why the deictic discourse derived from focal things and practices plays an initially crucial role by creating a striking contrast with the discourse of devices. In this sense, Borgmann shares with Grant the task of illuminating the darkness as darkness, but he also takes the next step of engagement as opposed to waiting. If such engaging action is to accomplish something more than illuming the dark circumstances of late modernity, then such action must be oriented and ordered focally. In Borgmann's words, "[i]f we are to challenge *the rule of technology*, we can do so only through *the practice of engagement*."[35] He contends that once the shallowness of the technological pattern is acknowledged, "the more evident it becomes to us that technology must be countered by an equally patterned and social commitment, i.e., by a practice."[36] Focal things and practices are therefore needed to restore depth and integrity to the patterns of daily life, for they provide "crucial counterforces to technology understood as a form of culture." Consequently, this restoration requires "a principled and fruitful reform of technology," which necessarily entails reforming the political background as well.[37] Crossing the postmodern divide offers a propitious moment for undertaking this reformation, and Borgmann proposes that it should be based on a "postmodern realism," emphasizing the characteristics of focal realism, patient vigor, and communal celebration.[38] The principal roles these characteristics play in reforming technology can be seen in Borgmann's critical assessment of the relationship between technology and democracy, and his constructive proposal for reforming it.

According to Borgmann, political discourse "constitutes the forum in which we transact our most important business."[39] As in Arendt's view, politics represents the most significant form of human association, and, like her, he worries about its late modern distortion. For Borgmann, however, the principal problem is not its predication on violence, but its reduction into the promotion

---

[35] Ibid., p. 207 (emphasis in original).
[36] Ibid., p. 208.
[37] See Borgmann, *Power Failure*, p. 22.
[38] See Borgmann, *Crossing the Postmodern Divide*, pp. 5–6. Borgmann contends that these characteristics are preferable to the weaker postmodern alternatives of respect for nature, particularity, and communitarianism (see p. 5).
[39] Borgmann, *Technology and the Character of Contemporary Life*, p. 86.

of mindless consumerism.[40] The bedrock democratic principles of liberty and equality, for instance, have been corrupted into commodities that are consumed by citizens. Government itself takes on a technological quality in producing and distributing its goods and services. More strongly, Borgmann asserts: "Politics has become the metadevice of the technological society."[41] So-called social services and entitlements are dispensed directly by government agencies and consumed by eligible recipients, and indirectly policies promote and support the production of material goods and services within the private sector. Consequently, employment, income, and GDP become the principal benchmarks for determining political success because they can be easily measured and distributed in ways resembling the consumption of commodities. Political debates are not over competing accounts or visions of the common good, but, rather, candidates are evaluated in terms of their ability to enable the delivery of commodities. Given this scheme, genuine political engagement is impossible, which is why cries for participatory democracy are virtually pointless and inconsequential. It is not surprising, then, that late modern politics have become a meta-device, for late modern "democracy is enacted as technology. It does not leave the question of the good life open but answers it along technological lines."[42]

We can now begin to see more clearly why the political background shapes or, better, misshapes the social foreground. In addressing the question of the good life along technological lines, the resulting answer is ambiguous and ambivalent because liberal democracies can neither promote nor defend any particular account of the good life since such discourse cannot be admitted to the public arena. This reticence stems from the supposed separation of morality and legality—you can't legislate morality—but this separation is itself morally charged by the very technological rationally of neutrality undergirding it. As a result, liberal societies are committed to a shallow pluralism, which in part accounts for the need for ubiquitous contracts and litigation. The political background is largely indifferent to the moral and social foreground so long as the central value of consumption, and its productive derivative, is maintained and practiced. As Borgmann contends, "when the supporting structure of daily life assumes the character of a machinery that is concealed and separated from the commodities it procures and when these become isolated and mobile, then it becomes possible to style and restyle one's life by assembling and disassembling commodities."[43] The political background of the meta-device effectively strips focal things and practices of their evocative power and formative influence. Policies protecting and managing wilderness, for instance, reinforce the primacy of human mastery rather than natural limits, reducing it to an amusement to be enjoyed by energetic consumers. And easy

---

[40] Presumably, Borgmann is also troubled by the extent to which violence permeates late modern politics, but he sees this as an effect, rather than a cause, of political failure.

[41] Borgmann, *Technology and the Character of Contemporary Life*, p. 107.

[42] Ibid., p. 92.

[43] Ibid.

access to divorce and abortion withdraws formal support for the family, reducing it to companionship instead of a "privileged and sacred" way "of expressing love."[44] Ultimately, all political policies, whether liberal or conservative, are designed to promote economic growth and prosperity through endless production and consumption of commodities, thereby transforming human communities into processes of "mindless labor and mindless leisure."[45] Ironically, the late modern democratic background erodes and dissolves the moral and social traditions of the foreground that make liberty and equality possible and sustainable.

The price paid for this political indifference is a highly diminished public life. According to Borgmann, a vibrant public life that is simultaneously modern and democratic has never been developed. This is a result of a constricted and unremitting fixation on affluence and prosperity, to the detriment of nearly all other values. He believes, like Arendt, that public life consists overwhelmingly of ravenous consumerism and mind-numbing entertainment, activities reinforced and exacerbated by modern technological development that has reshaped and reoriented work and labor. A fateful consequence is the displacement of the private sphere by an ill-defined commitment to privacy. For late moderns, privacy is confined to a small, and often changing, collection of friends and family. Yet, ironically, the idea of privacy has little meaning in the absence of a robust public context. To compensate for this contextual absence, the public sector is reduced to producing commodities while its public counterpart enables their consumption; hence the contraction of private life into secluded enclaves and an eviscerated public life. The moral and political consequences of this turn toward privacy and diminished public life are not benign, for the "trend to push production, consumption, and affluence ... makes us forget the poor and neglect the environment."[46] This forgetfulness and neglect are symptomatic of a larger decline of political and private landmarks of public decency and personal virtue—namely, the core democratic values of equality, dignity, and self-determination. The good goal of extending a universal justice to all human beings is, in effect, being denied by the relentless pursuit of affluence, and the essential social virtues of generosity and resourcefulness are atrophying due to inattention. The principal issue plaguing late modernity, therefore, is not, contrary to many pundits, "unruly diversity," but a "uniform mediocrity" that promotes a pervasive sullenness.[47] This mediocrity in turn stems from an insatiable, though largely invisible, consumerism, exerting a cancerous effect on public life, for the "subversive power of commodification is so strong because it is concealed, and it is concealed because it moves along a smooth gradient from good to bad and from harmless to injurious."[48]

---

[44] See ibid., p. 93.
[45] See ibid., p. 94.
[46] Albert Borgmann, *Real American Ethics: Taking Responsibility for Our Country* (Chicago, IL, and London: University of Chicago Press, 2006), p. 7.
[47] See ibid., pp. 8–12.
[48] Ibid., p. 161.

Borgmann insists that the two most popular options for purportedly solving this problem are both inadequate. On the one hand, traditional liberals cannot promote or defend a particular account of the good life—presumably one based on equality, dignity, and self-determination— because they lack a compelling normative vocabulary that is palatable in the denuded public sphere they helped to create. Moreover, "[o]rthodox liberalism has been left behind with modernism."[49] In crossing the postmodern divide, what is now needed is to provide everyone with meaningful work and adequate education. Without strong supportive communities—a prospect liberals cannot admit or envision—these central goals cannot be achieved. Liberals mistakenly presume that a good public life can be attained through an equal distribution of affluence. Civil disagreements therefore quickly degenerate into battles over conflicting rights. This reductionism, however, fails to address the more pressing issue of a common social and political order. The resulting arguments cannot be substantive, and as a consequence reformative, because they serve to the disguise the role technology plays in denigrating the character and quality of public life. The problems of inequality and poverty, for instance, remain unaddressed because late liberalism fails to establish a genuinely civil context in which they may be properly diagnosed and solved.

On the other hand, the proffered communitarian alternative is equally ineffective. Although communitarians are devoted to the ideal of community, they have failed to set a compelling social and realistic political agenda, in part because they also fail to critique the device paradigm as the principal formative feature of the social and political order they are attempting to reshape.[50] Given this critical failure, communitarians resort to concepts and arguments that the public cannot separate from a legacy of "paternalistic moralizing, suffocating provincialism, and totalitarian oppression."[51] Although liberalism admittedly conceals the most pressing moral and political issues, its minimalist convictions and viewpoints appear less threatening than communitarian alternatives.

In response to these liberal and communitarian option, Borgmann offers a third way—one that is better able to address and correct the turn to privacy and its correlative diminishment of public life His preferred solution is to establish focal communities. These communities, centered on focal things and their attendant practices, would have a twofold purpose: first, to create a genuinely public space in which the "[p]ractices of moral excellence flesh out the framework of equality, dignity, and self-determination"[52] as an antidote to the pervasive mediocrity plaguing late modernity; and, second, to engage the larger culture in recovering public discourse that is genuinely civil and political. These focal

---

[49] Borgmann, *Crossing the Postmodern Divide*, p. 127.
[50] The representative communitarians identified by Borgmann include Robert Bellah, Alasdair MacIntyre, Michael Sandel, and Michal Walzer; see *Power Failure*, pp. 35–36.
[51] See ibid., p. 36.
[52] Borgmann, *Real American Ethics*, p. 9.

communities will consequently be celebratory in nature since they are organized around a commanding presence or focal thing, rather than being self-referential. In modeling lives of excellence as opposed to mediocrity, they will prompt the broader public to recover and practice those political values and social virtues, as indicated above, which are required to sustain a genuinely democratic and civil community. Moreover, these focal communities must be granted protected spaces to pursue their requisite practices. If they are to flourish, and thereby serve the public by providing alternative models of social and political ordering, then they must be protected from being reduced to commodities to be consumed or dismissed as charming but irrelevant social experiments.[53] As Borgmann recognizes, the focal communities he envisions are relatively rare and fragile, for they are based on shared characteristics of work, residency, religion, ancestry, and communal celebrations, the kind of particularity that easily withers when subjected to the transformative power of the device paradigm.[54]

If it is paramount to provide protected spaces for focal communities, then it may be asked: what is the content of the focal things and practices that are celebrated by their respective communities, and why are the celebrations they embody important in forming and sustaining a good social and political order? According to Borgmann, focal practices are "required to counter technology in its patterned pervasiveness and to guard focal things in their depth and integrity."[55] Such practices acknowledge and ameliorate human frailty in and through the ordering of communal life centered on focal things, and the attendant practices disclose this inherent and necessary interdependency. Moreover, there are no substitutes, such as production and consumption commodities, that can replace focal things, for they are "concrete, tangible, and deep, admitting of no functional equivalents; they have a tradition, structure, and rhythm of their own."[56]

More importantly, a focal concern embedded in a particular focal thing is an end or purpose that centers and orients one's life. This is why a fruitful reform of technology must make room for focal things and practices, because they provide a *telos* that is served by the design and applications of various technologies. In the absence of this teleological ordering, reform proposals become ensnared and subsumed into the device paradigm. Consequently, a "focal practice engenders an intelligent and selective attitude toward technology. It leads to a simplification and perfection of technology in the background of one's focal concern and to

---

[53] Although Borgmann does not refer to the Amish to any great extent, they may serve as an example of a charming community that can be easily dismissed and commodified. Weekend Amish experiences—complete with buggy rides, plain-clothes shopping, and farm tours—are marketed to urban and suburban consumers. Although I am not aware of any computer games or simulations designed to offer a virtual Amish experience, the development of such a product is not inconceivable.

[54] See Borgmann, *Power Failure*, pp. 47–48.

[55] Borgmann, *Technology and the Character of Contemporary Life*, pp. 209–210.

[56] Ibid., p. 219.

a discerning use of technological products at the center of one's practice."[57] A communal life of focal practices centered on focal things thereby produces social wealth or capital, whereas a life fixated on the consumption of commodities results in individual affluence. Work performed on behalf of focal practices, then, incorporates technologies only to the extent that they enhance the quality of labor rather than the efficient production of goods and services, and such an approach and orientation in turn increases one's engagement with the focal thing at issue: a master carpenter, for instance, may use power tools as needed, not in order to produce more items to be sold, but to improve the quality of the furniture being constructed. In short, the reformation of technology will result in reduced affluence but increase the wealth of human association. This wealth promotes and undergirds a public life that is genuinely *civil* since it is premised on the core focal and cooperative values of generosity and resourcefulness, serving to counteract voracious consumption that promotes privacy, indifference, and incivility. It is, Borgmann hopes, through the witness of these focal communities that the general population will come to realize that the device paradigm must be resisted in order to live the good life.

Nowhere is this resistance more prominent than in the celebratory character of focal communities. Genuine celebration is simple and, although public in character, focused on mundane activities often involving "athletics, the arts, and religion." The ordinary character of celebration stems from its grounding in "reality, community, and divinity." [58] A celebration is not designed to draw attention to the creativity of the celebrants, but toward the focal thing and its formative and normative significance that is being celebrated. The wilderness, for instance, is a given reality that delimits human action in response to its inherent nature and fragility, rather than a protected space disclosing the wisdom and management skills of those designating it as such. A celebratory community emerges around a focal thing rather than being an artifact of its fabricators. The daily family meal promotes deliberate conversation and fellowship, and is not a mechanism for controlling the dynamics of the group gathered around the table. A celebratory community is oriented toward the *telos* of the good life it is endeavoring to practice, as opposed to pursuing horizons of its choosing and making. Consequently, celebrations are easily overlooked or dismissed by late moderns since they are looking to consume and be entertained. Given their penchant for the artificial, autonomous, and profane, they prefer spectacle over celebration. The spectacle highlights the ingenuity and power of the human will asserted through technological manipulation and mastery. The fabricated "reality" is more grand and stunning than the real counterpart it displaces. Autonomous and anonymous consumers gather for a time of amusement, and then leave with no expectation of any further contact with those who shared the thrill. There are no transcendents to direct and delimit expectations, only projected goals and objections originating in the insatiable will to consume.

---

[57] Ibid., p. 221.
[58] See Borgmann, *Crossing the Postmodern Divide*, p. 134.

The celebrations of focal communities offer a subversive alternative to the spectacles produced by the device paradigm. Rather than attending a major league baseball game, attend the local minor league or semi-pro game where, along with neighbors, you cheer on players most of whom will never make it to the majors but are motivated to practice their meager talents by a love for the game. Instead of listening to digitized music on a device of magnificent quality that cannot be matched in a live performance, attend a recital of local musicians who, no matter how much they practice, will never make it to Carnegie Hall but nonetheless create a social bond with the appreciative audience of friends and neighbors. Rather than attending a service in a mega-church with a cavernous sanctuary, massive HD monitors, and exquisite music and PA system, go to the local parish church and receive and celebrate the sacrament with the few believers who gather together each Sunday morning.

It could again be objected that Borgmann is merely commending the simple celebrations to espouse his personal preferences, but that they are little more than pointless gestures that do nothing to change or reform the political background. What this objection fails to recognize, however, is the subversive nature of these celebrations which are so easily disregarded. Celebratory communities embody the conviction that the enduring virtue of patience is ultimately stronger than the value of exerting short-term power, for the former is predicated on peaceful and persuasive speech whereas the latter presupposes the necessity of violence. When late moderns assert power, they impose political order "on the ruins of inconvenient circumstances" and suppress "uncooperative people." In contrast, patience, which is not synonymous with timidity, has the "time and strength to recognize complicated conditions and difficult people, to engage them in cooperation and conversation. The powerful provoke envy and fear; the patient earn admiration and affection."[59] As focal communities engage with the broader culture respectfully and interrogatively, late moderns will come to appreciate that wealth is preferable to affluence. In response, appropriate political reforms will be undertaken, slowly replacing the mega-device with a regime comprising a "community of communities" instead of autonomous consumers or tribes of culture warriors.[60] And these reforms in turn will redirect the development and deployment of technology in line with an emerging postmodern or focal realism.

Although Borgmann's proposal shares some similarities with Arendt's account of speech-based politics, he holds a much deeper appreciation for the constructive role that her despised society (albeit a reformed one) must play. Borgmann contends that a formal separation of politics and morality remains the lynchpin of liberal democracy. This separation, however, is not an absolute wall or chasm, but more along the lines of an informal division of labor. "The rule of law is *universal, compulsory, and morally minimal*, whereas "[p]rivate morality is …

---

[59] See ibid., p. 124.
[60] See ibid., p. 141.

particular, optional, and often maximal."[61] Everyone is subject to the rule of law, but law is not synonymous with the moral life. It is within focal communities that the moral life should be formed and practiced, and through their mutual and respectful engagement establish and preserve a civil public discourse. In this respect, civility is the bridge between legality and morality. Indeed, the rule of law is ineffective in the absence of civility, for mutual "goodwill and trust" are the "lifeblood" of a law abiding society.[62] Focal communities provide the moral, spiritual, and social resources that are needed to sustain a good, or at least decent, political and economic order. Or, in Augustinian terms, these communities reorder disordered desires in and through their focal practices.[63] Borgmann does not offer a detailed description of the reformed politics he envisions—indeed, he cannot if community is an emergent reality rather than a fabricated construct—but he does contend that it will entail policies promoting the protection or subsidization of artisans and craftsman producing higher-quality goods, decreased production and consumption of cheap devices and commodities, market and financial regulation, ameliorating the inequality between rich poor, and redistributing financial assets and income.[64] In short, a good or decent political and economic order that has been liberated from the tyranny of the meta-device will be less affluent, but he is hopeful, even cautiously optimistic, that if focal communities can be given sufficient time and social space, they can successfully reorder a desire for wealth over one for affluence.

Borgmann offers, in many respects, an engaging and compelling critique of the emerging technoculture. He frankly admits that late moderns cannot escape this culture, for it reflects the ontology of the age. Consequently, it can only be described and assessed from within and not from some external Archimedean vantage-point. Yet, unlike Grant, he does not refuse modernity in favor of antiquity, nor, unlike Arendt, does he draw on the ancients to offer an alternative modern narration. Rather, he attempts to subvert and reform late modernity as it crosses the postmodern divide. The device paradigm he describes provides a useful interpretive and evaluative tool in undertaking this subversion by initially directing attention toward the formative foreground of daily life that leads the critique inevitably to the supportive economic and political background. By exposing the shallowness and sullenness of late modern life in comparison to the rich life and practices of celebratory communities, the background of the meta-device cannot resist its own inevitable reform over time. Slowly, almost imperceptibly, the desire for the artificial, autonomous, and commodified is reoriented toward the real, communal, and divine. Allowing the device paradigm to disclose its own vacuity unleashes a process of evolutionary change, culminating in a revolutionary transformation of values.

---

[61] Borgmann, *Real American Ethics*, p. 25 (emphasis in original).
[62] See ibid., p. 26.
[63] Borgmann does not use Augustinian categories in any overt manner.
[64] See appropriate sections of Borgmann, *Real American Ethics*.

Borgmann's constructive proposal is less compelling and persuasive. One could quarrel, for instance, with his easy dismissal of affluence since arguably it provides, particularly for the most impoverished people on a global scale,[65] the financial stability and security that could help provide a more receptive political and economic background to the reforming efforts of the focal foreground.[66] Ironically, it may be the affluent that are most readily drawn to focal communities since they are not preoccupied with obtaining basic material necessities. Or it could be questioned whether the liberal democracy he champions can be separated from the production and consumption of commodities he decries.[67] The two may prove inseparable if a minimalist account of freedom is the prerequisite for preserving a modicum of public order. Although Grant's determinative portrayal of technology, as captured in the analogy of the package deal, goes too far, Borgmann has perhaps paid insufficient attention to inherent features that that cannot be unraveled, thereby limiting the prospects of reforming both the foreground and background. Uncivil discourse and sectarian strife may simply prove to be an inevitable consequence. A sullen and vacuous public life may be the price exacted by a liberal-democratic regime, a price that Borgmann may not be willing to pay since the implementation of many of his proposed political and economic reforms requires illiberal policies.

Additional objections and criticisms could be added to the list,[68] but assuming that Borgmann could mount an adequate defense so that none proves fatal to his proposal, two perplexities pertinent to this inquiry nonetheless remain. The first involves *how* the good life should be desired and ordered. The central task of a focal community is presumably to reorder its disordered desires in line with the *telos* of the focal thing that commands its attention and shape its requisite focal practices. Crossing the postmodern divide offers a propitious moment for undertaking this vital task. Modernity is being left behind, but postmodern realism does not indicate a rejection of the Enlightenment project but, rather, its culmination. This is a curious claim since arguably it is the Enlightenment project that created the mess which Borgmann wishes to clean up. It is a bit like turning to arsonists to put out the fire they started in the first place. Presumably, even arsonists can have a conversion experience, prompting them to change their ways. How might this conversion occur? Focal communities embody the pursuit of a

---

[65] See, e.g., Martin Wolf, *Why Globalization Works* (New Haven, CT, and London: Yale University Press, 2004); and Jagdish Bhagwati, *In Defense of Globalization* (New York: Oxford University Press, 2004).

[66] See, e.g., John R. Schneider, *The Good of Affluence: Seeking God in a Culture of Wealth* (Grand Rapids, MI and Cambridge, UK: Eerdmans, 2002); cf. John Kenneth Galbraith, *The Affluent Society* (Boston, MA, and New York: Houghton Mifflin, 1998).

[67] See, e.g., Michael Novak, *The Spirit of Democratic Capitalism* (Lanham, MD: Madison Books, 1991); cf. Robert Song, *Christianity and Liberal Society* (Oxford: Clarendon Press, 1997).

[68] See, e.g., Eric Higgs, Andrew Light, and David Strong, eds., *Technology and the Good Life?* (Chicago, IL, and London: University of Chicago Press, 2000).

good life. Individuals may perceive this more excellent way through reason, and will themselves to reform their lives accordingly. In appealing to the power of reason and the will to eventually reform the economic and political background, it is not surprising that Borgmann turns frequently to Immanuel Kant and his latter-day disciple, John Rawls. This Kantian framework provides an admittedly elegant framework for explicating how focal communities should undertake their practices for reforming the moral and social foreground, in turn leading to a reformation of the economic and political background. The framework, however, is opaque. For all of Borgmann's admonitions to pursue and practice the good life we are never told in much detail what the good is that should be known and willed. At this point we encounter an inertia not unlike that found in Grant, but rather than waiting for a waiting God, the proposal stalls in pursuing an unnamed good.

Why is Borgmann apparently reticent to offer a thick normative account of the good? This questions leads to the second perplexity, entailing *what* should be desired. On the one hand, this reticence could be endemic to the Kantian framework itself. It provides procedural guidelines and prohibitions enabling focal communities to pursue their practices, but offers little guidance regarding the subsequent normative judgments on the various goods being pursued other a few general guidelines such as the categorical imperative. For the sake of methodological consistency, Borgmann may feel compelled to honor this procedural focus, and when he does make normative assertions they are deviations rather than exemplars of the argument he is making. On the other hand, he deviates quite often, but his deviations tend to be moral declarations rather than demonstrative arguments. To expose the vacuity of the device paradigm does not necessarily render various focal things good. By and large we do not know why commended focal things are good in their own right, whether there is a hierarchy among these focal things, and whether or not there is a priority of focal practices internal to the respective things. For instance, why are the wilderness, running, family meals, and music good? What is the priority among these goods? Is it better to practice baroque rather than jazz? Borgmann's proposal, unlike that of Arendt, will prompt focal practitioners to leave their oases and travel widely throughout the surrounding, artificial desert, but it remains unclear how exactly they should engage with its nomadic inhabitants and what type of garden they are aspiring to create within this wasteland.

This reticence is all the more bewildering since Borgmann contends that divinity should play a prominent role within his postmodern realism. Presumably, divinity provides a transcendent *telos* that delimits and orders focal things and practices. To pass through technology, he claims, is to enter a realm of simplicity that is also the realm of the holy.[69] Yet, unless he is invoking polytheistic divinity, is not the divine the highest good which in turn delineates all lesser goods, things, and practices? Borgmann drops some hints that this may very well be the case. He baldly declares that the most worthwhile public values, such as compassion

---

[69] See Borgmann, *Power Failure*, p. 93.

and care, have religious origins, particularly Christianity in Western culture.[70] He presses for the development of a theology of contingency that nourishes the virtues of courage and fortitude in forming counter focal practices.[71] And, arguably, Borgmann draws on the Eucharist as the paradigmatic model of what is entailed in focal things and practices. He asserts that only a short step separates the fellowship of the familial table and the Lord's Table, and that the former is the "little sibling" of the latter.[72] Yet, again curiously, Borgmann does not take the next step of interjecting such religious and theological precepts into public discourse, once more falling back into his reticent default position. The reason why Christianity is greeted with indifference, he claims, is because late modern culture is hostile to the concept of grace.[73] Consequently, since the sacrament has no focal place within this culture, Christians must resort to the diffident, if not stealthy, strategy of supporting reverence and piety wherever they might find it, and he lists such examples as environmentalism, art, and science. There is nothing particularly wrong with this counsel, provided that it is not extended in any carte-blanche manner, and there is sufficient theological qualification and amplification to avoid supporting a "reverence" and "piety" that ought not to be commended and should, in some instances, be condemned. Without a doctrine of creation, for instance, environmentalism may appeal to an idolatrous elevation of nature that might be used as a political rationale for justifying oppressive and, at times tyrannous, policies.[74] Heidegger's appeal to the natural ordering and purity of blood and soil in defending the Nazi regime is an egregious example of this danger.

Borgmann could reply that I need not be perplexed. In criticizing the foreground of the device paradigm and outlining procedures for reforming the background of the meta-device he is doing his job as a philosopher. It is as a citizen, a member of various focal communities, and a Christian that he takes the next normative and practical step of pursuing this reform. If there is a need to develop a more overtly theological vocabulary that is intended to enrich public moral and political discourse, that is the job of theologians, and if his philosophical work aids and abets them, then so much the better. Fair enough! In the following chapters I will critically and selectively draw on Borgmann's work, as well as the work of Arendt and Grant, in exploring what developing such a theological vocabulary might entail.

---

[70] See Borgmann, *Crossing the Postmodern Divide*, pp. 143–147.
[71] See Borgmann, *Power Failure*, pp. 115–116.
[72] See ibid., pp. 125–128.
[73] See ibid., p. 65.
[74] See, e.g., Peter Manley Scott, *Anti-Human Theology: Nature, Technology and the Postnatural* (London: SCM Press, 2010).

PART II
Theological Construction

Philosophical Critique and Theological Construction

Part I entailed a philosophical inquiry into and critique of the emerging technoculture. Selected themes taken from the works of Friedrich Nietzsche and Martin Heidegger were examined as prescient explications of the philosophical principles underlying the emerging technoculture. Both contend that nihilism and historicism are the principal moral and political forces forming the late modern context in which the contemporary technoculture is emerging, and neither of them commend or endorse its eventual destiny. Both believe that these nihilistic impulses can be overcome and the historicist trajectories redirected. In the case of Nietzsche, this is achieved through a love of fate that enables the emergence of the Overman who has renounced the right of revenge, whereas, for Heidegger, the solution entails the recovery of a more natural and fitting habitat for humans within the midst of late modernity's technological enframement. Both, in this respect, appeal to the power of the will to reorient the will to power. Yet neither is very sanguine about the prospects of their respective proposals succeeding, and both set a tone of being resigned to a bleak fate—for Nietzsche, the victory of the last men and, for Heidegger, the ascendancy of the liberal consumer.

The works of George Grant, Hannah Arendt, and Albert Borgmann were in turn employed to assess the adequacy of Nietzsche's and Heidegger's accounts. For Grant, although both Nietzsche and Heidegger accurately depict the current circumstances and eventual fate of late modernity, both fail to name the encroaching darkness they describe *as* darkness. This failure stems from their rejection of the eternal good that brackets and orders the dictates of temporal and natural necessity. Consequently, neither can invoke any given norms to assess and reorient late modernity's fateful historicism and nihilism. All they can offer are alternative fabricated horizons to replace the fabricated versions they decry; they can only appeal to the will to overcome the will. It is a bit like arsonists using petrol to extinguish a fire. The resulting conflagration may eliminate the cave's shadows, but its late modern inhabitants remain oblivious to their condition of being cave-dwellers. For Grant, it is the late modern narrative described by Nietzsche and Heidegger that must be refused in favor of that offered by Athens and Jerusalem. In recovering the ancients' depiction and belief in the eternal good, the darkness can be recognized *as* darkness, an acknowledgment that in turn prepares late moderns to wait and be found by an eternally waiting God.

For Arendt, the problem is not the will *per se*, but what is being willed. In attempting to overcome the constraints of natural necessity, late moderns transposed the proper relation between labor and work. This transposition has effectively decimated the private *oikos* and public *polis* in favor of a vulgar society that is neither private nor public. This benighted space is populated by nomadic consumers who turn to technology to satisfy an insatiable appetite for ever greater mobility and consumption. The remaining political remnant is dedicated to protecting and enabling technological development and capability. Yet it is a deadly politics, for deploying such technology is itself a violent act of asserting human mastery over the world, reshaping it into an artifact of the will. Late moderns are thereby fixated on mortality or, more accurately, its evasion. Consequently, the work of crafting a human history is inevitably futile, since any and all hopes are by definition effectively stillborn in a society engrossed with a mortal fate it can neither accept nor avoid. For Arendt, the solution consists of redirecting the will away from overcoming mortality and toward enabling natality. This requires recovering the possibility of a second birth into the genuine work of politics that is predicated on peaceful speech. This work requires cooperation, promise-keeping, and forgiveness, which in turn creates an environment engendering new and renewing possibilities within the civil community. In contrast to Grant's view, this recovery does not entail a refusal of late modernity, but its reorientation. It is neither Athens nor Jerusalem, but Königsberg that is the vital source. Any prospect of a common wisdom or faith is a vain hope, but a universal Kantian reason may suffice, for only a modern can critically recover and reinterpret the ancient resources needed to reorient modernity's trajectory away from mortality and toward natality. It is, then, perhaps fitting that Arendt has placed her hope in a latter-day Immanuel.

For Borgmann, the principal issue at hand is neither refusal nor reorientation but reformation. What he calls the device paradigm has distorted both the social foreground and political background of late modernity. In many respects he agrees with Grant and Arendt that the modern project of mastering nature has degenerated into a process of voracious production and consumption; hence technology's ubiquitous presence and formative influence. The problem, however, is not inherent to the modern project, but reflects its loss of moral direction and compass. When technology is separated from any larger moral purpose, then the resulting device paradigm promotes a vacuous culture of rabid consumers who, in response to the very vacuity of their circumstances, perpetuate a society of indifferent and sullen incivility. Crossing the postmodern divide, however, presents an opportunity for reforming both the foreground and background. Although postmodernism admittedly can degenerate into hypermodernism, it also heightens an awareness of the futility of shaping the patterns of human life in compliance with the device paradigm. This heightened awareness should not be wasted, for it can motivate focal communities to practice those virtues which restore a moral compass to technological development by relegating it properly to a means rather than an end. As focal communities become more widespread and pervasive, the supportive economic and political background will also change accordingly. Consequently, technology need not be rejected or denigrated in any sweeping manner, but reformed to comply with prior human goals and objectives. No grandiose refusal or second births are needed, but rather a reshaping of desires and values which reshape daily, mundane practices that Grant tends to ignore and Arendt decries. In this respect, Heidegger is correct in contending that a suitable human habitat can be carved out in within late modernity's technological enframement; however, this does not entail a forceful assertion of the will but the sustained and disciplined reformation of desire and practice. The road to salvation, therefore, does not originate solely in Athens, Jerusalem, or Königsberg, but potentially in many communities wherever fertile soil for focal things and practices can be found—in such surprising places as Missoula, Montana.

My purpose for examining selected themes in the works of Grant, Arendt, and Borgmann is not to pursue an in-depth assessment of the acuity of their respective critiques and proposals. Rather, since this is a book on *Christian* moral theology within the context of an emerging technoculture, their themes are used as starting points and conversation partners for undertaking the task of theological construction and doctrinal exposition. This task is undertaken in the following three chapters, not in any comprehensive manner, but through some tentative and brief explorations. I have no pretense of launching an invasion and conquest of the emerging technoculture; my more modest aim is to conduct some reconnaissance within this perplexing terrain. Gathering intelligence, however, requires interpretive filters; otherwise, subsequent observation and reporting is merely a tiresome and fruitless exercise in compiling raw data. Early on, some criteria must be employed to separate the pertinent from the impertinent, and differentiate the important from the trivial. The interpretive lenses I employ are drawn from key moments of the liturgy—namely, judgment, confession, repentance, forgiveness, and amendment of life—in order to draw upon and refine, respectively, Grant's illumination of the darkness *as* darkness, Arendt's natality, and Borgmann's focal things and practices. And, as I hope the following chapters demonstrate, these moments are also formative in the Christian moral life.

Chapter 5
Confession: Admitting the Darkness as Darkness

The first task in constructing a Christian moral theology for engaging the emerging technoculture is, as George Grant insists, to illumine the darkness *as* darkness. Such illumination is required in order to deal with the world as it is. To a large extent, Grant has already accomplished this task. He describes, or to use his more favored term enucleates, the late modern world that, having drunk deeply from the wells of its own nihilistic and historicist pretensions, is dedicated to asserting a technological mastery over nature and human nature. Consequently, justice is eclipsed into a calculation and assertion of self-interests,[1] and historical necessity is debased into the good—a blasphemy used by the strong to justify themselves in crushing the weak.[2] Providence is thereby effectively denigrated into a historical account told by the victors while silencing the victims. The net effect is, as Nietzsche saw with great clarity, a transvaluation in which ugliness is declared to be beautiful, falsehoods become truths, and good becomes evil and evil becomes good.

Grant's primary critical tools are drawn from Platonic philosophy and Christian theology. In the former instance, the eternal Good is deployed as the standard of justice against which all human acts are measured. In the latter, the theology of the cross enables suffering to be taken on and endured rather than denied or justified on the grounds of necessity. When the late modern world is subjected to this cruciform scrutiny, it discloses the attempt at mastering nature and human nature as being encased in darkness, and when measured against the eternal standard of justice, the darkness is further exposed *as* darkness. It is this world which denies the eternal in pursuing the immortality of endless time, and which rejects the cross in favor of glory, that must be refused.

Although Grant's incisive critique provides an excellent starting point for a theological inquiry into, and moral assessment of, the emerging technoculture, it suffers from two fundamental weaknesses. First, it is not clear what exactly Grant is urging his readers to refuse. At times, he comes perilously close to suggesting that it is the darkness itself that should be refused. But this would be to mistake circumstances or consequences with causes. What is at issue, after all, is not assessing whether the darkness is good or evil, but what people do in the

---

[1] See, e.g., George Grant, *English-Speaking Justice* (Notre Dame, IN: University of Notre Dame Press, 1985), part II.

[2] See, e.g., George Grant, *Lament for a Nation: The Defeat of Canadian Nationalism* (Montreal and Kingston: McGill-Queen's University Press, 2000), ch. 7.

dark. At other times, Grant indicts, rather sweepingly and imprecisely, various political ideologies, economic systems, or technology itself. Yet, if these are the culprits causing the denial of justice, then it is not clear why they should be refused rather than reformed. This lack of precision stems from Grant's failure to offer, in any sustained manner, an account of *judgment*. Unless Grant is advocating a radical sectarian withdrawal of the truly enlightened, then the practical question of exercising judgment in a world that remains, at best, shadowy on this side of the eternal cannot be evaded. If, as Grant believes, the late modern world exists in the twilight of justice, then his reticence in addressing the necessity and practice of judgment is all the more perplexing, particularly if he entertains any hope of recovering the justice he is championing.

Second, Grant offers few, if any, suggestions on where to look for signs of hope and grace in a world encased in darkness.[3] It is a curious omission, given his core Christian convictions; indeed, he cannot declare the darkness *as* darkness in their absence. As a Platonist, Grant can expose the darkness, but it is only through the lens of the cross that the darkness is illumined *as* darkness and should thereby be refused. This refusal, however, begs a question that he never addresses: late modernity is to be refused, but in favor of what? Although the recovery of Athens and Jerusalem is a critical prerequisite, it is inadequate if the refusal is genuinely motivated by *Christian* convictions. Christianity is not a restorationist religion but is proleptic and eschatological; its hope is not placed in returning to the old Jerusalem, but in the New Jerusalem. But in Grant's scheme of waiting for a waiting God, all we have are memories of the old with few signs of what the new might entail. Christianity is, admittedly, a patient faith, but its waiting is expectant rather than passive; Christians wait for something in particular. In the absence of any substantive eschatological orientation, the hope and grace that sustains Christian faith become grim resignation and gritty pluck. Consequently, Grant can illumine the darkness *as* darkness but not confess it as such.

Given Grant's dependence on Simone Weil, it is not surprising that he can never quite move beyond the darkness he illumines. The late modern eclipse of justice is unremitting and irreversible because of the pervasive nihilism and historicism that denies any possibility of the eternal Good. Consequently, suffering is endemic and unending, and can only be faithfully endured and lamented. The problem with this account, however, is not Grant's employment of the Good and the cross as critical tools, but his incomplete Christology. The cross alone cannot reveal the fullness of God as the source of the Good, for all it discloses is the suffering often hidden by the world's darkness; hence, enduring and lamenting are about the best one can do. But the cross is not an isolated and self-sufficient event. Rather, it can only be properly understood in anticipation and confirmation of Christ's resurrection,

---

[3] Grant perhaps collapses grace and hope, as well as love, into his understanding of justice. But, if so, the resulting mixture is highly ambiguous. See Andrew Kaethler, *The Synthesis of Athens and Jerusalem: George Grant's Defense against Modernity* (Saarbrücken, Germany: VDM Verlag, 2009), ch. 5.

exaltation, and *parousia*. Together, they reveal given and anticipated signs of the eternal Good that Grant wishes to affirm. Late modernity's eclipsed justice is therefore neither unremitting nor irreversible, for judgments can be made in conformity to these signs, thereby ameliorating the injustice and resulting suffering endemic to the human condition, albeit to a limited degree. And it is precisely in this possibility that the new and not yet can enter and renew the old that hope and grace sustain the practice of judgment in the temporal pursuit of an anticipatory justice. Confessing the darkness *as* darkness necessarily entails a confession of culpability and possible renewal—the necessity of judgment, hope, and grace. In short, although Grant's critique of late modernity is incisive, it requires a more extensive and expansive Christology if it is to be effectual. The remainder of this chapter undertakes this task by developing a Christological framework, followed by constructive inquiries into the themes of judgment, hope and grace.

The Christological framework

The Incarnation is the centerpiece of this Christological framework.[4] In and through Jesus Christ the Word is made flesh; the eternal enters the temporal. In this act there is simultaneously a divine judgment upon the sins of the world and a bestowal of mercy, forgiveness, and grace. The significance of this act, however, is not confined to the birth, work, and death of Jesus. Rather, the crucifixion, resurrection, and exaltation of Jesus Christ constitute the *singular* but *trifold* culmination of the Incarnation.[5] Each respective act or instance presupposes and confirms the other two. Lingering exclusively, or too long, on Good Friday, Easter, or the Ascension distorts the theological significance of this interdependency. In the absence of resurrection and exaltation, Jesus' crucifixion is reduced to the tragic death of a heroic figure. Jesus' resurrection without his crucifixion and exaltation is a baffling display of divine power. And to exalt Jesus in isolation from his death and resurrection is an assertion of an arbitrary divine will. Together, these three instances complement, supplement, delineate, and thereby disclose the theological import of the Incarnation. Maintaining this integral and mutually dependent relatedness of these three instances is a crucial task if the Incarnation is to serve as a theological precept for a Christian moral engagement that is

---

[4] In developing the following framework, I am drawing on and revising themes from Brent Waters, "The Incarnation and the Christian Moral Life," in F. LeRon Shults and Brent Waters, eds., *Christology and Ethics* (Grand Rapids, MI, and Cambridge, UK: Eerdmans, 2010), pp. 5–31.

[5] I am indebted to the work of Oliver O'Donovan in developing this account of the Incarnation; see especially *Resurrection and Moral Order: An Outline for Evangelical Ethics* (Grand Rapids, MI: Eerdmans, 1986), Part I, and *The Desire of the Nations: Rediscovering the Roots of Political Theology* (Cambridge, UK: Cambridge University Press, 1996), Chapters 4–6.

both critical *and* constructive. Keeping this task in mind, each instance may be examined individually in further developing this Christological framework.

In the crucifixion of Jesus Christ the incarnate Word takes on the suffering of the world and condemns the willful sources of that suffering.[6] Particularly in respect to late modernity, it is the suffering resulting from its nihilistic will to power and self-justifying appeals to historical necessity that are principally at issue. We need not repeat Grant's exposition of the pervasive suffering resulting from late modernity's corrupting transvaluation of the eternal Good, especially as manifested in the emerging technoculture, but may move on to what the crucifixion anticipates. It anticipates a resurrection. Although suffering admittedly epitomizes, to a great extent, the human condition, it does not exemplify human destiny. The deadly suffering permeating daily life should be acknowledged and given its due, but that does not include its finality. In taking on the suffering of the world, Jesus Christ, in and through his resurrection, does not allow suffering a perpetual voice or the right to utter the final word. The world's destiny is not one of darkness, but of light. Consequently, the suffering of Good Friday instigates the hope of Easter Sunday. The crucifixion also anticipates an exaltation. The gospel does not end with an empty tomb but is the fulcrum initiating a new era—namely, that of the rule and reign of Christ. The One who took on the suffering of the world and died for its sake, the One who was raised from the dead is also exalted by God to be the Lord of the world. This era, however, is partly retrospective, for it is the reign of a suffering servant whose rule is oriented toward hope overcoming despair. Consequently, the suffering of Good Friday looks forward in gladness to the possibility that justice and grace will prevail.

In the resurrection of Jesus Christ from the dead, the created order is vindicated. Following Oliver O'Donovan, the resurrection does not merely validate Jesus' life and ministry.[7] Rather, as the central event of the tripartite culmination of the Incarnation, it vindicates the created order that the Word affirms in becoming flesh. Despite the darkness and distortions of sin, the world remains God's good creation. Consequently, the resurrection is simultaneously retrospective and prospective. It is retrospective in that it culminates the crucifixion's anticipation that suffering and death are not ultimately victorious. Any and all attempts at mastering creation, and thereby rejecting its created order which leads inevitably to suffering and death, are thwarted by God. In the resurrection humans are not "allowed to uncreate what God created."[8] All Gnostic and Manichean schemes, such as fabricating an immortal history or posthuman being, are thereby negated as futile endeavors or distractions. The resurrection is also prospective in that it anticipates that the One

---

[6] I am assuming that suffering resulting from natural finitude and mortality is taken on by Christ but not condemned. For a more extensive inquiry into human finitude and mortality, see Brent Waters, *This Mortal Flesh: Incarnation and Bioethics* (Grand Rapids, MI: Brazos, 2009).

[7] See O'Donovan, *Resurrection and Moral Order*, pp. 13–15.

[8] Ibid., p. 14.

who embodies God's vindication of created order will in turn be exalted as its Lord. Being raised from the dead is the prerequisite step for establishing Christ's reign. Christ will rule the creation that he affirmed through his Incarnation and vindicated in his resurrection. The vindication of created order, however, does not entail the restoration of creation. The rule of Christ is not oriented toward a recovery of creation's origin but toward its destiny. The resurrection, then, offers a hope that can sustain the world in the midst of its endemic suffering, for the crucified One was not abandoned by God. Yet it is not a self-referential hope, but one that redirects attention toward the new and renewing possibilities of justice and grace. The empty tomb anticipates a throne.

In the exaltation of Jesus Christ, the world is given its Lord and savior. In this respect, the rule and reign of Christ is retrospective. It fulfills the crucifixion's anticipation that suffering is neither endemic nor endless by pronouncing a judgment against its sinful causes. And it fulfills the hope anticipated in the resurrection that justice and grace are real and concrete possibilities in governing human affairs. The exaltation completes the culmination of the Incarnation by providing an ordering of creation over time. Or, drawing upon liturgical imagery, it is the long season of Ordinary Time following Lent and Easter.[9] This ordering, however, requires a strong prospective orientation, for the rule and reign of Christ does not lead the world back to Eden, but prepares it to receive the New Jerusalem. The exaltation of Christ is not the moment of the world's salvation, but inaugurates a time of preparation to be embraced by its savior in his *parousia*. The world's destiny is not a rule of endless time, but of eternal fellowship with its triune creator and redeemer. Consequently, the exaltation initiates Christ's lordship for the time being; it is a penultimate ordering of the time between the times.

When these the three culminating instances of the Incarnation and their corresponding emphases on suffering, hope, and grace are held together, they provide a fuller and richer grounding in which Christian moral engagement may be embedded. Together, they offer the possibility of a creative tension in their mutually retrospective and prospective orientations in which remembrance, attentiveness, and anticipation all play formative roles in moral engagement and discernment. How this creative tension is played out is examined in greater detail in subsequent chapters. The more immediate concern is to note how acknowledging and preserving the tension among crucifixion, resurrection, and exaltation serves to check the distortions that result when one instance is privileged to the detriment of the other two.

Fixating on the cross, for example, places an unwarranted significance on suffering. The cross amplifies that Jesus suffered with and for a suffering world. But when the cross is emphasized by effectively denying, ignoring, or muting the resurrection and ascension, suffering itself becomes redemptive. Consequently,

---

[9] I am aware that I have evaded Pentecost in this scheme. This omission should not be construed as a willful or unwitting dismissal of the Holy Spirit. Rather, I presuppose the work and gifts of the Spirit throughout the development of this Christological framework.

Christian faith and practice are reduced to perpetually re-enacting the crucifixion in a world in which suffering is pervasive, inevitable, and unremitting. Moral engagement becomes the pursuit of suffering. This fixation on the cross is, perhaps, best exemplified in the life and work of Simone Weil. She readily admits that "faith would be easier for me" if the Bible had "omitted all mention of Christ's resurrection," for the "Cross by itself suffices me."[10] As her writing and eventual death indicate, she steadfastly pursued a life of suffering, even wishing to join Jesus on his cross, if not replace him.[11] Although the cross may have sufficed for Weil, it alone is not sufficient. When the hope and grace of the resurrection and exaltation are denied or diminished, the justice she (and Grant) champions is effectively denied, and the pursuit of suffering is, at best, an empty gesture, and, at worst, an act of self-indulgent glorification. Ironically, in avoiding a theology of glory, the cross is glorified beyond recognition. Golgotha is not in itself salvific, but initiates the penultimate moments of Easter and Ascension, and the ultimate expectation of the *parousia*.

A similar distortion occurs in privileging the resurrection to the virtual exclusion of the crucifixion and exaltation.[12] The vindication of created order is rightfully celebrated, but to remain fixated on this act is to effectively reduce Jesus to a hero who has earned God's favor. Herein lies a subtle trap: if Jesus can earn Gods' favor, then so too can his followers. They can also be made heroic. God's vindication of created order is thereby corrupted into self-vindication. Easter merely demonstrates the power of the will to will the good. This stance, however, denies that much of the suffering leading to Good Friday is a consequence of all failed attempts at self-justification, as well as failing to recognize that the rule of the ascended Christ is predicated on mercy and grace and not desert. In elevating the vindication of the resurrection to the detriment of the suffering of the crucifixion and grace of the exaltation, Christians try to become, following Karl Barth, their own saviors.[13] Hope, in short, mutates into self-assertion, and justice into the will to power.

In focusing too exclusively on the exaltation there is a strong tendency to equate, if not replace, grace with power. Acknowledging Christ's rule and reign

---

[10] See Simone Weil, *Letter to a Priest* (London: Routledge and Kegan Paul, 1953), p. 55; see also Mario von der Ruhr, "Christianity and the Errors of Our Time: Simone Weil on Atheism and Idolatry," in A. Rebecca Rozelle-Stone and Lucian Stone, eds., *The Relevance of the Radical: Simone Weil 100 Years Later* (London and New York: Continuum, 2010), pp. 69–71.

[11] Weil implies that dying a violent death for Christ should be the desire of Christians and readily admits that "every time I think of the crucifixion of Christ I commit the sin of envy"; see Simone Weil, *Waiting for God* (New York: HarperCollins, 2001), p. 38.

[12] The following two paragraphs are adapted from Waters, "The Incarnation and the Christian Moral Life," pp. 7–9.

[13] See Karl Barth, *Church Dogmatics*, IV/1 (Edinburgh: T and T Clark, 1975), pp. 769–770.

becomes tantamount to placing oneself on the right side of history and identifying with the victors rather than the victims. In its worst form it embodies, as Grant correctly describes, a theology of glory in which good becomes evil and evil good. Consequently, whatever is purportedly said or done for the sake of Christ's rule is by definition good, a delusion easily contradicted by the stubborn facts of history. How may we account for this contradiction? It is a result of distorting grace into moral superiority. Such smug self-righteousness is insufficiently self-critical because of its underlying deficient eschatology which confuses or conflates the ascension with the *parousia*. The expectant orientation of Christ's rule is effectively lost, thereby muting its function as an interim reign. As a result, there is a failure to acknowledge that although suffering will be redeemed, that is not the present circumstance of the world; and it fails to comprehend that a vindicated created order is *not* synonymous with creation's full and complete redemption. The end of suffering and creation's redemption can only occur with the end of Christ's rule. For the end of reconciling the temporal and eternal is fellowship with the triune God in which all political metaphors such as kingdom and king (or republic and president, if the reader prefers) are discarded because they are no longer needed. Whatever necessary judgments and acts are undertaken in this interim rule of Christ, they are impermanent, penultimate, subject to critical appraisal and reform, and predicated on hope, grace, and forgiveness.

Together, the crucifixion, resurrection, and exaltation of Jesus Christ constitutes the singular yet tripartite culmination of the Incarnation, serving in turn to delimit and prevent distortions when any one of these instances are emphasized to the exclusion or diminishment of the other two. This delimitation, however, serves to enlarge and enrich rather than negate the particular focal point that is highlighted in each respective instance. The hope of the resurrection and rule of the exalted Christ are predicated on the necessity of a suffering servant. The vindication of created order neither denies the reality of present and past suffering nor anticipates a rule justifying its perpetuation. The reign of Christ's grace is that of a crucified and resurrected Lord—one acknowledging that suffering is not yet finally redeemed and that hope remains unfulfilled until the present time between the times comes to an end.

Although it is first necessary to illumine the darkness *as* darkness, it is not sufficient. To use Platonic imagery, the shadowy existence of cave-dwellers can only be fully assessed and engaged with not simply by acknowledging the existence of the cave, but also by asserting that it is not a fitting habitat. In this respect, illuminating the darkness must be accompanied by the eternal Good that is the light or source of the illumination. Description must be accompanied by confession; the darkness described as illumined by the Good must also be confessed as a darkness that is not suitable for the good ordering of human life and lives. Confessing the darkness *as* darkness, however, is predicated on a prior confession of the Good that illumines the darkness. To some extent, Grant makes this confession, for he is, after all, a self-avowed *Christian* Platonist. But his confession is partial and therefore inadequate. He confesses Christ as the crucified

Lord, but virtually ignores a resurrected and exalted Lord other than through an occasional cursory allusion. Presumably, this is the cost for avoiding a theology of glory, but the price is high for Grant can only offer resignation rather than hope, and suspicion instead of trust. Consequently, the eternal Good can only be approximated through a perpetual re-enactment of the crucifixion, meaning that suffering is endless and without respite. Ironically, Grant's incomplete confession blunts the power and insight of his criticism, for whatever critique is offered, it can only result in more suffering, albeit in differing forms and circumstances. Without a realistic prospect of hope and rule of grace, the justice he champions can never be enacted. In illuminating the darkness *as* darkness Grant does not anticipate the subsequent possibilities of repentance, forgiveness, and amendment of life. In the following two chapters I shall examine how the preceding Christological framework enables these possibilities. Before proceeding, however, I must first explicate more fully how confessing Jesus Christ as the crucified, resurrected, and exalted Lord entails confessing the darkness *as* darkness as an initial step in this process, and this exploration will be expedited by focusing on the themes of judgment, hope and grace.

Judgment

To make a judgment is to embark on a determinative course of action to the exclusion of other possible options. In most instances, such judgments are insignificant or trivial: I choose a hamburger for lunch rather than a salad. These kinds of judgments do not require extensive deliberation, and the consequences are not momentous: I do not agonize all morning on whether to eat a hamburger or a salad, and the resulting heartburn passes after a while.[14] Other kinds of judgment require prolonged deliberation, and the consequences are more extensive: one thinks long and hard about the prospect of becoming a parent, given the demanding responsibilities commitments accompanying such a decision. Still other kinds of judgments are made by, or on behalf of, various associations, and require more formal and collective processes of consultation and deliberation: a corporation compiles pertinent data, confers with various financial advisors and political leaders, and the board then deliberates before authorizing the CEO to announce a new venture. Political and judicial judgments are even more formal and public since they represent and encompass civil community: a legislative body debates and enacts certain laws, and juries determine the guilt or innocence of individuals accused of committing crimes.

The act of judgment entails a wide scope, ranging from the personal and private to the collective and public. Yet there are three characteristics that pervade

---

[14] This is not to suggest that the cumulative effects of such judgments may prove significant over an extended period of time. Decades of always choosing hamburgers over salads may have an adverse effect on my health.

the entire spectrum. First is determinative *foreclosure*. Making the judgment to pursue a particular course of action necessarily forecloses the pursuit of other options. If I choose to do this, then I cannot do that. I decide to eat a hamburger and not a salad. If a couple chooses to become parents, then they foreclose the option of remaining childless. If a corporate board determines that a new venture in manufacturing widgets is warranted, then it also chooses not to manufacture gizmos. If a law is passed permitting and protecting private property, then its forcible or fraudulent seizure is forbidden. If an individual is accused of stealing such property, then a jury must determine whether or not theft occurred. It should be noted that the foreclosure entailed in every act of judgment is not necessarily irreversible or permanent. I can, for instance, eat a salad today that was foreclosed yesterday, and a law prohibiting private ownership of gold can be repealed. The consequences of other acts of judgment, however, are irreversible and permanent. Once a person has become a parent that fact cannot be undone,[15] and an innocent person executed cannot be brought back to life. The point at hand is that making a judgment requires foreclosing other options, and refusing to foreclose disables or prevents an act of judgment.

The second characteristic is *authority*. Such authority varies from informal to formal, corresponding with the spectrum described above. In most instances, authority is exercised by individuals in a private and non-representative manner. As an adult, for example, I decide what I shall eat for lunch within the given options at my disposal. A couple has the authority to determine whether they use contraception, fertility drugs or in-vitro fertilization to either prevent or assist pregnancy. In some instances, authority is exercised by a group or individual on behalf of a larger association in a public and representative manner. A corporate board, for instance, is authorized by shareholders to determine whether or not to undertake a new venture. A legislative assembly is authorized by voters to enact or repeal laws on their behalf. A jury is empowered to determine guilt or innocence, and a judge has the authority to assign the punishment of convicted criminals. Exercising authority in each of these instances, however, is not unlimited, but constrained by a variety of factors that are either external or internal to the social setting in which the authority, and subsequent judgment, in question is properly exercised. I may start eating salads for lunch in response to admonishments by my wife and doctor, but I do not have the authority to compel other diners in a restaurant to do likewise. A couple may not be able to afford medical assistance in either preventing or assisting pregnancy, but they do not possess the authority to require more affluent couples to be similarly constrained. A corporate board may determine that a new venture could prove highly profitable, but nonetheless refrain in reaction to unfavorable public opinion. The majority of legislators may wish to enact a particular law but abstain from doing so due to perceived voter outrage. A

---

[15] Parents may abandon or surrender their children, or they may be seized by authorized agents of the states in cases of neglect or abuse, but none of these instances negates the prior fact of parentage.

jury cannot convict accessories for a crime they have not been formally accused of committing. The point being emphasized is that authority is never exercised (either properly or improperly) in isolation from internal and external pressures, which in turn shapes (again, properly and improperly) the ensuing judgments. In short, fitting judgments are rendered through a properly constrained authority, whereas unsuitable judgments are often made by either refusing to exercise authority or failing to honor its appropriate limits.

The third characteristic is *morality*. Exercising authority inevitably entails moral considerations and consequences that in turn shape or misshape subsequent judgments. This does not suggest that exercising authority is always an inherently moral act, only that many judgments entail an inescapable moral component; many judgments include an implicit or explicit determination that a particular act is either good or bad, right or wrong. Moreover, a properly authorized act of judgment does not in itself determine its morality. I have, for example, the authority to always eat a hamburger for lunch, but that does not mean that my decision is thereby good since such a diet may lead to ill-health that will jeopardize the well-being of my family who depend on my income. An infertile couple may contract the services of a surrogate, but that judgment does not endorse surrogacy as a good practice. A corporate board has the authority to launch a new venture, but that does not mean that its subsequent investment strategies and employment practices are necessarily ethical. A legislative body has the authority to enact laws confiscating private property, but it is another matter to determine whether such a judgment is right or wrong. A jury has the authority to determine guilt or innocence, but the judgment is not always correct. In short, although exercising authority includes an inescapably moral component, such an exercise does not necessarily make the ensuing judgment good or right. Rather, moral reflection on past acts of judgments and deliberation on prospective acts serve to delimit and orient judgments.

These delimiting and orienting roles may be seen, on the one hand, in the way in which moral reflection impinges on how subsequent judgments are enacted, thereby honing the proper exercise of authority, and, on the other hand, how moral deliberation on anticipated consequences of prospective acts may reorient the way in which authority should be exercised. Assessing the veracity and efficacy of prior judgments may impinge on how subsequent acts under similar circumstances are enacted. Such assessment may result in restricting the scope of future judgments, but such constraint frees the individual, representative, or group in question to exercise the appropriate authority in a more veracious and efficacious manner.[16] On reflection, for example, I choose a new diet of salads for lunch. Although this judgment restricts my culinary options, the resulting improved health (hopefully) enables a better exercising of personal authority in terms of my family's needs. An infertile couple may forego medically assisted treatments, freeing them to exercise

---

[16] See, e.g., Karl Barth, *Church Dogmatics*, III/4 §56 (Edinburgh: T and T Clark, 1961); and O'Donovan, *Resurrection and Moral Order*, Part II.

parental authority through the more restrictive options of adoption or foster care.[17] A corporate board that prohibits child labor may reduce the profit margin, but it is freed to govern in a manner that recognizes that labor cannot be reduced solely to a budget line.[18] Legislation privatizing the construction, maintenance, and provision of transportation reduces the scope of governmental action, but it is then free to exercise its regulatory authority in a more focused and limited manner. A judge may choose leniency over severity in assigning punishment in some instances, thereby freeing her to be an agent of mercy as well as retribution. It should not be assumed that the judgments described in the preceding examples are necessarily good or right. Rather, they illustrate that moral considerations and anticipated consequences can and should impinge on how acts of judgments are enacted, leading to constraints on asserting authority that serve to sharpen, delimit, and orient its exercise. In this regard, it is equally problematic when individuals, groups, and representatives refuse or refrain from exercising their rightful authority.

Moral considerations may also prompt a reorientation on how authority should be exercised. Moreover, this reorientation may result in judgments that affect a broad range of individuals and communities. I may come to believe, for example, that it is wrong to eat meat and become a vegetarian, a judgment that will affect, for good or ill, few, if any, other individuals. Should the owner of a meat-packing firm make the same judgment, however, leading him to close his firm rather than sell it since he does not wish to profit any longer from an immoral act, a far more expansive range of employees, suppliers, shippers, and consumers are affected. Similarly, the consequences of a couple choosing to remain childless are relatively limited, whereas the consequences of laws regulating procreation to achieve quantitative or qualitative outcomes will be widespread. Again, the point is not to suggest whether these judgments or right or wrong, but to illustrate that moral considerations impinging on particular judgments affect a relatively small or large number of other people beyond the individuals or representatives authorized to make the judgment. Rather, the issue at hand is to acknowledge that moral considerations may reorient the exercising of authority, but the ensuing judgments carry with them either the good or ill effects of a reoriented authority that is properly or improperly delineated and exercised. In this respect, power is not synonymous with authority. Government, for instance, has the power to regulate procreation, but whether or not it has the authority to do so is a different question.

To summarize: an act of judgment entails determinative *foreclosure*, exercising *authority*, and deliberative *morality*. It is precisely these three features that are eroded by late modernity's nihilism and historicism, and this erosion is seen most

---

[17] This does not imply that adoption and foster should be restricted to childless couples.

[18] This does not imply that reducing labor costs is not a moral consideration, particularly in respect to creating or maintaining employment opportunities, and costs to consumers.

poignantly in the emerging technoculture. To embark upon a course of action by foreclosing other possible options is perceived as an impediment to be surmounted rather than conceded. Late moderns prefer to have many options at their disposal and to keep them open for as long as possible. This was seen in Chapter 1 in terms of the various technologies enabling people to overcome the limits of time and place. A person need not be confined to doing one thing in one place at one time, but can be in one place while doing many things in many places. Moreover, this sense of virtual nomadic mobility and ubiquitous access permeates the late modern world and its emerging technoculture. I need not, for instance, give up my hamburgers since drugs can, to some significant extent, prevent their harmful effects. Any couple or individual can potentially use an expanding array of options in pursuing their respective reproductive options. A corporation need not foreclose entering or benefiting from a variety of new ventures through complex investment instruments that limit risk and liability. Legislative bodies may decry the harmful effects of tobacco while subsidizing its production, promoting its exportation, and procuring tax revenue from its sale. Judges purportedly uphold the rule of law through routinely overturning the legality of statues that constrain individual choices and preferences. For the nomadic residents of the emerging technoculture, the very notion that making a judgment requires saying "no" to this in order to say "yes" to that is unintelligible, or if intelligible nonetheless repugnant.

Authority in turn is effectively reduced to an assertive will. Individuals and groups have a self-originating authority to will whatever they wish, so long as what is willed does not entail deliberately harming others in the ensuing pursuit.[19] Particular judgments or choices are made by an agent or representative in accordance with what they will; they do not conform to the normative constraints and dictates of relevant spheres of human association and their corresponding ordering. Authority is not a given to be exercised, but a created artifact to justify acts required to attain a willed outcome. I choose a hamburger or salad, for example, because I prefer the taste of one over the other rather than considering certain obligations inherent to my roles of husband and father. A couple decides to have a child or remain childless based on the extent of anticipated disruption of their respective careers rather than aligning their decision with normative claims about marriage and family. A corporate board approves or disapproves a proposed new venture solely on a cost–benefit analysis rather than determining whether or not such a new product would meet the needs of the consumers it is dedicated to serving. A legislative body either refrains from or enacts legislation confiscating private property in reaction to its popularity rather than appealing to normative precepts regarding the proper size and scope of government. A judge may be either severe or lenient in assigning punishment not in order to vindicate the civil community, but to encourage or deter future prosecutions. For late moderns,

---

[19] This does not suggest that individuals and groups are guaranteed that they will obtain what they will, or that others may be inadvertently harmed in the process of obtaining what is willed.

authority is derived from what is willed rather than formative of what is willed; an act of judgment is not so much authorized as it is authored.

The immediate consequence of this reductive appraisal of moral considerations and consequences is that it corrupts the exercising of authority into a value judgment. The task is not to assess if a possible course of action is good or bad, right or wrong, but to assign relative value among various options. If one values A over B, then one will presumably do option 1 rather than option 2. Assigning and acting on such values, however, is often an arbitrary process, particularly when there is a reluctance to foreclose contradictory options. There is no external measure for determining why A should be valued over B, and the eventual assigning of value and corresponding judgment is little more than a thin rationalization. Or an option 3 is concocted that attempts to honor both A and B even if the resulting act is intrinsically incommensurable. I value tasty food and my family, and continue to eat hamburgers every day because of the immediate gratification they provide while insisting that the resulting happiness makes me a better husband and father. A couple values their respective careers and prospect of becoming parents. They intend on being actively involved parents, but neither one has any intention of cutting back on their 60-hour working weeks. A corporate board insists that its highest value is providing customers with innovative products, yet each year it trims the research and development budget to pay higher dividends to shareholders. Legislators value both justice and freedom, and proceed to enact employment statutes predicated on the principles of equal opportunity and discriminatory preferences. A judge or jury may assign a high value to the principle of "blind justice" in determining guilt or innocence, yet insist that the status of class, race, or gender should also be taken into account.

The point to be made is again not to portray the preceding value judgments as being necessarily bad or wrong, but to note that their determination originates within and enacts the will of the individuals, groups, or representatives in question rather than conforming to given standards of the good or right. Consequently, when the creation of options is exchanged for their foreclosure, when authority is reduced to a willing of what is valued, and when moral deliberation is debased into assigning value to what is willed, then the ensuing judgment is effectively warped into an act of power. I have the power to eat what I will; a couple has the power to obtain a child by whatever method they choose; a corporate board has the power to undertake whatever venture it desires; a legislative body has the power to enact any laws it fancies; judges have the power to assign whatever punishments they find fitting in respect to varying circumstances. There are admittedly a host of practical, economic, procedural, constitutional, and political constraints that constrict the assertions of such power, but they are subject to change and revision by those holding and asserting the power to do so, and conceptually it is the existence of such constraints on the will that the will to power seeks to overcome. As a result, the ensuing judgments enacting an assertive yet constrained power inevitably entail simultaneous satisfaction and frustration, thereby creating and perpetuating an expanding series of inherently contradictory desires and aspirations, a condition exacerbated by increasing recourse to technology in asserting the will in overcoming externally imposed constraints against it. The quest for autonomy leads to greater dependency; personal creativity is subsumed into mass consumerism; privacy dissolves into ubiquitous surveillance and voyeurism; the lines separating leisure, work, and labor fade and become unrecognizable; the private and political spheres coalesce into a bland concoction that can sustain neither. As late moderns become increasingly nomadic they decry their uprootedness; corporations are pressed not only to maximize profit and create jobs, but also to be socially responsible, all the while being increasingly regulated, monitored, and taxed; legislators must somehow preserve universal standards of justice and fairness while honoring the particularity of various individuals and communities within their jurisdictions.

The resulting judgments, then, assert a power to refuse the foreclosure of options that are willed and assigned value by various individuals, groups, and representatives. The ensuing conflicts and contradictions are thereby incessant, cumulative, and interminable, for in many instances their provisional resolution can only be achieved through explicit recourse to, or implicit threat of, coercion, and such provisional resolution can, in due course, be overturned at some future date if sufficient power can be marshaled. This tenuous character of making and asserting judgments helps explain, in part, late modernity's pervasive sullenness as described by Borgmann, as well as Arendt's chain of vengeance and refusal to assign or accept responsibility. More troubling, when judgment is reduced to power it is rendered unattainable except in a highly disfigured and unrecognizable manner, for it is despoiled into an artifact of the will to rationalize the assignment and enactment of values instead of a given standard against which what is willed is measured and assessed.[20] As Grant recognized, such artificial justice marks the triumph of the theology of glory over the theology of the cross in which good is made evil, and evil good. Yet it is not Nietzsche's rather tame transvaluation, but the more thoughtless and thoroughgoing mutilation of the true, the good, and the beautiful into valorized artifacts that are false, bad, and ugly that is the darkness in which late modernity and its emerging technoculture are encased. As noted, Grant's enucleation and assessment of this darkness is incisive. Yet, ironically, his judgment only serves to perpetuate the darkness, given his inadequate Christology. Grant can illumine the darkness with vivid clarity, but he cannot move toward the source of the illumination since all he has to offer is the cross and its suffering.[21] Although the cross is indispensable in dealing with the late modern world as it is, in itself it cannot lead its inhabitants out of their present darkness. Consequently, Grant does not escape the trap of reducing judgment to power, and he offers little more than an enfeebled gesture of indignant pique, for he cannot reorient judgment in a way that is simultaneously retrospective and prospective; he can confess the darkness *as* darkness but is unable to take the subsequent steps of repentance,

---

[20] See Grant, *English-Speaking Justice*, pp. 74–80.

[21] Cf. Brock's assessment of Grant's theology in Brian Brock, *Christian Ethics in a Technological Age* (Grand Rapids, MI, and Cambridge, UK: Eerdmans, 2010), pp. 99–101.

forgiveness, and amendment of life. Ultimately, he concedes that it is unlikely that justice will win out over technology.[22]

How might a judgment be made that is simultaneously retrospective and prospective, thereby resisting the pressure of reducing judgment to power? Following Oliver O'Donovan,[23] a "judgment is *an act of moral discrimination that pronounces upon a preceding act or existing state of affairs to establish a new public context.*"[24] An act of judgment, then, entails a moral determination of whether a particular act is right or wrong. I must determine, for example, whether it is right or wrong to always eat a hamburger for lunch; a legislative body must discern whether it is right or wrong to protect private property. As an act, judgment is always a retrospective exercise. A jury can only determine guilt or innocence in respect to a crime that has already been committed. Enacting a judgment, however, creates a new prospective context that orients subsequent deliberation and action. A corporate venture fails, but that determination promotes changes enabling future success. Consequently, the eventual objective of judgment is the creation of a new public space, regardless of how large or small it proves to be. Legislation prohibiting surrogacy creates a new space within which individuals become parents, and my decision to eat salads creates a new familial space in which I perform my responsibilities as husband and father.

This dual retrospective and prospective orientation of judgment creates a tension that mitigates the corrosive influences of late modernity's nihilism and historicism. In the first instance, in simultaneously pronouncing judgment on a past act and creating a space for a new course of action, the *necessity* of foreclosure is consented to rather than begrudged. Late moderns admit, at least tacitly, that they must eventually foreclose some options in order to implement a particular one; at some point they must finally choose not to do that in order to do this. This admission, however, reflects a surly concession to finite and temporal constraints that, at least for the time being, cannot be overcome through technological or political solutions. When a judgment is finally made it tends to be provisional and subject to immediate disavowal or revision should it result in unwanted outcomes. When foreclosure is itself a provisional act then there can also be subsequent closure, and in its absence no new space can be created. The late modern spaces in which judgments are made are never new, but tentative and endlessly undulating ambits in which the will is variously and provisionally asserted. Consequently, the efficacy of a judgment over time can only be maintained through an immediate, ongoing, and repetitive act of will: at each lunch I must will myself to eat a salad;

---

[22] See Grant, *English-Speaking Justice*, p. 89.

[23] O'Donovan's account of judgment is confined to the political sphere in which government's authority is derived from its practice as its core sense of purpose. The concept may be expanded to a broader range of individuals and associations without, I believe, diluting his analysis. See Oliver O'Donovan, *The Ways of Judgment: The Bampton Lectures, 2003* (Grand Rapids, MI, and Cambridge, UK: Eerdmans, 2005), esp. ch. 1.

[24] Ibid., p. 7 (emphasis in original).

each day the jury must be reconvened to pronounce its verdict. Ironically, for all their rhetoric on creativity and novelty, late moderns can never create anything new or allow it to be created, because the relentless assertion of the will requires imposing the tyranny of the immediate on the past and future. In contrast, to judge retrospectively is to create a new space of a prospective course of action. The past and future impose on and shape what is willed, thereby directing and orienting a new course of action. I make the judgment that, for a variety of reasons, my daily consumption of a hamburger for lunch should not continue. That judgment creates a new space for initiating a course of action that is not dependent on my ongoing will, but rather orients the will toward a future destination of improved health that eating salads enables. Likewise, the efficacy of a jury's judgment does not require the jury's ongoing or repetitive willing of the verdict, but, rather, its pronouncement on a past act of crime forecloses the option of innocence, thereby creating a new space for punishing (and perhaps promoting the reform of) the convicted criminal, and how such punishment is best pursued.

In the second instance, making a judgment is to act in a manner that is *authorized*. Contrary to the late modern portrayal of authority as the ability to pursue what is willed, a judgment is enacted by those exercising a properly delimited authority within a given associational sphere and set of circumstances. These given limitations and orientations shape what is willed and fittingly enacted rather than vice versa. An authorized judgment, then, entails sufficient power to be enacted. Parliament, for instance, has the authority to assign and assess taxes within its jurisdiction. Consequently, it must also have the power to collect revenue; otherwise, the act of taxation is an empty and ineffectual gesture. Parliament, however, does not have the authority to collect taxes within South Korea's jurisdiction, and attempting to do so would be to assert unauthorized power. Authority, however, does not bestow unlimited power in making judgments, but imposes restraints. These restraints may be constitutive or constitutional. Parliament has neither the authority nor the power to compel taxpayers to pay their taxes cheerfully rather than grudgingly, and the US Congress is forbidden from establishing any particular religion. External factors, such as custom or tradition, may also constrain or prevent the enactment of authorized judgments. Congress has the authority and power to tax non-profit organizations but has never done so. What should be clear from the preceding examples is that a judgment does not gain its authority from asserting sufficient power to enact what is willed; enacted judgment is not an artifact of the will. Rather, judgment is a suitable act that is authorized by and within the delimited confines of a given association or representative body and is congruent with its distinctive purposes; judgment is a fitting act that has been authorized by a particular association, either directly or representatively. Moreover, authorized judgments also entail a prospective orientation. In setting taxation policies, legislative bodies make certain judgments regarding what and who should be taxed and at what rate, partly to orient civil community in line with certain goals and objectives.

In the third instance, it is this prospective orientation that enables a judgment to simultaneously foreclose and create a new space. It is within this new space that moral deliberation plays its most prescient role. This deliberation is conducted within the association in question, ranging from informal reflection and conversation among individuals to formal processes of deliberative and representative bodies. The purpose of such deliberation is not to assign value, but to *distinguish* between good and bad, right and wrong in assessing prior and pending judgments. This determination is made in respect to the inherent nature, purpose, and teleological orientation of respective associations. These assessments may be made or changed gradually or quickly. A corporate board, for example, may determine that certain working conditions are wrong in response to mounting evidence gathered over time, or that it is good to recall defective products as swiftly as possible. Such assessments may also prompt the reform or reversal of prior judgments. A law or policy may be amended because it inadvertently permits wrongful discrimination, or a conviction may be rightfully overturned with the discovery of new evidence. More broadly, moral deliberation, discernment, and determination are needed when a judgment has foreclosed an option, thereby creating a space for new action. Once an infertile couple has made the judgment to foreclose remaining childless, they must then determine which options at their disposal are right or wrong. In many respects, moral determination closes the loop, prompting another round of foreclosure, authorized action, and further deliberation. Once I have made the judgment that it is wrong to eat hamburgers everyday for lunch, I must then subsequently foreclose other dietary options, in turn assessing, both retrospectively and prospectively, what further judgments should be made in this new space.

The circular process of making judgments described above can admittedly prove to be aimless or, worse, vicious. It may prove aimless in that a series of judgments is not following a particular trajectory, but is a series of haphazard responses to changing circumstances. A judgment does not initiate or sustain a new course of action but propels a succession of indiscriminate acts. The week following my judgment to become a vegetarian I switch back to hamburgers after reading an article lauding the benefits of a high-protein diet, only to return to salads the next week after experiencing mild chest pain. The circle is vicious when a judgment does not so much create a new space as replicate the old in a new guise. A legislative body makes the judgment that commercial surrogacy is wrong and passes a law prohibiting it, but permits generous gifts as expressions of gratitude. The aimless character of making judgments stems, in part, from a sense of frustration or futility because the admission that something is bad or wrong is relative and provisional if there are no given standards of what is good or right. One week it is good to be a vegetarian while the next it is not. The vicious character is derived, in part, when an attempt is made to reconcile conflicting values or varying assessments of good and bad, right and wrong within a single act of judgment. Most members of a civil community may believe that commercial surrogacy is wrong, but also believe that it is good to assist infertile couples in their desire to become parents. For some couples, surrogacy is a preferable option, but there is insufficient supply to meet demand in the absence of financial incentives. Both assessments of these relative wrongs and goods are presumably honored by prohibiting womb-renting while permitting gifts. This "judgment," however, does not foreclose surrogacy, thereby creating a new space in which to deliberate on assisting infertile couples or individuals, but creates an ambiguous ambit in which otherwise objectionable options can be repackaged and preserved. In short, the circle is made vicious when judgment itself is effectively foreclosed or suspended indefinitely, for no new course of action is actually undertaken.

Admitting that something is bad or wrong, then, is not in itself sufficiently strong enough to render a judgment that can sustain a new course of action. Such an admission does not necessarily require any subsequent change of behavior or action. What is needed is a stronger sense of acknowledgment and culpability as captured in the word *confession*, for, unlike admission, confession necessarily entails contrition. If, for example, I am given a speeding ticket (no doubt while driving to my favorite fast food restaurant to buy a hamburger), I can admit doing something wrong without being contrite, whereas if, while driving recklessly, I injure someone, my remorse may prompt me to try to right the wrong I have committed and undertake a new course of action by driving safely. Following judgment, confession leads to repentance and amendment of life. Confession, then, is necessarily a retrospective and prospective act. In confessing that a previous act is wrong or a state of affairs was or is bad, the ensuing contrition prompts a repentant response that reorients and reorders a subsequent sequence of acts in line with what is judged to be good and right. Confession initiates *metanoia*.[25]

Without this prospective orientation, confession cannot alleviate, much less remedy, the aimless and vicious circles described above. Confession alone is merely admission intensified by pathos, for in the absence of repentance and amendment of life, the resulting contrition has no place to go and is thereby misdirected. This misdirection can be seen by revisiting Grant. In illumining late modernity's darkness he not only admits but confesses the darkness as such, as reflected in his penetrating criticism and ardent discourse. Grant leaves his readers with little doubt that they live in a world that has gone terribly bad or wrong. Yet his resulting contrition does not prompt his audience to repentance and amendment of life, and indeed it cannot, given his inadequate Christology. In the virtual absence of the resurrection, exaltation, and *parousia*,[26] all he can offer is the cross that serves as a constant reminder that suffering is endemic to the human condition with no real prospect of amelioration this side of eternity. In confessing the darkness *as* darkness, Grant makes no attempt to reorient and reorder the course of late modernity and its emerging technoculture. Rather than making such a futile gesture, he instead refuses it.

---

[25] I am indebted to Ron Anderson for this insight.

[26] Other than a few cursory references.

The prospective orientation of repentance and amendment are examined and explicated in greater detail in the following two chapters. I will argue that they offer promising conceptual resources for formulating a Christian moral theology, one that is both critically and constructively engaging. Although Grant's critique of late modernity can and should be profitably deployed, it need not inevitably lead to refusal, but to reorienting and reordering the emerging technoculture. As will be seen, the pattern of the Christian moral life as one of judgment, confession, repentance, and amendment is explicable within the church and may easily inform a broader range of individuals, and small and informal associations. Admittedly, this potential influence becomes less obvious and more problematic in respect to more formal and representative associations. Yet I also argue that this pattern may nonetheless inform the ordering of the broader civil community, albeit in largely covert rather than overt ways. Before undertaking this task, however, something needs to be said about hope if the prospective orientation of this pattern is to avoid the traps of utopian dreaming, indolent fantasizing, or overzealous planning, or, worse, wrapping late modern historicism and nihilism within a thin veneer of Christian rhetoric.

Hope

Hope plays a paramount role in any act of judgment. At the most basic level human action is predicated on hope. Any action undertaken by an individual or group does so to create an improved or more desirable set of circumstances[27]; an infertile couple hopes that using IVF will result in a pregnancy and the birth of a child; a jury hopes that it has rendered a just verdict. Moreover, individuals and groups are, more often than not, drawn by multiple hopes; I hope that eating salads will improve my health, and I hope that the candidate I prefer will win the next election; a corporate board hopes its new venture will succeed. Following John Macquarrie, hope is always future-oriented toward achieving a goal or satisfying a desire.[28] It is a universal phenomenon, and cumulatively hope takes on a totality since human action is always future-oriented. It is only when there are no options open, or perceived to be open, that there is a corresponding incapacity to act. Or, in more poignant terms, despair is the opposite of hope. Hope, then, provides the freedom and anticipated space in which to act; hence the necessity of judgment to create this space.

Macquarrie warns, however, that hope does not inspire brash or reckless action but, rather, entails humility and tentativeness that results in provisional action. Hope is therefore not synonymous with progress but is a steady and patient "pursuit of the good."[29] Macquarrie's caution stems from the fact that humans

---

[27] See, e.g., Ludwig von Mises, *Human Action: A Treatise on Economics* (Indianapolis, IN: Liberty Fund, 2007), Vol. 1, Parts 1–2.

[28] See John Macquarrie, *Christian Hope* (New York: Seabury, 1978), ch. 1.

[29] Ibid., p. 9.

are often drawn by a bad or false hope, or a good hope might inspire deficient or inapt action. Unfulfilled or unrealized hope, then, may inspire constructive moral and social critique or, conversely, destructive warfare and violent upheaval. Consequently, although hope necessarily entails change, such change must have a good orientation or end in mind.

Macquarrie's account of hope begs an important question: what is a good hope? Or, better, what is the good that should be the object of hope? This is why Macquarrie admits that although hope is a universal phenomenon, it is not generic. Christian hope, for example, is different from other kinds, such as the hope inspired by progressive historicists. At this point we need not enter the debate over the extent to which various hopes incorporate truthful understandings of the good. Rather, for the purpose of this inquiry, we need to fix our attention on the particularity of Christian hope.

St Thomas identifies hope as one of the cardinal virtues.[30] He argues that a good act must correspond with a specific virtue. Hope is a virtue that helps the believer attain the good of God which is the ultimate object of hope. Faith, then, precedes hope for it is only in and through faith that God is known, and hope in turn expresses this faith. Since hope is a virtue, however, it is not a passion but a habit of mind. One must practice hope in order to become a hopeful person, whereas an impassioned hope may be vulnerable to utopian dreaming and reckless action.[31] Consequently, despair is not merely the antonym of hope but a deadly sin, for it inevitably results in aversion to God. According to St Thomas, sloth is the root of despair, for it disables a person's ability to take any action. Unlike the act of foreclosing *some* options in order to enact a judgment, despair entails the effective foreclosure of *all* options, thereby making the rendering of a judgment impossible. Foreclosing all options is a kind of final judgment, but it is nihilistic and destructive rather than creative and renewing; it annihilates space for any future action rather than creating new space for further action.[32]

Christian hope, therefore, is essentially eschatological, for it is in expectation of Christ's *parousia* as creation's *eschaton*, which both enables and constrains meaningful and purposeful action in the present—that is, teleological action ensuing from judgment. The *parousia* as God's final salvific act fulfills the deepest human longing because it provides eternal fellowship with the triune God. God's future is both the origin and end of creation, and the ensuing basis of hope is nothing less than the promise of God as Creator and Redeemer. Yet, if this hope is to enable real and effective action, then there must be some assurance that wrongs will be ultimately righted, otherwise proximate and penultimate acts of judgments incorporating and anticipating this expectation cannot be undertaken. Consequently, Christian hope is lodged in the promise of Christ's *parousia*, and

---

[30] The following discussion draws on Thomas Aquinas, *Summa Theologiae*, II–II, qq. 17–18, 20 (Blackfriars edn).

[31] Hence Macquarrie's insistence on patient and provisional action.

[32] Suicide is an example of a final foreclosure of all options.

the fulfillment of that promise requires a final judgment. In the meantime, the hope of renewing human life is sustained by this promise. When time is taken into eternity, the circle of judgment, foreclosure, action, and assessment comes to an end. And in this ending there is the final judgment of "truth and justice,"[33] but, unlike the counterfeit version stemming from despair, it is a judgment that purifies and does not destroy.

If Christian hope is to inspire judgments that create new and renewing spaces for concrete and effective action, then, as I argued earlier in this chapter, a more complete Christological framework for moral theology is needed. The singular yet trifold crucifixion–resurrection–ascension culmination of the Incarnation is needed to sustain hope in this period between the times of fulfilled and unfulfilled promise. As seen in Grant, when attention is fixated almost entirely on the cross the resulting hope is at best a forlorn one, resulting in refusal rather than renewal. Or, to invoke the pattern of the liturgy, there is confession but no subsequent repentance, forgiveness, and amendment of life. In the virtual absence of the resurrection there is no vindication of created order. Such vindication is needed to avoid a Gnostic disdain for the world, which can only embrace a hope in its negation rather than in its transformation. Yet, if Christian hope is grounded in a transformed creation, its antecedent ordering cannot be disparaged, and neither can such hope be sustained by disdaining the world. Rather, hope is directed toward the promise of Christ's *parousia* and is sustained by the exalted Christ who has entrusted sufficient authority and power to sustain and orient creation until the promise is fulfilled. It is the ascension, then, that validates and orients this hope, but this side of the final judgment it is hope that entails imperfect judgment and action, never quite entirely discerning right from wrong, good from bad. Consequently, it is a hope that cannot fixate solely on Jesus to the exclusion of Pilate, or any other humans exercising authority.[34]

It should be stressed that Christian hope is not merely a countervailing force to late modernity's nihilistic despair. The will to hope is not contending with the will to power, otherwise one would simply be the flip-side of the other. Rather, hope demonstrates God's promise to reorient the ordering of a vindicated creation over time toward its destiny in God's eternity. This orientation does not involve a Christian refusal or withdrawal from the emerging technoculture but an engagement that is both critical and constructive. In particular, in the following two chapters I argue in greater detail how this hope orients the circle of judgment, foreclosure, action, and assessment along a trajectory of confession, repentance, forgiveness, and amendment of life.

---

[33] See Wolfhart Pannenberg, *Systematic Theology*, vol. 3 (Grand Rapids, MI: Eerdmans, 1998), pp. 610–620.

[34] See O'Donovan, *Desire of the Nations*, pp. 121–122.

Chapter 6
Repentance: The Renewing Possibilities of Second Births

I argued in the previous chapter that judgment creates a new space in and through which the trajectory of moral action is reoriented. More importantly, judgment may lead to confession, prompting a more radical reorientation. This *metanoia* results from a sense of contrition: the recognition that wrongs must be righted. Confession, then, leads to repentance: the simultaneous acknowledgment that a past course and current trajectory of action must be broken, *and* subsequent acts redirected. Repentance, however, is predicated on hope, for if there is no belief that the past can be broken and the future reoriented for the better, then there is no need to repent. Moreover, if such hope is to be effectual, then it must instigate the real prospect of forgiving and promising. In order to right a wrong, the aggrieved and offending parties must be reconciled, and such reconciliation must also be accompanied by the promise of amended future conduct.

To a large extent, Hannah Arendt's account of forgiving and promising provides a moral and political space in which repentance and amendment of life can be operative.[1] Although she admits that attempting to right a wrong cannot undo past events or action, forgiveness can nonetheless break their spiraling aftermath of vengeance when accompanied by promises of altered behavior in the future. In the absence of forgiveness civil community remains mired in the past, and in the absence of promise it has no incentive to move on. The net result is a paralysis of new and renewing action, stemming from a fear, if not despair, that the past sequence of vengeance cannot be broken and promises cannot be made or kept. Together, forgiving and promising orients moral and political action toward the prospect of natality, thereby exchanging the certainty of repetitive vengeance for the uncertain hope of new and unexpected possibilities.

Although Arendt offers a rich conceptual scheme that may be used profitably in engaging with the emerging technoculture, it is nonetheless inadequate, as I argued in Chapter 3. Arendt's difficulty stems from her attempt to remove Jesus' teaching on forgiveness from its theological framework. She contends that reason can be substituted for a shared religious faith. People can forgive, be forgiven, and keep promises as good Kantians rather than as faithful Christians. This is, however, a curious argument, for, as Arendt admits, if forgiving and promising are to be efficacious, these closely related acts must be grounded in a recognized and binding authority. As Arendt also admits, it is precisely such authority that

---

[1] See Chapter 3.

has vanished from the late modern world, because it is predicated on common religious beliefs and practices. Yet she refuses to abandon hope, insisting that although universal reason may not have the same binding force as a common religion, it is nonetheless a sufficient substitute. But one is hard-pressed to find in her corpus a convincing argument, either conceptually or practically, that her scheme could work. In fairness to Arendt, this was a project she had initiated but was far from completing at the time of her death, but in the suggestive fragments she left behind there is little to suggest that she would have necessarily succeeded.[2] Moreover, late modernity's emerging technoculture is more corrosive of authority, in both its garbs of religion and reason, than Arendt imagined. The nomadic and fragmented character of this culture militates against any binding qualities of religion or reason, which in turn prompts an indifferent or hostile reaction to the prospect of forgiving and promising. The last men and nihilists populating this culture simply have no compelling reason to forgive or promise if they believe that their political, social, and economic mobility, as the source of their power, can insulate them from the ill-effects of their actions. The former see forgiving and promising as encumbering nuisances, while the latter disregard them as hateful vestiges of a slave morality. Consequently, natality is effectively reduced to a forlorn hope in stillbirths.

Despite these weaknesses, it is well worth the effort to preserve natality as a principle for orienting moral and political ordering, for it guides these tasks toward creating social and political spaces for new and renewing possibilities rather than foreclosing them in favor of certain vengeance and violence. As Arendt saw clearly, forgiving and promising must be intricately related practices if such a moral and political reorientation is to occur. This preservation, however, requires a recovery of the theological underpinnings that Arendt jettisoned. In the following sections I undertake this recovery by building upon themes developed in the previous chapter.

Forgiving and promising

As argued in the previous chapter, judgment should lead to confession. When a determination is made that a particular act is wrong, a space is created in which the wrong committed can be acknowledged and confessed. In addition, within this new space, the wrong may be addressed through assigning punishment, restitution, or some other recompense. Confession, however, is neither a necessary nor sufficient response to judgment. A person failing to confess guilt, for instance, does not prevent subsequent punishment, and confession alone does not guarantee reconciliation with those who have been wronged. When confession is made or is present, however, contrition leading to repentance may result. For the contrite

---

[2] See Hannah Arendt, *Lectures on Kant's Political Philosophy* (Chicago, IL: University of Chicago Press, 1992).

offender there is remorse for the wrong committed, accompanied by an equally deep acknowledgment and intent to right the wrong to whatever extent possible. It is in the simultaneity of regret and intent to rectify that repentance occurs—a *metanoia* reorienting the pattern of one's acts and trajectory of one's life.

Repentance authenticates the new space created by the prior act of judgment, by instantiating the possibility of the closely related acts of forgiving and promising. With repentance, forgiveness may be requested, offered, given, and received. But forgiveness is accompanied by the dual promise to seek reconciliation among offenders and offended and offenders amending their lives in order to avoid committing similar wrongs in the future. Forgiving and promising are thereby inseparable, and neither can be efficacious independent of the other. Forgiveness without any expectation of reconciliation and amendment of life is effectively an empty gesture of indifference, whereas promising without any thought of forgiving is tantamount to moral amnesia. Together, forgiving and promising open the prospect of new and renewing possibilities that not only reorient the lives of offenders and offended, but broader spheres of human association as well. A reconciled wife and husband, for example, benefits the entire family, and aggrieved racial or ethnic minorities receiving restitution reorients the larger civil community. In short, forgiving and promising create a trajectory oriented by the prospect of natality, to use Arendt's imagery, or, to use a theological concept, hope.

This pattern of judgment opening a new space for confession, contrition, repentance, forgiving and promising, which in turn opens up the possibility of natality or hope, occurs because of its simultaneous orientation toward, and attentiveness of, past and future. Forgiving is necessarily focused on the past. I can only be forgiven for deeds I have committed, and I cannot be forgiven in advance for acts I intend to commit. In contrast, promising is necessarily preoccupied with the future. I can indicate an intention to do or refrain from doing certain acts in the future, but promising cannot erase deeds done in the past. Yet forgiving and promising remain inescapably bound together; one presupposes and reinforces the other. If there is no promise of amendment of life, then effectively there is nothing in the past to forgive, and if forgiveness is withheld or refused, then a promise is reduced to empty pleading. In simultaneously forgiving and promising, the parties seeking reconciliation plot and commit themselves to a new course of action. It is important to stress, in this regard, that the giving and receiving of forgiveness is not conditional on fulfillment of the promise. Forgiving and promising is not a contractual relationship enforced by a greater coercive power, but an enduring affiliation based on an indeterminate trust and provisional certitude, subject to frequent reassessment and redirection. Hence the repetitious character of the pattern and reconfigured trajectory of judgment, confession, contrition, repentance, forgiveness and promise, and the prospect of natality imaginatively guiding how this repetition and reconfiguration are undertaken.

This need for repetition and reconfiguration is why Arendt insists that forgiving and promising cannot be based on certainty, and why she argues that human association, particularly political association, must in turn be based on uncertain speech rather than certain coercion. The pattern and trajectory of moral, social, and political ordering she inspires is not so much like a machine with a detailed design and predictable outcomes, but more like an instrument aiding the navigation of both familiar and unfamiliar moral terrain. Indeed, her schema has close affinities to the formation of human identity in general and Christian identity in particular. In his book, *Remembering the Future, Imagining the Past*, David Hogue conducts a suggestive inquiry into how the human brain, ritual, and story are crucially and inextricably related in forming one's identity.[3] The title is not a clever rhetorical device, but a succinct summary of Hogue's central thesis. Memory is the principal source of identity. People with amnesia, for instance, do not know who they are. Memory alone, however, is inadequate, for, in Hogue's words, "life and identity are not limited to the events of history; we constantly live on the cusp between past and future."[4] On this cusp, imagination grounds hope over time, and, unfortunately, it can also ground fear and despair. Memory and imagination, then, are closely related activities. Again, in Hogue's words, "[o]ur imaginations are as essential when we are recalling the past as when we are speculating about or planning for the future. Without memories, our dreams for what may yet be would be empty and impossible. We imagine the past and we remember the future."[5] Vision, as propounded in Scripture, is a close synonym of imagination, and the inability to imagine or envision new and renewing possibilities may lead to indifference, depression, or even suicide. Without memory there can be no future, and in the absence of imagination the past is random or pointless recall.

What holds memory and imagination together, and thereby identity, over time is narration. Human lives are stories in which certain patterns are traced and trajectories are plotted. These stories are accounts of the past and anticipated futures. They may unfold well or badly, may prove to be tragic or comical, stark or delusional, a source of fear or security. The telling of these stories may bring healing, they can be rewritten, and new stories can be discovered and incorporated. In any case they are highly complex stories, for, as Hogue emphasizes, we are simultaneously their authors and actors, and we appear and contribute as both to each other's stories. In addition, rituals both reinforce and challenge the adequacy of what is narrated.

This brief summary does not do justice to Hogue's thesis, particularly in respect to his analysis on how neuroscience, ritual, and story may inform pastoral theology and practice. It nonetheless serves to suggest some ways in which Arendt's account of forgiving, promising, and, more broadly, natality may simultaneously inform and be enfolded into a theological account of the Christian moral life, one that is better suited to both critiquing and engaging with the emerging technoculture. With some minor terminological tweaking, Hogue's proposal of remembering the

---

[3] See David A. Hogue, *Remembering the Future, Imagining the Past: Story, Ritual, and the Human Brain* (Cleveland, OH: Pilgrim Press, 2003).

[4] Ibid., p. 4.

[5] Ibid.

future and imagining the past provides a suggestive schema for thinking about moral deliberation, discernment, and action, especially in regard to charting the pattern and plotting the trajectory of the Christian moral life between the poles of *anticipatory remembrance* and *imaginative restlessness*.

The Christian moral life is formed and lived out between the Ascension and *parousia*—in this present time between the times. Consequently, Christian ethics has a Janus-like quality. Christians remember Jesus to glean key moral precepts and examples.[6] But, in remembering Jesus' life, teaching, and ministry, his crucifixion, resurrection, and ascension, they are necessarily redirected toward Christ's return—a return that they anxiously anticipate. Christians remember a history of anticipation: a history of the One who was, and is, and shall be—a history that is incomplete and still unfolding, awaiting its conclusion. In remembering Jesus they are jolted out of the past and directed toward the future.

Christians anticipate the culmination of creation in Christ in order to align their moral deliberation, discernment, and action with this end or *telos*. Yet, in contemplating this future, they never engage a clear image of what shall be, but instead encounter the restless anticipation of those who preceded them in the faith. They must imaginatively assess the adequacy of the extent to which this preceding anticipation aligned moral deliberation, discernment, and action with their proper end in Christ, and make any subsequent course corrections that might be needed. Christians, therefore, restlessly imagine a future that refracts their attention to an anticipatory remembrance.

Consequently, navigating the moral terrain in this time between the times is a challenging, inexact, and even perilous enterprise. It is analogous to a navigational technique used by ancient mariners and early airplane pilots that has come to be known as "dead reckoning." A pilot, for instance, flies an airplane toward a destination seen on, or envisioned beyond, the horizon without the aid of precise charts or instrumentation. A few prominent landmarks and some stars at night are the only assistance a pilot has in recording the flight pattern and plotting its subsequent trajectory, making necessary course corrections as needed. As far as I know, dead reckoning is not currently the preferred navigational method, but over a short distance, with clear weather, and an experienced pilot familiar with the landmarks, it will do; it can get you from Gatwick to Heathrow safely. But in bad weather, over a great distance of unknown terrain, or with an inexperienced pilot it is a dangerous way to travel. If you plan on flying from London to Hong Kong using dead reckoning, well, good luck. Even under the best of circumstances, highly skilled and experienced pilots can run into trouble by misreading a crucial landmark or overcompensating in making a course correction.

The only real option open to Christians for navigating the moral terrain in this time between the times is something akin to dead reckoning. The destination, the eschatological end or *telos*, lies beyond the horizon, perhaps a great distance, and

---

[6] See Allen Verhey, *Remembering Jesus: Christian Community, Scripture, and the Moral Life* (Grand Rapids, MI, and Cambridge, UK: Eerdmans, 2002).

they are already in the midst of a journey more similar to that of London to Hong Kong than Gatwick to Heathrow. Moreover, Christians do not know precisely where on the horizon they should be aiming, and they often encounter confusing landmarks and bad weather. Such navigation, however, is not merely guesswork or intuitive wandering. First, there is God's promise that there *is* a destination—an end to the journey. The details of this promise are, admittedly, vague. They do not know where the destination is or when exactly it will be reached. But they do have some hints that it will entail a reign of judgment, love, justice, peace, and reconciliation; that the hungry shall be fed, the naked clothed, and the sick healed; that the lion shall lie with the lamb; that good will prevail over evil. These are, of course, little more than puzzling images as seen dimly in a mirror, but they are nevertheless there, and they beckon beyond the horizon. Christians are pulled by a restless imagination.

Second, Christians are not bereft of any guidance. They have at their disposal the travel logs and journals of their ancestors in the faith who have journeyed before them. Although the landmarks they encounter are not identical, they are, more often than not, similar. They can learn something about what direction generally they should be heading and what course corrections might be in order through the good and bad examples, the wisdom and folly, the faithfulness and infidelity of those that have preceded them. And, like them, contemporary Christians will do the same for the journeyers that succeed them. Every generation is pushed by an anticipatory remembrance.

This admittedly sketchy portrayal of moral deliberation, discernment, and action as a kind of dead reckoning draws heavily from the Augustinian imagery of the Christian moral life as pilgrimage.[7] Christians are never entirely at home or at ease in the world, because they know this is not the destination they seek. Consequently, they are restless, wanting to get on with the journey. Yet it is not a restlessness that allows them to ignore or despise their present circumstances, for they know that their love of the God they seek cannot be separated from a love of the world and their neighbors in which and with whom they currently reside. Despite their longing, they know their destination will only be reached in God's own good time and not on their schedule.

Moreover, to return to Hogue's schema, the tension between anticipatory remembrance and imaginative restlessness incorporates elements of both story and ritual. In Scripture, for example, there are stories of God's promises to Israel and the church, many of which have been fulfilled and some of which have not yet been fulfilled. Christians, as well as others, participate both as actors and authors in this unfolding storyline, making wise and foolish, good and bad contributions. Additionally, liturgy reinforces the need to trace the pattern and replot the trajectory of navigating the terrain of this narration; hence the need for frequent repetition. In the Eucharist, for instance, the sequence of judgment, confession, contrition,

---

[7] See Augustine, *Concerning the City of God against the Pagans* (London: Penguin Books, 1984), Books 18–19.

repentance, forgiveness, amendment of life, and absolution is repeated week after week. The promise of amending one's life is not unlike a course correction—an admission that one is not heading in the right direction. And the frequency with which this promising must be repeated suggests that careful attention must be paid to aligning moral deliberation, discernment, and action with one's end or *telos* in God, regardless of the imprecision involved.

This ambiguity should not be construed as a disguised progressivism cloaked by indulgent or naive religious rhetoric. There is no reason to believe that contemporary Christians, or human beings more generally, are any wiser or more adept at navigating the moral life than their forebears. Every generation has the potential to be stubborn, foolish, ignorant, or wrong when it comes to moral deliberation, discernment, and action; every generation has the capability to be forgetful, unimaginative, or both. Rather, all that is being suggested is that although navigating the moral life is an uncertain enterprise, contemporary Christians, and human beings more generally, are not devoid of any clues about where they have been and where they should be headed. Consequently, they also, like every generation, have the potential to be wise, faithful, and imaginative—to be adroit navigators of the moral terrain.

It is because of this potential that we may draw on Arendt in constructing an account of the Christian moral life that both critically resists and constructively engages with the emerging technoculture. This utilization of Arendtian themes, however, requires that they be supplemented with appropriate theological claims in order to rectify certain weaknesses noted above. Arendt is right when she insists that a binding religious authority is virtually absent in the late modern world. Yet her proposed substitution of Kantian judgment derived from reason is neither convincing nor adequate. There is scant evidence of any common reason capable of binding late moderns together. Indeed, so-called postmodernists relish the very diversity of contending reasons that preclude any binding capability; hence the recourse to coercion or its threat to compel or restrain action. It is power, not reason or faith, which is the common currency of late modernity and its emerging technoculture. Late moderns can no more reason together than they can pray together. Moreover, if some kind of common reason could be adopted, it does not necessarily follow that it would result in the formation of good individuals or a good society. The reasoned judgment that Arendt borrows from Kant necessarily requires a political and public space that is presumably devoid of any normative claims because it is predicated on the right rather than the good.[8] Consequently, public morality or political ethics are procedural rather than normative, producing the kind of barren and banal mass society that Arendt decries. The *polis* is a public space of right, or more accurately rights, but it cannot be a good *polis* because there is no common good that it can embody or instantiate. Good societies are necessarily confined to secluded oases. Additionally, reasoned judgments do not necessarily

---

[8] See, e.g., John Rawls, *Political Liberalism* (New York: Columbia University Press, 1996), Lecture 5.

result in good judgments. Arendt is correct in arguing that evil often results from thoughtless acts, yet thoughtful deliberation is no guarantee of consequential good or even right action. There is substantial evidence of thoughtful people simply rationalizing immoral acts. Arendt pays insufficient attention to other factors, such as desires and aspirations, which also shape and orient judgments. The restricted scope of reason is partly why it cannot fill the void of moral authority that resulted from the decline of religion. Again, late moderns tend to fill this void with their varying and conflicting assertions of willful power.

Christians fill (or should attempt to fill) this void by appealing to the authority of Jesus Christ. As argued in the previous chapter, this authority is derived from his crucifixion, resurrection, and exaltation as the tripartite fulfillment of his Incarnation. He is the Lord of both the church and creation, and creation is thereby subject to his rule in this time between the times. In appealing to Christ's authority, Christians are not (or should not be) attempting to establish a theocracy or assert hegemony through a resuscitated Christendom.[9] Rather, the appeal to Christ's authority simultaneously affirms the legitimacy of temporal political rule while also insisting on the necessity of its limited scope and nature. Contrary to Arendt, the *polis* is not the highest form of human association, for its authority is not a product of its self-sufficiency but is derived from Christ's rule as creation's exalted Lord. Operatively, this means that the state is (or should be) limited, and never total or minimalist.

Such Christological authority is simultaneously retrospective and prospective or, in theological terms, both providential and eschatological. As noted above, in anticipating the *parousia*, Christians are redirected back toward their history, and in that history they encounter unfulfilled expectations reorienting them toward the future. Hence the tension between anticipatory remembrance and imaginative restlessness that provides the parameters within which the moral life is navigated. This tension invigorates Arendt's accounts of forgiving, promising, and natality by restoring the theological substance of Jesus' teaching that she discards. In the first instance, this restoration solves the three principal problems examined in Chapter 2. First, forgiving may, either overtly or inadvertently, promote the denial of justice. When forgiveness is posed as an alternative to punishment, expedient considerations for preserving the peace and order of the larger community may result in hollow gestures of righting wrongs. In short, wronged parties are effectively denied their due in order to obtain a cheap or eviscerated reconciliation. Despite Arendt's assurance that accompanying promises either prevent or mitigate this abuse, it is difficult to see how such prevention can be effectual, especially when prevailing individuals or groups define and implement particular acts of forgiving and promising. The reconciliation preferred by the strong, much less the wrongdoers, may not necessarily result in justice for the weak, much less the wronged. Arendt presumably assumes that sinners, through their reason, can

---

[9] Unless "theocracy" refers more modestly to rule under the authority of God. See Allen Verhey, *Remembering Jesus*, Part 5.

will themselves to act as angels once they are attentive to the error of their ways. Yet reason is often flawed and, even when it is not, the will may prove weak or disordered. This is why the theological essence of Jesus' teaching that Arendt discards must be recovered, for the forgiving and promising he propounds is not based on strengthening the will, but on the infusion of divine grace to sustain and reorient weak wills. It is in virtue of God's prior judgment and forgiveness in Christ that sinners are empowered to forgive, and to make and keep promises with one another. In this respect, forgiveness is not a substitute for punishment but, as an act of grace, the ultimate end of judgment.

Second, there is the problem of intergenerational reconciliation: the dead can neither forgive nor be forgiven. As Arendt admits, this is a vexing political issue, for how can wrongs originating in the distant past, and exacerbated by subsequent acts of vengeance, be righted in the present? How can the dead receive justice? Arendt concedes that the living and dead cannot be reconciled in any real sense. Nonetheless, if communities are to preserve and promote any semblance of civility, then something akin to forgiveness is required to break the cycle of vengeance, to displace the certainty of violence with uncertain speech. Although no one has the authority to speak on behalf of the dead who have been wronged or have wronged, promises to amend future action designed to break the cycle of vengeance can be offered and compelled. Policies and public gestures embodying the semblance of forgiveness can be enacted, signifying a break in past patterns and a reoriented future. What is really on offer, however, is a promise virtually devoid of forgiveness and completely dependent on the strength of will regarding its faithful keeping. Arendt has again paid a heavy price for her wholesale jettisoning of theology. As she insists, promising in the absence of forgiving is an empty and futile act, yet she cannot invoke any authority to reconcile the living and the dead. Consequently, her ensuing "promise" is a crude caricature of *creatio ex nihilo* in constructing a new future, one that is artificially cut off from its preceding causes and sustained by a strength of will that can easily degenerate into a threat of coercion, thereby creating a new cycle of vengeance. In Christ, however, the living and the dead are reconciled. In and through his crucifixion, resurrection, and exaltation, Jesus Christ is the Lord of creation and thereby also Lord over its providential unfolding over time. In Christ, all have already been judged and offered forgiveness and reconciliation. In this respect, forgiving and promising are acts seeking to conform to a given reality, rather than willing the efficacy and utility of a fiction. Forgiving and promising, in short, are at the heart of what it means to be human creatures rather than an artificial construct for ordering the civil life of the *polis*.

Third, Arendt wants to establish a political order predicated on speech rather than coercion; hence her appeal to the authority of reason for promoting forgiving, promising, and ultimately natality. Yet, as examined in Chapter 3, by restricting such speech to the *polis* she effectively transforms the acts of forgiving and promising into rights and duties that are enforced by the coercive power of the state. In the absence of any common religious or moral authority, political speech does not persuade by appealing to normative convictions but by signifying potential assertions of power. Late modern political speech is merely a rhetorical fig leaf providing some modicum of modesty for the state as it asserts its will to power. Despite her best efforts, Arendt cannot make a convincing case to exchange certain coercion for uncertain speech, because she ultimately cannot appeal to any theological or normative reason why such an exchange would be good rather than merely preferable. As a consequence, the late modern state and its emerging technoculture remain fixated on mortality and are oblivious, if not hostile to, natality. It is again the Christological orientation of forgiving and promising that makes possible a political ordering predicated on speech as opposed to coercion, and thereby rejuvenates the prospect of natality. By appealing to the authority of the exalted Christ from which all lesser political authority is derived in this time between the times, an order based on speech is not merely preferable but is requisite for human flourishing because it is good. In such a political order, forgiving, promising, and reconciling are not exceptional but routine acts, inspiring in turn openness to the Holy Spirit's creation of new and renewing possibilities. It is in and through the restless imagination guided and sustained by the Spirit that, to invoke Arendtian terms, reorients the late modern fixation away from mortality and toward natality. As explicated below and in the next chapter, it is the church that, in bearing witness to its Lord, also embodies and models a way of life predicated on speech, but before turning our attention to ecclesiology there is one more important issue regarding Arendt that must be addressed.

Although Christians may profitably draw on Arendt to enrich their understanding of the moral life as, in part, a pattern of forgiveness, reconciliation, amendment of life, and the renewing work of the Holy Spirit (natality), they must first, as indicated above, pursue some theological reconstruction. The importance of this reconstruction should not be underestimated, for it is not merely a task of overlaying her philosophical work with a veneer of theological rhetoric. Rather, such a theological account is needed to correct a far larger problem in her work that is only implied in the preceding criticisms regarding the denial of justice, intergenerational reconciliation, and political speech and coercion. Arendt's attempt to recover the ancient pagan ideal of the *polis* as the only, or at least the only worthwhile, form of public association is too limited. Despite her valiant attempts to enlarge the participatory franchise beyond a narrow range of heads of households, political ordering nonetheless remains an elitist and technocratic enterprise. Although the *polis* offers a public space in which individuals may participate as equals in political discourse, the resulting action is necessarily imposed on a broader civil community whose members, for a variety of reasons, are not participants in such speech. The problem, however, is not merely one of procedural or structural limitations. Rather, the issue at stake stems from the fundamental dichotomy that Arendt draws between public and private: the only public association of any significance is political, and all other associations are relegated to an inferior private status. Consequently, work is confined to political action derived from speech that endures over time, whereas private associations perform the labor of meeting the tedious demands of natural necessity. It is the second birth into the public life of the *polis* that makes humans human; hence her disdain for mass society that, under the cover of privacy, is dedicated to satisfying the natural needs and banal wants of the first birth.

Arendt, however, inverts an ordering of human life that is properly bottom-up rather than top-down. Ironically, her appeal to the ancient *polis* ends up being a thoroughly modernist program in which the political—and in late modernity this means the state—is the exclusive source of sanctioning, tolerating, and granting legitimacy to all other forms of social and private association. Yet, arguably, private associations are prior to political associations, so that the latter are derived from, sustained by, and embody the former. Or, in more colloquial terms, the purpose of the political is to serve the civil community it represents; the political is the child and not the parent of the private and social. It is also ironic that in this inversion Arendt dismisses the very spheres in which the practices undergirding her principle of natality are best formed and sustained. It is within private and social institutions that forgiving and promising are routinely practiced; indeed, their survival depends on the ensuing trust that they generate. By inverting the political over the social, Arendt effectively nullifies her proposal, for the natality she champions requires a formative and supportive community that the political cannot provide. The political sphere is adept at practicing judgment, but it is ill-equipped to sustain the practices of forgiving and promising.

Can Arendt's inversion be reversed, thereby perhaps rescuing natality from its ignominious fate? Yes, provided an alternative discourse privileging the social over the political can be composed, specifically one that is normative and theological in order to both resist and engage with the late modern nihilistic and historicist discourse of the emerging technoculture. One promising starting point for constructing such alternative discourse entails recovering the concept of *communication*. In contemporary parlance, the term has been debased to exchanging information, an apt image for technologically driven culture. Communication, however, has a far deeper meaning. According to Oliver O'Donovan, communication is the basic form of the social life, derived from its root in *koinōnia*, which can be variously translated as "community," "communion," or "communicate."[10] In O'Donovan's words, "[t]o 'communicate' is to hold some thing as common, to treat it as 'ours,' rather than 'yours' or 'mine.' The partners to a communication form a community, a 'we' in relation to the object in which they participate."[11] Although communication entails reciprocity, it is neither bestowal nor exchange. Something becomes "ours" without the parties surrendering their respective

---

[10] See Oliver O'Donovan, *The Ways of Judgment: The Bampton Lectures, 2003* (Grand Rapids, MI, and Cambridge, UK: Eerdmans, 2005), pp. 242–243. The following discussion of O'Donovan's account of judgment is based on a more detailed account from Brent Waters, "Communication," in Brent Waters and Robert Song, eds., *The Authority of the Gospel: Essays in Honor of Oliver O'Donovan* (Grand Rapids, MI and Cambridge, UK: Eerdmans, 2013).

[11] O'Donovan, *The Ways of Judgment*, p. 242.

claims. Rather, the principal purpose of communicating the goods of creation is to ground human equality in a given social reality, for in relation to God as Creator no single individual can be the basis of a communication. A man, for instance, cannot communicate with himself. Such things as gifts, meals, and property can be communicated among individuals, and there are social spheres of communication such as the church, family, and workplace within which communicating takes place. Civil society in turn comprises differentiated spheres of communication that share "enkaptic relations." Each sphere has an internal order that is relevant to the goods its members communicate with each other, and each overlaps with other spheres. But this interaction must be limited if the respective spheres are to remain differentiated. A family, for example, orders itself in line with the goods it communicates and is dependent on other spheres, such as medicine and the workplace, to sustain itself. This relation, however, does not suggest that a family should organize itself as if it were a hospital or business firm, or that hospitals and businesses should be organized as if they were families. It is precisely the differences among the differentiated spheres that enable communication or *koinōnia* as the form of the social life.

O'Donovan employs two crucial concepts in his account of a differentiated civil community. The first is that of a *people*. Civil community is not merely a collection of autonomous individuals, but the outgrowth of institutions and practices of a particular people. A people share an imaginative perception of a common good which they are, or should be, pursuing. This imaginative construct is not arbitrary, for it stems from a commonly held and binding tradition and culture, which in turn is instantiated in a series of "overlapping and interlocking" spheres of communication,[12] to a large extent echoing St Augustine's insistence that a people is bound together by its common objects of love.[13] A people tacitly agrees on what the goods of creation are, why they should be loved, and what social spheres are needed and how they should be ordered in communicating these goods. To begin with a people as the centerpiece of political ordering provides a necessary check to the nihilistic and historicist tendencies of late modernity. On the one hand, communicating the goods of creation requires a form of governance beyond a minimalist protection of civil rights, for such a structure cannot promote the common identity and good of a people. On the other hand, the priority of social communication resists unwarranted governmental encroachment that smothers the common identity of a people under the weight of bureaucratic regulation and control. In short, political ordering does not create civil community, but "discovers and defends the social order" of the people it governs.[14] Government represents a people, and a people sees itself in what

---

[12] Ibid., p. 150.

[13] See Augustine, *City of God*, XIX/24; see also Oliver O'Donovan, *Common Objects of Love: Moral Reflection and the Shaping of Community* (Grand Rapids, MI, and Cambridge, UK: Eerdman, 2002).

[14] O'Donovan, *The Ways of Judgment*, p. 157.

represents it, thereby resisting the "State-totalitarianism"[15] endemic to late modernity in both liberal and authoritarian regimes.

The second concept is that of *place* or *locality*. Territory and borders are definitive features of a people. Goods can only be communicated within a particular place or locale, and boundaries are needed to differentiate the "you" and "I" that become a "we." Practically, the spheres of communication require physical places in which their respective goods are communicated. A family needs a place to reside; work is performed in some locale. More broadly, a place incorporates the totality of diverse communications in which the particular spheres cohere in a singular locale. According to O'Donovan, it is a "high achievement to define society in terms of place, rather than blood-relationship," for such a "universal" conception embraces "all the forms of society that arise within a formally defined" place or bordered territory. This emphasis on place helps resist both the "platonic temptation" to abolish or escape the constraints of locality, which is amplified by the late modern drive to become dwellers of a worldless world and the liberal project of transforming any and all places into property that can be owned and traded.[16] Identifying a society with a particular place resists the "totalitarian pretensions" in both liberal and authoritarian guises. Such identification acknowledges a plurality of coexisting societies, each producing differing forms of governing their respective communications. Society is not a generic phenomenon, but entails a particular people in a particular locale producing a particular state and not idealistic models of political ordering that attempt to replace concrete locality with a vague and inclusive universality—a dangerous tactic of replacing bordered place with borderless space.

O'Donovan's account of communication draws on the work of Johannes Althusius who portrays civil community as a composition of private and public associations rather than autonomous individuals. Consequently, government represents, rather than creates, a people, suggesting a kind of proto-federalism. This structure embodies human nature that is incurably social. Humans cannot live a genuinely human life in isolation from one another. Moreover, God did not distribute evenly various gifts among human creatures. Consequently, specialization of labor and a need for cooperation is required, and it is worth quoting Althusius at length in this regard:

> He did not give all things to one person, but some to one and some to others, so that you have need for my gifts, and I for yours. And so was born, as it were, the need for communicating necessary and useful things, which communication was not possible except in social and political life. God therefore willed that each need the service and aid of others in order that friendship would bind all together, and no one would consider another valueless.[17]

---

[15] See ibid., pp. 155–156.
[16] See ibid., pp. 256–257.
[17] Johannes Althusius, *Politica* (Indianapolis, IN: Liberty Fund, 1995), p. 23.

Humans are necessarily "symbiotic" creatures, and the principal task of politics is to promote the "purpose of establishing, cultivating, and conserving social life among them," to the end of sustaining "holy, just, comfortable, and happy symbiosis, a life lacking nothing either useful or necessary."[18]

The basic components of a symbiotic community are private and public associations such as families, based on kinship, and collegia providing specialized labor, services, manufacturing, and other commercial transactions.[19] It is important to emphasize that, contrary to Arendt, these associations are not exclusively private and thereby devoid of any public significance because they are not political. Rather, each association has a private and public pole that must be taken into account in respect to political ordering. As a result, the city, as the most basic step in establishing "an inclusive political order," is "composed of many families and collegia living in the same place."[20] Although the relationship among people residing in a city is one of citizenship, such political ordering does not ignore or discount the prior affiliations of families and collegia, for the city exists to promote communication among these associations. Cities in turn form a province as a form of political association. The purpose of provincial governance is to support communication through the rule of law, specifically through legislative, judicial, and executive functions designed to provide defense, security, care of public goods, and promotion of commercial activities. Moreover, the rights, duties, and privileges of provincial citizenship are exercised through a person's membership in various secular or religious estates rather than as autonomous individuals.[21] An association of provinces constitutes a commonwealth governed by a supreme magistrate or monarch. Such a leader does not exercise his own power, but represents the will and identity of the commonwealth, thereby requiring consultation and collaboration with representatives of the various estates that in turn represent the private and public associations comprising civil community or, in Althusian terms, symbiotic society.

The preceding summary is a sparse rendition of lengthy tomes, omitting most of the structural minutia that Althusius describes in painstaking detail. My point, however, is not to plead a case for an Althusian framework as a superior alternative to that of late modern liberalism and its authoritarian variants. Rather, it is to demonstrate that there are strands within the modern liberal tradition in which the social has priority over the political in a bottom-up ordering designed to promote communication, as opposed to the political having priority over the social in a top-down ordering in which the state grants the right of private association. Or, more summarily, late liberalism is not necessarily predicated on the primacy of right over good. Consequently, to construct a counter-narrative to that of late modernity's nihilism and historicism in order to both resist and engage with the

---

[18] See ibid., pp. 17–18.
[19] See ibid., Chapters II–IV.
[20] See ibid., pp. 39–40.
[21] See ibid., Chapters VII–VIII.

emerging technoculture, one need not invent a novel discourse or appeal to the ancients in either refusing late modernity (Grant) or reorienting it (Arendt), but can glean and build upon neglected themes already present in the modern tradition. Although Althusius has, from time to time, enjoyed renewed scholarly and, to a much more limited extent, public interest, he has never really posed a viable alternative model of social and political ordering. Why? Answering this question requires a brief revisiting of the context in which Althusius worked.

Much of what Althusius wrote was provoked by his reaction against Jean Bodin. To oversimplify, Bodin proposed a top-down model of political and social ordering. The state creates civil society by assigning and granting selected duties, rights, and privileges to individual citizens. What holds a civil community together is the state's monopoly on coercive power rather than any particular tradition, culture, or locale as exemplified in expanding and contracting empires. As noted above, Althusius propounded a bottom-up model in which the state represents a differentiated society of private and public associations held together by a common tradition, culture, and locale that the state is obligated to honor and protect. Bodin obviously carried the day, and his general principle of the centrality of the state was refined by subsequent generations of political theorists such as Hobbes, Locke, Hegel, and Rawls.

Why did Bodin win the argument? There are a number of answers to this question, but the one I submit is that they presupposed two differing universal backgrounds against which they developed their particular and respective foregrounds of political and social ordering. Again, to oversimplify, Althusius presupposed the background of a universal Christian culture. There were admittedly severe disagreements over what this culture entailed, but it was an argument over a shared and given reality. Various civil communities were pluriform expressions of this universal culture, albeit in often conflicting ways; hence Althusius' insistence that the power of the commonwealth should be dispersed among the symbiotic associations comprising the civil community in order to protect their autonomy and preserve their respective communications. The borders of the commonwealth were roughly contiguous with that of the locality populated by a people that it represented. Althusius developed a splendid codification and philosophical justification for late medieval society at the very time when its formative Christian culture was in tatters and could not sustain what he was championing. What he offered was a description of Minerva's owl that was already well along its flight.

Bodin presupposed the universality of the state as an artificial and imposed reality, and in doing so turned the Althusian model on its head. Power should be centralized in the state and reallocated by granting selective duties, rights, and privileges. In this scheme, private associations could be ignored or tolerated so long as they did not unduly disturb the peace or directly threaten the authority of the state. Moreover, the state did not represent a particular people nor was it obligated to protect its locale. Rather, the state consisted of individual citizens or subjects, and its borders were determined by the territory it could either defend or seize. The state, then, with its monopoly of coercive power, could govern widely divergent cultures. Although subsequent generations of political philosophers argued over what form the state should take and the extent to which it should or should not encroach upon the private affairs of the individuals it governed, its necessity and universality has not been seriously challenged.

In constructing an alternative narrative that can resist and engage with late modernity's emerging technoculture, an Althusian-inspired account of social and political ordering dedicated to promoting communication offers a promising starting point. Yet, if such an alternative narrative is to have any purchase, the goal is not to develop a convincing argument, for this would result in an appeal to utility—the creation of a non-late liberal order based on pragmatic liberal principles. The state would simply grant the right to itself and its citizens to choose not to be late liberal. Rather, what is needed are communicative associations which, in their life and practices, bear witness to the priority of the social over the political, the good over the right—or, to borrow from Arendtian categories, communities oriented toward natality in which forgiving and promising are mundane, rather than exceptional, practices. Consequently, the witness of such communities stands in stark contrast to the surrounding technoculture and may therefore provide a base from which it may be simultaneously be resisted and engaged with. In this respect, Arendt is correct in her insistence on the need of second births, but it is the church as Christ's labor and not the *polis* as a human work into which one should be born again.

Life in the body of Christ

If Christians are to both resist and engage with the emerging technoculture, they require an alternative narration of the human condition and its contemporary circumstances in contrast to that afforded by late modern nihilism and historicism. Such a narration, however, is not merely descriptive but also exemplary; the story being told must also be embodied and enacted. This is true of any formative narration. The formative power of technology, for instance, does not stem from descriptions of how it works and what it accomplishes, but in the ways it is used. These then redirect the patterns and trajectories of daily life and the way in which social and political institutions adapt accordingly. These alterations and adaptations reveal in turn the identities of various people, both individually and collectively, and what they are aspiring to become. It is no different with Christian narration. The gospel is told or described in Scripture and refined in doctrine, preaching, and worship. Yet worship is also a symbolic and ritual enactment of the gospel, and since liturgy is literally a work of the people, its repetitive structure also forms (or should form) the mundane patterns and trajectories of how Christians live their daily lives, revealing what they value, who they are, what they are aspiring to or hoping to become.[22] But it is not a pristine story, for

---

[22] See, e.g., Bernd Wannenwetsch, *Political Worship: Ethics for Christian Citizens* (Oxford and New York: Oxford University Press, 2004).

its telling and enacting is deeply and inescapably interlaced within broader social and political contexts. Consequently, the Christian narration and enactment of the gospel must be simultaneously critical and constructive, able to both resist and engage with the emerging technoculture.

Communication, or how Christians communicate or should endeavor to communicate the goods of creation, is a principal embodiment and enactment of gospel narration, particularly in respect to forming the mundane patterns and trajectories of daily life and living. The primary theological elements of this embodied and enacted narration have been hinted at above and in the preceding chapter, and the task at hand is to put them together by way of a brief summation for the purpose of describing what this communication might or should entail, somewhat like putting a few pieces of a jigsaw puzzle together. Moreover, in the remainder of this chapter, I concentrate on the critical part of the puzzle that resists the emerging technoculture as a prelude to the constructive task of its engagement in the following chapter.

Judgment is the prerequisite of communication. By assessing a past act, judgment creates a space in and from which future action is undertaken. An individual or group must determine that a particular act was right or wrong, and subsequently to do this, rather than that, in response. More often than not, these judgments are made informally by individuals or small groups, and more formally within larger and more complex social and political associations. The goods of creation are communicated through these future-oriented acts. Consequently, communication is predicated on the new space created by judgment, for failing to assess the past forecloses the possibility of *metanoia* or reorientation of action. In the absence of judgment there is exchange but not communication, for without reconciliation, which judgment does not presuppose as a given outcome but creates the necessary space in which it can occur, what is mine and yours cannot become ours. This is why, in part, the church's narration of the gospel is ineffectual if it evades judgment, for the subsequent steps required in forming the pattern of the Christian moral life are effectively precluded. In short, without judgment there can ultimately be no forgiving or promising, for there is nothing to be forgiven or promised.

Judgment leads (or should lead) to *confession*. Although, as Grant makes clear, acknowledging the present darkness *as* darkness is a necessary prerequisite for resisting late modern nihilism and historicism, it is insufficient for sustaining such resistance. Rather, one's preference for, or complicity with, the darkness, either wittingly or unwittingly, must be confessed if the course of subsequent action is to be altered, for it entails *repentance* and *contrition*. There is an admission and confirmation that wrongs have been committed, prompting remorse. Yet regret alone cannot redress or reconcile those who have been wronged. Repentance is needed to initiate a process of righting the wrongs to the fullest extent possible. Consequently, contrition is not sentiment expressed through emotional intensity, nor is repentance a gesture used by perpetrators to buy the silence of victims. Contrition and repentance together reveal judgments against past acts, requiring a change of course in future action, if such action is to be properly aligned with the human *telos* in Christ.

Contrite repentance, then, prompts (or should prompt) *forgiveness* and *amendment of life*. Offering and receiving forgiveness is neither an agreement to forget the past nor a denial of justice. It is instead a shared commitment to reconciliation and restored fellowship—a reorientation or *metanoia* of a broken relationship. This is why receiving forgiveness must always be accompanied by the promise of amended lives. There is an intention that wrongs committed in the past will not be repeated in the future, and acknowledgment that ensuing wrongs, either willfully or unintentionally committed, are subject to subsequent judgment. As Arendt recognized, it is only through forgiving and promising that the cycle of vengeance can be broken and a community reoriented toward natality as opposed to mortality.

Christians may easily embrace Arendt's wisdom, embodying and exhibiting a life of forgiving and promising, and therefore a life oriented toward natality. They differ from Arendt, however, regarding the source of what makes forgiving and promising efficacious and the horizon that should command one's attention and imagination to make natality a real possibility. Contrary to Arendt, the pattern of the moral life is not directed by the will based on reason, but is set by grace aligning the will in obedience to Christ. The ensuing trajectory, then, is not aimed toward a horizon of the *polis* as the supreme human work but toward the *parousia* to be anticipated and received as a gift, ultimately culminating in the Incarnation of the Word of God. The contrast between these respective teleologies and eschatologies is significant. The horizon of the *polis* cannot be the means of promoting natality for, as a human work, it is limited to an extension of its temporal and finite origin. This origin delimits and distorts every human work as either a diversion or defiance of a mortality that cannot be escaped. The resulting "natality" cannot really offer any new or renewing possibilities other than a fleeting respite, defiant gesture, or counterfeit hope against the ever-present anxiety of impending death. This is especially vivid in the emerging technoculture in which the "new" is debased into the production and consumption of improved goods and services. Natality, in short, is effectively reduced to innovation. The horizon of the *parousia*, however, offers the hope of the temporal and finite being reconciled with and reconfigured within the eternal. Mortality, then, is not escaped but is, in Christ, taken up and reborn into the eternal. Mortality to a large extent continues to delimit human work, but it is no longer a pervasive anxiety corrupting such work. As a result there is a realistic and effectual prospect of new and renewing possibilities for they are not produced as the outcomes of human artifice but received as gifts of the Spirit. Work, therefore, is not a quest for immortality, but an expression of hope in aligning human life and lives in expectation of these gifts, and ultimately the gift of the *parousia*.

In this respect, Arendt is right to insist on the necessity of a second birth, even a rebirth into the *polis*, but she has chosen the wrong city. To invoke the imagery of her "old friend," St Augustine, it is the heavenly, rather than earthly, city in which our second births should occur. For the purpose of this inquiry, we need not undertake an exhaustive survey of the *City of God* but may highlight how the two cities are related and juxtaposed. Christians are citizens of the heavenly city, but they reside, for the time being, in the earthly city. They are resident because the two cities do not exist side by side, but, rather, the heavenly city is sheathed within the earthly city, for the two are intermingled in this time between the times.[23] Christians may be said to create spaces for the heavenly city within the places of the earthly city. Consequently, the church is not an institution requiring territory, but exists wherever two or three are gathered in Christ's name for relatively brief or extended periods of time. Christians are thereby restless and proleptic residents of the earthly city for they anticipate their eventual destination in the heavenly city. This anticipation, however, does not promote indifference or loathing of their current residency. Although Christians are not entirely at home in the world, they love creation and its creatures as God's gifts and work for the good ordering of communicating its goods. Moreover, in contrast to the nomadic citizens of the earthly city, who only require the provision of goods and services to enable their mobility, citizens of the heavenly city insist that such physical and imaginative mobility should be used to promote communication rather than being restricted to exchange. And such communication requires place and not just space.

Although the images of restless Christian pilgrims and late modern nomads may appear similar, the appearance is superficial. Pilgrims and nomads may be differentiated by two differing characteristics and orientation. First, pilgrims are not autonomous wanderers who create temporary spaces for brief exchanges or lengthier affiliations. Rather, they are bound together by the universal fellowship of the church that is manifested in the space which is created whenever and wherever two or three are gathered together in Christ's name. Yet the creation of such space depends on a particular place and designated time. The body of Christ cannot be constituted, for either brief or extended periods of time, by any so-called disembodied "presence" or participation of its members or parts, and the time of *koinonia* must be real and synchronous rather than virtual and allochronic. For the pilgrim, place is the prerequisite of space and time is formative, whereas, for the late modern nomad, place and time are encumbrances to be overcome through technological manipulation and mastery. For the nomad, spaces of exchange may be created virtually anytime, anywhere, and in no place in particular, and association with those sharing common interests or even intimates are not predicated by either physical proximity or synchronous time. Communication is thereby effectively reduced to the creation and consumption of information, which in turn forms the basis of narrating late modern nomadic identity.

The second difference is one of future orientation. Pilgrims are an eschatological and teleological people. Whenever and wherever two or three gather in Christ's name there is an intimation of the heavenly city that will not be fully realized until the *parousia*. Christians are thereby an expectant people, restlessly awaiting the time when this time between the times is culminated in Christ. Yet, as noted above, this restless anticipation does distract attention away from the present world, but

---

[23] See Augustine, *City of God*, 11/1, pp. 429–430.

prompts a preparation of creation to receive and welcome its creator and Lord. This preparation is pursued through the right ordering of communicating the goods of creation in line with its given *telos* in Christ. Pilgrims pursue a journey in which they are beckoned by a destination that awaits them. Consequently, the pilgrimage of the citizens of the heavenly city is immediate *and* proleptic, anticipatory *and* patient. In contrast, late modern nomads envision a future as either an artifact of their will or an inescapable fate. On the one hand, the future is solely an outgrowth or consequence of prior human action, a future that is highly contingent and, for practical purposes, infinitely malleable. The future is what they make of it. On the other hand, the future is dictated ultimately by a fate that cannot be altered or evaded. In the meantime, nomads are consigned to either futile gestures of resignation or attempts to discern what this fate is and align their actions accordingly. Consequently, the nomadic life of the earthly city is one of either willful or resigned mastery. Although these orientations are contradictory, they both reflect a fundamental fear of the future. The attempt to make the future an artifact of the will stems from the anxiety of finite and mortal limits that is overcome through the technological mastery of nature and human nature, whereas the resignation or acceptance of fate is expressed through a consumerism that provides temporary comfort and security. In both cases, however, the prospect of new and renewing possibilities is rejected out of hand, resulting in a narrative predicated on mortality rather than natality.

We may further elaborate this contrast between the pilgrim's narrative of natality and the nomadic narrative of mortality by revisiting the imagery of the Christian moral life as being roughly analogous to the navigational technique of dead reckoning examined above. To review briefly, the Christian moral life is lived out between the Ascension and *parousia*. Navigating the moral terrain in this time between the times is an inexact and perilous enterprise, but not devoid of any guidance. There are reliable landmarks that can be used to plot a course and trajectory toward the proper human end or *telos* in Christ. The pilgrims of the heavenly city are simultaneously pushed by an anticipatory remembrance and pulled by an imaginative restlessness toward a promised destination beyond the horizon; hence the eschatological and proleptic orientation of the resulting narration of natality. The contrast with the late modern nomadic narration of mortality can be made more distinct by briefly examining four prominent strategies for navigating the moral life. The four options described below are admittedly imprecise and hyperbolic. They are not latent typologies in which the reader may conveniently place his or her friends and enemies, but unwieldy clusters of similar late modern approaches to navigating the moral life. Nor do these clusters represent an ideological spectrum; in each instance, examples on both the left and right sides of various political divides should come readily to mind.

First, there are those who believe they can discern, perhaps through superior intellect or private revelation, an infallible course for navigating the moral life. These Gnostics have, so to speak, an infallible GPS device at their disposal to which the unenlightened can never avail themselves. Since they know the course history is taking toward its fated destination, it is merely a matter of placing themselves on the "right" side of every issue. What is perilous about this attenuated dispensationalism, in both its religious and secular garb, is that it has exchanged eschatology for history, and the resulting "certainty" often breeds an intolerance, and even contempt, for those who are on the "wrong" side of the issues. To claim that one knows what only God can know is to create a class of lesser deities who wreak havoc in their lives with mere mortals. Or, in philosophical terms, it is an appeal to historical necessity to justify deadly indifference or unspeakable cruelty. For this indifferent Gnostic narration, the end of history justifies whatever means are required along the way. The necessity of history becomes synonymous with its good, and the good in turn is corrupted into simply being on the winning side so that morality is effectively reduced to power. In the provocative words of George Grant, "Does this not make us cavalier about evil? The screams of the tortured child can be justified by the achievements of history. How pleasant for the achievers, but how meaningless for the child."[24]

Second, there are those who believe that through reason alone they can discern a reliable pattern in the landmarks that will guide them in the right direction. Moral landmarks are examined in meticulous detail from which enduring and universal ethical principles are abstracted. The resulting maps and charts they devise are elegant, and the precision of the ensuing travel plans inspire confidence. But it is a misplaced assurance, for the problem is that they almost never look at the horizon to see if they are actually heading somewhere. So fixated have they become on the landmarks that they cannot tell if they are simply in an endlessly circular holding pattern. They have fallen into the trap of believing that their abstraction *is* the reality they are charting. The moral life is effectively reduced to inflexible and timeless procedural rules derived from these abstractions. They have no need for natality, for the reliability of such rules must preclude the prospect of new and unexpected possibilities. Consequently, the ensuing narration stems from an uncritical moral myopia, for, in preserving the priority of the abstract over the concrete, they prefer a practice that seeks to be right rather than good. It is, in short, a marvelous plan for traveling endlessly but never arriving anywhere.

Third, there are those who are most attentive to the horizon. They don't have much need for landmarks because the moral life consists of an endlessly progressive movement into unchartered territory. The problem, however, is that after a while they grow weary, perhaps even dismayed, by a horizon they never reach. So they land at the next safe haven they come upon, and declare it to be the destination to which they had been heading all along. Yet, for all the self-congratulatory bravado about going where no one has gone before, it is actually a strategy predicated on a fear of the future. Since the horizon can never be reached, the only reasonable solution is to find a relatively secure place, hunker down, and be content with the best possibility at hand. Consequently, the resulting story is fixated on security

---

[24] George Grant, *Lament for a Nation: The Defeat of Canadian Nationalism* (Montreal and Kingston: McGill-Queen's University Press, 2000), p. 100.

and comfort as the predominant values derived from expedient calculations and rationalizations in which any genuinely new possibility is rejected as a threat to be avoided. Ultimately, it is little more than a cowardly and halfhearted Pelagianism chasing after a highly debased notion of a pseudo-perfection that is not worth pursuing in the first place.

Finally, there are those who have no time or need for moral landmarks, for the horizon that looms ahead is not real but a mere projection of one's will. Where one aims upon that faux horizon is therefore irrelevant, for one spot is as good as another. There is, then, no need to navigate because there is no good destination to be had; every journey ends in a crash from which no pilot ever walks away. There are no good or bad, right or wrong choices in any normative sense to be made, merely preferences to which high or low valuations are assigned. Consequently, it does not matter whether the horizon is approached cautiously or carelessly, for there is no reason why prudence should be valued over recklessness in pursuing what is willed. Indeed, the moral life consists of asserting one's will over that of another, and ethics is little more than a rhetorical exercise for justifying the preferences of the strong over the weak—cumbersome attempts at placing ill-fitting loin cloths on the idol of naked power, a curious waste of time prompted by a residual modesty. This is, of course, the narration resulting from a nihilistic will to power or, perhaps more accurately, the despair and rage stemming from the belief that there is nothing ultimately good or noble to be willed.

In describing these four strategies in contrast to the dead reckoning approach I am proposing there are seemingly five options for navigating the moral life that need to be evaluated. Yet there are actually only two options in play: a choice of orientation between mortality and natality. The four approaches described above are varying strategies for overcoming the so-called problem of mortality. Their differences on navigating the moral life are one of degree rather than kind. All four strategies are purportedly future-oriented, and the past is thereby merely an account of terrain that has been traversed and of little immediate value. The targeted futures range from Gnostic certainty to nihilistic illusion, but the entire range of strategies is fixated on futile attempts at overcoming the fate of mortality. Despite the futuristic rhetoric, this fixation on overcoming mortality collapses attention almost exclusively upon a "now" cut off from past and future. The moral identity of late moderns is at best ambiguous, because they are ill-equipped to either imagining the past or remembering the future. Any resulting remembrance is therefore a source of anxiety rather than anticipation, and the ensuing restlessness is based on fear rather than imagination. Late moderns do not so much navigate the moral life but stumble through the terrain as best they can in varying directions. Consequently, the prospect of any genuinely new and renewing possibilities is either dismissed as delusions, or resisted as threats. In order to further explicate the principal difference between the orientations of mortality and natality, and to also contrast what difference they might make in navigating the moral life, I turn, fittingly, to two stories.

The first is the novel, *An Accidental Man*, by Iris Murdoch.[25] The story takes place in England in the late 1960s at the height of the Vietnam War. As is true with all of Murdoch's novels, an intricate storyline entangles a wide variety of intriguing characters, but we may profitably focus on two. Ludwig Leferrier is a promising American student finishing his studies in London. He has accepted a fellowship at Oxford that will begin in a few months and is engaged to a charming and rich young English woman. By all appearances he has a bright, even idyllic, future ahead of him. But the appearance is deceiving. Ludwig has been drafted and summoned to report for military service. He ignores the summons and destroys his draft card. He cannot apply for CO status because he is not a pacifist; he simply believes that this particular war is unjust. Due to a quirky set of circumstances he can avoid extradition as a draft-dodger. Ludwig is the only son of immigrant parents who fled Europe at the outbreak of the Second World War. They eventually became American citizens, but prior to that were refugees in England where Ludwig was born. He can therefore become a British subject and will thus no longer be eligible to be drafted. Ludwig can avoid the war, have his marriage and cherished academic career, but at the price of renouncing his American citizenship and facing a trial and jail term should he ever return. It is a price he is willing to pay. His parents are not happy with his decision, and they plead with him to come home. He can place his career on hold, marry later, and he has a duty to serve a country that has been good and generous to him and his family. Their pleas are to no avail; Ludwig is seemingly resolute in his choice to forsake his homeland and remain in England.

Austin Gibson Gray is a middle-aged man who drifts from one accident to another. He has always lived in the shadow of his highly successful older brother who he fears, resents, but on whom he remains emotionally and financially dependent. His first wife drowned under suspicious circumstances, he is separated from his second wife who also eventually dies as the result of a curious accident, and he is living with a woman who adores him but he does not love in return, and she unsuccessfully attempts suicide when he leaves her. He is barely on speaking terms with his son, and he is broke and unemployed. It gets worse, for Austin seems to go out of his way to create misfortune for himself and others. He destroys his brother's valuable china collection. While driving his brother's car he hits and kills a young girl who suddenly darts out into the street, and he later assaults and hospitalizes her stepfather who was trying to blackmail Austin because he did not tell the police that he had been a bit drunk while driving. Austin, of course, suffers the effects of his accidental life, but he also constantly wounds those around him. Yet he is never forced to take responsibility for the chaos he creates. Family and friends cover for him, lie for him, protect him, or conveniently overlook and explain away his faults; and he is lucky that when the man he assaulted recovers from his coma he has no memory of who attacked him or why he was attacked. Presumably, an accidental man cannot be held accountable for his deeds, for Austin believes that he is nothing more than a victim of unfortunate circumstances, and victims, he insists, can never be blamed.

---

[25] Iris Murdoch, *An Accidental Man* (London: Penguin, 1971).

There is seemingly a stark contrast between Ludwig and Austin—a clear distinction between one who is responsible and one who is irresponsible. But the story is not quite finished. Ludwig receives a letter from his parents indicating that they are now reconciled to his decision. They urge him to stay in England and pursue his academic career rather than return to the United States and face a trial and jail sentence. They are looking forward to attending the wedding and meeting their new daughter-in-law. Ludwig sends a telegram telling them not to make any travel plans. He has broken off the engagement, notified Oxford that he will not be accepting the fellowship after all, and has booked a passage on a boat to return to the United States where he plans on doing some time in jail.

It may be tempting to believe that, despite this 180-degree turn, there is still a big difference between these two characters, for Ludwig is at least on a course of taking responsibility for his actions. But is he? It is never quite clear why he broke the engagement, other than a hint that he wishes to flee from a woman that fails to live up to his ideal image. Although he grieves losing Oxford, he is young and assumes he can pursue it at a later date. Although he is not looking forward to the prospect of sitting in jail, opposing an unpopular war might professionally and personally prove beneficial in the future. What is entirely absent is any sense that he is returning because it is good to honor the wishes of his parents or fulfill his duties as a citizen. All Ludwig discloses is that he is returning because of who he will be in the future; he reveals nothing about what future is envisioned or what he is aspiring to become, perhaps because there is nothing there to reveal. He is also an accidental man, stumbling from one accident to another. The difference between Ludwig and Austin is not one of kind, but degree—a bit like comparing a Category 1 hurricane with a Category 5.

For Murdoch, it could not be otherwise. She reminds her readers again and again in her 26 novels that the difference between good and evil is never seen in the light of any vivid clarity, but always in a twilight blurring the distinctions. Consequently, the characters in her stories are rarely obviously virtuous or vicious. They are common and ordinary people, such as Ludwig and Austin, who for reasons such as inattention, ego, ignorance, stupidity, bad luck and the like are morally clumsy and thoughtless. They stumble about creating accidents for themselves and others, and, as a Platonist, Murdoch cannot describe the moral life any differently. There is a real horizon of the Good, but very few people ever see it with any degree of clarity, and the so-called landmarks for navigating the moral terrain are not real but shadows on the wall of the cave in which they are encased. In a shadow-land of unremitting twilight, the best one can do is to try to stumble a little less often. The difference between the four options described earlier is also one of degree and not kind; varying strategies for coping with moral clumsiness. Consequently, confession and forgiveness are virtually devoid of any real meaning, for how can accidents be either confessed or forgiven? Any promise of amending one's life is an empty gesture, because accidents, and accidental people, are by definition unpredictable and unreliable. How can one promise that no more accidents will occur? It should also be noted that Murdoch's stories are largely fixated on the now. The past is mere backdrop, memories are ghosts of past failures and regrets that haunt the characters, and the future looms as a cruel fate which cannot be evaded. For accidental people there is little remembrance or anticipation, because both are pointless activities.

The emerging technoculture mitigates the ill-effects of this moral clumsiness and thoughtlessness by reinforcing the notion that the moral life is ultimately an accidental life, thereby broadening the scope of victimization. The undesirable consequences of moral action stem largely from errors of judgment, the capricious limitations of nature and human nature, or the vagaries of complex social and political systems. For late moderns, there is the growing perception that so-called immoral acts are not the result of fault or failure, but accidents that can be prevented or rectified; hence the recourse to asserting mastery over nature and human nature. Yet this growing perception of moral accident is accompanied by a shrinking notion of culpability and responsibility, in turn lessening the need for judgment and punishment, and thereby diminishing the need for forgiving and promising as well. The emerging technoculture creates the illusion of navigating a moral terrain in which no landmarks are presumed to be fixed or given, so that compensation instead of reconciliation becomes the preferred response to moral accidents; exchange effectively displaces communication. It is a strategy particularly well suited to the nomadic inhabitants of the emerging technoculture, for it offers temporary and shifting spaces of freedom demarcated and controlled by appropriate threats of coercion. Gnostics are free to await their end of history so long as they do not forcibly include unwilling others in apocalyptic conflagrations. So-called permanent landmarks may be examined and charted so long as they are not imposed on other unwilling nomadic journeyers. Progressives are permitted, indeed encouraged, to pursue their respective utopias so long as they are proffered as embodying value preferences and not the good. Nihilists are provided safe, often virtual or media–manipulative, venues to vent their rage. The emerging technoculture, in short, strives to create relatively safe spaces in which moral accidents may occur with minimal damage, and largely devoid of any necessity to judge or punish, to forgive or promise.

Although Murdoch's depiction of late modern moral life is largely accurate, it is inadequate because Christians believe the moral life can be navigated despite their clumsy stumbling. Yet to argue why this is the case requires an alternative narration, one that illumines the twilight and shortens the shadows. Such an alternative is provided by Marilynne Robinson's *Gilead*.[26] Gilead is a small town in Iowa. There we find John Ames and his friend Boughton, sometime in the early 1950s. They grew up together in Gilead, were classmates at the same seminary, and returned to serve their respective congregations for over 40 years. *Gilead* is an account of this relationship and community told from John's viewpoint, and a subsequent novel, *Home*,[27] relates Boughton's perspective as told primarily by his daughter.

---

[26] Marilynne Robinson, *Gilead* (New York: Picador, 2004).
[27] Marilynne Robinson, *Home* (New York Picador, 2008).

The relationship between these two men has been long, close, and tightly interwoven. Boughton was John's best man at his first wedding. A few years later his wife died in childbirth, and a few days later his newborn daughter died as well. Boughton baptized her shortly before her death. A little later John baptized Boughton's new son who he named after his best friend to compensate for the loss of his wife and daughter. He comes to be known as Jack to differentiate him from his namesake. John has recently married a much younger woman, and they have a son who John, given his age and failing health, will never see grow into a man. Much of the story is taken from the journal that John is writing for his son—a voice from the past that will hopefully help his son in a future they cannot share. Since this is a story told by a minister, it is fitting to pause for a moment and glean some of the theological insights that are offered. People can and do change. Grace can bridge the gap between estranged people, and it reduces life to its essentials. And, in John's words, "[i]f the Lord chooses to make nothing of our transgressions, then they *are* nothing."[28] These aphorisms, however, are sorely tested in John's and Jack's relationship.

John has never felt very close to his namesake, and he takes most of the blame for their strained relationship. John knows he must be gracious to Jack, and he often prays for him. But in his journal he warns his son to stay away from Jack; he is bad news and hurts those around him. Many years ago Jack got a local girl pregnant, and then ignored and neglected her and his daughter. John cannot forgive him for squandering his fatherhood. Jack wants to live a better life, to be more like his father, but he has no faith. He is a liar, a cheat, a thief, a drunk, and a coward. Jack now has a wife and daughter who he has left for a while. He has never told his own family for they are not legally married because they live in a state that prohibits mixed-race marriage. They could move to Iowa where they could legally wed, but her parents oppose the idea, and John doubts that they would be welcomed in Gilead. The town has a bad history in terms of race relations; there are, apparently, limits to what a community can accept and embrace. There is much more that could be told, but it suffices to say that this is a story about moral failings and deeply strained relationships stretching over decades.

The apex of the story occurs at a bus stop. John and Jack are sitting on a bench waiting for the bus to arrive. Jack is leaving and will never return to Gilead. John will tell Jack's sister not to judge her brother for running away again, and he will say goodbye to his father for him. As they sit on the bench, John is reminded that the Greek word for "saved" can also mean healing. Grace manifests itself in many ways, and no one should be as lonely as Jack. In Robinson's words:

> John said, "If you would accept a few dollars of that money of mine, you'd be doing me a kindness."
>
> He laughed and said, "I suppose I could see my way clear."

---

[28] Robinson, *Gilead*, p. 189 (emphasis in original).

So I gave him forty dollars and he kept twenty and gave twenty back. We sat there for a while.

Then I said, "The thing I would like, actually, is to bless you."

He shrugged. "What would that involve?"

"Well, as I envisage it, it would involve placing my hand on your brow and asking the protection of God for you. But it would be embarrassing—" There were a few people on the street.

"No, no," he said. "That doesn't matter." And he took his hat off and set it on his knee and closed his eyes and lowered his head, almost rested it against my hand, and I did bless him to the limit of my powers, whatever they are, repeating the benediction from Numbers, of course—"The Lord make His face to shine upon thee and be gracious unto thee. The Lord lift up His countenance upon thee, and give thee peace." Nothing could be more beautiful than that, or more expressive of my feelings, certainly, or more sufficient, for that matter. Then, when he didn't open his eyes or lift up his head, I said, "Lord, bless John Ames Boughton, this beloved son and brother and husband and father." Then he sat back and looked at me as if he were waking out of a dream.

"Thank you, Reverend," he said, and his tone made me think that it might have seemed I had named everything I thought he no longer was, when that was absolutely the furthest thing from my meaning, the exact opposite of my meaning. Well, anyway, I told him it was an honor to bless him. And that was absolutely true. In fact I'd have gone through seminary and ordination and all the years intervening for that one moment. He just studied me, in that way he has. Then the bus came. I said, "We all love you, you know," and he laughed and said, "You're all saints." He stopped in the door and lifted his hat, and then he was gone, God bless him.[29]

Robinson's account of the moral life is no less untidy than that of Murdoch's. *Gilead* is full of morally clumsy people, stumbling from one mess to the next, adversely affecting everyone around them; even the concluding blessing is awkward. But there is a difference: the characters in *Gilead* are not accidental people. They may better be described as people who are attempting to navigate the moral life, but often do so badly. They make as many bad choices as good, and their subsequent course corrections are sometimes right but also often wrong. One principal reason is that *Gilead*, unlike *An Accidental Man*, is not focused on the "now," but is largely a story of remembrance and anticipation—of imagining the past and remembering the future. It is in the many regrets and failed aspirations, and in the moments

---

[29] Ibid., pp. 241–242.

of unexpected mercy and grace that these characters do not stumble alone but together. They do not claim to be blameless victims assigning fault to others or fate nor do they flee from one set of unwanted circumstances to another, in both instances consigning the past to a dustbin best forgotten. Even when Jack leaves on the bus, he is still embraced by a love that will not let him go. Unlike accidental people who easily drift apart, the characters of *Gilead* remain tied together through unbroken bonds of imperfection. They remember and they anticipate; they forgive and they promise. They live in a "now" demarcated by the poles of these tensions. Why? Because Robinson laces her story with the landmarks of faith, hope, and love for navigating the moral life. These landmarks are often missed, ignored, or misread, but they are nonetheless there. Consequently, for Robinson, the repetitive storyline of the moral life is one of judgment, confession, repentance, contrition, forgiveness, and amendment of life, albeit imperfectly and clumsily performed. The difference between Murdoch and Robinson is that for the latter there are the landmarks of an abiding faith, hope, and love that can direct people toward a horizon beyond which lies blessing. And it is in the tension between anticipatory remembrance and imaginative restlessness that the Holy Spirit does its work of helping us read those landmarks that direct us toward that benediction beckoning beyond the horizon.

To adopt a strategy of dead reckoning is to espouse a counter-narrative to that offered by late modernity, for it requires being formed and guided by the hope of natality instead of the fear of mortality. It entails rejecting an accidental victimization in favor of judgment, forgiving, and promising. Consequently, it encompasses a navigation of the moral terrain that emphasizes course corrections, amendment of life, and *metanoia*. The moral life is not a narration of avoiding, preventing, and repairing accidents, but accepting responsibility, repentance, contrition, and the acceptance of grace. To espouse and be formed by this narrative is to be genuinely countercultural to the dominant technoculture, for the moral life is not one of either precise or reckless technique, but one more akin to art and disciplined improvisation. To be countercultural, however, does not require either total rejection or perpetual resistance, but, rather, engagement, reformation, and, perhaps, even conversion. To pursue such engagement requires that we shift the focus of this inquiry, necessitating greater elaboration of the content of this counter-narrative and its ensuing formative practices. Such a shift is undertaken in the following chapter by further investigating Borgmann's account of focal things and practices, particularly in respect to ecclesial space and place within the emerging technoculture.

Chapter 7
Amendment of Life: Desiring the Good

In the celebration of the Eucharist, the promise of amendment of life is the final prerequisite before absolution is pronounced. In such promising, Christians reorient themselves to the gift of God's grace and Christ's *parousia* which are enacted and anticipated in the sacrament. Such promising may be said to culminate in a repetitive and reorienting series of acts entailing both remembrance and anticipation; judgment leads to forgiveness. As I have argued in the preceding chapters, a similar pattern in repeated in the Christian moral life. We do not need to revisit that pattern, except to emphasize the penultimate step of amendment of life. The amending of life is needed to reorient the trajectory of moral deliberation, discernment, and action in accord with its proper end or destination in Christ, thereby promoting an ongoing *metanoia*. The exact location of this destination is imprecise. Subsequently, navigating the moral terrain is often misdirected, thereby necessitating course corrections that are akin to a kind of dead reckoning. It is these course corrections that are embodied in the promise to amend one's life.

This promise, however, begs an important question: what is the good life that these amendments are attempting to achieve? To answer this question, Christians must offer an account of this good life and therefore must be taught how to desire the Good or, better, God in fitting ways. Yet these desires cannot be satisfied immediately, for their complete satisfaction is depends on the *parousia*. The Incarnation *is* the desire of the nations that God has satisfied, but subsequent understanding and acknowledgment remains unfulfilled in this time between the times. Consequently, the Christian moral life is one of both remembrance and anticipation—simultaneously retrospective and proleptic, eschatological and teleological. The ensuing moral life, however, is not one of indefinite suspension. The imagery of dead reckoning is predicated on movement over and through time—a journey headed in a particular direction. Christians do not so much await the *parousia* as they are beckoned by and drawn toward it. Consequently, Christians are called to participate in ordering the communication of the goods of creation along their journey, albeit as pilgrims who know that their sojourn is not the satisfaction of their desires.

In the remainder of this chapter I further develop the concept of communication that was initiated in the previous chapter. I argue that communication, or communicative association, offers a promising venue for initiating a shift in emphasis in this inquiry from criticism to engagement. It is an engagement, however, that remains critical, even resistant, for it is an account of communication embedded in a narration of pilgrimage and is therefore never fully at ease with the nomadic life of the emerging technoculture. There is inevitably a tension between communication and late modernity's fixation on exchange. The goal of this engagement is not necessarily to ease this tension, but to orient it in a more constructive direction. In undertaking this engagement I first examine the problematic relationship between place and space in the emerging technoculture and the attendant troubled relationship between narration and information. In particular, the questions I am posing and pondering are: can space supplant place as the principal mode of being, and, if so, what are some of the moral, social, and political consequences of this displacement? Can information supplant narration as the principal expression of identity, and, if so, what are some of the moral, social, and political consequences of this displacement? In addressing these questions I pose and ponder the counter-categories of remembrance and anticipation. I argue that both being in the world and expressing the identity of that being require particular places and narratives. Although, admittedly, space and information need to be created to express this identity, place must embed space and information must be embedded in narration if there is to be any coherency of expression over time. Consequently, there is an inherent need for remembrance and anticipation to prevent the moral life from collapsing into a series of momentary "nows," effectively cut off from any past direction or future orientation—a scheme well suited to the nomadic life of the emerging technoculture predicated on exchange rather than communication. In theological terms, place and narration derived from remembrance and anticipation are needed to preserve the proleptic, eschatological, and teleological orientation of the moral life; or, to change the imagery, in the absence of anticipatory remembrance and imaginative restlessness, no reliable landmarks can be identified for navigating the moral terrain. In short, without remembrance and anticipation that are narrated in particular places there can be no amendment of life.

In addressing these questions, I draw, more often than not implicitly rather than explicitly, on conceptual themes developed by Albert Borgmann. There is, again, no need to extensively revisit these themes, which were developed in Chapter 4, other than to note the chief conceptual imagery that is employed. First and foremost is the conception of focal things and practices. A focal thing is a commanding presence that captures the attention of various individuals, in turn ordering their subsequent action in appropriate ways. This ordering results from the necessity of focal practices that are required to sustain a focal thing. For example, fine dining requires that hosts and guests must arrange their schedules to be present at a specified time and place. The food is thoughtfully selected and prepared, and the table carefully set. Good hosts are hospitable to their guests, ensuring they are put at ease, given opportunities to enter into conversation, and are not ignored, and good guests in turn follow customary etiquette and express gratitude to their hosts. Moreover, focal things and practices are not ends in themselves or self-referential, but promote a greater good. The consumption of food is not the overriding purpose of a meal; fine dining promotes the good of fellowship. Borgmann further contends that larger associations can be dedicated, for either relatively short or long periods of time, to focal things and practices, in turn creating focal communities. A small town organizing an annual celebratory event or a monastery would be examples of such communities.

I argue that the church is (or should be) a focal community with attendant focal practices. These practices do not draw attention to themselves or to the practitioners, but bear witness to Christ as Lord of the church and creation. Such practices also form the desires and lives of followers of Jesus Christ. It is, for example, in practicing charity that people become charitable. These practices necessarily embody remembrance and anticipation, for, in remembering Jesus, Christians not only order their desires with what he desired, but also desire and anticipate his *parousia*. Consequently, the church is not only a focal community, but also an eschatologically-oriented community—in short, a pilgrim community. I examine, in particular, baptism, Eucharist, and Sabbath as practices that capture the focal and eschatological qualities of Christian fellowship and witness.[1] In sum, the life of the church is (or should be) one of communication rather than exchange, and in and through its communion, its *koinonia*, it is driven by an unending amendment of life until life's end. It is as a focal and eschatologically-oriented community that the church engages the emerging technoculture, and in doing so reorients (or should reorient) the trajectories of its own moral life and that of the culture it engages toward their common end in Christ. My inquiry into what this engagement might entail is initiated in the remainder of this chapter and continued in greater detail in Part III.

Place and space; narration and information

Place is always a physical and particular locale. An object or a person is always somewhere, someplace. The duration of these locales may be brief, such as standing in a queue at the supermarket, or lengthy, such as Mount Everest. Place is also always singular and exclusive. If I am here, I cannot be there. Although I may move from here to there, I cannot be in both places at the same time. Moreover, place demarcates human life. A person is born and dies in particular places, and in between there are places where one resides, works, and visits. Traditionally, place has often been most closely associated with land, and such territory has boundaries. These borders may be rigid, such as a wall, or porous, such as a meandering trail where hikers come and go. Property in turn may be regarded as a private place that is entered only by right or invitation, such as a house, or a public place where entrance is permitted to everyone, such as a park. Consequently, the boundaries of place are set by both inclusion and exclusion. The sizes of territorial places vary, ranging, for instance, from an isolated mountain cabin to an expansive nation-state. Varying significance is also assigned to these places: the patriot, for

---

[1] Throughout this book, I frequently use the term "Eucharist" without the definite article as a paradigmatic device for summarizing the repetitive pattern of the Christian moral life rather than referring to a particular act of worship. Likewise, "Sabbath" connotes leisurely reception as opposed to willful mastery, connoting a mode of being rather than a particular day of the week.

example, may love her country but despise the city in which she resides, whereas the recluse may love his mountain cabin, while hating the country in which it is located. Every person and association of people must be in some place at any given time and cannot be in no place at all. Although some individuals may be on the run, wandering about, exiles, or refugees displaced from locales where they claim they belong, their temporary locales nonetheless exist in particular places. So long as humans are physical creatures, they can only exist in place.

To a great extent, accommodating the necessity of place has been a dominant factor in ordering the patterns of human life, often in beneficial ways. Since humans are social creatures, place provides bordered locales in which associations are created and sustained. These places are concentric, of varying expanses in accordance with the nature and purposes of differing associations, and ranging from the intimate to the political. Yet what is common is the recognition that humans cannot live as unassociated beings, for even the hermit requires a society to withdraw from, or as an undifferentiated mass, for there is no such thing as a global humanity. Human association simultaneously requires an appropriate inclusivity and exclusivity, and it is often, if not largely, place in which this requisite need is met. A family, for instance, requires a sequestered locale, free from public gaze or interference to attend to its affiliative and affective needs. Not just anyone can choose to join a particular family. A university needs a place to teach its students, and it selects which applicants to include and exclude. A nation-state is in part defined by the territory it governs, and it determines who is allowed and not allowed to cross its borders and reside within its jurisdiction. Moreover, it is in and through particular places that a civil community is sustained and enriched. Goods are produced, bought, and sold in particular places; theaters, museums, and sporting facilities are located on particular parcels of land; cities and countries are situated in particular locales. In short, it is in and through place that people communicate.

Despite the many benefits derived from sustaining and ordering particular places, the accompanying disadvantages and limitations must not be denied. These ills may stem from wrongful inclusion or exclusion. A conquered people, for example, may be unwillingly included in an empire, or a nation-state may exclude individuals or groups from exercising their political rights. Or maintaining place may be used to justify injustices. The privacy of the household hides the abuse being committed within its walls, aliens may be treated inhumanely, or some groups may be given unwarranted advantages over others. Place, particularly territory, can be the source of frequent conflict: much blood has been spilt in seizing and defending land or property. Moreover, place imposes severe constraints on the will. Being confined to a particular place restricts the number of individuals I may interact with, the associations I may participate in, commerce, the arts, and many other worthwhile activities and pursuits. To be fixed or grounded in place is to settle for a greatly diminished quality of life. Mitigating the limits of time and distance, the constraints of place, would greatly enlarge the range of opportunities that humans could pursue.

As argued in Chapter 1, easing or overcoming these constraints against the will prompted, in part, the development of modern technology, particularly in terms of transportation and transmission of information. Rapid transport has made travel and trade among remote locations accessible, and telecommunication enables a global and instantaneous exchange of information among multiple locales in either real or virtual time. Although such technological development does not eliminate the constraints of place, it has mitigated them to a substantial extent. This mitigation has in turn prompted a concomitant preference of *space* over place. A space entails the creation or identification of a point in time where an action or transaction is pursued. Two business colleagues, for example, specify a time, thereby creating a space in which to converse. The particular location of these spaces is often irrelevant. The two colleagues may talk in an office, airport, or café. Designated space may be physical, distant, or virtual. Our colleagues may be conversing face-to-face, over their telephones, or in a chatroom. The duration of a space may be relatively brief or lengthy—a few minutes exchanging emails or a day-long webinar. The time a space needs to exist may be singular or repetitive—an interview or a weekly conference call. A space may incorporate the features of proximity, virtuality, and distance over time. Our colleagues are members of a working group comprising individuals located around the world. Following their initial face-to-face meeting, they view and comment on documents posted on a secure website, exchange emails, and participate in a concluding live videoconference. Such created space, be it physical, distant, virtual or some combination, can range in "size" from small and intimate to large and public. A few old college friends stay in touch through a virtual social network and a get-together at homecoming; a learned society convenes its annual meeting each year in a different city, and its members stay informed in the interval through the society's website and other media.

Space is preferable to place in the emerging technoculture, for conceptually it purportedly mitigates the constraints of place, in turn simultaneously enabling and reinforcing a nomadic mobility that is both physical and imaginative. For late modern nomads—those individuals having access to the requisite transportation and information technologies—the particularity of place becomes increasingly supplanted by malleable space. The creation of temporary space, both physical and virtual, gives individuals greater control over how they conduct their business, spend their leisure time, and construct and express their identities. Locale, distance, and time are no longer defining features of the human condition, but inconveniences to be surmounted in differing and idiosyncratic ways. In a matter of hours an individual may arrive at almost any airport in the world, and in a matter of seconds inform friends and family that she has arrived. Following her business meeting, she shares with them virtually her well-deserved holiday at an exotic resort through posting her daily blog and photos. Alternatively, another individual never leaves his flat, conducting his business through a variety of information technologies. He spends his well-deserved holiday on a lonely island in an online simulated world, sharing a rendezvous with another avatar. In both instances, individuals have seemingly overcome the constraints of place by creating spaces that fulfill their respective preferences.

The creation of space, however, does not really lessen the necessity of place, but makes it more opaque and hidden. The perception of enjoying a liberating displacement is largely illusory. Although particular places may seem less relevant to the way in which daily living is conducted, they nonetheless remain, and remain necessary. It may not matter where I am when I phone my wife, but both of us must be located someplace. It may not matter where or when I post a blog,[2] but I have to be somewhere to post, and the various computers, servers, routers, and readers (if any) are located in particular places. I may travel here, there, and everywhere, but I nonetheless require places for the airplane to land, and to sleep and eat. The creation of space, however transient and temporary, cannot escape its dependence on place. But late modern nomads are coming to perceive place not as a formative reality they must accommodate, but as a nuisance to be managed and ignored as much as possible through the employment of various technologies. This perception marks a significant shift in emphasis in the ordering of human desires and subsequent action. If it is determined that human flourishing is best enabled through the creation of willed spaces, then physical, virtual, and imaginative mobility are absolute prerequisites, and hence the preference for a nomadic life. To return to Arendt's imagery, anyone with sufficient access and capabilities can fashion oases virtually anytime, anywhere, and no place in particular. Place becomes increasingly a means to be mastered and used in accomplishing the end of creating space. In this nomadic preference of space over place, the latter is no longer a dominant foreground in which restricted spaces are carved out, but has faded into the background of a supportive infrastructure enabling a frenetic opening and closing of spaces. Although this privileging of space does not represent a total mastery of place, it nevertheless indicates a partial triumph of the will over necessity. The spaces created by late modern nomads indicate habitats of their design and desire, and the resulting technoculture is thereby an artifact of their will to satisfy this desire.

Concurrently, late modern nomads favor *information* over *narration*. To narrate is to give a congruent account of identity over time; it is to situate oneself in a description of what has transpired and what is aspired. Such a narrative may be simple and relatively brief. A couple, for instance, come home after work, tell each other how their day went, and plan what they will do in the approaching weekend. Yet these seemingly insignificant episodes contribute to the more expansive narration of their relationship over a more extended period of time. A narrative may also be complex and of long duration. A school or nation has existed for generations and continues to do so in the future, and in both instances various interactions, events, acts, and deeds express what these associations have been and what they are aspiring to become. Although narrations are accomplished within

---

[2] In the spirit of transparent disclosure, I do not blog, tweet, maintain a Facebook page, or otherwise participate in social media.

created spaces—such as relationships, classrooms, and high streets—they are also tied to particular places. A particular home (or homes), campus, and location are needed to narrate a marriage, school, or nation. Expansive political narratives are often tied to land. One cannot narrate being an Athenian or an American without referring to a particular locale. Moreover, these narrations overlap and are interdependent. I am simultaneously a husband, a teacher, and a citizen. My personal narrative depends on these associations: I cannot be a husband without a wife, a teacher without students, or a citizen without a country, and conversely these associations cannot be narrated without the contributions of countless individuals. Narration, then, may be said to be story-like. An ideative narrative, like a story, is simultaneously retrospective and prospective, unfolding in the nexus of past and future. Consequently, both interpretation and imagination are required to make a narration coherent and formative over time. In being attentive to an imaginative interpretation of past and future, narration, like a story, locates the present between remembrance and anticipation, and is therefore not fixated on the immediate or the "now."

Narration, like place, necessarily includes and excludes. If everyone is either included or excluded, a narrative cannot unfold. Like place, narration defines by delimiting and confining. To narrate, for example, a particular family, school, or nation requires varying degrees of inclusion and exclusion. A family includes *these* children, but not every child; a school includes *these* students, but not every applicant; a nation includes *these* citizens, but not everyone crossing its borders. Inclusive and exclusive parameters are not necessarily fixed, however, and the resulting narration may be reinterpreted over time. A familial narrative may come to include individuals not related by blood or marriage; a school may include a more expansive range of ethnicities among its students; a nation may change its laws determining who is excluded from voting or immigrating. Editing such narratives also changes the identities of those who are formed by them. The death of parents creates an orphan; becoming coeducational changes the identity of a student body; an individual ceases to be a Soviet citizen and becomes Ukrainian. The issue at stake is not whether the inclusive and exclusive parameters of formative narrations should be narrow or broad, relatively stable or in flux, but to highlight that they are necessarily subject to "editing" over time, and to warn that extreme inflexibility or plasticity in this editing process can result in either truncated or insipid narrations. On the one hand, for example, when conservative Christians defend the "traditional family," they usually do not have in mind the polygamous households of the Old Testament patriarchs. An appeal for closed borders to preserve a traditional way of life may fail to recognize that the nationalism being invoked is a modern invention. The so-called traditional familial and national identities being evoked may, then, actually prove malformative since the truncated traditions in question may not adequately narrate what "family" and "nation" mean in any normative or formative sense. This does not mean that the proposed ordering of families and borders is necessarily wrong, but only that it fails to recognize that what is being proposed is an editing, not preservation, of the narratives in question. On the other hand, when a "family" simply designates two or more individuals living together under the same roof, or a nation cannot control its borders, the resulting identities cannot be regarded as familial or national to any significant extent. Again, this does not mean that the living arrangements and porous borders in question are wrong, but that what is being pursued is not editing, but the creation of new narratives that in turn will be formative in ways that are not familial or national in any normative or traditional sense.

Narration presupposes and reinforces the notion of place, both conceptually and concretely. A narrative requires points of reference in order to unfold, for it records, interprets, and anticipates movement, so to speak, from here to there. Although impermanent, a narrative is enduring and transitional. A narration cannot exist in the absence of sequential points of departure and arrival, which in turn grants it both a determinative and formative power. Those narrating both form and are formed by what is narrated. In this respect, narration is grounded in place, because what is narrated occurs in particular locales. Dislocation can be narrated, but there cannot be dislocated narration.

Unlike narration, information can be displaced. Although information may refer or contribute to narration, it is not necessarily dependent on any enduring narrative structure to convey its meaning or utility. In this respect, information has an instrumental value, but no determinative or formative power of its own. An investor, for instance, requires information about potential investments, but it is the narrative about financial goals and objectives that determines and forms the eventual decision and not the information *per se*. Information, then, does not presuppose any enduring quality; it is created, exchanged, consumed, and disposed of. Moreover, information is not grounded in place, but is free-floating. Again, information may be gleaned from, or describe, a particular locale, but its utility is operable virtually anywhere. It does not matter to the investor where data is created, exchanged, and consumed. Information, unlike narration, is thereby highly malleable and transient. It need not be sequential or transitional, for information does not itself reveal any purposeful unfolding of events that constitutes a narrative. Merely recording financial transactions does not tell the investor's story.

Late modern nomads prefer information over narration. This preference is related directly to the privileging of space over place. As the finite limits of embodiment are regarded as unwanted restraints against the will, so too are the constraints of narration seen as unfortunate encumbrances. Narrative is limited by what is being narrated, and subsequent editing and aspiration, however extensive and novel, must nonetheless cohere if the storyline is to endure over time. In contrast, information is under no such constraint. It is produced, exchanged, and consumed in fragments that presuppose no coherence other than that which is assigned to it by its users. The endlessly crawling stock-ticker does not disclose a story. As late moderns turn to technology to overcome the finite limits of place, so too is technology employed to overcome the conceptual constraints of narration. Late modern nomads treasure information because it is a useful instrument in creating the various, often virtual, spaces where they congregate to exchange whatever they crave for relatively brief or lengthy periods of time. In short, information is the superstructure that enables and supports the late modern nomadic life, and the principal mode of that life is one of exchanging ideas, goods, and services. There is nothing new about such exchange, except that in the emerging technoculture it occurs anonymously in spaces rather than places. If, for example, I want to read a book on investing, I need not bother haggling with the owner of a local bookstore; instead, I can find the information that enables me to purchase it, using my computer, and download it instantly to my e-reader. I need not share any common narrative with a merchant in a community; I have no desire to communicate since all I want is a space to exchange. In the emerging technoculture the market*place* is being displaced by market *spaces* that its nomadic inhabitants quickly create and discard. It is no coincidence that late modernity can be characterized simultaneously and aptly as an age of information and global markets.

Like the presumption that place has been supplanted by space, the notion that information is displacing narration is also largely illusory. Although various technologies enable the creation and rapid dissemination of voluminous information, a requisite narrative framework for its selection and interpretation is inescapable. Disorganized and uninterrupted data is useless. Information is not simply raw conceptual material that can be used in infinite ways. Its production, exchange, and consumption presuppose particular narrated contexts. The information provided to investors assumes certain narrations about how wealth should be created and for what purposes it should be employed. The providers and participants in spaces created for anonymous exchange remain beings that narrate and are narrated. Indeed, exchange is impossible if one cannot narrate what is wanted or needed, and these wants and needs are shaped by preceding narratives which shape the desires and aspirations that such exchange presumably facilitates. To even designate late modernity's emerging technoculture as an age of information and global markets is to narrate, albeit in an attempted, dislocated dialect. Late modern nomads may cherish their unprecedented physical and imaginative mobility, but they cannot escape the necessity of narrating their wandering.

Although information cannot evade narrated contexts, its preferred status in the emerging technoculture has redirected the purpose and diminished the quality of narration. The late modern nomad does not try to lodge her particular identity within a series of expanding social and political narratives. Rather, personal identity is narrated in ways that attempt to selectively allow and prevent these larger narratives from intruding. This partly explains the preference for information that helps individuals to rapidly construct and deconstruct spaces that enable and protect mobility and easy exchange as key elements of a dislocated nomadic identity. One resulting consequence is a narration emphasizing the identity of consumer over citizen, and autonomous individual over broader associations. The quality of this ensuing narrative is diminished because of its narrowing fixation on the individual as both the author and principal object of the narration. As a consequence, space is used to exclude the many and include the few who are of immediate interest or utility, which in turn requires a narration of limited scope and duration. Ironically, the ready availability of more information and greater mobility may actually serve to diminish an appreciation of difference, resulting not so much from fear or hostility but indifference, for the spaces constructed within the emerging technoculture largely comprise individuals sharing a narrow and immediate range of common interests or mutually beneficial exchange. In short, the narrations of late modern nomads are more analogous to highly personal diaries (or blogs to update the imagery) than well-crafted novels or philosophical tomes that attempt to address the human condition within social and political associations enduring over time.

The late modern privileging of space over place, and information over narration, in order to support the nomadic life of the emerging technoculture, prompts three crucial questions in respect to Christian moral theology. If humans are to flourish as creatures created by God, can space be an adequate substitute for place? Can information be an adequate substitute for narration? Can exchange be an adequate substitute for communication? These questions set the agenda for the remainder of this book. My answer in each instance is "no," but it is not an unqualified reply. To merely offer a blanket condemnation of the emerging technoculture is to condemn a world created by God. Rather, to engage in the world is to pursue a relationship that is simultaneously critical *and* constructive. It should be critical in that there are certain aspects of the emerging technoculture that Christian moral theology should reprove, or at least call into question, because they distract attention away from pursuing the good, thereby impeding human flourishing. It should be constructive in that there are certain characteristics of the emerging technoculture that Christians can affirm and embrace as being in line with creation's providential unfolding and teleological trajectory toward its eschatological end in Christ. Or, in theological terms, engagement entails judgment oriented toward the amendment of life. In the absence of engagement that is both critical and constructive, Christian moral theology can neither effectively demonstrate the inadequacy of the various moral schemes outlined in the previous chapter nor argue on behalf of its own moral vision and assessments. To return to the imagery of dead reckoning, without such engagement the church can neither contend that the late modern options of smug Gnosticism, unwarranted certainty, cowardly progressivism, or nihilism are perilous and best avoided, nor offer, with any credibility, reliable moral landmarks and corresponding course corrections.

It is for the sake of such critical and constructive engagement why the principal interlocutors of this inquiry are, individually, inadequate. Although Grant provides an invaluable service in illuminating the darkness *as* darkness, his refusal of late modernity prevents any substantive amendment or reform of, and hence engagement with, the emerging technoculture. Arendt's account of forgiving and promising is potentially fruitful for breaking the cycle of vengeance that plagues late modernity, but her unfounded reliance on reason divorced from religion results in a stillborn hope. Borgmann is correct in insisting that the emerging technoculture can be reformed through the adoption of key focal things and practices, but he offers little guidance about what their moral content might and should entail. Consequently, each of these contributions must be revised and incorporated into a more expansive moral and theological framework in order for the church to critically and constructively engage with late modernity and its emerging technoculture. For the purpose of this inquiry, this framework is encapsulated in the narration of *pilgrimage*. This Augustinian imagery has been introduced previously,[3] and the following elaboration expands some of its chief concepts in order to engage with the emerging technoculture in a directly critical and constructive manner. In many respects, pilgrims and nomads share much in common. Neither, for instance, is tied to particular physical or imaginative locales, and such a restriction is regarded by both as inimical to pursuing a good life. Consequently, mobility *per se* is not the issue at stake. Rather, what are disputed are the purposes for which mobility should be employed. Should such mobility be used to construct and narrate rapidly changing and fluid identities? Or, to the contrary, should mobility help align one's actions and subsequent identity with a formative narrative? Or, stated more prosaically, despite their similarities, there is a sharp difference between late modern nomads, who wander where they will, and Christian pilgrims attempting to align their journeys along a teleological and eschatological trajectory. This similarity and difference, as well as their differing moral, social, and political implications, may be seen with greater clarity by revisiting, briefly, the themes of place and space, narration and information, and exchange and communication.

To a large extent, pilgrims share with nomads a preference for space over place. Both tacitly acknowledge that the temporal life of mortal creatures is necessarily impermanent and transient. To prefer place over space exclusively is to grant the former an unwarranted formative power that could prove perilous, even idolatrous. Both pilgrims and nomads, then, are never entirely at home when in place, resulting in an urgency to be on the move, both physically and imaginatively. It is the creation of space, as opposed to the maintenance of place, which enables this movement. The difference between nomads and pilgrims is one of how and why space is privileged over place. Christianity is not a territorial religion, for Christ is present wherever two or three are gathered in his name; it is ultimately space, and not place, that is sanctified by the Holy Spirit. Yet the place where such space is created is neither an irrelevant consideration nor an encumbrance. When Christians gather in Christ's name they do so as embodied creatures, and as such they cannot escape being in a particular and shared place. Such gathering not only acknowledges the impermanent and transient character of temporal creatures, but also affirms the finitude of creaturely life as a good gift of the creator. Consequently, although place does not determine Christian identity, it is not necessarily regarded as a limitation but as a requisite context for ordering the Christian life. It is a particular place that enables the creation of a holy space and, more importantly, gives it a commanding and formative presence. This is why a

---

[3] See Chapter 6.

space to worship is often associated with a particular place that endures for years, decades, or centuries, and why, as pilgrims, Christians are commanded to pray for the peace of whatever place they may be in, be it Babylon or some more congenial locale. In this respect, Christians do not attempt to supplant place with space, but embed the latter in the former.

Pilgrims do not dispute the need for information to create the space in which they worship and have fellowship. They must be informed about when and where to gather, and how their life together is formed and sustained. They also must be informed about the world they are called to engage in, serve, and evangelize. In short, they require information in order to form and narrate their identities as followers of Jesus Christ. Where Christian pilgrims differ from late modern nomads is over the malleability of information and how it can and should shape subsequent narration. As was noted above, information is not simply raw data that is infinitely malleable. Rather, a prior narrative context filters, interprets, and utilizes information in subsequent narration. What is at stake, then, is the adequacy of the narrative frameworks within which information is processed. Late modern nomads, for instance, tend to prefer narrations that are highly individualistic and idiosyncratic—purportedly unique or novel fabrications that express one's identity over time. Creating and exchanging information is therefore not unlike picking and choosing items in a supermarket. As was noted above, narratives are subject to editing over time, often in response to new or neglected information. Yet editing is subject to certain rules and limitations; otherwise, it ceases to be formative. In this respect, Grant is correct in insisting that some narrations are "package deals" that are not subject to picking and choosing.[4] An individual, for example, cannot pick and choose various practices in the pattern of the Christian moral life that begins with judgment and ends with amendment of life without in turn eviscerating its formative power. An individual is not at liberty to choose forgiveness but reject judgment, or embrace amendment of life while refusing repentance and contrition. Consequently, Christians should challenge the adequacy of these nomadic, and thereby displaced, narratives, insisting that although information is needed to create spaces of interaction, it alone is not sufficient to sustain associations that enable human flourishing.

This assessment of the inadequacy of information to sustain human flourishing, however, begs two important questions: first, why exactly is information alone insufficient?; and, second, why is narrative required to sustain human flourishing? First, information is well equipped to facilitate exchange, but ill-equipped to sustain communication. Humans are constantly creating spaces to exchange such things as ideas, goods, and services. Much, if not most, of our time is spent exchanging because it is a vital activity in sustaining human life. Although exchange does not require any enduring or intimate relationships, it is nonetheless the requisite condition for all forms of human association. A family, for instance, requires

---

[4] See George Parkin Grant, *Technology and Justice* (Notre Dame, IN: Notre Dame University Press, 1986), p. 32.

labor, financial, and commercial exchanges beyond its associational boundaries to satisfy its physical and material needs. Familial intimacy depends on countless exchanges with numerous strangers on a daily basis. A family, however, cannot be reduced to or sustained by exchange. This is not to say that exchanges do occur frequently among members of a family, for as social creatures reciprocity is a ubiquitous feature of human life. Yet a family is not the sum total of exchanged goods acquired by its individual members. The good of a family is not exchanged but shared, or better, communicated, and, concomitantly, communication is formed and sustained by narration. Through emerging and repetitive patterns of interactions and practices, an association narrates what it has become, is becoming, and aspires to be. These narrations are often inadvertent and inarticulate, but they nonetheless disclose the goods that are communicated. Such disclosure occurs, more often than not, in ordinary activities, for it is in and through the mundane that the narration takes shape and in turn forms its participants. It is, so to speak, in the taken-for-granted spaces in its life together that an association communicates. For instance, a family sharing a daily meal or gathering together to celebrate a holiday is simultaneously narrating the good that binds it together while also sustaining the space for its *koinonia* and its subsequent, emerging narration.

Communication, unlike exchange, requires a particular locale; to communicate one must be in place and not displaced. This is not surprising since, as already noted, narration must also be in place and not displaced, and communication can only occur within a narrative framework entailing much more than exchanging information. This does not imply the necessity or even preference for static permanence. A family, for instance, does not stop communicating or narrating when it moves into a new house. Rather, a family requires a particular place to reside, to share meals, and gather together at holidays in order to communicate, and their communication is sustained by their formative narration. In the absence of place, communicative spaces cannot be created, sustained, and narrated.

The emerging technoculture does not so much destroy or prevent communication as it erodes its requisite foundations of place and narration. The challenge faced by communicative associations is not open and overt hostility but inattention and indifference. Given the nomadic preference for space, information, and exchange, communication and narration are reduced to commodities that are produced and consumed by idiosyncratic individuals. Narration is simply a creative accumulation and interpretive presentation of information, and communication is the sum total of exchanges over time. Consequently, place, other than as an element of personal taste or preference, is irrelevant so long as spaces for exchanging information are readily available. In this respect, it does not matter if a family shares its meals in a restaurant, or gathers at a resort for a holiday. There is, admittedly, a modicum of truth in the casual dismissal of place, for a restaurant or resort can provide a setting where a space for familial fellowship is temporarily created. Although such places may support familial bonds, they are ill-equipped to facilitate familial communication in a full or enduring sense, for they do not connote particular places where a particular family belongs. Dining in a restaurant is not the same as sharing a meal day in and day out at roughly the same time in the same room; enjoying each other's company at a resort is not synonymous with gathering together in a place that some family members call home.

Again, these differences do not suggest the necessity of any relative permanence. A family may move from house to house thereby changing the locale of their daily meals, or extended family gatherings may be rotated among various households. Yet, despite this transiency, both instances demarcate places where a family belongs and communicates their mutual belonging. The same cannot be said for such places as restaurants and resorts. A family may use these locales to achieve certain purposes, such as fellowship or entertainment, but they are not places to which a family may be said to belong. They are not, in short, places that can be called "home" as the chief place where a family communicates its shared goods. This is not to romanticize, but to observe that, when stripped of its sentimentality, the phrase "there's no place like home" correctly identifies the particular and proper place where familial communication is formed, sustained, and narrated. "Home" connotes the predominant locale where a family belongs in communicating its shared goods, and although other locales, such as restaurants and resorts, may assist a family in this process, they cannot be substitute homes. Moreover, the resulting narrative may not prove to be an entirely happy one, for it often involves an ongoing association with intolerable siblings, parents, aunts, uncles, and cousins with whom one would prefer not to belong. Or, far worse, the ensuing narration may entail distorted or corrupt communicative practices to justify neglect, cruelty, or abuse. The point to be stressed is simply that familial communication and its subsequent narration, however good or bad it may prove to be, is inescapably embedded in particular places, as are all other forms of symbiotic association.

The principal underlying difference at issue is one of time: exchange is fixated on the immediate, whereas communication is oriented simultaneously toward past and future. Since exchange does not presuppose the necessity of prior or subsequent relationships, the need for particular venues, narration, and shared goods are thereby greatly diminished, if not eliminated altogether in some circumstances. In contrast, communication is predicated on sustained relationships requiring particular locales, accompanying and formative narration, and preservation of shared goods. Exchange, unlike communication, requires no enduring memory or extensive anticipation. Consequently, the emerging technoculture erodes the supportive structures of communicative association, given its preference for nomadic mobility. Exchange, in short, is simply easier and less constraining. It is more convenient, for example, for individuals to grab something to eat at a time and place of their choosing, or perhaps together at a restaurant should various calendars allow, than to gather together at a specified time and place to prepare and share a meal, and clean up afterward. It is less demanding for members of an extended family to pursue their discrete holiday celebrations at more convenient locales, rather than gathering together at a house (or even a resort), and retain some semblance of commonality through phone calls, "face time," or posting videos on a social network. The same may be said for other communicative associations: a school offering an online course in virtual time is far more convenient than attending lectures in designated classrooms at specified times. Watching a religious service on streaming video, or participating in a simulated worship service is easier than getting dressed and traveling to gather with fellow worshippers at an inconvenient place and hour. In each of these instances the preference of space, information, and exchange erodes the necessity of place, narration, and communication.

Should this erosion concern us? Does not the convenience of exchange enlarge one's scope of freedom, or at the very least allow one to avoid unwanted circumstances such as wasting time with disagreeable family members, fellow students, or co-religionists? Do the constraints purportedly required by communication demonstrably enhance the quality of individual lives? These questions wind back to the second question posed above: is narration, and therefore communication, needed to sustain human flourishing, or, more generally, can space, information, and exchange provide adequate substitutes? This is a far more complex question, and it requires a more elaborate answer—indeed, an inquiry— which will take us through the remainder of this book. We begin this exploration by revisiting the relation between remembering and anticipating.

Remembrance and anticipation

If the emphasis on space, information, and exchange cannot sustain associations that are crucial to human flourishing, then a recovery of place, narration, and communication is thereby required. The nomadic life of the emerging technoculture may be easy and convenient, but it cannot preserve the supportive social bonds that are crucial in orienting human life and lives toward their proper teleological and eschatological ends. This recovery, however, should not entail either a conservative refusal or sectarian withdrawal, for to do so is tantamount to either denying, in the former, the providential and timely unfolding of God's creation, or, in the latter, denying that God's creation is good. Rather, what is needed is an engagement with the emerging technoculture that is simultaneously critical and constructive, and thereby able to recover the formative and sustaining elements of place, narration, and communication in a manner that does not simply refuse or reject the broader culture. The principal objective is to reorient the creation and uses of space, information, and exchange in ways that do not erode, and may in some instances promote, these formative and sustaining elements; hence the counter-imagery of the pilgrim as opposed to the nomad.

The first step in this engagement is to shift the late nomadic fixation away from the immediate and toward both past and future—to challenge the nomadic obsession with the "now" in favor of remembering and anticipating. The principal reason for this shift is that without remembrance and anticipation human associations cannot be adequately sustained, and in the absence of strong and robust associations humans cannot flourish in the ways that God intends. If such an engagement is to be Christian, however, then the remembrance in play is anticipatory, which in turn draws on and reinforces an imaginative restlessness. These twin foci are focused on the crucifixion, resurrection, and exaltation of Jesus Christ as the tripartite culmination of the Incarnation of the Word, and which in turn portends his *parousia*. It is this not entirely fulfilled culmination that inspires a remembrance that is anticipatory. Whenever Christians remember Jesus as the incarnate Word of God, their attention is necessarily redirected toward the promised return that they anticipate. And such anticipation entails a restlessness stemming from an imaginative interpretation of what the presence of the Word— past, present, and future—means and requires of Christ's disciples in this time between the times. In this tension between remembrance and anticipation, the immediate is neither neglected nor negated, but is properly located as the nexus linking what is remembered and anticipated; the "now' is effectively stripped of its idolatry and restored as a time and space of interpretation, deliberation, and discernment. It is also within this tension that the pattern of the Christian moral life, beginning in judgment and ending in amendment of life, is frequently enacted. Although this pattern is repeated frequently, it is not merely cyclical but is also drawn toward its end in the *parousia*; hence the ensuing teleological and eschatological trajectory of the Christian moral life. This pattern is drawn from the pilgrimage narrative which I have likened to a kind of dead reckoning that pilgrims may use to navigate the moral terrain in this time between the times, for they are neither stuck in the constraints of place, narration, and communication, nor lost in the fluidity of space, information, and exchange. It is as pilgrims that Christians may engage the emerging technoculture and its nomadic inhabitants, for they do not deny the necessity of mobility predicated on exchange, information, and space, but insist that they cannot adequately replace the necessities of communication, narration, and place. Consequently, in their earthly pilgrimage, followers of Jesus Christ cannot ignore, refuse or despise the emerging technoculture and its nomadic inhabitants, for it continues to be the creation in which its creator was pleased to abide as the Word made flesh.

Borgmann's account of focal things and practices offers a promising venue for engaging the emerging technoculture in both a critical and constructive manner. This account need not be revisited other than to highlight the most prominent features that are employed below. A focal thing is a commanding presence that captures the attention of a particular person or group, such as a family meal or household hearth. Focal practices are a series of acts that are required to sustain the focal thing, such as preparing a meal or maintaining a supply of wood. These practices require individuals to orient their daily lives in respect to particular times and locales; a person must be in a particular place at a specified time to participate in a family meal, and wood must be cut, split, and stored in a timely manner. These practices are both teleological and formative. A focal practice is teleological in that it is oriented toward serving a prescribed purpose: a menu is planned to meet the dietary needs and culinary preferences of family members, and wood is chosen and prepared to provide heat and comfort. A focal practice is formative in that it shapes certain patterns of behavior: a family meal incorporates and promotes table fellowship in which conversation often includes both remembrance and anticipation, a pattern repeated by those warming themselves around the hearth. Focal things and practices acknowledge the necessity of place that enables subsequent narration and communication. In contrast, the nomadic inhabitants of the emerging technoculture prefer devices that facilitate easy and quick consumption of commodities, such as microwave ovens and central heating. Neither of these devices may serve as focal things because they are not intended to assert a commanding presence but are designed to be effectively invisible, thereby requiring no attentive focal practices. Consequently, they are well equipped to promote the nomadic preferences of space, information, and exchange. Borgmann's focal things and practices, however, offer a promising platform from which to engage with the emerging technoculture, for his goal is neither to reject nor withdraw, but to selectively and simultaneously resist, reform, and reorient. On the one hand, members of a family who restrict their mobility to participate regularly in shared meals could exemplify resistance. On the other hand, removing central heating and returning to the hearth would be a pointless and futile act of refusal. Yet are there other focal things and practices that central heating, in conjunction with the reformed and reoriented uses of other various technologies, could help promote and sustain?

For the purpose of inquiring into some of the illustrative aspects this engagement entails, we may concentrate on two *focal orientations*. The first is *focal remembrance*. One cannot be a Christian without remembering the life, ministry, death, resurrection, and exaltation of Jesus. This memory is preserved is Scripture, refined in doctrine, enacted in worship, and celebrated in the sacraments. Yet, as I have argued in the preceding chapters, remembrance is an imaginative act. To a great extent, remembrance is remembering the memories of predecessors; the past is imagined in and through tradition. Tradition may be thought of as a way in which a community captures and narrates its arguments over time. Consequently, tradition is subject to revision, refinement, and correction. To say that tradition changes over time is not a contradiction in terms, but an indication of health and vibrancy. If the Holy Spirit is at work in the church and world, then remembrance is not a static or inert activity. Such change, however, is not arbitrary or capricious, for what is imagined is shaped and constrained by the collective memory and subsequent narration of the community over time. Moreover, when Christians imaginatively remember their predecessors in the faith remembering Jesus, they also encounter their anticipation of his *parousia*; their remembrance is not only recollective but also anticipatory; they remember the future.

The second focal orientation, then, is *focal eschatology*. The work initiated by God in the Word made flesh is not yet complete, or, to change the metaphor, the final chapter of this story is not yet written: hence the ensuing restlessness of the Christian moral life; its sense of unsettled but patient pilgrimage. This eschatological orientation inspires an awareness that new and renewing possibilities for ordering human life in this time between the times can and do occur, precisely because it acts as a mirror casting attention back to the remembered Jesus. But it also inspires reticence, for the fulfillment of Christ's promised future cannot be foreknown with complete certainty. Thus, the need for Christians to make course corrections in their pilgrimage, to amend their lives as needed and required. And, thus, in engaging with the emerging technoculture their action cannot be confined to refusal or condemnation, but must include the entire range initiated by judgment and concluding in amendment of life.

In undertaking this critical and constructive engagement, Christians must attend to focal things and practices derived from these focal orientations. Such focal things and practices embody patterns of daily living and life that call into question many of the nomadic values of the emerging technoculture, particularly the adequacy of its preferences for space, information, and exchange. In the following subsections I examine three focal things and practices. This list is not exhaustive but illustrative of how focal things and practices serve as a conceptual base for critical and constructive engagement. Nor is the exposition of these three examples comprehensive. I presuppose that each are interlocking and mutually reinforcing, but do not describe this overlap in much detail. Instead, I highlight selected emphases that help to tie together key theological and conceptual strands that have been developed in the preceding chapters. These brief forays into baptism, Eucharist, and Sabbath provide a basic conceptual contrast between the pattern of the Christian pilgrimage and that of the nomadic life of the emerging technoculture, while the practical details of engagement derived from this contrast are developed in Part III.

Baptism

Through their baptism, believers share in the death and resurrection of Jesus Christ. In the water of the baptismal font or baptistery, a person dies with Christ and is raised with Christ. Baptism is a second birth; the one baptized is born anew. Why the need to be born again? Although everyone is born within God's good creation, they are also born into a world constructed by their human predecessors. Consequently, it is also a world constructed by sinners and thereby a fallen world deeply disordered and disfigured by sin. The first-born cannot, if left to his or her own devices, recognize fully the world for what it is, or reshape it into what it should be. Thus baptism is also the admission that the world, as it is, is not, at present, a place where humans, as God's creatures, may flourish as intended by their creator.

In this respect, we may say that baptism is a focal thing that illumines the darkness *as* darkness. The world, as it is, is one of twilight and shadows. Sin distorts and entangles human life into so-called realities that are in fact illusions, for good is often disfigured into evil, and evil into good. Such distortion is subtle, ordinary, and frequently unrecognized because it is accomplished under a veil of darkness and unexposed for what it is. This is why, in part, the cross is a premier symbol of both baptism and the baptized, for it is the beacon that illumines the darkness and exposes the world for what it is. The baptized bear witness to this illumination, helping to explain why they are never entirely at ease or at home in the world.

Baptism, however, does not (or should not) result in despair or a hatred of the world. Although baptism begins by sharing in Christ's death, it ends by sharing in Christ's resurrection. The empty tomb is thereby the complementary premier symbol of baptism to that of the cross, acknowledging that although being a follower of Jesus Christ necessitates death, it pre-eminently entails being born anew. This second birth is into the church as Christ's body in and for the world. The proper response of the baptized to the world, as it is, is not one of despair or hatred, but of love and service, for it was on behalf of this world that the Word became incarnate as an act of divine love and grace. The focal practices stemming from, and attending to, baptism affirm and embody, albeit imperfectly, this steadfast love for the world. The space the church creates within the world not only illumines the darkness, but also dispels the shadows and twilight.

In this respect, we may say that these focal practices enact anticipatory remembrance. The very act is predicated on a remembrance of what Jesus, as the incarnate Word of God, has done and continues to do through the Holy Spirit in reconciling the eternal with the temporal, the infinite with the finite. Jesus' salvific work and ministry in particular are recalled, and believers of every generation respond to his call to become his disciples, following him in his death. Yet dying in Christ already presupposes and anticipates his resurrection which his followers also share. But they are not resurrected as autonomous believers but into the body of Christ. Consequently, baptism is also a rite of initiation into the church. It is the church that is most directly formed by, and oriented to, this anticipatory remembrance. But that which the church remembers and anticipates is not self-referential, for the church simultaneously celebrates the presence of Christ and his absence. The church does not place its hope in itself but in the return of its Lord. This penultimate status is captured in St Augustine's imagery of the two cities. The earthly city, at present, encases the heavenly, and its citizens are dispersed throughout it. They are, then, dual citizens of both cities, but it is an unequal citizenship. Baptism is a declaration that although a penultimate respect is owed to the earthly city, ultimate loyalty is given to its heavenly counterpart. More precisely, their status in the earthly city is more akin to that of aliens that reside for a while during their pilgrimage, for their primary citizenship is based on their second, rather than first, birth. The church, then, is not the city of God but more like its embassy, helping Christians to properly order their ultimate loyalty with penultimate duties and responsibilities. Baptism is thereby the demonstrative *metanoia* entailed in the Christian life and pilgrimage.

In this respect, we may further say that baptism provides the basis of Christian narration—a rudimentary but requisite vocabulary, syntax, and grammar. In the absence of baptism as a declarative act, subsequent discourse sacrifices its distinctive ultimacy and is enfolded into the world's narrations as rhetoric ranging from appealing to whimsical, or, worse, as mere information to be ignored or used in whatever ways nomadic consumers might choose. Without the platform of baptism, Christians may soothe, ridicule, or scold the nomadic inhabitants of the emerging technoculture, but they cannot critically and constructively engage them for they lack any compelling countervailing loyalty that may prompt a substantive and teleological reordering of desire. In the absence of baptism Christians can describe the world as it is, but they cannot ascribe how it should be. And, without this ascriptive power, Christian narration cannot coax the needed *metanoia* for navigating the moral terrain in this time between the times.

We may finally say that baptism encapsulates the virtue or practice of *faith*. Following Josef Pieper, the object of faith is a given rather than a determination or artifact.[5] Faith is not general or ethereal, but directed toward a particular person or object; one believes someone or in something. Faith thereby presupposes a relational quality entailing disclosure or revelation. Consequently, faith cannot establish its legitimacy on the basis of demonstrable facts, nor can its truth be "definitively proved by any rational argument."[6] In this respect, faith is more an act of will than cognition, and it is the will that attempts to acknowledge that the particular object of faith is good. In Pieper's words: "We believe, not because we see, perceive, deduce something true, but because we desire something good."[7] Baptism is a concrete demonstration of the desired good that is God.

Although faith cannot be predicated on exact knowledge or certainty, it can nonetheless be explicated in ways that can be understood. It is the explicability of faith that enables a Christian engagement with the emerging technoculture that is simultaneously critical and constructive. Since belief is primarily an act of will, then faith, of some sort, is inescapable. As Herman Dooyeweerd observed, the choice is not between belief and unbelief, but judging the veracity of various, and at times conflicting, beliefs.[8] The nomadic inhabitants of the emerging technoculture will particular things, and hence they presumably believe them to be true and good.[9] The emerging technoculture is not devoid of belief, but contains many faiths. As Pieper notes, the true antonym of belief is not unbelief, but inattention.[10] This question of the veracity of a particular faith provides an opening for Christian engagement. Critically, it may be asked if sufficient attention has been given to the necessities of place, narration, and communication in sustaining human flourishing, as a consequence challenging the faith placed in space, information, and exchange as adequate substitutes. Constructively, it may also be asked whether various technologies, as the principal means of enacting the will as an expression of faith, may be reoriented in ways that better serve and sustain human flourishing.

---

[5] See Josef Pieper, *Faith Hope Love* (San Francisco, CA: Ignatius Press, 1997), pp. 18–26.

[6] Ibid., p. 72.

[7] Ibid., p. 36.

[8] See Herman Dooyeweerd, *Roots of Western Culture: Pagan, Secular, and Christian Options* (Toronto: Wedge Publishing Foundation, 1979), pp. 7–15.

[9] Despite Nietzsche's insistence that such willing is delusional, a judgment that, ironically, is based on his own faith in the impossibility of anything being good or true.

[10] See Pieper, *Faith Hope Love*, p. 16.

But what exactly are Christians proposing or attempting to accomplish in engaging with the faith of the emerging technoculture? Christians contend that faith is largely conforming one's life to God. This requires that one desires the good and orders one's life accordingly. Consequently, the Christian life in general, and moral life in particular, must demonstrate what such desiring and ordering entails, which brings us to the next focal thing and practice.

Eucharist

In the Eucharist, the life of the baptized is encapsulated. As argued in previous chapters, this sacrament embodies a pattern and trajectory entailing judgment, confession, contrition, repentance, forgiveness, and amendment of life. As a pattern, it is repeated frequently in anticipatory remembrance of Jesus. As a trajectory, it orients restless pilgrims toward their destination in Christ. For the purpose of this inquiry, then, we may say that if baptism highlights the crucifixion and resurrection of Jesus Christ, then the Eucharist underscores his exaltation and *parousia*. Its liturgical structure and rhythm exemplifies and prompts how life should be lived in this time between the times. Three instances in particular need to be briefly recalled and emphasized. First, the Christian moral life acknowledges the pervasiveness of sin, and hence the need for judgment to differentiate right from wrong, subsequently creating a space for confession, contrition, and repentance to begin the reconciliation of offenders and offended. Second, the Christian moral life acknowledges the need to amend human action, both to instantiate prior judgment and to reorient life toward its *telos* in Christ. Third, and most important in terms of this inquiry, there is the possibility of offering and receiving forgiveness that serves as the principal bridge between judgment and amendment of life.

In this respect, we may say that Eucharist is the focal thing that exemplifies the imaginative restlessness of the Christian pilgrimage. The baptized are called to love and serve the world in remembrance of Jesus as the Incarnate Word of God. Yet, since this remembrance is anticipatory, such love is partial and penultimate, for the world, as it is, is not what it should and shall be. Hence the imaginative restlessness of the Christian moral life that is lived out in the world but is not of it—the life of pilgrims who reside in the earthly city but long for its heavenly counterpart. This is why, in part, forgiveness plays a central role, for it is literally the linkage in between judgment and amendment of life. Forgiving presupposes promising, and promises are empty in the absence of forgiveness. Forgiveness is the centerpiece holding together, while not negating, the tension between remembrance and anticipation, and, moreover, it creates a space in which new and renewing possibilities may be born.

This promise of natality is crucial for countering the two extreme moral orientations often plaguing the emerging technoculture. On the one hand, it challenges the presumption that the prospect of new or renewing possibilities is nothing but a naive and empty fantasy, for human action can never escape the eternal recurrence of the same. The potential efficacy of forgiving and promising is thereby effectively dismissed as a futile and disingenuous gesture. The Christian moral life in contrast restores a teleological orientation and movement through time to its repetitive pattern, in turn opening a space for natality to occur—of being attentive to the possibility of something genuinely new. On the other hand, it counters the belief that creativity is a good in its own right. New or novel possibilities are being created routinely and incessantly. What is willed or desired can increasingly be fabricated within various real or virtual spaces. The emerging technoculture is a hotbed of new and novel possibilities. In creating and actualizing these possibilities, some individuals are inevitably wronged or injured. Subsequent forgiving and promising, however, are effectively reduced to gestures of compensation or buying off, because no enduring relationship is necessarily presupposed. In short, reconciliation is not needed in a relationship of exchange as opposed to communication. If the creation of new possibilities is routine and ubiquitous, however, they are stripped of their power to renew and reorient for if creativity is a good in its own right, it cannot redirect subsequent action in any normative manner, and the resulting possibilities cannot thereby be renewing. The creation of such possibilities is literally pointless because these possibilities have nothing to point to beyond their own creation. In contrast, the repetitive pattern of the Christian moral life tethers creativity to a particular teleology and eschatology. When genuinely new possibilities emerge, they renew by reorienting moral action in its proper direction; they renew by prompting a course correction. Consequently, forgiving and promising are indispensable to the moral life, because their repetitive pattern is practiced and their trajectory is plotted over time not by autonomous individuals, but by a community or *koinonia* bound together by a shared narration. Reconciliation is therefore vital since the community is based on communicating rather than exchanging. More importantly, forgiving and promising are crucial prerequisites for natality, for it is in graceful acts of reconciliation that a space for new and renewing possibilities is also created. In brief, the Christian moral life reinstalls remembrance as the rudder of anticipation.

In this respect, Eucharist provides the template of communication. The liturgical celebration of this sacrament cannot capture and portray in any complete detail the rich complexity of communicating the goods of creation. Yet, in highlighting the moments of judgment, confession, contrition, repentance, forgiveness, and amendment of life, guidance is nonetheless provided for how human life and lives should be lived. Through its sheer repetition, Christians are formed as restless pilgrims, remembering Jesus and anticipating his *parousia*. Consequently, Eucharist encapsulates the virtue of *hope*. In highlighting the focus on exaltation and *parousia*, Eucharist enacts the hope that drives the restless lives of Christians in this time between the times, sustaining the hope that the "between" shall be replaced by the anticipated "end." Drawing on Pieper again, hope entails a "steadfast turning toward the true fulfillment" of being human—an orientation toward the good that "has its source in the reality of grace" that is drawing humans into fellowship with God.[11] The virtue of hope upholds humans in communicating the goods of creation over time, for in its absence humans are effectively reduced to producers and consumers.

Hope may serve as an antidote to the indifference, sloth, and despair that are endemic to the emerging technoculture in which exchange is displacing communication. A pervasive indifference stems from the momentary and episodic exchanges on which the nomadic life of the emerging technoculture is predicated. Since nomads have little at stake in preserving particular associations, an indifferent attitude toward the various, and often invisible, parties to an exchange is needed to both promote efficiency and protect mobility; hence the growing preference for the Internet over the High Street as a convenient venue for entering the misnamed global market*place*. This indifference leads to a less obvious but equally pervasive sloth. To accuse the frenetic nomads of the emerging technoculture of committing the sin of sloth may strike the reader as being a bit daft. Sloth, however, is not synonymous with laziness. Rather, sloth is the belief that there are no available options for changing an ongoing course of action toward a more satisfying or fulfilling direction. Consequently, any substantive amendment of life is impossible, and forgiving and promising are thereby delusional. Sloth may be manifested in lethargy, but it can also prompt frenzied activity to distract attention away from the ensuing void that sloth creates. The ceaseless nomadic meandering of the emerging technoculture may simply be an admission that life is little or nothing more than endless and unfulfilling exchange. More troubling, sloth often leads to despair. As Pieper notes, sloth results in a "joyless, ill-tempered and narrow-mindedly self-seeking rejection of the nobility of the children of God with all the obligations it entails."[12] It is a small step to a more encompassing despair that denies that ultimately human life has no purpose or direction, and hence no goods to be communicated. In short, despair is the denial of redemption, and therefore the rejection of hope. There is simply no prospect of new and renewing possibilities, because there is nothing to change or renew in the first place. The so-called time between the times is merely time bracketed by oblivion.

Hope is an antidote to despair not because it can offer certain knowledge concerning human destiny and therefore any ultimate Good or purpose, but because it can offer the faith on which it is based. By at least entertaining the possibility that there is a fulfilling Good to be attained, and created goods to be communicated in the meantime, hope can also resist the indifference and sloth preceding despair. In this respect, a recovery of hope strengthens Arendt's claim that evil, particularly in its late modern guise, is not so much the outcome of wicked willfulness as it is the result of banal inattention. And, more importantly, it is in hope that promising and forgiving—amendment of life—is made effectual. Hope, therefore, is the premier virtue of the pilgrim, for it lies literally between the virtues of faith and charity. Hope presupposes and is born out of faith, but it is destined by, and prefigures, a future of love.

---

[11] See ibid., p. 99.
[12] Ibid., p. 119.

Sabbath

The third focal thing and practice is *Sabbath*. Unlike baptism and Eucharist, Sabbath is neither a sacrament nor does it have any formal liturgical expression. Its purpose and practice, as I argue below, thereby differs, but first I must explain how I am interpreting and using this term. Sabbath is usually understood as a day of rest when people focus their attention on worship, prayer, or devotional reflection, often associated with laws and rules restricting what kinds of activities can be undertaken. With the exception of Sabbatarian laws, an odd outgrowth of the unfortunate proclivity of some influential Protestants to conflate Sunday with Sabbath, I am ambivalent about such a rigorous and regulated practice of Sabbath. A day of Sabbath rest, for instance, may indeed provide an important occasion for ordering one's spiritual life by offering an oasis for weary nomads traversing the desert of late modernity, but it is not an absolute necessity for engaging with the emerging technoculture. Rather, I am proposing a broader conceptual schema that preserves, for instance, the priority of place over space but requires practices that do not diminish or denigrate the importance of the latter.

In this schema, "rest" is not the word more closely associated with Sabbath. There is, of course, nothing wrong with resting; even God rested after creating the world. But when "rest" and "Sabbath" become virtually synonymous, the practice of keeping Sabbath can easily degenerate into episodic and nostalgic attempts at recapturing a slower and less hectic pace of life. The word that should be closely associated with Sabbath is *leisure*. By this I do not mean a hobby, recreation, or a vocational pursuit. It is a stance or orientation that is receptive rather than proactive, an "attitude of mind, a contemplative attitude, and ... not only the occasion but also the capacity for steeping oneself in the whole of creation."[13] According to Pieper, leisure is the affirmation of one's being,[14] an act that is effortless for it entails receiving as opposed to making or creating. In our leisure we are given knowledge or understanding of ourselves and creation, requiring an openness that refrains from intervening and manipulating. What Pieper is challenging is the peculiarly modern, specifically Kantian idea that knowledge is the result of work or effort, and that there is nothing to it that is given.[15] Late moderns have come to believe that anything worthwhile can only result from their own effort and creativity, ultimately even debasing love into an artifact of their work.

Pieper's account of leisure provides a more expansive understanding of Sabbath that preserves the priority of place over space while resisting the temptations of consigning it to a particular day and corrupting it into another form of work. If knowledge of self and creation is a given to be received, then a space must be created for its reception. But such a space cannot be separated from place, for it

---

[13] Josef Pieper, *Leisure, the Basis of Culture: The Philosophical Act* (San Francisco, CA: Ignatius Press, 2009), pp. 46–47.

[14] See ibid., p. 46.

[15] See ibid., pp. 30–34.

is only when a person is in place that she can be still in order to receive. Being still in place need not be not be confined to a specified day or enacted through precise regulations. Stillness is required as means of being at leisure in order to be receptive. In the absence of this openness, Sabbath is disfigured into work—one more artifact of the will to power and mastery. It is true that humans were not made for the Sabbath; it is also not their invention, but a divine gift that is not a means but an end in its own right.

Although Karl Barth unfortunately conflates Sabbath with the "Lord's Day,"[16] he nevertheless captures reception as the core practice of keeping Sabbath. This conflation is unfortunate because Sabbath is not worship, for the former is akin to leisure while the latter, as very word "liturgy" makes clear, is a public work. Sabbath, however, presupposes and requires the support of worship because, as Pieper insists, leisure "is not possible unless it has a durable and ... living link with the *cultus*, with divine worship."[17] Celebration is ultimately the source of leisure, and worship is the basis of celebration. Consequently, as Barth contends, Sabbath is a reminder that life is a free gift of grace rather than a human work, thereby forbidding humans from placing their faith and hope in their own plans and efforts, for genuine knowledge and understanding are given and not made. Again, as Pieper notes, the English word "school" is derived from the Greek and Latin terms for leisure,[18] which serves as a damning indictment of the educational institutions of the emerging technoculture that have been mutilated into spaces for creating information rather than places of leisurely contemplation. God has given the Sabbath to interrupt the routine of work, in order that we might know and understand his creation and its destiny. The requisite stillness, however, is not inactivity; sleeping is not keeping Sabbath. Being in place and being still is an act of reception that breaks, but does not negate, the pattern of the routine. Those keeping Sabbath must return to work, and in doing so narrate and communicate what they have been given. Or, as Marva Dawn notes, Christians need a "Sabbath way of life for serving the world."[19]

Sabbath is a time and place where our desires are assessed and reformed. In receiving what we should know and understand, we learn what we should desire and how they should be properly ordered. Sabbath is also a time and place in which the patterns of the moral life are realigned in accordance with the promises made in amending one's life. To return to the analogy of dead reckoning, keeping Sabbath affords opportunities for making necessary course corrections. In being still and in place key landmarks may be more adequately appraised for helping

---

[16] See Karl Barth, *Church Dogmatics*, III/4 (Edinburgh, UK: T and T Clark, 1961), § 53.1, pp. 47–72.

[17] Pieper, *Leisure*, p. 15.

[18] See ibid., pp. 19–20.

[19] Marva J. Dawn, *The Sense of the Call: A Sabbath Way of Life for those Who Serve God, the Church, and the World* (Grand Rapids, MI, and Cambridge, UK: Eerdmans, 2006), p. xi.

one navigate the moral terrain of the emerging technoculture. As any pilot knows, sometimes holding patterns are needed to avoid navigational errors.[20]

We may say, then, that the focal thing and practices of Sabbath amplify the virtue of charity. The reason why the knowledge and understanding received through the leisure of Sabbath is narrated and communicated is love. Presumably, what is received when one is still and in place is good, for one has become steeped in creation as a whole, a creation created and loved by God. To horde the knowledge and understanding that one has been given is a self-indulgence that fails to appreciate that the command to love God is inseparable from the love of one's neighbor. Love is inherently relational; it seeks to bind rather than isolate and separate. If Christians practice Sabbath, then they must also engage their nomadic neighbors in a charitable manner. Moreover, it is love that makes the possibilities of forgiving, promising, and amendment of life realistic prospects. In the absence of love these acts would be merely perfunctory and expedient. It is ultimately love that provides the bonds of imperfection that sustain human associations, and it is therefore a reconciling love that Christians are ultimately narrating and communicating with their neighbors. Charity, however, is not a superficial kindness entailing unconditional acceptance or approval. Charity is simultaneously approbation and reprobation, requiring a relationship that is both critical and constructive. Without these polarities, forgiving, promising, and amendment of life are voided of any real content. In and through charity, grounded in the knowledge and understanding received in Sabbath practice, we learn that the proper ordering of desire cannot be separated from knowing when and to what a "no" or "yes" must be uttered. It is only by first saying the former that the latter may be expressed with any strength or conviction. Consequently, discerning the requisite negations that make affirmations possible lies at the heart of the Christian moral life.

It may rightfully be asked how charity—in conjunction with hope and faith—enables one to know when and to what a "no" or "yes" should be voiced. Or, more pointedly, what practical moral difference do these virtues—especially in conjunction with the insistence on preserving the priority of place, narration, and communication over the alternative preferences of space, information, and exchange—make in navigating the moral terrain of the emerging technoculture? These are the questions prompting the inquiries of Part III.

---

[20] I am indebted to Jim Noseworthy for this insight.

PART III
Moral Engagement

Theological Construction and Moral Engagement

The following chapters examine how the theological construction undertaken in Part II may inform Christian moral engagement with the emerging technoculture that is both critical *and* constructive. Collectively, they serve as a brief account of navigating the moral terrain. My purpose, however, is not to provide a detailed map of this terrain, or prescribe rules of engagement. Rather, I offer some reflections and commentary on both the challenges entailed in reconnoitering the ever-changing landscape of the emerging technoculture.

Since these chapters draw on arguments explicated in preceding ones, a brief précis might prove helpful. Part I was devoted to philosophical description and critique. The descriptions of late modernity provided by Friedrich Nietzsche and Martin Heidegger portray the culmination of the will to power, particularly as exemplified in a pervasive historicism and nihilism. These dominant themes help explain the privileging of space, information, and exchange within the emerging technoculture, and its resulting nomadic life. Three critiques were examined in turn. George Grant offers a bleak assessment of late modernity, exposing it as age of darkness that must be illumined as such. His response to the emerging technoculture is to neither reform nor replace it, but to refuse it. Hannah Arendt's chief complaint with late modernity is its fixation on mortality. An insidious fear of death prompts various attempts to construct works or artifacts that survive the demise of their creators, and increasingly late moderns turn to technology as the principal means of achieving this purported immortality. These attempts, however, often prove destructive, if not deadly. Arendt's solution is to reorient civil community, particularly politics away from mortality and toward natality in order to create an openness to genuinely new and renewing possibilities. According to Albert Borgmann, the daily patterns of late modern life are shaped by the device paradigm. A growing collection of devices or technologies has greatly increased the range of commodities that are easily produced and consumed. Although these devices have admittedly improved the quality of life for many individuals, they also promote greater autonomy and individualism that have a withering effect on families, communities, and other forms of human association. In response, Borgmann argues that individuals and communities should adopt focal things and practices that would reform and reorient technological development in ways that enable rather than diminish human flourishing.

Part II built upon the critiques of Part I. Although each of these critiques provides a good starting point for engaging with the emerging technoculture, they require further theological construction in order to form a Christian moral assessment that is both critical and constructive. Grant's illumination of the present darkness *as* darkness must be confessed rather than merely acknowledged. The prerequisite for confession is judgment that in turn opens new spaces in which hope can emerge. Although Arendt's preference for a politics focused on natality as opposed to mortality is a welcome shift in emphasis, it requires a richer theological account of forgiveness that is grounded in both repentance and the promise of renewing grace. As Arendt insists, natality, along with its new and renewing possibilities, requires a second birth, but one properly occurring in the body of Christ rather than the *polis*. Borgmann's account of focal things and practices offers a fruitful way of engaging with the emerging technoculture in both a critical and constructive manner. Focal practices enable communities to resist the prevalent device paradigm that diminishes the quality of daily life, while at the same time exhibiting an alternative for how a good life should be lived. Borgmann, however, does not specify what focal things and practices should be undertaken. In response, I argued that focal practices should promote the amendment of life, entailing a reordering of desire. This ordering requires maintaining the priority of place, narration, and communication as opposed to the nomadic preferences of space, information, and exchange. This privileging is exemplified in the focal practices of baptism, Eucharist, and Sabbath and their corresponding virtues of faith, hope, and charity.

Part III builds upon the arguments developed previously to probe how Christians might engage with the emerging technoculture—a culture in which they are enmeshed but also not fully at home. The following inquiry is not comprehensive. Rather, I concentrate on three selected instances or contexts that exhibit the late modern nomadic preferences for space, information, and exchange. Specifically, I focus on issues involving the Internet, politics, and economics. I have selected these settings for two reasons. First, each exerts a pervasive influence in both shaping and sustaining the emerging technoculture. This ubiquity is simultaneously extensive and subtle, so the extent to which they shape the mundane patterns of daily life often goes unrecognized and therefore unchallenged. Second, I need to address the question of what difference the arguments I am developing might make to the Christian moral life within the present circumstances of the emerging technoculture. Moral theology is, after all, a discipline of practical reasoning, and if it cannot assist Christians in discerning what they should and should not do, it is of little value. The following chapters, however, do not provide detailed instructions on how to engage; there is no checklist of dos and don'ts. In short, my interest is neither strategic nor tactical, but suggestive; I am more concerned with exploring ways in which Christian desire and moral imagination are (or should be) formed, than concocting a manual of how-to-do-it techniques.

In each instance, my method of inquiry involves highlighting the contrast between nomadic preferences of space, information, and exchange with the counter-priorities of place, narration, and communication. It should be stressed that the following chapters entail highlighting rather than segmenting. Although

I focus on a particular contrast in each chapter, pertinent theological and moral themes are also interwoven throughout, for my goal is to demonstrate a pattern of the Christian moral life rather than reporting isolated episodes. It should also be noted that many of my interlocutors in the following chapters are often "popular" authors rather than philosophers and theologians, who dominated Parts I and II. This is, I think, appropriate, since my objective is to engage with an emerging culture that is being formed almost everywhere other than the academy. This does not imply a lack of acuity, but acknowledges that these authors, often saddled with the derisive qualifier "popular," write in an idiom that both captures and shapes public mores with a clarity of thought and understanding that often eludes the peculiar dialect and jargon of academic ghettos.

Chapter 8
The Translucent Self In an Age of Transparency: Parasitic Self-Fulfillment

The late modern nomads traversing the emerging technoculture imagine that they are the *avant-garde* of a revolutionary way of living. Never before have so many people enjoyed such mobility, had so much information at their fingertips, or been able to converse with so vast an array of fellow wanderers virtually anytime and anywhere. In taking the first steps toward conquering the constraints of time and distance, endless possibilities begin to open for how individuals may go about inventing and reinventing themselves. With unprecedented technological power at their disposal, late modern nomads are constantly constructing and reconstructing the physical and virtual spaces in which they effortlessly appear and reappear, and in doing so are redefining how human life and lives can and should be lived. The old phrase "ends of the earth" is a poor metaphor to describe the extent to which humans can indulge their imaginations in creating their realities and also refashioning themselves in the process. For some of the more exuberant prognosticators, the emerging technoculture is the first step toward finally realizing Teilhard de Chardin's dream of the "noosphere" and its "Ultra-Humanity."[1]

This belief is, of course, nonsense. Far from being revolutionaries, late modern nomads are compliant conformists to a culture that precedes them by more than a few generations. Rather than being on the forefront of a new way of being human, they are riding the crest of innovation that has been gaining momentum for quite some time. This is especially the case with the vaunted technologies that are purportedly ushering in the new age of overcoming the limits of time and place. If a revolution may be said to have occurred, it took place with the steady stream of inventions in the nineteenth and early twentieth centuries. The introduction of the train, automobile, and airplane, coupled with the telegraph, telephone, and motion pictures were the revolutionary means of greatly reducing the constraints of time and place to an unprecedented extent.

The principal difference is the ubiquity, availability, and refinement of preceding technological developments, stemming primarily from three innovations: wireless transmission, digitization and miniaturization. The ability to transmit data through the airwaves led to the introduction of radio, television, and the mobile phone. The digitalization of data, when coupled with miniaturized electronic components, prompted the manufacture of smaller and portable devices for creating, storing,

---

[1] Pierre Teilhard de Chardin, *The Phenomenon of Man* (London: Collins, 1959), and *The Future of Man* (London: Collins, 1964).

and transmitting information. The creation of supportive infrastructures prompted burgeoning mass markets for these devices, making them increasingly affordable and readily available. This informational mobility in turn reinforces and spurs greater physical mobility, for people can now travel extensively or relocate and still remain in touch with colleagues, friends, and family.

The current innovation underway entails integrating once discrete technologies into a single and easily portable device. The so-called "smart phone" exemplifies this trend, for telephony is merely one among many functions that it performs. Although it is an impressive and useful gadget, even the smartest phone contains nothing new, but comprises refinements of initial ideas that prompted prior technological development. Text messages, emails, and tweets are not appreciably different from a telegram. The video, photo, and music galleries bear striking resemblances to television, scrapbooks, and phonographs. The Internet provides a quick and easy means to undertake activities that used to require such time-consuming tasks as perusing catalogs, scouring libraries, writing and mailing checks, or having a face-to-face conversation. The digital camera can trace a lineage back to the Polaroid®, and the GPS is an improved TripTic®. There is nothing novel about the smart phone; it merely provides quick and portable access to an array of technologies that current and previous generations have grown accustomed to. Arguably, a Victorian visiting present-day London would suffer far less future shock than an eighteenth-century Londoner visiting Victorian London.

Consequently, the nomadic life of late modernity is not a unique phenomenon, but the latest chapter of an unfolding cultural saga. It could be easily assumed that a novel entitled *Wired Love* is a tale of the steamy world of online dating and virtual affairs. But it is a story written in 1879 about two telegraph operators falling in love with each other, or, as the subtitle proclaims, a romance of dots and dashes.[2] People have been pursuing, as well as questioning, the propriety of online relationships for quite some time. What is different about this current phase are the ubiquitous and hyper qualities of information technologies, and the greater extent to which they are used in forming and expressing the identities of their users. These technologies are now readily available. Wired love, for instance, is not confined to relatively few telegraph operators, but open to anyone having access to the Internet or other communication networks. The quality and sophistication of the available technology is also exponentially greater. Some claim that we are beginning to collapse the real and virtual into a hyper-reality. Even if such a claim is dismissed as hyperbole, an alluring nexus of proffered online intimacy and social networks is available, which few can resist and some prefer. Two avatars walking hand-in-hand through Second Life® is a different experience from two telegraph operators exchanging dots and dashes.

---

[2] Ella Cheever Thayer, *Wired Love: A Romance of Dots and Dashes* (New York: C.W. Carleton, 1879; see also Maggie Jackson, *Distracted: The Erosion of Attention and the Coming Dark Age* (Amherst, NY: Prometheus Books, 2008), pp. 29–30.

Most importantly, technology is becoming the principal means of forming, expressing, and sustaining the identities of late modern nomads. With the aid of various gadgets, individuals organize their daily schedules, conduct their business, stay in contact, monitor news, events, and people, network with colleagues, friends, and family, post photos and personal information, and blog their opinions, rants, and raves. The accumulative effect of these mundane activities is the formation and expression of who one is and aspiring to become. The growing dependence on—one might be even tempted to say symbiosis with—these technologies is captured in the ensuing anxiety when individuals are deprived of their gadgets. Without the requisite technologies, late modern nomads lose the ability to easily open and close spaces that enable them to overcome the limits of time and place.

Yet the sense of identity, one might even say self-fulfillment, coming from purportedly exerting greater control over time and place is not only fluid but also fragile. Ironically, the autonomy and mobility prized by late modern nomads are growing increasingly dependent on others. I cannot, for instance, schedule meetings, conduct my business, stay in contact, monitor, network, or blog, if there is no one with whom to interact. These interactions, however, grow increasingly episodic, temporary, and impermanent. And, in executing these exchanges, late modern nomads must necessarily consume each other in constructing and expressing their respective identities. This necessity poses some troubling concerns: do the transient spaces—real, virtual, and hyper—comprising the emerging technoculture enable the construction of true identities, or do they also help produce simulacra that deceive and mislead? Do my exploits in a simulation make me a great baseball player? The spaces that are opened and entered must also be filtered, monitored, and tended if they are to fulfill the goals and desires of their users. Something, however minimal, must be known about those sharing a space, however temporary. Consequently, since spatial exchanges entail quick and partial expressions of identities that can reveal, conceal, or mislead, there is an accompanying need for scrutiny, suspicion, and surveillance, promoting a fundamental and mutual distrust. Is the person with whom I am exchanging an email really the woman she claims to be? Focusing attention on these spaces also requires inattentiveness to place and those occupying it. Most of the individuals with whom one comes into physical contact are often regarded as impediments or distractions that divert time and attention from the important spaces that are frequently distant or virtual. If I am talking on the phone, I cannot be attentive to those around me.

To raise these concerns, however, is to anticipate, and before examining them in greater detail, some praise should be offered for the emerging technoculture and its nomadic life. The technologies enabling greater mobility should not be taken for granted, much less despised. Easing the constraints of time and place has improved the lives of many individuals. The liberation of individuals from parochialisms often stemming from being sequestered in a particular locale, both physically and imaginatively, is to be welcomed. The ability to quickly and instantaneously exchange information globally has improved the material well-being of millions of people by creating employment opportunities and greater purchasing power. Christians especially—restless pilgrims that they are—share, to a certain extent, the preference of space over place, for their faith is practiced wherever two or three are gathered, and is not restricted to any hallow ground. Saint Paul, after all, was an itinerant evangelist. Despite the frequent complaints about the frantic pace, shallowness, and banality of the nomadic life, there are no serious proposals for banning the technologies that make it possible. Nor should there be.

Nevertheless, nomadic mobility comes at a price. All is not well in the emerging technoculture, as its critics make clear. The remedy, however, is not refusal, which for all practical purposes would offer little more than nostalgic escape. This is especially the case for Christians, for refusing the emerging technoculture would also be to refuse God's creation—a refusal to understand and serve the thing as it is. The challenge is one of reorientation, of reorienting the trajectory of the emerging technoculture away from its historicist and nihilistic illusions and toward a good *telos* or end; or, more pointedly, of reforming the nomadic life to one of pilgrimage. But before exploring what such reformation might entail, we must first probe further into the shadowy side of the nomadic life.

Shadow dancers in the twilight

As might be expected, late modern nomads spend a lot of time in airports. These are not only staging areas for travelers, but also beehives of frenetic activity. There are swarms of people rushing to and from gates, and a din of conversations pervades nearly every corner. But few are interacting with anyone in the building. Most are on their smart phones or tablets, talking, emailing, texting, tweeting, surfing, reading, writing, or listening to music. It seems that the only poor souls relegated to talking to another person are pensioners, frustrated customers haranguing airline employees, and parents of infants and toddlers too young to have their own phones or tablets.

The inattention to immediate place and those occupying it is a result of preserving the spaces in which nomads create their identities and exchange information. Technology is employed to effectively create borders to maintain spaces that are not predicated on either common locale or time. Consequently, those in close and temporary proximity are not admitted to these protected spaces because they are not needed or relevant. The resulting indifference or even rudeness, however, is not the principal issue at stake. The advent of ever more efficient gadgets aiding the preservation of private space is, in many respects, a welcome revenge of the introverted against the gregarious.

More troubling is what the cumulative effects of persistent inattentiveness to immediate place and those occupying it might prove to be. When space is consistently and routinely privileged over place, is the subsequent meaning of human identity and association substantially redefined? And is it redefined in ways that may serve more to diminish than promote human flourishing? Since, as noted above, the emerging technoculture is entering its third or fourth generation, there are some signs, albeit largely anecdotal, that this disturbing prospect may be the case.

There is, for instance, a pervasive sense of displacement—of not being connected to anywhere in particular. This loss of place, however, is not mourned but embraced as a liberating necessity in crafting one's sense of identity and well-being. While conducting an interview, Maggie Jackson asked a business executive if it was difficult to become rooted in the new suburb to which she had recently moved. "'I don't have any interest in being rooted here, honestly,' she said slowly. 'My safety net is made up of individuals. So while I need to have associations with time and space, I can be anywhere.' And she laughed."[3] In another interview, "global nomad" Fleura Bardhi admits: "[It is] 'important for me to establish a quick sense of home. You can leave the next day and not miss your neighbors. I can't allow myself to fully be comfortable, feel at home and identify with a place'."[4] This preference for a free-floating identity is necessary if one is to be a nomadic resident of the emerging technoculture because it is well suited to coping with and taking advantage of its afforded mobility. As Jackson notes, the "infatuation with nomadic life has grown in direct proportion to the rise of highly complex, circumscribed, and crowded societies."[5] Protected space is both needed and highly prized in a culture populated by strangers for whom exchange, rather than communication, is wanted and valued. Temporary and virtual space is preferred because it helps overcome the constraints of time and place, but the ensuing "life of perpetual movement reshapes our relationship to *place* and what it means to be in the world."[6]

To be in the world now requires one to be less attentive to the most immediately proximate. What differentiates late modern nomads from their ancient counterparts is that they do not need to be very aware of where they are most of the time. Indeed, being attentive to place is a distraction from the more pressing task of creating and preserving a preferred space. Nomads must often render themselves and others within a particular place effectively invisible in order to conduct exchanges or maintain intimate associations with individuals either in temporarily sequestered locales or at a distance. The issue at stake is not that this invisibility necessarily promotes incivility among strangers. Given the technoculture's sheer complexity, hectic pace of life, and interactions with unfamiliar people, large doses of anonymity and inattentiveness are needed to accomplish worthwhile objectives. Idle chit-chat with any and every stranger can be a mind-numbing waste of time, and a presumed familiarity of a chance encounter can prove foolish or even dangerous.

---

[3] Jackson, *Distracted*, p. 99.
[4] Ibid., p. 113.
[5] Ibid., p. 108.
[6] Ibid., p. 99 (emphasis in original).

More troubling are the distorting effects on identity and its dependence on relationships stemming from prolonged and routine inattentiveness to place and proximity. To preserve distant or temporary spaces of selected intimates, late modern nomads must, ironically, exchange invisibility for transparency because relationships require one to form and express one's identity. A self needs other selves to be a self. Interaction, exchange, and reciprocity undergird this formative and expressive process. This requires, however, that the self consumes what is offered by other selves, and that what the self offers is in turn consumed by other selves. Unlike those sharing a place, those admitted into shared space cannot be ignored because of the consumptive utility they presumably offer, and the degree of intimacy being sought dictates not only the scope and longevity of, but also admission to, the created space in question. Hence the need for transparency to examine and assess what is being offered in forming and expressing various identities.

But it is not full transparency. Like relationships within a shared place, those admitted to virtual spaces, for instance, both disclose and conceal. The information posted by an individual on a social network is selective and designed to both project a chosen identity and attract certain types of other individuals as possible candidates for admission into a shared space; friending and defriending are filters for constructing and defending virtual space. Such partial disclosure therefore requires requisite scrutiny and surveillance. Especially as greater intimacy is exchanged within a virtual space, the veracity of the disclosed information must be verified, a task made easier by the increasing volume of available information on individuals, and over which they have little or no control. Increasingly, the nomads of the emerging technoculture feel entitled to access such raw data, and feel cheated when it is either not available or they are denied access, for it impedes the construction and expression of identity.

Virtual formative and expressive spaces, then, are no more reliable or any less risky than those occurring in proximate places. And reliability and risk avoidance are valued highly, for dealing with disappointed expectations stemming from undisclosed or deceptive information is a waste of precious time. Consequently, there is an incentive to restrict the scope of virtual space in which greater control can be asserted. Avatars representing a range of experimental identities, for instance, may be unleashed to wander through virtual worlds encountering other fabricated identities. The need for transparency is diminished for the initially projected identities are often entirely fictitious constructs, but opportunities for exchange are increased. Mirroring their life in the real world, nomads are free to wander the vast expanses of cyberspace. These entirely virtual worlds, however, are not free from disappointment and risk. One's avatar can encounter deceptive, mean, and even vicious avatars.

Online games and computer simulations offer a safer option. Unlike avatars, the "others" one encounters are often software-generated figments. Within these virtual environments there is little, if any, need for transparency, but ample opportunities for exchange are provided that can be more easily controlled by the user; if a game or simulation goes wrong, hit reset. Still another option is socially programmed robots. An attractive or cuddly toy, often resembling a real or fictitious animal, contains a fairly sophisticated AI program. It has limited mobility, can read how it is being treated, and with a rudimentary vocabulary and other sounds simulates emotional reactions, indicates how it wants to be treated, and interacts with its users. Over time, its "behavior" adapts or changes in response to how it is "neglected" or "cared for." In sum, it is a combination of hardware and software that creates a suitable illusion of a "creation" that provides "companionship" and is "loved" by a large and growing number of satisfied customers, particularly among the young and elderly.[7]

Since identity is formed and expressed in association with others, the trajectory described above is troubling. In privileging space over place, the scope of association grows increasingly smaller. Relationships based on proximity are replaced by social networks, which are displaced by atavistic cohorts, which in turn are supplanted by simulations, games, and robotic companions. A winnowing process beginning with social networks concludes with projections of oneself onto virtual "objects," or, in the case of robots, a virtual space is accompanied by tactile stimulation. The self creates the associates which form and sustain the identity of the originating self. To invoke an admittedly unflattering image, what begins with a circle of snakes consuming each other's tails ends with a single snake eating its own.

It may be objected that my unease is overstated or misplaced. What I described above complements and supplements the process of forming and expressing the identities of flesh-and-blood human beings. Late modern nomads know the difference between the real and the virtual, despite the privileging of space over place and corresponding fascination with technology. Yet, as Sherry Turkle contends, "Technology proposes itself as the architect of our intimacies. These days, it suggests substitutions that put the real on the run."[8] Increasingly, more people are comfortable with a fabricated world, and are happy with the illusion of intimacy it provides and the ease with which technology can mitigate loneliness. Virtual and robotic companions are reliable and less likely to disappoint, thereby providing "relationships the way we want them."[9] And since in the virtual world identity is reduced to nothing but performance, these "companions" are "alive enough" to fit the bill.[10] To simply reassure that the nomadic inhabitants know the difference between the virtual and real is naive, for Turkle baldly states: "Gradually, we come to see our online life as life itself."[11] This change in perspective prompts the question: "Does virtual intimacy degrade our experience of the other kind and, indeed, of all encounters of any kind?"[12]

---

[7] See Sherry Turkle, *Alone Together: Why We Expect More Technology and Less from Each Other* (New York: Basic Books), Part One.
[8] Ibid., p. 1.
[9] Ibid., p. 12.
[10] See ibid., pp. 28–29, 35–66.
[11] Ibid., p. 17.
[12] Ibid., p. 12.

Should the answer to this question prove to be "yes," then alterity is diminished, if not threatened. Alterity is basically the recognition of the other *as other*. The other is a person we encounter, not an object we create in our own image and likeness. This other cannot be entirely mastered or manipulated, and regardless of how long or how well this other is known she or he retains a mystery and opaqueness that remains always hidden. If alterity is diminished or lost, then the quality of personal and social identities is degraded, for the associational contexts supporting their formative and expressive spaces are also weakened. People, of course, have often violated, rather than honored, alterity. I may wittingly or unwittingly, for instance, project upon friends or colleagues what I wish they would be rather than engaging with them for who they are. But, more often than not, my attempts are steadfastly and stubbornly resisted. This is why intimate relationships are filled with both joy and frustration. The resistance to such projection, however, weakens dramatically in digital domains. Participants in social networks can be removed from a virtual space; atavistic identities can be easily constructed, dismantled, and ignored; games and simulations can be entered, reprogrammed, and exited at will. The virtual or robotic "companion" provides an illusion of alterity since it is programmed to respond and offer requests or demands, but it is a simulacrum of intimacy for, over time, it comes to reflect the wishes and desires of its user. The virtual or robotic other is merely a technologically sophisticated mirror.

There is also some troubling anecdotal evidence that the answer to Turkle's question is in fact becoming "yes." In conducting interviews with teenagers over a 25-year period she notes a distinct shift in how the prospect of robotic companions are perceived.[13] Early on there was an insistence that robots could perform certain tasks in a highly efficient manner. What differentiated humans from robots were the relational and emotional imperfections of the former. Robots were not to be admitted into this realm of imperfection because they were incompetent to offer anything useful. In the latest interviews, there were teenagers wishing for robotic companions with whom they could discuss their most intimate issues, such as dating and friendships. It was assumed that since human behavior can be reduced to its underlying information, robots would have extensive databases from which they could provide more reliable advice and trustworthy counsel than that afforded by parents. Intelligent robotic confidants, it was assumed, would provide better guidance by avoiding mistakes stemming from limited information and human fallibility. In short, people are "risky" while robots are "safe."[14]

The newest generation of the emerging technoculture, the so-called digital generation, may be forming and expressing their nomadic identities somewhat like mirrors gazing at mirrors. Growing up in a world in which the virtual and robotic is often both preferred and easily accessible, they may not be able to recall or imagine the necessity of alterity in forming and expressing healthy identities, resulting in narcissistic tendencies which technological companions are unlikely

---

[13] See ibid., pp. 49–52.
[14] Ibid., p. 51.

to be able to counter. What the effects of these tendencies might be if they go unchecked or intensify over an extended period of time is currently unknown, but the initial signs are not encouraging. Maggie Jackson warns of an "impending dark age" characterized by "veneer and form," devoid of "depth and content."[15] Her prophecy is hopefully too dire, but as people sharing a place grow increasingly invisible and as the virtual is the preferred space where identity is formed and expressed, the emerging technoculture becomes a twilight zone inhabited by shadow dancers. The challenge for Christians is how they should engage with such a culture.

Opaque neighbors

Turkle contends that technology is beginning to shape our most intimate relationships and worries that they in turn are eroding the social bonds that bind people together. If this is the case, can technology be reoriented in ways that help sustain relationships and strengthen social bonds? Note that in posing this question there is no suggestion of refusing technology or withdrawing from the culture it is forging. The question is not a preamble of condemnation, but an invitation to engagement and reformation. It is especially important for Christians to keep this invitational tone in mind. Theologically, to pursue a blanket condemnation and withdrawal is tantamount to writing off the emerging technoculture as irredeemable, a curious claim to make, to say the least, about God's creation that Christians affirm (or should affirm) as good, despite its disfigurement by sin. Practically, if Christians were to surrender their computers, smart phones, and other gadgets, it is difficult to imagine how they or the world would be any better off. But what do Christians have to offer in engaging with the emerging technoculture? In short, they can persuade its nomadic inhabitants to become pilgrims.

Although the goal of the engagement being proposed and explored is not condemnation, the first step is nonetheless judgment. Judgment is a necessary prerequisite because it creates a space in which possibilities for a new and renewing ordering of human life and lives can be undertaken. For the purpose of this inquiry, two judgments may be briefly highlighted. First, prolonged or routine inattentiveness promotes moral indifference to that which is most immediate. When those sharing a proximate locale are perceived as hindrances in preserving one's preferred space, they are effectively rendered invisible, thereby promoting indifference. Such indifference in turn diminishes moral regard. Following Simone Weil, to attend to others is to be attentive to their good.[16] Focusing on

---

[15] Jackson, *Distracted*, p. 26.
[16] See Michael Ross, "Transcendence, Immanence, and Practical Deliberation in Simone Weil's Early and Middle Years," in E. Jane Doering and Eric O. Springstead, eds., *The Christian Platonism of Simone Weil* (Notre Dame, IN: University of Notre Dame Press, 2004), pp. 45–48.

the good of others requires a corresponding suspension of being self-oriented. Attentiveness, then, does not seek to dominate but is receptive, for the purpose is to know the good of the other, and to encounter that good *as it is* and not as might be preferred.[17] In this respect, attentiveness is similar to Josef Pieper's account of leisure.[18] Unlike preserving space, being attentive is *not* work but being openly receptive—being aware of what is most immediately at hand. For Weil, attention is ultimately the act of consenting to the world as it is, and learning to love it as such. Again, such love does not entail an immediate intimacy with every stranger one encounters, but it is an orientation that resists rendering the nearby invisible and reducing the needs and necessity of place to distractions to be avoided. Late modern nomads often devote considerable time, money, and interest in faraway causes and disasters while being oblivious to the crushing destitution a few blocks from where they currently work or reside. This effectively transforms those remote places into another chosen space requiring little prolonged attention, while rendering the proximate and immediate invisible.

The second, closely related, judgment involves the erosion and denial of alterity. When others are not given their due or fitting attention they are not afforded a corresponding moral consideration and obligation. The other makes moral demands, either implicitly or explicitly, to which I must respond. The one making these demands, however, is opaque, and I must be attentive in order to discern a response that is fitting to the good of this other. Consequently, I must also be attentive in a manner that allows the good of the other to be disclosed while preserving the opaqueness that protects the other *as* other. Otherwise, attentiveness is corrupted into a controlling act in which the other is reconstructed into my image, and the other's good reduced to a mere reflection of my good. As Murdoch, following Weil, contends, moral change can only occur by being attentive to the world, and the resulting decrease in egoism prompts an increased sense of that world consisting primarily of other people.[19] She goes on to argue that such attentiveness is a "just and loving" gaze that seeks to engage, rather than control, the other,[20] evoking a response that she characterizes as "obedience."[21] To be moral is to obediently respond to the good of a world that is encountered as a given other and not as a construct and projection of what we will it to be. When the other *as* other is lost, so is the possibility of moral change. The nomadic life, both wittingly and unwittingly, diminishes alterity. The other in a proximate place is effectively rendered an inert object to be ignored, thereby disclosing nothing of the good capable of making a moral demand. The other of preferred space is

---

[17] See Simone Weil, *Waiting for God* (New York: HarperCollins, 2001), pp. 99–117.

[18] See Chapter 7.

[19] See Iris Murdoch, *Metaphysics as a Guide to Morals* (London and New York: Penguin Books, 1993), pp. 52–53.

[20] See Iris Murdoch, *The Sovereignty of Good* (London and New York: Routledge, 2001), p. 33.

[21] See ibid., p. 39.

increasingly stripped of its opaqueness, eventually becoming the mirror of the one gazing. As Murdoch warns, as attentiveness and alterity declines, so too does the prospect for moral change—the amendment of life.

With these judgments a space is presumably created for recovering attentiveness and alterity and thereby creating the possibility of moral change or reorientation. But how best to take advantage of this new space? The language of baptism as a focal thing and practice may assist us. We may say that the act of baptism creates a space that preserves the necessity of place, and, in doing so, acknowledges the need for recovering attentiveness and sustaining alterity. The sacrament of baptism is a commanding presence within the space created by the church that is gathered in its Lord's name. Although the gathering of the church is not restricted to designated locales, it nonetheless must gather in a particular place. It must be gathered because the sacrament requires that it be attentive to the one being baptized, and such a loving gaze forbids the creation of any intrusive or competing spaces. The physicality of the act reinforces the requisite necessity of embodied presence in real time and shared place. The communicant, parents or sponsors, and priest must be gathered at the same particular place and time. Actual flesh and blood must past through real water. The congregation is gathered and attentive in this shared place and time. There can be no baptism at a distance, for it is not an act that can be performed remotely, nor should it be. There can be no substitutes or surrogates; a representative doll may not take the place of an infant. Baptism cannot occur in virtual space and time; baptizing an avatar is at best a simulacrum and at worst a parody, for no flesh, blood, or water is involved.[22] The gaze of the congregation must be immediate, for watching a video transmission in either real or virtual time at remote locations is to degrade the sacrament into a spectacle to be consumed at one's convenience. To be a focal thing, baptism requires attentiveness at a particular and shared place and time.

Baptism is also a rite of initiation into a community or, better, a communion (*koinonia*). Communication requires sustained attentiveness to the good of one another, for the principal operative pronoun is neither "you" nor "me," but "us." Baptism, however, delineates and delimits communication. In baptism an infant or believer is given back to God as the giver of life. This giving confirms that it is only before God that one is fully transparent, for it is God, and God alone, who can know one fully. The baptized one is returned and entrusted to the care of the community. This trust in turn requires that the opaqueness of the other with whom one communicates must be respected, for to strive for complete transparency that is reserved to God alone is both futile and destructive. To encounter the other *as other* requires a reserve or restraint from manipulation and control; the "us" of

---

[22] For a defense of "virtual baptism," see Douglas Estes, *SimChurch: Being the Church on the Virtual World* (Grand Rapids, MI: Zondervan, 2009), pp. 123–128. I do not find Estes' argument convincing because of his latent Manichean tendency to disparage the body in contending for the superiority of the soul or spirit that is not confined to constraints of place or time.

communication negates neither "you" nor "me." Alterity, then, necessarily entails mystery, for the other can never be known fully. And in such mystery lies the possibility of taking delight in the other *as* other, the outcome of a just and loving gaze that is receptive rather than dominating. Honoring an opaque alterity resists the futile quest for transparency often undertaken by the nomads of the emerging technoculture. As individuals sharing a created space disclose themselves, they inevitably disappoint, and one turns to creating an other that reflects back the self. Attentiveness is thereby effectively twisted into narcissistic inattention; the just and loving gaze becomes consuming, initially parasitic but eventually self-devouring. This inattention spills over into places whose inhabitants are distractions that are best ignored and rendered invisible. The focal practice of baptism helps recover an attentiveness to the world that is not populated by mirrors and specters, but by opaque others whom we can and should receive and communicate with as such.

Furthermore, baptism is an act of faith. We are prompted by faith to give our lives back to God as the giver of life. It is in faith that we are returned to live the life of the baptized. It is by faith that the community receives those whom God has entrusted into its care. Baptism embodies and confirms the belief that we are not our own, but belong to God; we are not self-made artifacts, nor are the others we encounter artifacts reflecting what we will them to be. As noted in Chapter 7, faith demonstrates our desire for the good that is God, and thereby entails a reordering of our lives in accordance with this desire. To desire God, for instance, requires that we also desire the good of others, for the love of God is inseparable from the love of neighbor. It is in and through faith, then, that attentiveness is enabled and alterity is respected. In confirming that our lives are not our own, the resulting just and loving gaze brings us out of ourselves to receive the other *as* other rather than as an object to be manipulated, controlled, and consumed. And, in being faithfully attentive, we also respect the other as an opaque person who, like ourselves, is transparent only to God and no one else. More broadly, we communicate the goods of creation with people that rightfully resist a consuming gaze that seeks to dominate, for since we do not belong to ourselves, then neither do we belong to anyone else. In short, the life of the baptized is one of faith and freedom, for in affirming that we belong *to* God we are freed to belong *with* others; others whom we may encounter and take delight in *as* other and not as projections and reflections of ourselves.

What difference does all this talk of baptism and faith make in how we might order our lives? Would such ordering result in a good life? And, for that matter, would preserving alterity and attentiveness necessarily promote moral change for the better? These are fair questions. Christians have often ordered their lives in ways that cannot be said to be good, and used their baptism and faith to justify acts that are unjustifiable. Attentiveness is often not welcomed, for the gaze fashions the recipient into an object of loathing and disgust. There is no reason to deny the validity of these objections. Yet, if they are accepted as reminders of traps to be avoided, these questions may be provisionally answered.

In offering such a response I return to the stories penned by Iris Murdoch and Marilynne Robinson.[23] In Murdoch's *An Accidental Man*, we met two characters, Austin and Ludwig. Austin stumbles from episode to episode, creating havoc in his wake. He has lost his job and moved in with a woman he does not love, pilfering her meager funds. His marriage is in shambles, and he is estranged from his son and older brother. Moreover, he is indirectly implicated in two suicides, and inadvertently kills a young girl while driving and covers up his culpability. Austin never admits responsibility for any of his acts, and in the end describes himself as a "victim," an "accidental man."[24] Ludwig's life is less chaotic, but nonetheless unsettled and episodic. As the story begins, he is engaged to a rich young woman and has a promising future as a gifted scholar. But he is a draft dodger, and his parents plead with him frantically to break off the marriage and return to America, a request he steadfastly refuses. At the end, however, he capitulates and returns home for reasons that are never entirely clear. Although it appears that he is ready to do his duty and honor his parents, his decision has also been shaped by a series of chance encounters and torturous indecision. Although Ludwig's moral wandering is less destructive, he too is an accidental man. Together, these two characters exemplify the accidental character of the late modern nomadic life in general and moral life in particular. They are insubstantial shadow dancers drifting from temporary space to temporary space, using those they come into contact with in cobbling together their haphazard lives. In their consistent and mutual inattentiveness there is also an incessant loss of alterity that reduces the other to little more than an object of passing necessity, a pattern that comes more pronounced when the cast of characters that Murdoch weaves together in her complex tale is enlarged.

Charlotte, the aunt of Ludwig's fiancée, is regarded by her family as a woman incapable of taking care herself. Consequently, they turn her into a project in which she can perform useful family duties such as housework and babysitting. Charlotte is rarely consulted while these plans are made, but she bitterly accepts a "family bond" that makes "her life seem arbitrary by comparison," and resigns herself to the prospect that she has "no private destiny."[25] Dorina, Austin's estranged wife, is another project. There is a scheme for how she might "save" Austin,[26] and while the conspiracy is being planned—one in which Dorina is assumed to play a major role—she wonders why they "behave as if I was not here."[27] The relationship between Mavis and Austin's older brother erodes, and she devotes herself to taking care of Austin. Despite his plea of victimhood, she knows he is a "vampire." Yet he cannot be blamed, for everyone uses others in constructing their "own kind of truth." Mavis will simply try to prevent his kind of truth from being "crushed."[28]

---

[23] See Chapter 6.
[24] See Iris Murdoch, *An Accidental Man* (London: Penguin), p. 429.
[25] See ibid., pp. 100–101.
[26] See ibid., p. 225.
[27] See ibid., pp. 208–209.
[28] See ibid., p. 429.

And, after all, she enjoys taking caring of Austin, for she had "always so much wanted a brother."[29] George, the father of Ludwig's fiancée, summarizes the loss of alterity in this story most succinctly while reflecting on his own marriage: "We've each surrendered our soul to please the other. Perhaps this doesn't matter. Perhaps this is love."[30]

The characters of this story may be said to meander from one temporary space to another in which they emotionally feed upon one another. In the process they are morally clumsy, creating one accident after another, in turn forming themselves and others as accidental people. Their mutual parasitism, however, does not nourish, but diminishes. As these characters consistently fail each other, they flee or discard the other, or reduce it to an object or project. In the end, each character is a soulless, shadowy, self-attentive wandering specter, devouring and being devoured. In their incessant drive to feed the ego, to be self-fulfilled, the characters become malnourished and unfulfilled, isolated and self-absorbed. Yet, can there be a self in the absence of a genuine other to whom one must be attentive? Murdoch's story—written before the advent of ubiquitous information and mobile technologies—is masterful because it discloses that these technologies have not created the nomadic drive for predatory self-fulfillment but exacerbate a diminishing attentiveness and alterity that was already operative. Imagine how *An Accidental Man* could be retold in light of smart phones, social networks, simulations, and robotic companions in which virtual spaces complement, supplement, and even supplant real places. At least in Murdoch's telling, the characters must make the effort and take the time to be in the same place to prey upon one another.[31] Yet what is most sobering about this story is that Murdoch suggests that accidental people is about the best that can be expected of late modern nomads. Clumsy, self-diminished parasites are at least preferable to crafty and wicked ones.

Is such pessimism warranted? If technology does not create accidental people but amplifies the problem, then perhaps it can be reoriented toward ameliorating the predicament by focusing attentiveness and thereby safeguarding alterity. Such a story, however, cannot be told on Murdoch's terms, for it is an account effectively devoid of faith. What is needed is an alternative narration in which the creation of real and virtual spaces does not supplant the priority of place. Robinson offers such an alternative narration.

Recall the relationship between John Ames and his namesake Jack.[32] John is 76 years old, and has lived all but two years in Gilead except when away attending college and seminary. This town has shaped him, for both good and ill. It is in this

---

[29] See ibid., p. 426.
[30] Ibid., p. 370.
[31] In fairness it should be noted that Murdoch often uses letter-writing as a means of interaction among her characters. Letters for Murdoch, however, presume a level of familiarity between the correspondents and prosaic craftsmanship that are frequently absent in emails, texting, tweeting and the like.
[32] See Marilynne Robinson, *Gilead* (New York: Picador, 2004).

place that he was born and raised, formed lifelong friendships, and was a minister to generations of residents. It is here where he married and buried his wife and daughter. He embodies both the virtues and vices of this community; he is generous and kindly, yet also shares its parochialism, judgmental outlook, and prejudices. John draws his life from this town. Jack has also been shaped by Gilead but, unlike John's experience, it has not been life-giving but life-taking. The town has imposed a moral standard against which Jack has been found wanting. He is judged to be an untrustworthy rogue and failed father, a destructive person best avoided. And since Jack either refuses or fails at any proffered attempts at reconciliation, he must leave. For John, Gilead is a hospitable place where he easily creates the spaces in which he lives and works, whereas for Jack it is a hostile place forcing him to wander and construct whatever temporary spaces he can manage.

When Jack tries to return to Gilead, John can only perceive and treat him as the failure he has been judged to be. All John sees in Jack is the embodiment of behavior he fears and loathes. Consequently, Jack can only be treated as the image of John's fear and loathing, and since the judgment is unceasing, no new space is created to perceive Jack as anything other than John's projection; he sees exactly what he is looking for, what he has created, and nothing more. In the absence of this new space there is also no prospect of forgiveness and reconciliation. It is only when John, much to his own surprise, begins to listen to Jack narrating his life since leaving Gilead that this new space begins to emerge. It is only when John begins to attend to Jack, consenting to who he is and not what John would prefer him to be, that he begins to see him in a just and loving gaze; he begins to receive Jack, rather than dominate and manipulate him. In that gaze, a judgment is pronounced against John's inattentiveness, and Jack becomes an other to be encountered as such.

The reader does not know what triggers John's new-found attentiveness, but it nonetheless preserves an alterity and creates a space in which reconciliation and forgiveness are made possible. Unlike the accidental characters of Murdoch's story, John and Jack leave, sharing a benediction that, in faith, preserves their bonds of shared place. Jack never becomes entirely transparent to John, and rightfully so, for judgment is only effective when the opaqueness of the other is preserved. In the absence of genuine alterity, judgment can only condemn and is unable to create a space in which new and renewing and possibilities might emerge. Jack's deeds are never dismissed, ignored, or indulged, but, in the just and loving gaze, forgiveness, reconciliation, and amendment of life are made possible. The story does not tell us whether or not these possibilities are ever realized. We do not know if Jack accepts the forgiveness offered to him, or if he seeks reconciliation and amends his life accordingly. But in the absence of a binding faith that is, at least in part, grounded in a particular place, no space for creating these possibilities would be forthcoming.

It may be objected that although Robinson has written a good story, it is largely irrelevant to the nomadic life of the emerging technoculture. It recalls a bygone age, technologically unsophisticated and less harried—a time when the constraints of place had not yet been effectively surmounted. The few direct allusions to technologies beginning to erode these limits are almost always negative. John, for instance, derides television as a device that gets in the way of friendship, and loathes the religious programs that simplify theology and diminish local ministry. Not a promising starting point for engaging late modern nomads.

To some extent, the objection is valid, but *Gilead* nonetheless offers a sobering reminder of the problem of distraction. When one is distracted, one cannot be attentive to the other, and in the absence of attentiveness the other is disfigured into the projected image of the beholder. Contemporary technologies merely amplify the ability to disfigure the other into a projected image, eventually dispensing with him altogether in favor of a more pliable and desirable robotic or virtual substitute. Moreover, *Gilead* reminds us that attentiveness requires a shared space that is lodged in a particular place. The just and loving gaze requires a mutual *and* physical presence.

Turkle insists that technology often masks what we really want, and we are therefore disappointed when it fails to satisfy relational needs that it is ill-equipped to fulfill. Consequently, we come to "expect more from technology and less from each other," resulting in a palpable neglect of the very relationships we crave.[33] In short, technology puts its users to work in creating and maintaining the spaces that distract our attention away from the places where we should be most attentive. Turkle rightfully has no desire to entertain any broad rejection or refusal of technology. Rather, she urges the adoption of "*realtechnik*," a skepticism of any "linear" notion of technological progress.[34] Such skepticism can help redirect technology in ways that do not hide our real wants and desires, that work for its users rather than vice versa. As Turkle asserts, "We deserve better. When we remind ourselves that it is we who decide how to keep technology busy, we shall have better."[35] The remaining chapters explore some possible ways to reorient technology toward keeping it busy in ways we decide, particularly in respect to the focal practices of Eucharist and Sabbath.

---

[33] See Turkle, *Alone Together*, pp. 294–295.
[34] See ibid., p. 294 (emphasis in original).
[35] Ibid., p. 296.

Chapter 9
Creation into Nothing: Nihilistic Power

The preceding chapter accentuated the personal. Individuals use various technologies to create spaces of selective intimacy, keeping at bay unwanted intrusions by strangers occupying common places. The scope of these spaces steadily shrink until eventually they are "shared" with virtual or robotic companions. The risky other is exchanged for a safer projected image of the self.

The personal is not unrelated to the political. The loss of alterity not only distorts relationships, but also disfigures civil governance. The problem at hand in this instance, however, is not a preference of space over place, but the privileging of information over narration. The task is not to create a political space, but to procure the requisite power to assert the will over and against competing assertions. In the emerging technoculture such power is obtained through the creation, dissemination, and manipulation of information. Politics is not telling and enacting the story of a good civil community, but constructing and portraying data that can garner sufficient consent and silence opposition.

A change in imagery may help to illustrate this shift in emphasis from the personal to the political. The preceding chapter began with the image of a busy airport in which individuals are talking or otherwise exchanging information incessantly, but not with each other. In contrast, imagine a large chamber in which people have gathered for a town-hall meeting. Presumably, they will have to talk with each other in this shared place. When the gavel is struck, the room is filled with a deafening cacophony of assertions and counter-assertions, often reduced to simple slogans. Global warming is catastrophic and needs to be stopped before it is too late. No, the problem is global cooling. The issue is climate change and how to prevent it. There is no such thing as cataclysmic climate change. It does not matter how climate may or may not change since technology will enable us to adapt as needed. Energy should only be produced from renewable sources. Drill wherever fossil fuels are extractable. Nuclear power is the answer: abundant energy with minimal environmental impact. Yeah, right, just pray there are no more earthquakes, tsunamis, design flaws, or human errors. And so on and so forth on virtually any and every conceivable issue.

The situation is exacerbated by media coverage and commentary by interested parties. Reporters describe what is occurring, spinning their reports either subtly or overtly in line with ideological commitments, or capturing attention and generating greater revenue. Bloggers churn out an endless stream of blogs, readers post comments, individuals tweet their preferences, and those with little time to spare merely click a thumbs up or down to indicate whether or not they like a particular assertion.

The cacophonous character of politics in the emerging technoculture stems from the goal of imposing the will by overwhelming contending assertions. This is accomplished by enhancing the superiority of a particular assertion to the detriment of alternatives. Public attention is captured and subsequent opinion shaped by those who concisely communicate their message and manipulate the ensuing debate. In short, the politics of the emerging technoculture is a twofold strategy of increasing the volume of one's voice while silencing opposing voices.

The problem is not that these contending assertions are uninformed. To the contrary, they are derived from an abundance of information. Data is collected regarding, for instance, global warming, cooling, climate change, environmental concerns and the like, and then interpreted and presented in ways that promote the interests of those making a particular assertion. Counter-interpretations and presentations promoting conflicting interests are in turn propounded. Hence the need to increase the volume in promoting one's assertion while also muting that of the opposition. There is, however, little, if any, opportunity to make normative evaluations of the contending assertions because there is no common narration against which such an assessment can be made. The ensuing disputes are not over the good of civil community, but over whose will shall prevail. The victors in these disputes are usually those who master the techniques of creating and disseminating information that demonstrate whose interests are purportedly benefited or harmed in a given assertion. Politics is essentially a battle fought with information designed to either persuade or discredit.

Nothing in the preceding paragraphs suggests that the emerging technoculture has corrupted politics. Rather, it exacerbates inherent tensions within the modern liberal political tradition in which the technoculture originated and is now coming into fruition. Within the modern liberal tradition there is a perennial tension between the one voice and the many.[1] Liberalism is committed to a plurality of voices or narrations of what constitutes the good life. Yet, in the absence of a single voice or narration that determines the good of civil community, it is plagued with the perpetual strife of the many, eventually degenerating into anarchy. Imposing one narration through sheer force is tyrannous, the chief anathema of liberals. The singular narrative required for political ordering is obtained through the consent of the governed as seen in such schemes as Hobbes' Leviathan, Rousseau's Social Contract, and Rawls' overlapping consensus. The liberal solution allows the many voices to narrate their contending accounts of the good life within private spaces through the right of association, and even allows their voices to be heard publicly through the right of free speech, but ultimately the many voices cannot trump that of the one. The singular political narration can, for various reasons, be amended or expanded to include certain claims of selected voices among the many so long as there is sufficient consent within the civil community.

---

[1] See, e.g., Colin Gunton, *The One, the Three, and the Many: God, Creation and the Culture of Modernity* (Cambridge, UK: Cambridge University Press, 1993).

What is troubling is the prospect that the emerging technoculture cannot sustain such consent because it effectively prevents the requisite substantive narration in the public sphere, filling the ensuing void with information. In debates over energy production, for instance, there is little appeal made to how various sources are most in line with shared values and common goods. Rather, there are varying assessments of competing costs and benefits—less pollution, for instance, versus cheaper energy—and various interests assert their preference by shaping public opinion and lobbying or otherwise influencing legislative bodies or other relevant governmental agencies.

The effective exclusion of normative narration in the political domain does not mean that it does not occur, only that it is confined to private spheres. Private associations may narrate normative accounts of the good of civil community. If such associations enter the political domain to implement their respective accounts, however, their normative narrations must be reduced to information demonstrating desirable benefits and advantages. To return to the example of energy production, the dispute is not between proponents contending that ecological harmony is the good of civil community thereby requiring green sources of energy, as opposed to those contending that affluence is the predominant good, thereby requiring cheap sources of energy. Rather, both must reduce their respective narrations to information asserting comparative costs and benefits: going green will save the members of the civil community from catastrophic climate change; fossil fuels will save them from economic contraction and declining standards of living. Hence the ensuing strategy of simultaneously disseminating persuasive information and discrediting counter-information.

It may be argued that what I am describing is not the absence of a common or dominant political narration, but the narrative of rights. In order to avoid tyranny, the state should refrain from imposing a normative narrative on members of the civil community. It instead provides neutral procedures in which the rights of individuals and groups may be asserted and assessed. Should a consensus emerge, the state in turn protects the exercise of certain prescribed rights. Normative narrations of the good may be told within the confines of private associations, but any forthcoming political assertions must be translated into the language of rights. For example, the narration of a good civil community as a green one is couched in the language of individuals having a right to clean air and water, whereas the counter-narrative of affluence appeals to cheap energy as enabling the right of economic opportunity. Since these assertions of rights are often in conflict, the state provides procedures for peaceful resolution, and uses its coercive power to protect any ensuing rights that might emerge from these resolutions. Hence the cacophonous character of late modern politics, since rights emerge out of the power to assert the will of one over another rather than appealing to normative standards or convictions regarding the good of civil community. In short, the narrative of late liberalism is that right trumps good in the political sphere.

The language of late liberal political rights, however, is *not* narration in any formal sense. A narrative requires an end or *telos* that is judged to be good, and requisite acts must accord with achieving this good. A green civil community cannot be achieved by drilling anywhere and everywhere, nor can an affluent civil community be achieved by constraining economic growth. The procedural establishment and protection of rights requires no such teleological grammar and normative vocabulary, for they are based on what civil community wills and not necessarily what many of its members believe to be good. Indeed, exercising rights requires the suspension of any formal moral judgment by the state. Representatives of the state do not (or should not) scold those building windmills or oil derricks if they have a right to do so. Since rights are established through the power of those asserting their will and are protected by the coercive power of the state, they are akin to information that has been distilled from private narrations that are inadmissible in the political realm.

Again, the emerging technoculture is not the inventor of rights language. Rather, it instantiates the trajectory of political liberalism within which it originated, and exacerbates the proliferation of contending private goods from which political rights are derived. As argued in the previous chapter, in privileging space over place, the emerging technoculture comprises ever more temporary, quixotic, and narrowing associations predicated on the changing needs and desires of nomadic individuals. The resulting narrations of the good are thereby highly fluid, tentative, and increasingly diminutive. The scope of the various narrations of the good inevitably shrink for, given the nomadic life of the emerging technoculture, such discourse cannot be about "we" but "me." The resulting politics is a perpetual contest of contending rights, conducted by temporary and expedient coalitions of like-minded people. Consequently, the politics of the emerging technoculture is one of constant flux, action and reprisal; the greens get their policies this legislative session, only to have them reversed in the next, prompting a new round of conflict. In this political scheme there is a lot of talking, both to assert and discredit, but little conversing in order to persuade or dissuade—an abundance of information but no narration.

The politics of late modernity stems from its underlying nihilism and historicism.[2] The will to power, as expressed predominantly through attempts at constructing history, is played out through an endless cycle of resentment and revenge. Those gaining power are resented by those losing it, who in turn plot their revenge to seize it back, in turn creating another round of resentment and revenge, and so on. The liberal solutions noted above were designed to prevent these cycles from breaking out into extensive acts of violence. This task was entrusted to the universal and homogenous state. Initially, the role of the state was to order political governance in accordance with the good of civil community. Since there was often a broad consensus regarding the normative content of the good, the role of the state, at least ideally, was to prevent such narration from either atrophy or unwarranted imposition on often very small or weak, minorities through legislation, policies, and protection of civil rights. As the consensus of

---

[2] See Chapter 1.

a dominant political narration began to weaken through the growing power of minorities and other self-interested private associations, the role of the state shifted to ensuring procedural mechanisms for identifying, legislating, and protecting a growing range of rights for groups and individuals. The proliferation of such rights is often perceived to be imposed at the expense of other self-interested parties, promoting a seemingly escalating and endless cycle of resentment and revenge. In such a scheme the state can, at beast, contain the more virulent aspects of this cycle, but, as Arendt recognized, cannot break it.[3]

The emerging technoculture again exacerbates this situation. In addition to diminishing and disbursing the scope of private normative narrations of the good that are translated into political information in respect to establishing and protecting rights, it also erodes the coercive power of the state. Nomads do not want to be fettered by political constraints on their mobility, be it physical, economic, social, or imaginative. The scope and intensity of this desire is reflected in the state's growing incapacity to protect, much less control, the flow of capital, finance, and labor across its borders without recourse to illiberal policies and practices. At the very moment when the coercive power of the state is needed to contain a growing range of political conflicts, the nomadic inhabitants it is attempting to govern are effectively withering its capability to exercise such power. At worst, this diminished capability may lead to pervasive cultural conflict on a global scale,[4] or at best promote the demise of the nation-state in favor of the market-state[5] to better accommodate the needs of late modern nomadic inhabitants. Even if this presumably better option should prevail, however, it is still fraught with a daunting political challenge. Since late liberal politics cannot break the cycle of resentment and revenge, political governance will be hard-pressed to contain, much less diminish the intensity of, a simmering, sullen anger underlying and pervading the politics of the emerging technoculture as reflected in its increasingly vitriolic and uncivil rhetoric. Should the heat of this anger reach a critical temperature, the temptations of either permitting what is tantamount to anarchical struggles among competing narrations of the good to determine which shall dominate or tyrannically imposing a selected narration will be hard to resist.

The cause of this predicament, in part, is a result of the mistaken belief that information is an adequate substitute for narration as the principal means or tool of political ordering. In the following sections I examine why this mistaken belief is dangerous, and argue for an approach that enables derivative narrations of the good back into political discourse, but in a manner that avoids either anarchical struggle or tyrannical imposition.

---

[3] See Chapter 3.

[4] See, e.g., Samuel P. Huntington, *Clash of Civilizations and the Remaking of World Order* (New York: Touchstone, 1997).

[5] See, e.g., Philip Bobbitt, *The Shield of Achilles: War, Peace, and the Course of History* (New York: Knopf, 2002), and *Terror and Consent: The Wars for the Twenty-First Century* (New York: Knopf, 2008).

Creativity, indifference, and sullenness

The political ordering of the emerging technoculture combines banal cheerfulness with simmering anger. On the one hand, its nomadic inhabitants treat politics with casual disregard. Many often do not bother to participate in political processes unless their self-interests are directly at stake. Politics is, at best, a nuisance to be endured and avoided whenever possible. On the other hand, when these interests are threatened, the resulting political action discloses a deep, underlying anger. The ensuing political rhetoric is often vitriolic and hyperbolic; Tea Partiers, for instance, are written off as reactionary supremacists while Wall Street occupiers are dismissed as lazy whiners. Or, more occasionally, protests escalate into violent riots. When interests collide like this, politics as a process of discerning the ordering of civil community degenerates into a Manichean, even apocalyptic struggle between purported forces of good and evil.

This seemingly contradictory combination of banal cheerfulness and simmering anger should not be surprising. There is nothing novel about the politics of the emerging technoculture. The historicism and nihilism that has dominated modernity have not been dethroned or even seriously challenged. Late modern nomads continue to construct their history, albeit in more fragmented and tenuous ways, and they continue to assert a nihilistic will to power, albeit in a shriller and more brazen manner. Although historicism and nihilism are related, inevitably tensions arise when there is little consensus over what kind of history should be constructed, or insufficient power can be mustered to impose one will over another. As noted above, the liberal solution was to sublimate a potentially destructive nihilism with political procedures that do not privilege one moral preference for a particular history over another; in the political sphere, right trumps good. And as also noted above, the emerging technoculture is effectively fraying this liberal solution as a growing scope of rights are enacted, derived from an expanding range of narrowing narrations of the good. In short, the emerging technoculture amplifies the cycle of resentment and revenge.

What is new about the politics of the emerging technoculture is the premise that information can be entirely substituted for narration in sustaining a political order, or, in other terminology, in constructing a history and sublimating underlying nihilistic impulses. The liberal procedural solution worked in the past because political rights were derived from the narration of a dominant private good, or an overlapping narration of compatible goods. With an expanding range of narrated but narrowly construed private goods, however, the procedural mechanism is taking on an increasingly heavy burden that it is ill-equipped to bear. As the scope of private narrations of the good decline and come into conflict, a corresponding proliferation of conflicting political rights in the political sphere occurs. Consequently, politics is not taken seriously as a mechanism for ordering the good of civil community, for it is correctly perceived as little more than a public arena in which contending nihilistic wills to power compete through a series of temporary and expedient coalitions. The political structures within the emerging technoculture simultaneously grow more pervasive and eviscerated, for in their dispersion to accommodate greater amounts of information required in establishing and protecting rights, they in effect grow weaker in terms of governance. When politics pervades virtually every aspect of life because it is the principal means of asserting, rather than sublimating, the nihilistic will to power, then it effectively governs nothing of any lasting importance.[6] The emerging technoculture exacerbates a rapid depletion of normative capital stored in private narrations of the good while paying virtually no attention to their renewal. The ensuing acerbic and endless cycle of resentment and revenge is, again, not surprising.

Information alone cannot sustain civil community. Following Arendt, if a civil community cannot narrate its political order, then its politics deteriorates into, at best, uncivil bickering, and, at worst, perpetual strife. Politics is no longer deliberative discourse seeking discernment, but declarative assertions intent on imposing and silencing. Politics is no longer speech but power exercised to the satisfaction of those seizing it. As Arendt warns, when politics displaces speech with power, the cycle of resentment and revenge cannot be broken, for the uncertainty of forgiving and promising derived from speech cannot be seriously entertained as an alternative to the certainty of vengeance as an unadulterated display of power. Moreover, the emerging technoculture cannot prevent this late liberal slide into cyclical resentment and revenge, for it has no narrative to offer to restore the primacy of political speech. Indeed, it accelerates the momentum by privileging information to the virtual exclusion of any substantive narration that can bind civil community together. Consequently, its nomadic inhabitants bounce back and forth between banal cheerfulness and simmering anger, hoping that a politics of asserting conflicting rights can somehow maintain itself without overt recourse to the coercive power of the state.

There are three indicators that disclose this strained tension between cheerfulness and anger: creativity, indifference, and sullenness. *Creativity* is arguably one of the hallmarks of the emerging technoculture.[7] Information is easily created and readily disseminated, and it is shaped and projected in ways that express who one is, or at least how one wishes to appear to others. Some individuals, for instance, spend a great deal of time carefully designing and crafting their personal websites in order to make a good impression on visitors, or others invent elaborate avatars to express their alter egos. More generally, the consumption of goods and services are vital components in creating one's lifestyle. The selection of a particular bistro, car, computer, clothing, and so on reveals something about the preferences or taste of the owner, or may indicate a modest or radical change of lifestyle. Using technology in creatively crafting and presenting who one is, or aspires to become, has emerged for late modern nomads as a widespread and laudable undertaking.

---

[6] See Oliver O'Donovan's account of "totalizing politics" in *The Ways of Judgment: The Bampton Lectures, 2003* (Grand Rapids, MI, and Cambridge, UK: Eerdmans, 2005), ch. 13.

[7] For a more extensive and critical assessment of creativity, see Brent Waters, *This Mortal Flesh: Incarnation and Bioethics* (Grand Rapids, MI: Brazos, 2009), ch. 9.

This undertaking is, in most respects, harmless. Creating and maintaining one's image may prove time-consuming, but there are certainly worse ways to spend one's time. Yet the seemingly innocuous quality may hide a more troubling concern. Jacques Ellul insists that late moderns have displaced the word with image.[8] This displacement does not merely reflect a change in preference, but indicates a more encompassing cultural transformation that is not only unable or unwilling to narrate, but is also hostile to narration itself. Imagery is what the nomads of the emerging technoculture demand, for the image is temporary, lacking duration and placement. Since the image is oriented to sight, it enables action, possession, and mastery, thereby committing humans to the dominance of manipulative techniques. Or, in Ellul's words, "[s]ight leads us simultaneously along the paths of separation and division, of intervention and efficiency, and of artificiality."[9] It is through artifice that late moderns create their world and themselves in the process.

The problem, according to Ellul, is not that the image is not real, but that late moderns conflate reality with truth.[10] It is a dangerous conflation, for the image is related to reality, whereas the word is ordered to truth. The word, unlike information, communicates rather than conveys, for it, unlike an image, is directed toward particular people, anticipating a response. Truthful discourse can therefore never be reduced to underlying information. The world—through speech, language, and, most importantly, narration—interprets reality. In the absence of the word, the ensuing social life becomes increasingly fragmented, consumerist, and ultimately violent in reaction to an uninterpreted world. This fragmentation, consumerism, and violence are reinforced by media and information technologies that have come to dominate entertainment, business, and education. The emerging technoculture is literally saturated by images, and this saturation produces "visually oriented people,"[11] nomads increasingly dependent on techniques to support their mobility and project their self-images. Moreover, technique is not confined to personal pursuits and interpersonal relationships, but pervades more expansive social and political associations. Politics, for instance, is reduced to a process of assessing inputs and outputs rather than implementing any moral considerations.

The triumph of image does not merely reflect a preference, but, as Ellul warns, also indicates contempt for language and hatred of the word.[12] The contempt is seen in the reduction of language to the transmission of information, stripping discourse of any normative meaning and transforming it into an instrument of power and domination. The hatred is expressed, ironically, in a purported love for freedom. Yet, since the word is hated, the truth to which it is ordered is also

---

[8] See Jacques Ellul, *The Humiliation of the Word* (Grand Rapids, MI: Eerdmans, 1985).
[9] Ibid., p. 12.
[10] See ibid., pp. 27–28.
[11] See ibid., pp. 149–150.
[12] See ibid., ch. 4.

effectively despised. Consequently, the love of freedom becomes an endless expression of creativity. Everyone is encouraged to always and everywhere be creative and is celebrated for this, but the outcome is not important. Since truth has been rejected, there is no standard by which to judge if a particular act is or is not creative. It is the effort, the act itself, that counts. Yet, when everything is creative, then nothing is, resulting in a series of empty outbursts of self-indulgent expression, and culminating in public spectacles that merely flatter its participants because there is no greater truth to capture their attention. Political spectacle in the emerging technoculture, for instance, is little more than its nomads pausing to celebrate themselves as the ones for whom they have been waiting.

As Arendt contends, banality is a fertile field for spawning a thoughtless evil, and the initial sprouting is *indifference*. The issue at stake is not indifference *per se*. There are many things about which one can and should be apathetic. It should make no difference, for example, if my colleague's favorite color is red or blue. This is not a preference requiring any judgment on my part, much less that of the broader civil community. What is at stake is a pervasive indifference that promotes a myopic moral vision restricted to narrowing spheres of immediate association. This indifference stems partly from privileging space over place, as noted in the previous chapter. Highly mobile individuals assume that the places where they live and work are temporary and transient. Consequently, they may not be personally invested in these locales while having an interest in more remote locations. I may not care, for instance, whether energy comes from green or fossil sources so long as my favorite resort remains unaffected.

Associations based on temporary spaces of shared interests expand the range of indifference. Since the interests of individuals and groups often conflict, the ill-effect on others caused by asserting one's preference is unfortunate but necessary collateral damage incurred when asserting one's will. There is, in short, an indifference to those who must bear the costs of necessity in constructing a desirable history. Green energy policies, for example, are required to prevent climate change, and slower economic growth and less affluent lifestyles are a necessary cost. The counter-contention is that cheap energy is needed to promote economic growth and greater affluence for more people, and pollution is thereby an unavoidable cost. The trajectory of these spaces of association, however, is one of contraction. Eventually, they may culminate in little more than a projection of oneself. Consequently, the politics of the emerging technoculture may degenerate to one conducted by habitual mirror-gazers; the personal becomes political with a vengeance. I may be entirely ambivalent about energy policies and completely indifferent to their social and economic consequences so long as I don't have to look at windmills or oil derricks on a daily basis.

The implicit belief that information can suffice for narration again helps to explain, in part, this contraction of moral vision and accompanying expansion of indifference. Information expedites judgment. In the absence of information, judgments can either not be made or become little more than random determinations. If we do not know whether or not renewable sources can provide an adequate supply of energy or how much fossil fuel is available and exploitable, how can a judgment be made between competing policies? In addition, the value of information increases in proportion to its immediate utility. So-called "information" about environmental degradation or energy needs 500 years in the future is of virtually no use in making judgments about current policies because it is little more than conjecture. Information about these concerns a decade into the future is of greater utility, and information concerning a recent bankruptcy of a solar energy firm or an oil spill is even more useful. Receiving information on how much I owe the gas and electricity companies is highly useful in determining where I set the thermostat. As the value of information increases, the scope of moral vision narrows, thereby increasing the range of indifference in making required judgments. If one were to indulge in speculation about environmental and energy needs 500 years into the future, virtually every imagined human and, for some, virtually every living creature would fall within an expansive moral vision; the zero utility of such information produces a corresponding indifference. To set an energy policy prohibiting coal-mining within 10 years requires indifference to those whose livelihood depends on this industry, or a policy allowing unbridled drilling in wilderness areas entails indifference to those wishing to preserve its pristine nature; conflicting data must be weighed in making policy judgments, and such judgments necessarily entail varying rates of indifference. When I reset my thermostat, I am indifferent to where everyone else is setting theirs; high utility produces widespread indifference.

Although information is needed in making judgments, it is neither permanent nor indisputable. Information changes over time, thereby altering its utility and subsequent judgments. Technological innovations show much promise for producing more reliable and cheaper energy from solar sources within 10 years, while breakthroughs in producing coal-based fuels that produce little pollution are equally promising. After a few months I note that the price of gas and electricity has fallen, so I reset my thermostat to a more comfortable level. New information alone, however, does not resolve disputes regarding ensuing judgments, for conflicting values still come into play. Technological innovation does not determine whether green or fossil fuels should be produced because there is still an array of conflicting values and interests in both options. My wife and I may argue about where to set the thermostat in light of falling gas and electricity prices, for I value comfort while she prefers frugality. Consequently, new information does not resolve conflict, or, more broadly, break the cycle of resentment and revenge. Following an election, a new energy policy favoring one option over the other is adopted, and is changed again in a subsequent election; my wife and I are constantly resetting the thermostat at different levels. And on and on it goes.

Given the preference of information over narration, the irresolute and acrimonious character of political debate is intensified, particularly given the growing proficiency at quickly creating and disseminating information. Information is a culprit because it has become a principal political tool in asserting the will to power over contenders; or, following Alasdair MacIntyre, interminable moral and political disputes are tantamount to civil wars fought with other means.[13] Since information is only a means or, in MacIntyre's analogy, a weapon, in asserting one's will over another, it has no inherent normative claim on the user, beneficiary, or target. Information is used, abused, disputed, or ignored, and then disposed of by disputants in endless cycles of resentment and revenge. In contrast, narration makes a normative claim on both the narrator and audience, and therefore cannot be as easily manipulated and tossed away. When confronted with a narrative of the good of civil community, for instance, we cannot simply ignore it; some judgment regarding its veracity must eventually be made. Narration must be either, affirmed, rejected or refused. As such, narration becomes further removed from the political sphere of the emerging technoculture; its derivative moral claims grow increasingly faint and unintelligible to nomadic disputants. As information is used increasingly to fill the resulting void, not only do political conflicts grow more interminable and shriller, but the range of indifference also expands.

Indifference, however, both cloaks and prompts a more insidious sullenness.[14] In many respects, the sullen mood of the emerging technoculture is the underlying source for the seemingly contradictory characteristics of banal cheerfulness and angry indifference described above. According to Borgmann, "[s]ullenness is both passive and aggressive, both indolent and resentful. It manifests itself both in obvious and social maladies and in diffused and individual symptoms."[15] These symptoms include rising levels of private and public debt, mushrooming deficits, declining voter turnout and political participation in general, rising unemployment, acerbic conflicts over a variety of divisive social issues, drug abuse, declining birthrates, and greater recourse to litigation.[16] On the one hand, these symptoms disclose a pervasive indolence. To be indolent is not to be merely lazy or lethargic, but denotes a sense of powerlessness, despondency, and cynicism that is seen in an aversion to assume responsibility for one's actions, because ultimately it makes no difference how one acts. Hence the passive behavior of not bothering to vote because it does not matter which inept or corrupt politicians are in power. On the other hand, these symptoms reveal a deep resentment that is manifested in two ways. First, individuals resent the imposition of unwanted burdens, such as parental obligations, resulting in growing numbers of couples in affluent societies that are childless by choice. Second, individuals shift blame away themselves, as seen in characterizing the unemployed as lazy or villainizing investors for creating unemployment.

This resentment is played out in and through a politics that is simultaneously defensive and retaliatory. One group attempts to protect its interests through enacting

---

[13] See Alasdair MacIntyre, *After Virtue: A Study in Moral Theory* (Notre Dame, IN: University of Notre Dame Press, 2007), ch. 2.

[14] The following description of sullenness draws on and expands the summary of Borgmann's account in Chapter 2.

[15] Albert Borgmann, *Crossing the Postmodern Divide* (Chicago, IL, and London: University of Chicago Press, 1992), pp. 6–7.

[16] See ibid., pp. 7–11.

favorable legislation, policies, and rights. Contending groups react by attempting to block these initiatives while also promoting their own causes, prompting further retaliation and intransigence by the first group, and so on. Consequently, the political battles of defensive maneuvering and retaliatory strikes are interminable for no law, policy, or right is permanent and they can be overturned in line with the vicissitudes of changing circumstances, manipulation of public opinion, and shifting power configurations. No issue is ever closed because, with sufficient power, it can always be reopened. In the politics of the emerging technoculture, judgment does not create a new space, but merely indicates that one round of conflict has ended and a new one is beginning. Moreover, should some perceive that a late liberal political process is an ineffective means of asserting their will to power, then the battle can be taken to the streets. Generally, these spectacles are peaceful and harmless, designed to capture the attention of the media but, with sufficient provocation and pent-up resentment, the streets become the scene of violent rioting and confrontation. This anarchic state of affairs, however, is intolerable over a prolonged period of time, and eventually either the mob or the state prevails, and whichever side wins, it will, most usually, impose illiberal measures to consolidate and assert its power.[17]

Ironically, the emerging technoculture promotes a politics that cannot sustain the mobile and autonomous nomads it seeks to support. The freedom that greater mobility and autonomy purportedly enables is dissipated in an endless cycle of resentment and revenge. Since this cycle cannot be broken, individuals may withdraw into increasingly small, insular, associations that seek to ignore the surrounding political struggles. Or the freedom afforded by greater mobility and autonomy may be surrendered for the sake of security. Although the cycle of resentment and revenge cannot be broken, it can be contained by the coercive power of the state. The emerging technoculture sets the stage for, as Grant feared, the tyranny of the universal and homogenous state, or worse, as Arendt worried, a thoughtless slide into totalitarianism. As Arendt contends, extreme individualism, isolation and "lack of normal social relationships" precede tyranny.[18] More pointedly, she insists: "Totalitarian movements are mass organizations of atomized, isolated individuals."[19] The nomads of the emerging technoculture appear to be on their way to becoming candidates for such organization. Again, ironically, the same technologies that enable nomadic mobility and autonomy can just as easily be used to constrain and control through ubiquitous surveillance and monitoring.

It must be stressed that the politics of the emerging technoculture is a trajectory and *not* a fate. A change in course is possible. But if such a change is to occur, then it is paramount to find a way of breaking the cycle of resentment and revenge. Exploring such a possibility is the topic of the following section.

---

[17] See, e.g., Hannah Arendt, *On Revolution* (New York: Viking Press, 1965).

[18] See Hannah Arendt, *The Origins of Totalitarianism* (San Diego, CA: Harvest Books, 1968), pp. 316–317.

[19] Ibid., p. 323.

Narration and natality

As Arendt argues, the cycle of resentment and revenge can only be broken by the twin practices of forgiving and promising.[20] To be effective, however, these practices must be embedded in a fitting narrative. This is precisely the problem with late liberal politics: it is embedded in the narration of overcoming mortality through the construction of an immortal history. This construction requires an assertive will to power that is exhibited through mastery, resulting in an endless cycle of resentment and revenge since there are contending narrations regarding how history should be constructed.

Arendt's solution is to recover speech as the basis of politics. Such a recovery requires a narration of natality instead of power and mastery. An orientation toward natality opens up the prospect of new and renewing possibilities, for the ensuing political action is not dedicated to the futile effort of overcoming mortality. Since political action is no longer predicated on the will to power, forgiving and promising can break the cycle of resentment and revenge, for they are practices that open a space for new and renewing possibilities. Arendt is aware that her proposition is disquieting, for she is proposing that the certainty of vengeance be exchanged for the uncertainty of forgiving and promising—people are, after all, often unforgiving and frequently break their promises. It is a hard sell to late moderns who are unable to imagine a politics in which the threat of coercion is not ever-present. It is a harder sell within the emerging technoculture, given its privileging of information over narration. Since speech is ordered to truth, narration is immalleable but ambiguous because truth can never be known in its entirety and thereby mastered.[21] In contrast, information is distinct but pliable, and therefore a useful tool in asserting power, control, and mastery. Consequently, the emerging technoculture unwittingly reinforces a preference for the certainty of vengeance over the uncertainty of forgiving and promising.

Despite these daunting challenges, Arendt's proposal is well worth pursuing. As was noted in Chapter 3, however, there are two weaknesses that need to be addressed. First, Arendt tries to extract Jesus' teaching on forgiveness from its theological milieu and transplant it into a Kantian host, presuming that although people can no longer pray together, they can reason together. Yet she fails to acknowledge the extent to which any common reason has been sequestered from the political realm. Given the primacy of the will to power that inevitably leads to conflict, there is no common reason enabling late moderns to think together. Consequently, the requisite narration for supporting the practices of forgiving and promising is not forthcoming, and they are reduced to ineffectual political rights and duties enforced by the coercive power of the state. Second, Arendt dismisses society as a modern wasteland of banal production and consumption. Her curt dismissal is derived from her bifurcation of civil community into the superior

---

[20] See Chapter 3.
[21] See Ellul, *The Humiliation of the Word*, pp. 22–26.

political and inferior private spheres. All public associations are therefore by definition political while all others are private. This means, however, that there are effectively no public spaces free from unending and divisive conflict, so again there is no space in which a political narration enabling forgiving and promising may occur.

In order to demonstrate the potential efficacy of forgiving and promising, we must turn our attention to the society Arendt despises, reconceptualizing it as comprising a series of overlapping *public* associations that are neither political nor private. These associations are not unrelated to politics and private interests, but they are public spaces mediating them. Ironically, it is the oases that Arendt laments as isolated pockets of civil life that provide the most promising locales for rejuvenating the surrounding political desert of the emerging technoculture. It is within these oases that an account of the good oriented toward natality may be narrated and lived out. The goal is not to impose this narration on the surrounding desert, but to demonstrate ways in which speech, rather than power, may be recovered derivatively, thereby opening the possibility for forgiving and promising to emerge as political practices. Or, to use Borgmann's terminology, focal communities can provide public places that simultaneously reorder the values and desires of private individuals and reorient, through exemplary demonstration, political policies and practices accordingly.

The church is an example of such a focal community, and it commands most of my attention in the remainder of this chapter. I am examining the church not only because I regard it as my principal audience, but also to demonstrate why forgiving and promising cannot be separated from their theological moorings. As I argue below, this is the case, in brief, because these practices are predicated on the gift of divine grace and not the handiworks of human willing and action. In this respect, a community oriented toward natality and the prospect of new and renewing possibilities is one that is leisurely receptive rather than frenetically creative. I hold up the church as an example of a focal community with much humility, even embarrassment. Throughout much of its history the church has often failed to embody the forgiveness it champions, or exemplify the accompanying need for promise-keeping. Moreover, the church has, on both its left and right wings, largely aped the emerging technoculture's banal cheerfulness and simmering anger, purportedly justifying the former as creative evangelism[22] and the latter as prophetic indignation.[23] Yet these failings stress all the more the need for a theological narration of forgiving and promising as gifts of grace and not Pelagian-inspired willpower. It is, perhaps, as a treasure in an earthen vessel that makes the church a potentially compelling and suggestive focal community.

---

[22] See, e.g., Douglas Estes, *SimChurch: Being the Church in the Virtual World* (Grand Rapids, MI: Zondervan, 2009); for an excellent critique, see Tim Challies, *The Next Story: Life and Faith after the Digital Explosion* (Grand Rapids, MI: Zondervan, 2011).

[23] See, e.g., Jim Wallis, *God's Politics: Why the Right Gets It Wrong and the Left Doesn't Get It* (New York: HarperCollins, 2005).

As the phrase suggests, a "focal community" is an association that is organized in accordance to what Borgmann describes as "focal things" and sustains itself through fitting "focal practices."[24] A family is an example of a focal community that is organized around focal things, such as meals, and its members perform focal practices to sustain the things in question, such as preparing the meals, setting the table, and cleaning up afterward. Sharing a meal with one's family is admittedly a mundane activity, but it promotes practicing such virtues as cooperation ("I'll cook, you clean up"), attentiveness to quality (good recipes require attending to details and skillful execution), self-denial (even though I hate broccoli I'll prepare this dish because my wife loves it), and hospitality, especially when guests are present. Most importantly, the meal promotes conversation. A good family meal is not shared in silence.

I am not suggesting that if a family eats together, all will be well. Rather, in combination with other mundane household practices, it exemplifies the ordering of an association based on speech rather than coercion. Family members do not gather for a meal because they fear being incarcerated if they fail to do so; there is no law forcing me to cook my wife's favorite broccoli dish. This does not mean that parents do not have the authority to compel the behavior of their children, including appropriate discipline. If Sally and Sam refuse their mother's instruction to stop playing the video game and set the table, they lose their playing privileges for a few days. This does not imply that families are free from any coercion or even abuse, but this should be regarded as a failure to be avoided and not a model to be emulated.

Moreover, since households are predicated on speech, they create social settings in which forgiving and promising are routinely practiced. It is difficult to imagine how a family could function in a setting in which forgiveness is never offered or received. The familial setting also demonstrates vividly why forgiving is vacuous and ineffective if it is not linked with promises to change one's behavior. I cannot expect my wife to forgive me for botching the broccoli dish unless I promise to quit sabotaging the recipe. A parent cannot forgive a teenage son for wrecking the car, if he refuses to stop texting while driving. No one can command another to forgive unconditionally; otherwise, it is reduced to an empty gesture or, worse, a coerced indulgence.

Two objections may be raised that purportedly disqualify the family as an exemplar of forgiving and promising as potential political practices. First, the family is one of many private associations that are tainted with particular normative convictions that should not be admitted to the public arena. This arena is restricted to procedural considerations regarding the establishment and protection of rights through the coercive power of the state. Individuals are free to draw on their experiences in these private associations when participating in these procedural debates, and they may even demonstrate the personal benefits derived

---

[24] See Chapter 4 for a detailed summary of Borgmann's account of focal things and practices.

from such practices as forgiving and promising, but the normative bases of their support or opposition to proposed or enacted rights are inadmissible. Or, to invoke the terminology of this inquiry, individuals may glean relevant information about forgiving and promising from their participation in private associations such as families, but narrating the good of such associations is publicly irrelevant.

The family is one of many associations that are admittedly and rightfully private. Private associations *per se*, however, are not devoid of any public role or relevancy. They have what may be described as a "public pole," for otherwise they cannot contribute to, or benefit from, interactions with the various spheres comprising civil community. Families, for example, are related to, and depend on, schools, healthcare facilities, sports clubs, businesses, and the like to sustain themselves.[25] These public poles disclose not only the goods ordering these associations, but also what they need from civil community to pursue these goods, and derivatively how the coercive power of the state should be aligned and constrained in enabling or preventing these pursuits. In order to perform this task, the narration of these respective goods must be assessed in order to make appropriate judgments, a task that is distorted when undertaken with distilled information alone.

Moreover, private associations may be said to create "public spaces." These spaces are often narrowly delineated and temporary, but nonetheless comprise individuals pursuing a common purpose, task, or activity. A family meal, for instance, is a public setting where individuals are sharing a common pursuit for a brief period of time. The mistake that late liberals (and Arendt) make is to conflate "public" with "political." In doing so, they fail to recognize that public space is created more by exclusion than inclusion. Unlike most political space, not everyone or anyone has the right to be admitted to a public space. If they could be admitted, then no barriers or boundaries defining a space could be erected. This need to exclude is even tacitly admitted by liberal regimes through immigration policies and the restriction of legislative bodies to elected representatives. Civil community is simply not a town meeting writ large. Rather, it comprises various publics of varying scope and duration, and it is within these public settings that the goods of these associations are narrated. These narrations, and not merely their derivative information, may in turn offer suggestions for broader questions of political ordering, such as the practice of forgiving and promising. The purpose of the state, therefore, is not to create public space, but to enable—most often through constraining, rather than asserting, its coercive power—these publics to narrate and pursue their respective goods. More importantly, this conflation means that, for late moderns, public association is based on coercion or its threat. Hence the incessant conflict stemming from the perpetual cycle of resentment and revenge, effectively negating any prospect of forgiving and promising as a political practice.

---

[25] For a more detailed account of the private and public poles of the family, see Brent Waters, *The Family in Christian Social and Political Thought* (Oxford: Oxford University Press, 2007), pp. 192–206.

The second objection is that the private associations I am highlighting are too diminutive to be exemplary. Their restricted scope, limited diversity, and narrow purposes disqualify them as suggestive sources for how forgiving and promising might become political practices. These practices serve the affiliative needs of private associations, and although they may promote the performance of civic virtues and political duties, these benefits are derivative rather than direct. Families, for instance, may provide a suitable social setting for practicing forgiving and promising that is necessitated and enabled by both their familiarity and informality. These crucial features, however, are irrelevant to far larger and more complex political associations that presuppose unfamiliarity among its citizens and formal procedures for ordering their civil conduct. The late modern state, in short, is *not* a family writ large.

This objection is correct to insist that the state is not a very large family, and any attempt to govern it as such should be steadfastly resisted. However, it fails to entertain the possibility that there are *public* associations of sufficient scope, complexity, and formality that can inform political practices. The church exemplifies such a possibility. In making this claim I not arguing that the church is a counter-political order. Rather, the church's complex and pluriform sociality is constituted by certain formal structures and practices that have a potential purchase for political ordering.[26] In respect to forgiving and promising, these ecclesial practices would not be simply replicated in the political realm, but might serve as suggestive resources for fashioning similar, but appropriate, political practices. In order to make this argument, the church's sufficient scope, complexity, and formality must first be demonstrated. For the purpose of the following inquiry, a systematic or extensive ecclesiology is not needed, but some minimal framework is nonetheless required, and the four traditional claims that the church is one, holy, catholic, and apostolic will suffice.

The church is *one* because its singular founder and head, Jesus Christ, is one. There are, of course, numerous disputes among and within differing polity camps on how best to organize this unity. Yet, despite these differences Christians, in at least their more chastened moments, acknowledge that they worship, serve, and are bound together by the same Lord, and regret the divisions that prevent them from worshipping this One as one.

The church is *holy* because its bears witness to God who alone is holy. Since the church is part of the present secular age, this time between the times, it cannot be holy *per se*. Rather, the church is made holy by the tasks that God has entrusted to it: namely, to evangelize and serve the world. Consequently, the church, through its life and ministry, not only affirms God's good creation and enables the communication of its goods, but also bears witness to its end. In this respect, the church is an inkling of creation's destiny in which all temporal associations are displaced by eternal fellowship with God.

---

[26] See Bernd Wannenwetsch, *Political Worship: Ethics for Christian Citizens* (Oxford and New York: Oxford University Press, 2004).

The church is *catholic* because it comprises people drawn from every race and nation. It is a universal association that is not formed by birthright or common interest, but by calling and confession; it is not an association based on flesh and blood, but on water and the Spirit. Consequently, through baptism the church is one but also pluriform, reflecting the diversity of those who gather in Christ's name. The church, then, does not comprise individuals who have chosen each other, but those who have been called and are now bound together by their faith and life together in the Spirit. Consequently, the church is not confined to any particular places, but exists wherever two or three gather in its Lord's name.

The church is *apostolic* because it has endured over time at the initiative of its founder, Jesus Christ, and guidance of the Holy Spirit. One need not embrace a formal doctrine of apostolic succession to affirm apostolicity: an unbroken chain of belief and practice passed on from generation to generation. In this respect, we may say that apostolicity is the form of the church's narration. It is a narrative expressed through Scripture, doctrine, practice, preaching, and worship, and such narration has changed over time, sometimes faithfully and sometimes not. Yet this ongoing narration helps the church navigate the world over time, by providing both landmarks and reference points for plotting trajectories.

There are various focal things and practices that embody the church's unity, holiness, catholicity, and apostolicity. In this respect, Eucharist is a paradigmatic focal thing and practice, exemplifying the pattern and trajectory of the Christian moral life. The ritual performance of judgment, confession, contrition, repentance, forgiveness, amendment of life, and absolution simultaneously embodies, reinforces, and enacts the central scriptural and doctrinal precepts that form the Christian moral life, and this formation in turn is inexplicable and ineffectual in the absence of the church's narration of its four marks noted above. Ordering one's life and the life of the community to the focal practices of Eucharist is to also order accompanying desires and hopes to the church's narration of the gospel, both in terms of remembrance and expectation.

The practices of forgiveness and amendment of life (promising), in particular, instantiates and engenders the virtue of hope. Following Josef Pieper, hope orients people toward the fulfillment of their true nature as creatures created and loved by God. Hope is therefore needed to prevent despair as the denial of redemption—the refusal to allow new and renewing possibilities to reorient the lives of individuals and communities. Despair breeds resignation and fear, prompting in turn premature and inappropriate judgments that perpetuate a cycle of resentment and revenge rather than creating a new space for the possibility of reconciliation. Hope, in short, is the expectation of God's promises that illumine the present reality of creation by revealing its future.[27] It is such a divine promise that makes forgiving and promising possible among people estranged by cycles of resentment and revenge.

---

[27] See Jurgen Moltmann, *Theology of Hope: On the Ground and the Implications of Christian Eschatology* (Minneapolis, MN: Fortress Press, 1993).

How might the church's practices of forgiveness and amendment of life inform other associations comprising civil community and their political governance? Or perhaps, more pointedly, has the church anything to offer, given the fact that it often fails to forgive and amend its life as promised, invoking an empty rhetoric of hope to cloak its own underlying despair? It is precisely this failure that makes these practices potentially informative and formative, because they are predicated on grace. Forgiving and promising entail the stewardship of a gift rather than the construction of an artifact. It is this gifted quality that inspires a hope that can embrace the prospect of new and renewing possibilities, whereas an artifact or work is always built with a prior outcome in mind.

Arendt recognizes the giftedness entailed in forgiving and promising. She admits that all work undertaken by humans in constructing their world entails the violent extraction and refashioning of raw materials.[28] Subsequent principles of political ordering are extrapolations that are necessarily based on coercion. Consequently, she offers her account of natality as a means of reorienting politics toward speech rather than violence, and a baby serves as the principal metaphor of her argument that is *given to*, and not constructed by, civil community. It is only on the basis of a gift that natality can promote the prospect of new and renewing possibilities, and sustain the accompanying practices of forgiving and promising. Yet in replacing the religious rationale for forgiving and promising with Kantian reason, Arendt inadvertently transforms the gift into one more artifact, effectively miring natality in the very cycle of resentment and revenge that it was proffered to break. The baby is no longer given but is the outcome of work, inspiring an ensuing and coercive struggle over to whom it belongs.

If forgiving and promising are to become political practices, then a more robust recovery of their gifted qualities is needed. This recovery cannot occur within the late modern political sphere, for there is no dominant narration to make these practices intelligible, much less sustain them. Rather, it is within the public and private associations comprising civil community that forgiving and promising are routinely practiced, and their members, as citizens, can interject pertinent political expectations, albeit in derivative ways. In other words, these associations can provide narrated filters to help interpret the myriad information inundating the political arena. This does not mean that the politics of the emerging technoculture would be any less contentious, for there are many competing narratives regarding the good of civil community. But civil narration is predicated on speech leading to persuasion, rather than coercion promoting resentment and revenge. As noted previously,[29] the prospect of forgiving and promising as a political practice is highly problematic, particularly when predicated on a religious belief in the gift of grace. Yet, if this gift proves untenable or unpalatable, political judgment, tempered by mercy, is at least explicable. To be clear, introducing derived

---

[28] See Hannah Arendt, *The Human Condition* (Chicago, IL, and London: University of Chicago Press, 1998), Part IV.

[29] See Chapter 3.

narrative accounts of forgiving and promising will not, and should not, eliminate the necessity of coercion for political ordering. But they can, perhaps, mitigate the pervasive recourse to coercion in settling political disputes, reorienting politics in part toward speech instead of raw power.

The preceding paragraphs do not suggest that the church's narrative should dominate civil community, or should even enjoy a privileged position. Rather, I used the church to counteract the curt dismissal of the narrations of public and private associations as devoid of any political purchase or relevancy. The church, in fact, is potentially well suited to engaging with, and informing, the politics of the emerging technoculture, for it too is predicated on space rather than place. It too is a pluriform association, drawing people from every race and nation. But the church is *not* nomadic. It recognizes that space and information are inadequate substitutes for place and narration in sustaining a healthy public domain that can in turn nourish the political and private spheres. The church is *not* therefore a competing *polis*, but more akin to a *civitas* helping to define and maintain the proper boundaries demarcating the political and private that surround and draw on the public.

The church is not the only association that should comprise this public realm. To invoke Arendt's imagery, it is one of the many oases within the vast desert of late modern politics. She insists that these oases are not havens for escaping the desert, but "life-giving sources that let us live in the desert without becoming reconciled to it."[30] Preserving these oases is therefore an urgent task, because although "we suffer under desert conditions we are still human and still intact; the danger lies in becoming true inhabitants of the desert and feeling at home in it."[31] It is in these oases that we continue to love the world despite its desertification. It is such love that prompts the task of preservation. Preserving these oases requires resisting any further encroachment, and, more ambitiously, their assistance in reclaiming and shrinking the desert. Undertaking this task requires that the oases be populated by what Borgmann describes as focal communities that are dedicated to life-giving practices—such as forgiving and promising—in a purposeful and sustained manner. This task, of course, begs the question of what life-giving purposes these focal communities should serve, and it is the question that prompts the next and final chapter.

---

[30] Hannah Arendt, *The Promise of Politics* (New York: Schocken Books, 2005), p. 203.

[31] Ibid., p. 201.

Chapter 10
Dissembling the Other: Consuming Predation

The previous chapter ended with Hannah Arendt's stark imagery of the vast desert of late modern politics in which a few life-giving oases are scattered about. Although these oases are vital for sustaining life in the desert, they are small and isolated, creating a nearly perfect environment for the nomadic inhabitants of the emerging technoculture. Arendt insists, however, that the purpose of these oases is not only to provide respite, but more importantly to serve as reminders that we never feel at home in the surrounding desert. She suggests, therefore, that the desert can and should be reclaimed in order to provide a more suitable political habitat.

Although Arendt is correct to insinuate that reclamation of the desert should be undertaken, it is not clear what she has in mind. The late modern desert cannot sustain a politics predicated on speech, for presumably too much time is expended commuting back to life-giving oases. Yet neither can she be suggesting an expansion of the oases that eventually transform the desert into one large oasis, for the political would then be merely the private writ large. As Arendt insists, humans need a second birth into politics. Late moderns must leave their private oases to enter a political terrain that is anything but life-giving, resulting, more often than not, in a stillbirth rather than a second birth. Hence the need to reclaim the desert, but we are never told what this more sustaining environment might look like.

The problem is not that Arendt lacks the intellectual and imaginative skills to offer, at the very least, an impressionistic landscape of a reclaimed desert. Rather, the problem stems from the categorical constraints she imposes on her analysis of late modernity. By insisting that only the political and private spheres are crucial in ordering the human condition, she cannot overcome the dilemma of the desert and oases, for neither is equipped to nourish sustained political speech. The former is too parched and monotonous, while the latter is too lush and particular.

Arendt needs a third category, one that mediates the private and political because it is related to both while being neither one nor the other. Given her allergic reaction to the word "social," we may use *public* to identify this third category. Public associations are uniquely positioned to draw on and support the strengths of private associations, while also fashioning and contributing to political discourse. Unlike its private counterpart, a public association is not based on intimacy, familial affinity, or narrowly defined interests. Moreover, it tends to endure over time, establishing in the process certain customs, traditions, and formal structures of governance. Unlike its political counterpart, a public association is not predicated on the non-exclusionary status of right or citizenship.

Consequently, it has neither the authority nor power to legislate, adjudicate, or coerce the behavior of individuals within a political jurisdiction; it cannot tax, incarcerate, or wage war.[1]

Collectively, public associations mediate and enrich the relationship between the private and political spheres. On the one hand, public associations do not comprise only autonomous individuals who choose to be affiliated for relatively brief or extended periods of time. Rather, it is recognized that individuals also participate in other, more intimate private associations. Consequently, a public association draws on these life-giving sources of affinity, and also supports them as its sustaining source of nourishment. On the other hand, public associations are not state-approved agencies that exist to promote the state's policies and dictates. Rather, the state is (or should be) organized to govern in ways that promote the flourishing of public associations, thereby recognizing that civil community does not consist solely of a relationship between the state and individuals, but of a complex web of overlapping associations, or what Althusius describes as a symbiotic society.[2] Moreover, within these public associations certain practices, such as forgiving and promising, can be undertaken and sustained, having in turn, at least potentially, a derivative influence on political practices based on speech instead of power. To return to Arendt's imagery, a locale is needed between the oases and desert, one that that is sufficiently habitable to sustain public interaction while being neither too barren nor too lush.

This public locale offers the most promising venue for the church, as a public association, to engage with the emerging technoculture. If civil community consists of only the private and political spheres—the oases surrounded by a vast desert—then a nomadic life is not only explicable, but also necessary. The privileging of space and information, as described in the preceding two chapters, are requisite, because neither the oases nor the desert can nourish the more demanding requirements of public place and narration. As argued previously,[3] these substitutions cannot sustain robust private and political associations, thereby devolving the emerging technoculture into a collection of increasingly isolated individuals bound loosely only by an increasingly contentious and acerbic politics.

This bleak prospect becomes even more pronounced when the third preference of exchange over communication is added to the list, which is the principal topic of this chapter. In the first section I argue that exchange is an absolute necessity for sustaining the private, political, and public associations comprising civil community. In the absence of exchange any possibility of human flourishing is rendered mute. Yet exchange alone is not sufficient to sustain such flourishing, for when consumption becomes its own end, it leads to predation. In the following section I argue that communication is needed to resist this tendency. Building

---

[1] A private association may, however, collect dues, discipline its members, and compete with other public associations.

[2] See Johannes Althusius, *Politica* (Indianapolis, IN: Liberty Fund, 1995).

[3] See Chapter 9.

upon the more detailed account in Chapter 6, I contend that communication is not only predicated on the necessity of exchange, but also serves as its *telos*, thereby preventing the corruption of consumption into predation. Ideally, communication should occur prominently in public associations, and, again ideally, these associations should be what Borgmann portrays as focal communities. These focal communities engender a robust public venue that in turn fosters the private and political associations that it mediates. The church is one such focal community, and can engage the emerging technoculture through its focal thing and practice of Sabbath. This practice is exemplified in the virtue of charity, and it is through charity that communication is sustained. Consequently, this chapter both complements and completes discussions of baptism, Eucharist, and the corresponding virtues of faith and hope undertaken in the preceding two chapters. Together, they constitute my central thesis on how Christians should engage with the emerging technoculture: namely, by preserving the necessity of place, narration, and communication in a culture that is tempted to replace them with space, information, and exchange.

The necessity and insufficiency of exchange

Exchange is a prerequisite of human survival. Individuals could endure alone and isolated for brief periods of time, but the human species would soon become extinct. Procreation and child-rearing require numerous exchanges among progenitors and offspring over an extended period of time.[4] Moreover, larger groups require a more expansive range of exchanges in order to procure the necessities of food and shelter.

Exchange is a prerequisite of human flourishing. In the absence of people exchanging ideas, goods, and services, human life would be bereft of any meaning or purpose other than obtaining what is needed for daily survival. People both support and enrich one another through numerous interactions, and, more expansively, exchange enables a common life. Following Thomas Hobbes, in the absence of exchange there are "no arts; no letters; no society," and life in the so-called state of nature is "solitary, mean, nasty, brutish, and short."[5] In brief, humans are social creatures; they are drawn to one another and must cooperate to both survive and flourish. Or in the words of Johannes Althusius, "[c]learly, man by nature is a gregarious animal born for cultivating society with other men, not by nature living alone as wild beasts do, nor wandering about as birds."[6]

---

[4] See Don S. Browning et al., *From Culture Wars to Common Ground: Religion and the American Family Debate* (Louisville, KY: Westminster John Knox Press, 1997), ch. 4; and Don S. Browning, *Equality and the Family: A Fundamental, Practical Theology of Children, Mothers, and Fathers in Modern Societies* (Grand Rapids, MI and Cambridge, UK: Eerdmans, 2007), ch. 9.

[5] Thomas Hobbes, *Leviathan* (Oxford and New York: Oxford University Press, 1996), p. 84 (I/13).

[6] Althusius, *Politica*, p. 22.

Since humans are born to cultivate society, they must also learn how to work with one another to sustain their social interactions. Such exchange, however, does not eliminate self-interest. As Adam Smith famously observed, "[i]t is not from the benevolence of the butcher, the brewer, or the baker, that we expect our dinner, but from their regard to their own interest."[7] Unlike other animals, humans possess or own things to satisfy their wants and needs. They also do not have everything they want or need, but others do. How might this deficiency best be resolved? Again, unlike other animals, humans should not resort to theft or seizure to satisfy their wants and needs, for this would resort back to Hobbes' infamous state of nature—squirrels constantly plundering each other's hidden food troves. Rather, humans can exchange respectively desired items so that what is mine becomes yours, and what is yours becomes mine. The butcher and baker exchange meat and bread. Through these exchanges individuals help each other, but this assistance is accomplished by appealing to their respective interests rather than depending on a benevolent bestowal of unreciprocated gifts or aid. This appeal to self-interest is not synonymous with selfishness,[8] but recognizes that mutual assistance is most efficiently and peacefully accomplished by satisfying the particular wants and needs of individuals. An individual can flourish only by cooperating with others.

Smith's great insight is that trade is the best mechanism for enabling these exchanges. When individuals produce things that other people want or need, they can trade them for what they want and need. This means, however, that there must be a diversity of production, for if everyone produces the same thing, then there would be nothing to trade, and wants and needs would remain unsatisfied. Hence Smith's second, and closely related, insight: specialization of labor. By producing one thing rather than many, individuals are much more likely to satisfy a greater range of wants and needs. If, for instance, I want to eat well and try to be simultaneously a butcher, brewer, and baker, I will need to maintain a herd and cultivate hops and grain, and by the end of the day I will probably be too exhausted to prepare and enjoy dinner. Rather, it is by producing something that the butcher, brewer, and baker need or want that I can exchange them for my desired menu items. The specialization of labor increases both the volume and ease of exchange, thereby freeing up time for individuals to pursue other interests.

Smith recognized with great clarity the underlying necessity of exchange for human flourishing, and therefore the need to sustain mechanisms of sufficient scale. Consequently, markets are needed in which trade can be easily conducted. People needing to eat must have easy access to butchers, brewers, and bakers, and money was invented as a more efficient means of exchange than barter.[9] In these markets, consumers obtain a greater variety of ingredients for making their

---

[7] Adam Smith, *An Inquiry into the Nature and Causes of the Wealth of Nations* (Indianapolis, IN: Liberty Fund, 1981), pp. 26–27 (I/2).

[8] See Adam Smith, *The Theory of Moral Sentiments* (Indianapolis, IN: Liberty Fund, 1982).

[9] See Smith, *Wealth of Nations*, I/4.

dinners, and efficient producers generate greater profit which they in turn use to facilitate more exchanges. Moreover, markets should not be confined to local venues, but can and should be global. It is better for all concerned if the Scots drink Portuguese wine and the Portuguese wear Scottish wool.[10]

Although markets enable human flourishing through promoting trade, they are also predicated on competition. Consumers have limited financial resources and must allocate them in accordance with those needs and wants they wish to satisfy: do they want a diet consisting primarily of meat, beer, or bread? Butchers, brewers, and bakers, then, compete not only with each other, but also with competitors in their respective specialties. Competition benefits consumers in two ways. First, it keeps prices low, thereby increasing purchasing power. Butchers, brewers, and bakers cannot stay in business if they price their products too high. Second, competition spurs innovation, resulting in new or improved products. To gain an advantage over competitors, butchers, brewers, and bakers create more efficient and less costly methods or production, or introduce new product lines.

The principal benefit of competitive markets is that they generate a greater number and range of exchanges, a key factor in promoting human flourishing. Competition, then, does not negate but promotes cooperation. If exchange is seen as a cooperative act—I give you what you want and you give me what I need—competition is a driving force in pursuing this good. Cooperation and competition are not contending forces, but are more akin to two sides of the same coin. Butchers, brewers, bakers, and hungry and thirsty customers need each other. This is why Smith excoriated the mercantile policies of his day, because their monopolistic practices diminished the range and quality of exchanges.[11]

Smith's once controversial discourse on political economy has now prevailed. Generations of subsequent disciples have refined his arguments, and competitive markets, based on trade and specialization of labor, are now taken for granted as the only realistic game in town. Even purported socialist and communist regimes have become adept at playing the financial and energy markets, and old-fashioned artisans have discovered lucrative niche markets. And these markets are now global in scale. For late moderns it does not seem odd to see a Hyundai driving through a McDonalds in Pittsburgh or a Mercedes parked at a KFC in Tokyo. One can go on a shopping spree and obtain an item with a "made in" label from a country for every letter in the alphabet (with the exception of x). The inhabitants of the emerging technoculture take it for granted that the world is their marketplace, and it is a spacious and fluid locale enabling a plethora of exchanges on a daily basis. This is no small accomplishment to be disdained, for in these countless mundane daily exchanges, humans have crafted for themselves an environment in which they may flourish because their material needs are met with relative ease. Moreover, it is a cooperative environment based on trust. This, again, is a remarkable accomplishment. Unlike any other animal, humans are comfortable

---

[10] See ibid., IV/2.
[11] See ibid., Book IV.

being in the company of strangers, and in the absence of such comfort and trust, ubiquitous exchanging could not be pursued. In Paul Seabright's evocative words:

> Within a few hundred generations—barely a pause for breath in evolutionary time—[humans] had formed social organizations of startling complexity. Not just village settlements but cities, armies, empires, corporations, nation states, political movements, humanitarian organizations, even internet communities. The same shy, murderous ape that had avoided strangers throughout its evolutionary history was now living, working, and moving among complete strangers in their millions.[12]

There are two reasons why I have concentrated on economic exchange. First, it is a ubiquitous global reality in the emerging technoculture. It is also a reality made possible and sustained by various technologies and interlocking infrastructures. Without sophisticated and coordinated transportation and telecommunication systems enabling the prompt and efficient delivery of goods and services to consumers, global markets could not exist to any great extent. In this respect, technology has enriched the material well-being of literally billions of people worldwide.

The second reason is that global economic exchange enables and exemplifies other social trends within the emerging technoculture. The world is now perceived as a single marketplace—or more accurately, market*space*—that, with the aid of a device and supportive network, can be "entered" with a click (or touch for those preferring a tablet or smart phone). Once this market has been entered, one is virtually free to wander the world in search of wanted or needed goods and services. This wandering, however, is not confined to economic exchange. Rather, exchange becomes the preferred, if not exclusive, paradigmatic mode for all interactions within the nomadic life of the emerging technoculture.

This paradigmatic penchant can be seen more clearly by briefly revisiting the privileging of space over place and information over narration that were examined in the preceding two chapters. The creation of virtual spaces that ease or negate the constraints of physical places is almost entirely predicated on exchange for relatively brief or extended periods of time. These spaces are necessarily fluid in terms of purpose, and restricted in respect to admission and participation. In a conference call or videoconference, business associates review sales data and share gossip about clients and absent colleagues. After the meeting each participant uses various devices to create subsequent virtual spaces to conduct follow-up tasks and spread gossip.

In each of these spaces information is readily exchanged. Indeed, if there is no information to be exchanged, there is no compelling reason to create or participate in the virtual space. This is particularly true in respect to social media. Information

---

[12] Paul Seabright, *The Company of Strangers: A Natural History of Economic Life* (Princeton, NJ, and Oxford: Princeton University Press, 2004), p. 1.

about oneself is constantly being generated and then posted or distributed in the expectation that it will be consumed and responded to in turn. There is also the further expectation that such information should be exchanged concisely, in some instances limiting the number of characters that can be transmitted in any single burst. Without such informational reciprocity social media would not exist.

What is wrong with exchanging information in virtual spaces? Nothing *per se*, for, as I noted above, exchange is a prerequisite of human survival as well as flourishing. Yet, although exchange is necessary, it is not sufficient for the pursuit or sustenance of what may be described as a good life. As a number of critics argue, spending a lot of time in virtual spaces exchanging information promotes aberrant behavior, stilted relationships, and superficial thinking.[13] Some individuals—perhaps a growing number—view virtual space as "home turf" and are ill at ease in physical places; they prefer technologically mediated encounters to their face-to-face counterparts, and see sustained or deep thinking as a burden to be avoided.

Exchange is subtly corrupted from a means of satisfying needs and wants to enabling insatiable consumption. This is especially the case in the absence of a normative narration that orders a hierarchy of needs and determines what should be wanted. Without such a narrative, consumption becomes an end in itself. We exchange in order to consume, or, more accurately, we consume for the sake of consumption. When consumption becomes its own self-referential purpose, the obtained item or information no longer satisfies a perceived need or want but becomes a device for concocting whatever additional desires the consumer might assign. Adept advertising carries the recognition that it is not selling a good or service but a derived experience—marketing the desire of desire.[14] A 2008 Cadillac television commercial serves as an example. Kate Walsh tells viewers, "In today's luxury game, the question isn't whether or not your car has available features like a 40 gig hard drive. It isn't about sunroofs or sapele wood accents, popup map screens or any of that. No, the real question is when you turn your car on, does it return the favor?"

The desire of desire is, alas, insatiable, for there is always something new to be desired—a better way to have the favor returned. Consequently, the voracious consumption driven by such desire is endless, relentless, and consuming. More troubling, such consumption becomes predatory. In their ceaseless quest to satisfy insatiable desires, the nomadic inhabitants of the emerging technoculture consume each other.

---

[13] See, e.g., Nicholas Carr, *The Shallows: What the Internet is Doing to Our Brains* (New York and London: Norton, 2010); Maggie Jackson, *Distracted: The Erosion of Attention and the Coming Dark Age* (Amherst, NY: Prometheus Books, 2008); and Sherry Turkle, *Alone Together: Why We Expect More from Technology and Less from Each Other* (New York: Basic Books, 2011).

[14] I am indebted to Bernd Wannenwetsch for this observation.

This predatory consumption, however, is not malicious. It is more akin to Arendt's account of thoughtlessness, and hence to its potential for mischief. Moreover, predatory consumption is *not* irrational given the preferences entailed in living a high-tech nomadic life. When any place and no place in particular is home so long as a real or virtual space can be created for the time being, and when there is no perceived need to narrate what should be desired but only information to promote the desire of desire, then what else is left other than consumption? Although predatory consumption is a rational outcome of the late modern nomadic life, it is not sustainable. It is a bit like a nest of snakes eating each other's tails.

The task of Christian moral theology is not merely to condemn predatory consumption or scold the nomads of the emerging technoculture for being thoughtless consumers. Rather, the task is to admit and affirm the necessity of exchange, but to reorient away from promoting consumption for its own sake toward enabling communication.

Communication

As presented in Chapter 6, *koinōnia* may be variously translated as "community," "communion," or communication." It is a form of human action entailing the proper ordering of the goods of creation. In communicating these goods a people is formed and sustained. Unlike exchange, what is mine does not become yours and yours mine; it becomes ours. The goods that are communicated form and sustain what may be characterized as a communicative association. Moreover, such associations are not the sum total of the goods communicated, but take on an identity and way of life that are greater than the sum of their parts. Families and churches are examples of communicative association. Both comprise the goods of individuals that become common or shared.

Communication and exchange are not synonymous, but they are intricately related. In the absence of exchange, communicative associations could not exist because basic needs could not be met. A member or members of a household must engage in some kind of exchange to obtain such necessities as food and shelter, and likewise a church is constituted and sustained indirectly by the exchanges of its members.[15] In this respect, all communicative associations are dependent on, and embedded within, a broader nexus of exchange.

Although communicative associations depend on a series of underlying exchanges, exchange is not practiced formally within the association. Rather, exchange enables communication. Family members do not barter their respective goods. Affection is not exchanged for patience, but affection and patience are communicated among household members. Similarly, church members do not

---

[15] The early Christians in Jerusalem serve as a sobering example of what happens to a church that fails to attend to the necessity of exchange; see Acts 2:42–47.

purchase spiritual goods and services. A worshipper does not buy forgiveness; it is a good communicated among those gathered in Christ's name.

Communicating the goods of creation requires time. What is mine and what is yours cannot instantly become ours. Certain goods are assumed to belong to a family and not any particular member over time. A church begins to conceive itself as a whole rather than an aggregate of parts over time. Communicating the goods of creation requires narration. It is a story that binds a communicative association together over time, narrating, to return to David Hogue's imagery, an imagined past and remembered future.[16] Moreover, the narration is not merely recalled, retold, and revised, but also enacted, often through informal and formal rituals. A family gathers on a holiday repeating certain patterns of apropos behavior and conversation. A church's liturgy enacts the telling of the gospel. Communicating the goods of creation requires a place. Physical location and proximity are required if goods are to become ours over time; there can be no virtual communication. Both family and church need a place to gather to communicate and narrate the goods that have become theirs.

Sustaining a communicative association requires requisite and recurring practices that are routine and mundane, and therefore vital. The place where a family gathers over time must be cleaned and kept in good repair, as should the place where a church gathers to worship. Appropriate settings for ritual narration must be prepared. A home is decorated and a dinner cooked for the holiday family gathering. Seasonal paraments adorn the sanctuary, and the bread and wine are placed on the altar for worship.

Communicative associations may also be what Albert Borgmann characterizes as focal communities. As examined in greater detail in Chapters 4 and 7, a focal community is ordered around formative focal things and practices. A focal thing has a commanding presence that orders, in part, the life of the community that recognizes it as such. In addition, requisite practices are required to support and reinforce the formative influence of the focal thing. These practices in turn are often embedded in traditions relating to their performance. Mom prepares the holiday dinner using the family's favorite recipes. The priest stands behind the pulpit when preaching. Focal practices, however, are not fixed or unchangeable, and may be altered in ways that better serve to support and reinforce the formative influence of the focal thing. Dad cooks the holiday dinner, and tries a new recipe or two. The priest abandons the pulpit to use a less formal style of preaching.

For the purposes of this chapter, three aspects of focal things and practices need to be highlighted. First, if focal things and practices are to form and sustain a community, then they must be *communal and material*.[17] The focal thing needs

---

[16] See Chapter 7.

[17] Borgmann does not insist that focal things and practices must be communal. Running, fly-fishing, and woodworking are examples that are highly individualistic. I do not disagree, but in respect to focal communities the formative things and practices must involve their members as a group and not as individuals.

a particular locale where the attendant practices are undertaken; a community requires a place to gather. Otherwise, the resulting ritualized narration is deformed into a simulacrum. Family members participating in a videoconference while eating is not a dinner, and watching a video-recording of a service of worship and eating a piece of bread followed by a sip of wine is not receiving the sacrament.

Second, formative focal things and practices are not self-referential, but *redirect attention to a greater good*. Although a focal thing is a commanding presence, it is a means and not an end; it is more akin to an icon than an object. Otherwise, the related focal practices become exercises in idolatry. The purpose of the holiday dinner is not to celebrate the culinary expertise of the cook but to enable the greater good of fellowship, and the purpose of worship is not to celebrate the musical skills of the choir but to direct attention toward God. This does not mean, however, that the quality of focal things and practices is unimportant. Undertaking focal practices in a shabby manner makes the practitioners less receptive to the formative influence of the focal thing. Careful, thoughtful, and attentive practice is required if it is to be both focal and formative. A well-prepared dinner is better equipped to promote fellowship than one haphazardly thrown together, and the same can be said about a homily in respect to directing attention toward God.

Third, formative focal things and practices both *reinforce and reorient*. People undertake focal practices because they believe they help preserve something important, even crucial, to their lives. The ensuing ritualized narration reinforces this conviction. Family members gather for the holiday dinner despite any inconveniences encountered. Worshipping reinforces the belief in the need for forgiveness and grace. Focal practices, however, are not inflexible or unchanging. They may be altered in ways that reorient toward better serving the greater good that the focal thing discloses and enables. Rather than expecting mom or dad to do everything, the tasks of setting the table, cooking, and cleaning up are more evenly distributed, in turn enriching the ensuing fellowship. The Eucharist is celebrated every week rather than occasionally, emphasizing the constant need to amend one's life.

Yet focal things and practices *per se* do not necessarily change behavior that challenges and engages in troubling cultural trends. In particular, a family gathering for a holiday dinner or a church gathering to worship may do nothing to contest predatory consumption, and may in some instances unwittingly intensify it. The content and greater good that focal things and practices enable are important. What kinds of focal thing and practices are therefore needed to combat the predatory consumption of the emerging technoculture? Addressing this question requires briefly revisiting Sabbath as a focal thing and the related or paradigmatic virtue of charity.

As noted in Chapter 7, Sabbath is not confined to, or encapsulated in, the proscription of certain acts or activities. Rather, as a focal thing, Sabbath is more akin to Josef Pieper's account of leisure as a "receptive attitude of mind" reinforcing the "capacity for steeping oneself in the whole of creation."[18] In leisure there is reception but no exchange, and in receiving there is a subsequent communication with the whole of creation. In practicing Sabbath, the goods of creation become ours. Karl Barth reinforces this central practice of reception by portraying Sabbath as a celebration of life as God's free gift of grace.[19] In celebrating the reception of this gift, the community again communicates the good of their life as creatures. This notion of reception is crucial for, contrary to the chief tenet of the emerging technoculture that communities are artifacts of the will, a community cannot be built, as Borgmann contends, but only emerge around a focal thing.[20]

It may be objected that practicing such leisurely Sabbath does little to challenge predatory consumption, much less reorient exchange toward communication. If anything, the exclusive emphasis on reception intensifies consumption without any residual benefits of exchange. How can the goods of creation be communicated when reciprocity has been displaced by unidirectional reception? In linking Sabbath with leisure all I have done is edit an old adage: it is better to receive and never give.

This objection fails to recognize that although there is no reciprocity, the reception entailed in Sabbath is not unidirectional. Although leisure is a "receptive attitude," it does not mean that what is received becomes the possession of the recipient. Rather, as Pieper emphasizes, it serves to steep one in the whole of creation. In receiving, one is drawn out and into a greater reality than the self. In practicing Sabbath, one receives and is drawn out and into a creation that cannot be consumed but can be communicated. Moreover, further linking the focal thing of Sabbath with the virtue of charity prevents leisurely receptivity from becoming mere consumption. Love cannot remain contained. It is an inherently relational quality that draws one toward the other. Although love involves reciprocity, it is not an item or thing to be exchanged. One does not propose "Let us exchange love," but, rather, one falls in love. Practicing charity is, in short, oriented toward the "ours" and not the "mine" and "yours."

In this respect, Sabbath is not the act of communicating the goods of creation, but helps enable it. Becoming steeped in the whole of creation affords opportunities to assess whether various exchanges serve, neglect, or diminish communication, and to amend subsequent exchanges accordingly. Such assessment requires a narrative framework to determine what these goods are and how they should be communicated. The absence of such a framework does not mean, however, that narration is absent in how exchange is pursued. Since humans are story-telling

---

[18] See Josef Pieper, *Leisure, the Basis of Culture: The Philosophical Act* (San Francisco, CA: Ignatius Press, 2009), pp. 15–47.

[19] See Karl Barth, *Church Dogmatics*, III/4 (Edinburgh, UK: T and T Clark, 1961), §53.1, pp. 53–55.

[20] See Albert Borgmann, *Crossing the Postmodern Divide* (Chicago, IL, and London: University of Chicago Press, 1992), pp. 134–138.

creatures, they cannot help but narrate.[21] But when exchange is assumed to be sufficient in its own right, then it is simply oriented to facilitate further exchanges, and a curious story unfolds. The narrative of the emerging technoculture is one of insatiable desire in which predatory consumption becomes the dominant storyline.

We may capture a glimpse of this narrative by revisiting, one last time, Iris Murdoch's novel, *An Accidental Man*.[22] In Chapter 6 we encountered two characters, Ludwig Leferrier and Austin Gibson Gray, as exemplars, respectively, of a courageous and cowardly approach to the moral life. Yet, in the end, both strategies fail because Ludwig and Austin are both accidental men. Murdoch's story is largely an account of characters creating and suffering the ill-effects of various moral accidents stemming from thoughtlessness, unintended consequences, jealousy, and occasional malice.

Murdoch also tells her story as a series of episodic exchanges among the various characters. Usually, these exchanges prove unsatisfactory, because the respective characters are driven by desires that can never be satisfied; hence the resulting accidents in the wake of relentlessly but fruitlessly trying to satiate the insatiable. Austin's older brother, Matthew Gibson Gray, is an exemplary character in this regard. He has taken early retirement from a highly successful career as a diplomat and is in the process of relocating in London after spending much of his adult life in Asia. As a shrewd investor and collector, he is wealthy but regarded as a generous, benevolent, and kind man, eager to help others.

Matthew displays this reputation on a number of occasions. He frequently gives his destitute brother money, and tries to mitigate the ill-effects of his irresponsible behavior. He counsels and befriends Ludwig while in the process of breaking his engagement and returning to America. He renews a friendship with an old flame, Mavis, and supports her work with "distressed girls." When Charlotte, Ludwig's fiancée's aunt, is disinherited by her elderly mother, he chairs a committee of concerned family members to provide financial assistance. Matthew also allows Dorina, Austin's estranged wife, to live with him for a while until she is able to be on her own.

Matthew's assistance, however, never proves helpful to the purported beneficiaries. His brother resents what he perceives to be Matthew's attempts to dominate and manipulate him. His advice to Ludwig tends to confuse rather than clarify. Mavis lets the renewed friendship wither as Matthew grows increasingly remote and detached. Charlotte is furious with the condescending way in which she is treated by so-called concerned people. Dorina flees from a man who treats her as if she were a helpless and hapless child.

We learn that, despite his benign repute, Matthew is driven by a desire to use and even own other people, stemming from his sense of natural superiority over others. He is on a "quest" to be reconciled with his younger brother, but it is a

---

[21] See Jonathan Gottschall, *The Storytelling Animal: How Stories Make Us Human* (Boston, MA, and New York: Houghton Mifflin Harcourt, 2012).

[22] Iris Murdoch, *An Accidental Man* (London: Penguin, 1971).

venture having nothing to do with Austin; it is simply the burden of fulfilling an empty "duty" that the superior must bear.[23] Ludwig admits that he has easily "given his heart" to Matthew.[24] Once Mavis begins to warm to the idea of renewing a past love with Matthew, he quickly loses interest in the newly collected trophy. Charlotte is little more than a project to Matthew, triggering in her a "pure" hatred of him and her family because they "pity" her.[25] After Dorina and Matthew have become intimate, she tells him that she loves him and "belongs" to him, to which Matthew replies, "'If I am to have helped you at all I must abandon you completely.'"[26]

Matthew, Murdoch tells her readers, wants "to have people forever."[27] They are possessions to be used and discarded at will. Dorina, in this respect, is simply paradigmatic of Matthew's insatiable desire to add "another marvellously beautiful object to his collection."[28] Although Matthew's behavior is deplorable, it is not unusual. Matthew merely magnifies how all the characters in this story relate to one another: they consume each other. Matthew's younger brother, Austin, is described as a vampire, sucking the life out all those he encounters.[29] But it is also an apt description of his older brother, and therefore emblematic of all the other characters to greater or lesser degrees. Moreover, these characters are not wicked, but rather ordinary, driven by common and mundane desires. But, unfortunately, they are bereft of any normative standards for assessing and ordering what and how they should desire. Consequently, they thoughtlessly consume each other to fill a void that cannot be filled. Murdoch tells a fitting tale of late modern nomads engaging in a series of, often uneven, exchanges. But when exchange is merely oriented to further exchange and no greater good, then the resulting consumption is effectively relentless and predacious. It is a story of individuals incessantly trying to make yours mine, but nowhere is there any attempt at making something ours.

In contrast, Marilynne Robinson tells a story of exchange oriented toward communication instead of consumption. In her novel, *Gilead*, we again encounter two characters, John Ames and his namesake Jack Boughton.[30] It is a troubled relationship characterized by failings and misunderstandings on the part of both. But the novel is also a powerful tale on the need for forgiving and promising. In this chapter we return, one last time, to this story but told from the Boughton perspective as recounted in the sequel, *Home*.[31] Again, we may focus on two characters, Jack and his younger sister, Glory.

---

[23] See ibid., p. 128.
[24] Ibid., p. 278.
[25] See ibid., p. 310.
[26] Ibid., p. 312.
[27] See ibid., p. 317.
[28] Ibid., p. 296.
[29] See ibid., p. 429.
[30] Marilynne Robinson, *Gilead* (New York: Picador, 2004); see also Chapters 6 and 8.
[31] Marilynne Robinson, *Home* (New York: Picador, 2008).

Glory has been away for 13 years, teaching English. She returns to Gilead partly to care for her dying father, but also to escape the aftermath of some personal and professional misfortunes. Growing up in a preacher's home, she has retained many of her religious habits, such as daily prayer and Bible reading. For Glory, faith is habit, loyalty, and reverence. "She was pious, no doubt, though she would not have chosen the word to describe herself."[32] As Robinson elaborates, "She did not know what it meant to be pious. She had never been anything else."[33] This unacknowledged piety helps Glory to remember her home and where she is from. It also helps her face a future in which she knows she will never have her own home, husband, or children.

Upon her return to Gilead, "Glory and her father and settled into a tolerable life of its kind."[34] This tolerable life, however, deteriorates when a letter from Jack indicates that, after 20 years, he too is returning home, at least for a while. She tells her father, expecting him to be overjoyed, but he warns her that they should not be hopeful about the impending visit. "What followed were weeks of trouble and disruption, dealing with the old man's anticipation and anxiety and then his disappointments, every one of which made him restless and sleepless and cross."[35] Glory shares her father's distress and is angry because of all the work she needs to do to prepare for Jack's arrival. Her fond memories of home are souring.

Finally Jack arrives late, disheveled and suffering a hangover. When father and son embrace, Jack is in no condition, physically or emotionally, to receive the kindness that has been prepared for him. What subsequently unfolds is one failed attempt after another to make Jack's homecoming successful. Jack's father insists that forgiveness precedes understanding, but the more he tries to understand his son the less able he is to forgive. Jack in turn is unable to accept his father's offer of forgiveness, because he knows he will unable to keep any accompanying promise to live a better life, and he does not believe that God's grace was ever, or will ever be, extended to him. Broughton believes that Jack never felt at home in his own house, and that he has not been a good father, and Jack believes the same about fitting in and not being a good son. The father wonders why he continues to care for his son, and his son shares his bewilderment. Eventually, Jack knows that although he wants to come home, he cannot, and his father treats him as good as dead.

Glory is exasperated by these failed attempts at reconciliation. She encourages her father, ever so gently, to accept Jack as he is. She scolds Jack for believing he is the only bad member of a good family, exclaiming, "'How could you think you were the only sinner in the family? We're Presbyterians!'"[36] She pleads with him to repent, accept his father's forgiveness, and change his ways. Yet all the time, perhaps unknowingly, she harbors grievances against some who had wronged

---

[32] Ibid., p. 110.
[33] Ibid., p. 109.
[34] Ibid., p. 13.
[35] Ibid., p. 28.
[36] Ibid., p. 124.

her or her family in the past, and refuses to forgive them. Such inconsistency does not diminish her idealism, however, for being "naive" was her source of personal "authority."[37] At one point, when Glory is fuming that her older brother had returned and done nothing more than disturb the tolerable life she has cobbled together, she falls into her habit of praying. "As she considered the prayer she was not disconsolate enough to put into words, the unwelcome realization came to her that she loved Jack and yearned for his approval."[38] Why else had she defended him for as long as she could remember, and would continue to do so? She knows she is Jack's only friend and is incapable of remaining angry with him.

Glory's prayer and its unwelcome realization discloses the communication she shares with Jack. As the story unfolds, their respective mines and yours become ours. Glory and Jack are inescapably linked to the extent that one is nearly unintelligible without the other in terms of the narrative that has formed and continues to form them. This formative narrative is also inescapably embedded in the town of Gilead and the Broughton home; this story could not occur and be told anywhere else. Communicating the goods of creation requires both a formative and binding narration, and a particular place in which the narrative forms and binds.

Robinson's novel is not a sentimental story about family ties and warm memories of home. Arguably, Jack would be happier if he were to sever all contact with his family and Gilead that only serve to remind him of his many failures. Glory is appalled when she learns that she will inherit the house when her father dies, for she has no desire to live in Gilead and is afraid she will never have a life of her own. Yet neither Jack nor Glory can pursue the escape they dream of, for the town and the house are intricate parts of who they are and have become—focal and vital things of their communication. This is why Glory also discovers in her prayer that the great, unspoken fear of her family is that Jack may actually find a way to remove himself beyond their "endless, relentless loyalty to him."[39]

The contrast with Murdoch's *An Accidental Man* could not be more striking. There is no relentless loyalty to escape, only accidental collisions in which the characters consume one another. There is no narrative that, for good or ill, forms and binds, but only brief reports of random and brief encounters that almost always end badly. Where this story takes place is irrelevant. Although Murdoch uses London as her locale, almost any late modern city would do. *An Accidental Man* is an account of imperfect people trying, as best they can, to survive their imperfections, whereas *Gilead* and *Home* insist that it is precisely these imperfections that bind people together and keep them human and humane. In this respect, Robinson offers a fitting benediction on the human condition: as God's creation it remains good.

---

[37] See ibid., pp. 17–18.
[38] Ibid., p. 69.
[39] Ibid., p. 247.

A postscript, of sorts

Some readers are undoubtedly frustrated that I never describe how a focal community might be built and maintained. As I bring this book to its end they will remain annoyed, perhaps accusing me of authorial malfeasance for withholding the goods, so to speak. I plead guilty for two reasons. First, I am not particularly gifted in the art of planning and implementation. Or, more prosaically, I am not very good at getting things done; I am, after all, an academic. Second, I have purposely resisted the temptation to indulge any semblance of a "how-to-do-it" or DIY genre. Such indulgence would be to succumb to the very spirit of the emerging technoculture that I find most troubling: namely, a relentless quest for mastery of virtually everything and anything. In pursuing this mastery, technique becomes the operative mode for ordering the lives and affairs of individuals, human associations, and civil communities. It would be a travesty if something resembling a Dummies® book on focal things and practices were ever published.

Why would it be a travesty? Because a focal community is more akin to a gift received than an artifact constructed; hence the contrasts that have been woven throughout the final chapters. The preference for space, information, and exchange lend themselves easily to techniques of mastery, whereas the necessities of place, narration, and communication resist such presumptuous supremacy. The former are like raw material to be used in creating artifacts of the will, whereas the latter are gifts that carry with them given or prescribed ways in which they are to be received and cared for. Mastery settles for the ease of manipulation, whereas a gift requires the hard work of safeguarding.

There is admittedly a superficial resemblance between technique and practice, but they stem from differing motivations and orientations. A technique is judged by the utility of its performance, whereas a practice is formative. In a marriage, for example, one spouse is often tempted to be unfaithful but has mastered the technique of self-control, while the other has been formed by the practice of fidelity and is not therefore tempted. Both are technically faithful spouses, but there is an important difference. To employ the contrasts mentioned above, the former uses information to protect the marital space in which mutually beneficial exchanges may be pursued, whereas the latter narrates the communication of goods entailed in a good marriage. As Rebecca Konyndyk DeYoung suggests, isn't the practice of fidelity better than the technique of self-control?[40]

The most troubling aspect of the relentless pursuit of mastery is the belief that nature, human nature, relationships, civil communities, anything and everything are infinitely malleable. All of reality, be it material or virtual, should and shall eventually be an artifact of the will. It is only a matter of time until technology is developed that will give us full and complete mastery. This presumptive malleability even extends to the human body, which leads us back to where this

---

[40] See Rebecca Konyndyk DeYoung, *Glittering Vices: A New Look at the Seven Deadly Sins and Their Remedies* (Grand Rapids, MI: Brazos, 2009), p. 16.

book began. The posthumanists decry the body as a pathetic prosthetic of the will. Consequently, technology can and should be developed and used to build a superior one. There is admittedly a plethora of important issues regarding the extent to which technology should be used to augment physical and cognitive abilities. They are issues that deserve informed, thoughtful, and sustained deliberation. But, as I mentioned at the beginning of this book, posthuman discourse is also a distraction. It redirects attention away from navigating the moral terrain of our present circumstances toward the promise that all will be well because eventually both the terrain and those traversing it will be radically refashioned into what we will them to be. The promise, however, is gratuitous, for, more often than not, the quest for mastery produces accidental people who are unable to will what is good. In this respect, the most likely destiny of the emerging technoculture is neither a glorious utopia to be embraced nor a cataclysmic apocalypse to be avoided, but banal and predatory consumption—the fruitless and endless striving to satisfy insatiable desires.

My principal goal in writing this book is to help Christians selectively resist, engage, and reorient the direction of the emerging technoculture and the lives of its nomadic inhabitants. To do so requires redirecting attention away from the posthuman distraction and toward focal communities as places where communicating the goods of creation are narrated. It is in such communities that some suggestive ways for achieving the goal of resisting, engaging, and reorienting might emerge. If they do, however, it will be a gift of grace and not the result of mastery; hence my refusal to offer any how-to-do-it scheme. There is a good reason why Christians believe in the gifts and not techniques of the Spirit, for it is only in and through the Spirit that genuinely new and renewing possibilities are given to us. And we need communities that are able to receive and care for such good gifts.

Bibliography

Althusius, Johannes (1995), *Politica*, Indianapolis, IN: Liberty Fund.
Aquinas, Thomas (1964–73), *Summa theologia*, Blackfriars edn, trans, Thomas Gilby et al., 60 vols., London: Eyre and Spottiswoode, and New York: McGraw–Hill.
Arendt, Hannah (2006), *Between Past and Future: Eight Exercises in Political Thought*, New York and London: Penguin Books.
Arendt, Hannah (1972), *Crises of the Republic*, San Diego, CA, and London: Harcourt Brace.
Arendt, Hannah (1992), *Eichmann in Jerusalem: A Report on the Banality of Evil*, New York: Penguin Books.
Arendt, Hannah (1994), *Essays in Understanding, 1930–1954*, New York: Harcourt Brace.
Arendt, Hannah (1998), *The Human Condition*, Chicago, IL, and London: University of Chicago Press.
Arendt, Hannah (1992), *Lectures on Kant's Political Philosophy*, Chicago, IL: University of Chicago Press.
Arendt, Hannah (1978), *The Life of the Mind*, 2 vols., San Diego, CA, and London: Harcourt.
Arendt, Hannah (1996), *Love and Saint Augustine*, Chicago, IL, and London: University of Chicago Press.
Arendt, Hannah (1993), *Men in Dark Times*, San Diego, CA: Harcourt Brace.
Arendt, Hannah (1968), *The Origins of Totalitarianism*, San Diego, CA: Harvest Books.
Arendt, Hannah (2005), *The Promise of Politics*, New York: Schocken Books.
Arendt, Hannah (2007), *Reflections on Literature and Culture*, Stanford, CA: Stanford University Press.
Arendt, Hannah (2003), *Responsibility and Judgment*, New York: Schocken Books.
Arendt, Hannah (1965), *On Revolution*, New York: Viking Press.
Arendt, Hannah (1970), *On Violence*, New York: Harcourt, Brace and World.
Athanasiadis, Harris (2001), *George Grant and the Theology of the Cross: The Christian Foundations of his Thought*, Toronto and London: University of Toronto Press.
Athanasiadis, Harris (2006), "Waiting at the Foot of the Cross: The Spirituality of George Grant," in Ian Angus, Ron Dart, and Randy Peg Peters, eds., *Athens and Jerusalem: George Grant's Theology, Philosophy, and Politics*, Toronto and London: University of Toronto Press.

Augustine (1984), *Concerning the City of God against the Pagans*, trans. Henry Bettenson, London: Penguin Books.
Barth, Karl (1961), *Church Dogmatics*, III/4, Edinburgh: T and T Clark.
Barth, Karl (1975), *Church Dogmatics*, IV/1, Edinburgh: T and T Clark.
Beiner, Ronald (1996), "George Grant, Nietzsche, and the Problem of Post-Christian Theism," in Arthur Davis, ed., *George Grant and the Subversion of Modernity: Art, Philosophy, Politics, Religion, and Education*, Toronto: University of Toronto Press.
Bhagwati, Jagdish (2004), *In Defense of Globalization*, New York: Oxford University Press.
Bobbitt, Philip. (2002), *The Shield of Achilles: War, Peace, and the Course of History*, New York: Knopf.
Bobbitt, Philip (2008), *Terror and Consent: The Wars for the Twenty-First Century*, New York: Knopf.
Borgmann, Albert (1992), *Crossing the Postmodern Divide*, Chicago, IL, and London: University of Chicago Press.
Borgmann, Albert (1999), *Holding On to Reality: The Nature of Information at the Turn of the Millennium*, Chicago, IL, and London: University of Chicago Press.
Borgmann, Albert (2003), *Power Failure: Christianity in the Culture of Technology*, Grand Rapids, MI: Brazos.
Borgmann, Albert (2006), *Real American Ethics: Taking Responsibility for Our Country*, Chicago, IL, and London: University of Chicago Press.
Borgmann, Albert (1984), *Technology and the Character of Contemporary Life: A Philosophical Inquiry*, Chicago, IL, and London: University of Chicago Press.
Bowen-Moore, Patricia (1989), *Hannah Arendt's Philosophy of Natality*, London: Macmillan.
Brock, Brian (2010), *Christian Ethics in a Technological Age*, Grand Rapids, MI and Cambridge, UK: Eerdmans.
Browning, Don S. (2007), *Equality and the Family: A Fundamental, Practical Theology of Children, Mothers, and Fathers in Modern Societies*, Grand Rapids, MI, and Cambridge, UK: Eerdmans.
Browning, Don S. et al. (1997), *From Culture Wars to Common Ground: Religion and the American Family Debate*, Louisville, KY: Westminster John Knox Press.
Carr, Nicholas (2010), *The Shallows: What the Internet is Doing to Our Brains*, New York and London: Norton.
Cayley, David (1995), *George Grant in Conversation*, Concord, Ont: Anansi.
Challies, Tim (2011), *The Next Story: Life and Faith After the Digital Explosion*, Grand Rapids, MI: Zondervan.
Chiba, Shin (1995), "Hannah Arendt on Love and the Political: Love, Friendship, and Citizenship," *Review of Politics*, 57/3, pp. 505–535.
Christian, William (1978), "George and the Terrifying Darkness," in Larry Schmidt, ed., *George Grant in Process: Essays and Conversations*, Toronto: Anansi.

Christian, William, ed. (1996), *George Grant: Selected Letters*, Toronto and London: University of Toronto Press.

Davis, Arthur (1996), "Justice and Freedom: George Grant's Encounter with Martin Heidegger," in Arthur Davis, ed., *George Grant and the Subversion of Modernity: Art, Philosophy, Politics, Religion, and Education*, Toronto: University of Toronto Press.

Dawn, Marva J. (2006), *The Sense of the Call: A Sabbath Way of Life for Those Who Serve God, the Church, and the World*, Grand Rapids, MI, and Cambridge, UK: Eerdmans.

DeYoung, Rebecca Konyndyk (2009), *Glittering Vices: A New Look at the Seven Deadly Sins and their Remedies*, Grand Rapids, MI: Brazos.

Dooyeweerd, Herman (1979), *Roots of Western Culture: Pagan, Secular, and Christian Options*, Toronto: Wedge Publishing Foundation.

Ellul, Jacques (1985), *The Humiliation of the Word*, Grand Rapids, MI: Eerdmans.

Ellul, Jacques (1964), *The Technological Society*, New York: Vintage Books.

Estes, Douglas (2009), *SimChurch: Being the Church in the Virtual World*, Grand Rapids, MI: Zondervan.

Fairclough, Gordon (2009), "The Global Downturn Lands With a Zud on Mongolia's Nomads," *Wall Street Journal*, 20 April.

Forbes, Hugh Donald (2007), *George Grant: A Guide to his Thought*, Toronto and London: University of Toronto Press.

Fukuyama, Francis (2002), *Our Posthuman Future: Consequences of the Biotechnology Revolution*, New York: Farrar, Straus and Giroux.

Galbraith, John Kenneth (1998), *The Affluent Society*, Boston, MA, and New York: Houghton Mifflin.

Gottschall, Jonathan (2012), *The Storytelling Animal: How Stories Make Us Human*, Boston, MA, and New York: Houghton Mifflin Harcourt.

Grant, George (2012), "The Computer Does Not Impose on Us How It Should Be Used," in Arthur Davis and Henry Roper, eds., *Collected Works of George Grant: Vol. 4, 1970–1988*, Toronto and London: Toronto University Press.

Grant, George (2000), "The Concept of Nature and Supernature in the Theology of John Oman," in Arthur Davis and Peter Emberley, eds., *Collected Works of George Grant: Volume 1, 1933–50*, Toronto: University of Toronto Press.

Grant, George (1985), *English-Speaking Justice*, Notre Dame, IN: University of Notre Dame Press.

Grant, George (1998), "An Ethic of Community," in William Christian and Sheila Grant, eds., *The George Grant Reader*, Toronto and London: University of Toronto Press.

Grant, George (1998), "The Great Society," in William Christian and Sheila Grant, eds., *The George Grant Reader*, Toronto and London: University of Toronto Press.

Grant, George (1998), "Interview on Martin Heidegger," in William Christian and Sheila Grant, eds., *The George Grant Reader*, Toronto and London: University of Toronto Press.

Grant, George (2000), *Lament for a Nation: The Defeat of Canadian Nationalism*, Montreal and Kingston: McGill-Queen's University Press.

Grant, George (1995), *Philosophy in the Mass Age*, Toronto: University of Toronto Press.

Grant, George (2002), "St Augustine," in Arthur Davis, ed., *Collected Works of George Grant, Volume 2: 1951–1959*, Toronto: University of Toronto Press.

Grant, George (1969), *Technology and Empire: Perspectives on North America*, Toronto: Anansi.

Grant, George (1986), *Technology and Justice*, Notre Dame, IN: University of Notre Dame Press.

Grant, George (1995), *Time as History*, Toronto and London: University of Toronto Press.

Grant, George (1998), "The Triumph of the Will," in William Christian and Sheila Grant, eds., *The George Grant Reader*, Toronto and London: University of Toronto Press.

Grant, Sheila (1996), "George Grant and the Theology of the Cross," in Arthur Davis, ed., *George Grant and the Subversion of Modernity: Art, Philosophy, Politics, Religion, and Education*, Toronto: University of Toronto Press.

Gunton, Colin (1993), *The One, the Three, and the Many: God, Creation and the Culture of Modernity*, Cambridge, UK: Cambridge University Press.

Havers, Grant (2006), "Leo Strauss's Influence on George Grant," in Ian Angus, Ron Dart, and Randy Peg Peters, eds., *Athens and Jerusalem: George Grant's Theology, Philosophy, and Politics*, Toronto and London: University of Toronto Press.

Hayles, N. Katherine (1999), *How We Became Posthuman: Virtual Bodies in Cybernetics, Literature, and Informatics*, Chicago, IL, and London: University of Chicago Press.

Heaven, Edwin B., and Heaven, David R. (1978), "Some Influences of Simone Weil on George Grant's Silence," in Larry Schmidt, ed., *George Grant in Process: Essays and Conversations*, Toronto: Anansi.

Heaven, Ted (2006), "George Grant on Socrates and Christ," in Ian Angus, Ron Dart, and Randy Peg Peters, eds., *Athens and Jerusalem: George Grant's Theology, Philosophy, and Politics*, Toronto and London: University of Toronto Press.

Heidegger, Martin (1993), *Basic Writings*, San Francisco, CA: HarperCollins.

Heidegger, Martin (1991), *Nietzsche*, 4 vols., San Fancisco, CA: HarperCollins.

Heidegger, Martin (1976), "Only a God Can Save Us: Der Spiegel's Interview with Martin Heidegger," *Philosophy Today*, 20/4, Winter, pp. 267–285.

Heidegger, Martin (1977), *The Question Concerning Technology and Other Essays*, New York: Harper and Row.

Higgs, Eric, Light, Andrew, and Strong, David, eds. (2000), *Technology and the Good Life?*, Chicago, IL, and London: University of Chicago Press.

Hobbes, Thomas (1996), *Leviathan*, Oxford and New York: Oxford University Press.

Hogue, David A. (2003), *Remembering the Future, Imagining the Past: Story, Ritual, and the Human Brain*, Cleveland, OH: Pilgrim Press.
Hughes, James (2004), *Citizen Cyborg: Why Democratic Societies Must Respond to the Redesigned Human of the Future*, Cambridge, MA: Westview.
Huntington, Samuel P. (1997), *Clash of Civilizations and the Remaking of World Order*, New York: Touchstone.
Jackson, Maggie (2008), *Distracted: The Erosion of Attention and the Coming Dark Age*, Amherst, NY: Prometheus Books.
Jiggins, Alan (2007), "Book Review: *From Human to Posthuman*," *Science and Christian Belief*, 19/2.
Kaethler, Andrew (2009), *The Synthesis of Athens and Jerusalem: George Grant's Defense Against Modernity*, Saarbrücken, Germany: VDM Verlag.
Kass, Leon R. (2002), *Life, Liberty and the Defense of Dignity: The Challenge for Bioethics*, San Francisco, CA: Encounter Books.
Krell, David Farrell (1991), "Introduction to the Paperback Edition," in Martin Heidegger, *Nietzsche*, 4 vols., San Francisco, CA: HarperCollins.
Kurzweil, Ray (2005), *The Singularity is Near: When Humans Transcend Biology*, New York and London: Penguin Books.
Lampert, Laurence (1978), "The Uses of Philosophy in George Grant," in Larry Schmidt, ed., *George Grant in Process: Essays and Conversations*, Toronto: Anansi.
McCarroll, Pam (2006), "The Whole as Love," in Ian Angus, Ron Dart, and Randy Peg Peters, eds., *Athens and Jerusalem: George Grant's Theology, Philosophy, and Politics*, Toronto and London: University of Toronto Press.
MacIntyre, Alasdair (2007), *After Virtue: A Study in Moral Theory*, Notre Dame, IN: University of Notre Dame Press.
Macquarrie, John (1978), *Christian Hope*, New York: Seabury.
Moltmann, Jürgen (1993), *Theology of Hope: On the Ground and the Implications of Christian Eschatology*, Minneapolis, MN: Fortress Press.
Moravec, Hans (1988), *Mind Children: The Future of Robot and Human Intelligence*, Cambridge, MA, and London: Harvard University Press.
Moravec, Hans (1999), *Robot: Mere Machines to Transcendent Mind*, Oxford and New York: Oxford University Press.
Murdoch, Iris (1971), *An Accidental Man*, London: Penguin.
Murdoch, Iris (1993), *Metaphysics as a Guide to Morals*, London and New York: Penguin.
Murdoch, Iris (2001), *The Sovereignty of Good*, London and New York: Routledge.
Niebuhr, H. Richard (1970), *Radical Monotheism and Western Culture*, New York: Harper and Row.
Nietzsche, Friedrich (1974), *The Gay Science*, New York: Vintage Books.
Novak, Michael (1991), *The Spirit of Democratic Capitalism*, Lanham, NY: Madison Books.
O'Donovan, Joan E. (1984), *George Grant and the Twilight of Justice*, Toronto and London: University of Toronto Press.

O'Donovan, Oliver (2002), *Common Objects of Love: Moral Reflection and the Shaping of Community*, Grand Rapids, MI, and Cambridge, UK: Eerdmans.

O'Donovan, Oliver (1996), *The Desire of the Nations: Rediscovering the Roots of Political Theology*, Cambridge, UK: Cambridge University Press.

O'Donovan, Oliver (1986), *Resurrection and Moral Order: An Outline for Evangelical Ethics*, Grand Rapids, MI: Eerdmans.

O'Donovan, Oliver (2005), *The Ways of Judgment: The Bampton Lectures, 2003*, Grand Rapids, MI, and Cambridge, UK: Eerdmans.

Pannenberg, Wolfhart (1998), *Systematic Theology*, vol. 3, Grand Rapids, MI: Eerdmans.

Pieper, Josef (1997), *Faith Hope Love*, San Francisco, CA: Ignatius Press.

Pieper, Josef (2009), *Leisure, the Basis of Culture: The Philosophical Act*, San Francisco, CA: Ignatius Press, 2009.

Pitkin, Hanna Fenichel (1981), "Justice: On Relating Private and Public," *Political Theory*, 9/3, pp. 327–352.

Rawls, John (1996), *Political Liberalism*, New York: Columbia University Press.

Robinson, Marilynne (2004), *Gilead*, New York: Picador.

Robinson, Marilynne (2008), *Home*, New York: Picador.

Ross, Michael (2004), "Transcendence, Immanence, and Practical Deliberation in Simone Weil's Early and Middle Years," in E. Jane Doering and Eric O. Springstead, eds., *The Christian Platonism of Simone Weil*, Notre Dame, IN: University of Notre Dame Press.

Savulescu, Julian, and Bostrom, Nick, eds. (2009), *Human Enhancement*, Oxford and New York: Oxford University Press.

Schmidt, Larry (1978), "George Grant and the Problem of History," in Larry Schmidt, ed., *George Grant in Process: Essays and Conversations*, Toronto: Anansi.

Schmidt, Larry ed. (1978), *George Grant in Process: Essays and Conversations*, Toronto: Anansi.

Schmidt, Lawrence (1996), "George Grant on Simone Weil as Saint and Thinker," in Arthur Davis, ed., *George Grant and the Subversion of Modernity: Art, Philosophy, Politics, Religion, and Education*, Toronto: University of Toronto Press.

Schneider, John R. (2002), *The Good of Affluence: Seeking God in a Culture of Wealth*, Grand Rapids, MI, and Cambridge, UK: Eerdmans.

Scott, Peter Manley (2010), *Anti-Human Theology: Nature, Technology and the Postnatural*, London: SCM Press.

Seabright, Paul (2004), *The Company of Strangers: A Natural History of Economic Life*, Princeton, NJ, and Oxford: Princeton University Press.

Sitton, John F. (1987), "Hannah Arendt's argument for Council Democracy," *Polity*, 20/1, pp. 80–100.

Smith, Adam (1981), *An Inquiry into the Nature and Causes of the Wealth of Nations*, Indianapolis, IN: Liberty Fund.

Smith, Adam (1982), *The Theory of Moral Sentiments*, Indianapolis, IN: Liberty Fund.
Song, Robert (1997), *Christianity and Liberal Society*, Oxford: Clarendon Press.
Strauss, Leo (2000), *On Tyranny*, Chicago, IL, and London: University of Chicago Press.
Teilhard de Chardin, Pierre (1964), *The Future of Man*, London: Collins.
Teilhard de Chardin, Pierre (1959), *The Phenomenon of Man*, London: Collins.
Thayer, Ella Cheever (1879), *Wired Love: A Romance of Dots and Dashes*, New York: C.W. Carleton.
Turkle, Sherry (2011), *Alone Together: Why We Expect More from Technology and Less from Each Other*, New York: Basic Books.
Umar, Yusuf K. (1992), "The Philosophical Context of George Grant's Political Thought," in Yusuf K. Umar, ed., *George Grant and the Future of Canada* (Calgary: University of Calgary Press.
Verhey, Allen (2002), *Remembering Jesus: Christian Community, Scripture, and the Moral Life*, Grand Rapids, MI, and Cambridge, UK: Eerdmans.
Villa, Dana R. (1996), *Arendt and Heidegger: The Fate of the Political*, Princeton, NJ, and Chichester, UK: Princeton University Press.
von der Ruhr, Mario (2010), "Christianity and the Errors of Our Time: Simone Weil on Atheism and Idolatry," in A. Rebecca Rozelle-Stone and Lucian Stone, eds., *The Relevance of the Radical: Simone Weil 100 Years Later*, London and New York: Continuum.
von Mises, Ludwig (2007), *Human Action: A Treatise on Economics*, vol. 1, Indianapolis, IN: Liberty Fund.
Wallis, Jim (2005), *God's Politics: Why the Right Gets It Wrong and the Left Doesn't Get It*, New York: HarperCollins.
Wannenwetsch, Bernd (2004), *Political Worship: Ethics for Christian Citizens*, Oxford and New York: Oxford University Press.
Waters, Brent (2013), "Communication," in Brent Waters and Robert Song, eds., *The Authority of the Gospel: Essays in Honor of Oliver O'Donovan*, Grand Rapids, MI, and Cambridge, UK: Eerdmans.
Waters, Brent (2007), *The Family in Christian Social and Political Thought*, Oxford: Oxford University Press.
Waters, Brent (2006), *From Human to Posthuman: Christian Theology and Technology in a Postmodern World*, Aldershot, UK, and Burlington, VT: Ashgate.
Waters, Brent (2010), "The Incarnation and the Christian Moral Life," in F. LeRon Shults and Brent Waters, eds., *Christology and Ethics*, Grand Rapids, MI, and Cambridge, UK: Eerdmans.
Waters, Brent (2009). *This Mortal Flesh: Incarnation and Bioethics*, Grand Rapids, MI: Brazos.
Weil, Simone (1953), *Letter to a Priest*, London: Routledge and Kagan Paul.
Weil, Simone (2001), *Waiting for God*, New York: HarperCollins.

Wolf, Martin (2004), *Why Globalization Works*, New Haven, CT, and London: Yale University Press.

Zimmerman, Michael E. (1990), *Heidegger's Confrontation with Modernity: Technology, Politics, and Art*, Bloomington and Indianapolis, IN: Indiana University Press.

Index

action
    Arendt's notion of 59–63, 67–73, 131, 219
    judgment and 116–27, 129, 147, 155
alterity 198, 200–205, 207
Althusius, Johannes 12, 143–5, 228–9
amendment of life
    confession and 123, 126, 129, 148
    forgiveness and 133, 159, 181, 224–5
    judgment and 168, 170, 176
    liturgy and 107, 137, 179–80, 224
    remembrance and anticipation and 160, 174
    repentance and 158
anticipation and remembrance 135–6, 138, 150, 155, 157–8, 159–61, 165, 173–7, 179–80, 224
Aquinas, Thomas 128
Arendt, Hannah 2–3, 33–4, 57–80, 81–2, 85, 91, 93, 97–8, 100–101, 105–7, 122, 131–4, 137–41, 144–8, 164, 168, 181, 187–8, 211, 213, 215, 218–20, 222, 225–6, 227–8, 234
aristocracy 66, 71, 73
Aristotle 67
amor fati (love of fate) 23, 25, 27, 38–9, 51–2, 105
art 25–6, 30–32, 38, 41, 101
Augustine 59–61, 68–9, 98, 136, 142, 148, 169, 177
authority 22, 76–8, 117–21, 124, 129, 131–2, 137–40
autonomous agent/individual 29, 32, 63, 65, 70, 85, 96–8, 142–4, 149, 167, 177, 180, 218, 228
autonomy 3, 7, 9–10, 122, 145, 187, 193, 218
avatar 163, 192, 196, 201, 213

baptism 4, 161, 176–9, 182, 188, 201–2, 224, 229

Barth, Karl 114, 183, 237
beautiful, beauty 30, 35, 38–9, 44, 52–5, 66–7, 109, 122
Bodin, Jean 145
Borgmann, Albert 2–3, 33–4, 81–101, 105–7, 122, 158, 160, 168, 174, 175, 187–8, 217, 220–21, 226, 229, 235, 237

Chardin, Teilhard de 191
charity 161, 181, 184, 188, 229, 236–7
Christ, *see* Jesus
Christian theology, *see* theology
Christianity 37, 40, 45, 50–55, 61–3, 101, 110, 169
Christology, Christological 3, 78, 110–12, 116, 122, 126, 129, 138, 140
church
    baptism and 177, 201
    Christ and 79, 138, 177, 223
    Christian moral life and 127, 169
    focal community and 161, 220, 229
    gathering of Christians and 149, 224
    mortality of 62
    public association and 223, 226, 228
    second birth and 146, 177
    speech and 140
    suffering and 56
civil community
    Althusius' notion of 143–5
    O'Donovan's notion of 142–3
    the public and 222, 228
coercion
    authority and 76, 137
    forgiveness and 75–6, 133–4, 139
    judgment and 122
    public order and 70, 75, 79, 139, 145, 209, 218–19, 225–6
    speech and 140, 221, 225

commanding presence 89, 95, 160, 174–5, 201, 235–6
commodity 54, 84–7, 89–93, 95–6, 98, 99, 171, 175, 187
communication
    communication technology 7–16, 19, 86, 192
    exchange and 3–4, 68, 141–50, 155, 159–62, 167–84, 188, 195, 201–2, 223, 228–9, 234–9, 241–3
communitarian 63, 65, 94
compassion 73–4, 100
confession 3, 34, 56, 107, 109–11, 115–16, 126–7, 129, 131–3, 136, 147, 154, 158, 179–80, 188, 224
consumerism 37, 63, 67, 75, 85–6, 90, 92–3, 112, 150, 214
consumption 65, 67, 84–5, 89–9, 106, 148–9, 167, 175, 196, 213, 219, 228–9, 233–4, 236–9, 243
contrition 126, 131–3, 136, 147–8, 158, 170, 179–80, 224
created order 56, 78–9, 112–15, 129
creatio ex nihilo 67, 69, 139
cross, crucifixion 52–6, 78, 109–16, 122, 126, 129, 135, 138–9, 174, 176–7, 179
cybernetics 30–32, 40–42, 44, 48

Dawn, Martha 183
dead reckoning 135–6, 150, 152, 158–9, 168, 174, 183
deictic discourse 90–91
democracy 54, 71, 81–2, 91–3, 95, 97, 99
desire
    body and 12, 16, 67
    consumption and 233–4, 238, 243
    hope and 127
    love and 62
    ordering of 98–100, 107, 159, 161, 164, 178–9, 183–4, 188, 202, 220, 224, 239
    technology and 8–9, 17–18, 26, 58, 81, 164, 180, 193, 198, 206, 210–11
despair
    baptism and 177
    hope and 127–9, 134, 181, 224
    mortality and 58
    nihilism and 2, 23, 37, 44, 48, 152
    overcoming of 112
    sloth and 128, 181
destiny
    destiny of creation 113, 129, 183, 223
    destiny of liberalism 46, 49
    destiny of modernity 21, 29, 31–3, 41–4
    destiny of technology 29, 42, 44, 46–7, 49, 52, 63, 105, 243
    human 1, 35, 53, 63, 65–7, 79, 82, 112, 181
    nihilism and 30–31, 44
device paradigm 3, 83–5, 90–91, 94–101, 106, 187–8
DeYoung, Rebecca Konyndyk 242
digital generation 198
Dooyeweerd, Herman 178

ecclesiology 3, 56, 140, 223
Ellul, Jacques 82, 214
equality 70
    economic 88, 94, 98
    friendship and 72
    natural 44, 48, 70, 142
    opportunistic 48
    political 3, 64, 70–71, 73, 92–4
embodied, embodiment 11, 149, 166, 201
eschatological, eschatology 3, 55–6, 110, 115, 128, 135, 138, 148–51, 159–61, 168–9, 173–5, 180
eternal recurrence 24–7, 33, 38, 180
Eucharist 4, 101, 136, 159, 161, 176, 179–80, 182, 188, 206, 224, 229, 236
exaltation 55, 56, 78–9, 111–16, 126, 129, 138–40, 174–5, 179–80
exchange 3, 4
    communication and, *see* communication and exchange
    economic 171, 230–32
    information 9, 13, 19, 87, 141, 163, 166–7, 170, 193–4, 207, 232–3
    technoculture and 3, 160, 167–8, 181, 196

fabrication
    historicism and 19, 23, 27, 32, 37, 105
    nihilism and 22, 105

technology and 7, 17, 26, 44, 66–7, 76, 96, 98
faith
  Christian 4, 62–3, 110, 114, 128, 135–7, 158, 175, 178–9, 181, 183–4, 188, 194, 202, 224, 229, 240
  forgiveness and 79, 106
  religious 77, 131
family 93, 120, 142–4, 162, 165–6, 170–75, 221–3, 234–6
family meal 84, 90–91, 96, 100–101, 174–5, 221–2
focal community 94–101, 106, 160–61, 220–21, 226, 229, 235, 242–3
focal eschatology 175
focal practice 89–90, 95–101, 160, 174–5, 188, 221, 235–6
  sacrament as 3, 161, 177, 188, 202, 206, 224
focal remembrance 175
focal thing 3, 34, 89–96, 99–101, 107, 158, 160, 168, 174–6, 179, 187–8, 221, 235–7, 242
  church and 179, 182, 184, 201, 224, 229, 237
foreclosure 117–32, 147
forgiveness, forgiving 132–3, 155, 158, 170, 228
  Arendt's notion of 3, 34, 71–80, 81, 106, 131, 133–4, 138–9, 141, 146, 168, 213, 219
  Christian 78–9, 107, 111, 115–16, 123, 129, 137, 139–40, 147–8, 154, 159, 179–81, 184, 188, 219–20, 223–5, 235–6
  forgiveness in family 221–2
  political practice of 222–3, 225–6
friendship 59, 70, 80, 143

Gnostic 36, 55, 112, 129, 150–52, 155, 168
gospel 112, 146–7, 224, 235
Grant, George 2–3, 8, 20, 33, 35–56, 58, 81–2, 85, 91, 98, 100, 101, 105–7, 109–11, 114–16, 112, 126, 129, 145, 147, 151, 168, 170, 187, 218

Hegel, Georg Wilhelm Friedrich 35–7, 39, 41, 67, 145

Heidegger, Martin 2, 20–33, 36, 38–41, 44–5, 49, 56, 57–9, 66, 79–81, 83, 101, 105, 107, 187
Heaven, Ted 54
historicism 3, 18–20, 26, 29, 33–4, 36–7
  Arendt's view of 80, 141
  Grant's view of 3, 33–4, 37, 40–41, 44–6, 49–50, 56, 81, 109–10
  late modern 11, 18–21, 119, 123, 127–8, 142, 144, 146–7, 187, 210, 212
  technoculture and 21–2, 26–7, 29, 31, 105, 194
Hobbes, Thomas 145, 208, 229–30
Hogue, David 134, 136, 235
Holy Spirit 56, 77, 140, 148, 158, 169, 175, 177, 224, 243
homogenization 40, 42, 47, 56, 78
homogenous state 41, 46, 48–9, 52, 56, 63, 210, 218
hope, Christian 4, 68, 110–16, 127–9, 133, 148, 158, 177, 180–81, 184, 188, 224–5, 229
hyperactivity 86–8
hyperintelligence 86–8
hypermodernism, hypermodernity 83, 85, 106
hyperreality 86–8, 192

identity
  Christian 134, 169–70
  expression of 160, 163, 170, 192, 196–9
  formation of 134, 165–6, 169, 195–9
  identity of a people 142, 144
  nomadic 149, 164, 167, 193–6, 198
immortality
  mortality and 60–61, 219
  Overman and 28
  posthuman and 17, 112
  quest for 33–4, 61–4, 68, 109, 148
  technology and 67, 79, 187
Incarnation 3, 59–60, 111–15, 129, 138, 148, 159, 174, 177, 179
individualism 83, 85, 86, 90, 170, 187, 218
information
  narration and 3, 160–61, 164, 166–71, 173–8, 184, 188, 207, 209–17, 219, 222, 226, 229, 232

nomad and 167, 177, 187–8
information technology 8–10, 15–16, 86, 163, 192, 194, 214

Jackson, Maggie 195, 199
Jaspers, Karl 68
Jesus
   birth of 68
   Christians and 3, 135, 138, 161, 170, 174–7, 223–4
   crucifixion of, *see* cross, crucifixion
   exaltation of, *see* exaltation
   forgiveness and 71–2, 76, 78, 131, 138–9, 219
   incarnation of, *see* Incarnation
   remembrance of, *see* remembrance
resurrection of, *see* resurrection
joy 78, 88
judgment 72
   amendment of life and 168, 170, 174, 176, 179
   communication and 147
   confession and 116–27, 131, 147, 188
   Eucharist and 136, 179–80, 224
   forgiveness and 72–4, 78–9, 158–9, 170
   hope and 127–9
   information and 215–16
   punishment and, *see* punishment and judgment
justice 49–50
   forgiveness and 74–6, 138–40, 148
   late liberalism and 44, 46, 48–9
   technology and 40, 42, 44

Kant, Immanuel 76–9, 100, 106, 131, 137, 182, 219, 225
koinōnia 141–2, 149, 161, 171, 180, 201, 234

labor 64
   Arendt's view of 64–7, 80, 106, 140, 146
   Borgmann's view of 85–7, 93, 97
   specialization of 12, 144, 230–31
last man 2, 27, 37, 46, 48, 58, 105, 132
late liberal, late liberalism
   historicism and 46

   last man and 37–8
   politics of 144, 146, 209, 211, 218–19, 222
   technology and 47–9, 94, 213
leisure
   Borgmann's view of 85–7, 93
   Sabbath and 182–4, 200, 236–7
lifestyle 7–8, 10, 90–91, 213, 215
liturgy 107, 113, 129, 136, 146, 179–80, 182–3, 235
Locke, John 145
love
   Arendt's view of 60–62, 68, 72, 73, 80, 226
   Grant's view of 50–53, 55–6, 59
   virtue and 4, 158, 177, 179, 181, 184, 237
love of fate, *see amor fati*

MacIntyre, Alasdair 216–17
Macquarrie, John 127–8
Manichean 112, 212
mass culture 65
mastery 3, 7, 11, 17, 19, 24–32, 36–41, 45–53, 56, 58–9, 90, 92, 96, 106, 109, 149–50, 155, 164, 183, 214, 219, 242–3
metanoia, *see* repentance
mercy 73, 78–9, 111, 114, 119, 158, 225
mobility
   Christian 174
   nomadic 3, 29, 106, 120, 149, 163–4, 167–9, 181, 191, 193–5, 211, 214, 218
   technology and 7, 12–13, 15, 19, 84, 172, 192, 218
moral theology 109, 127, 129, 168, 188, 234
morality
   judgment and 118–19
mortality; *see also* immortality
   Christ and 148
   human finitude and 33, 39, 45, 53
   late modernity and 3, 20, 34, 50, 58, 106, 140, 187, 219
   natality and 60, 148, 152, 158, 188
   nomad and 150
   technology and 16–18

Murdoch, Iris 153–5, 157–8, 200–201, 203–5, 238–9, 241
mystery 198, 202

narration, narrative
   Christian and 136, 146–7, 150, 158–9
   identity and 134, 160
   information and, *see* information and narration
   natality and 219–26
   nihilism and 39–40, 44–5, 53–6, 105, 144, 152
   nomad and 149, 150
   politics and 4, 69, 71, 78–9
   ritual and 235–7
   technology and 32, 238
natality
   Arendt's notion of 3, 34, 57–60, 68, 70–71, 75–6, 79–81, 106, 131–4, 138–41, 146, 148, 187, 220, 225
   Christian notion of 140, 148, 150, 180, 188
   mortality and, *see* mortality and natality
   narration and, *see* narration and natality
natural law 56
the necessary and the good 45, 50, 52
necessity
   historical necessity 46–7, 51, 109, 112, 151
   natural necessity 12, 65, 69, 85
      constraint of 45–7, 50, 64–5, 105, 140
      technology and 17, 43, 70; *see also* technological necessity
Nietzsche, Friedrich 2, 20–29, 33, 36–9, 44–5, 49, 56–8, 67, 79–81, 105, 109, 122, 187
nihilism, nihilist 2–3, 18–34, 37–40, 44–52, 56–60, 80–81, 105, 109–10, 112, 119, 123, 127–9, 132, 141–4, 146–7, 152, 155, 168, 187, 194, 210, 212–13
nomad
   alterity and 200–202
   exchange and 181
   homelessness of 37, 122
   information and 164, 166–8, 171, 196, 217
   mobility of, *see* mobility, nomadic
   pilgrim and 149–50, 169–70, 173–6, 199
   politics and 212, 215
   space and 164, 167, 171, 194–6, 200
   technoculture and 3–4, 106, 120, 132, 155, 159–60, 173, 177–8, 187–8, 191–3

oasis 80, 81, 100, 137, 164, 182, 220, 226–8
O'Donovan, Joan 20, 55
O'Donovan, Oliver 11, 112, 123, 141–3
oikos 64–5, 67, 75, 106
oligarchy 71
opaque, opaqueness 198–202, 205
opinion 70, 117, 208, 209, 218

Paul, St 194
parousia 55, 78–9, 111, 113–15, 126–8, 135, 138, 148–50, 159, 161, 174–5, 179–80
penultimate 113–15, 128, 159, 177, 179
Pieper, Josef 178, 180–83, 200, 224, 236–7
pilgrim, pilgrimage 4, 136, 149–50, 159, 161, 169–70, 173–7, 179–81, 194, 199
Pitkin, Hanna Fenichel 75
pity 73–4, 239
place
   civil community and 143
   late moderns and 32–3
   narration and 165–6
   space and 3, 143, 149, 158, 160–73, 182, 188, 193–7, 201, 207, 210, 215, 226, 232, 242
   technology and 8–9, 11, 16–19, 84, 86, 120, 191, 193
   time and 11–16, 68, 89, 90
Plato, Platonism 115, 143
   Arendt's view of 59, 71
   Grant's view of 40, 44–5, 50–51, 54–5, 109–10, 115
   Murdoch's view of 154
   Nietzsche's view of 28, 57
plurality 71, 78–9, 143, 208

pluriform 145, 223, 224, 226
polis
   Arendt's view of 3, 57, 61–5, 69, 71, 75–6, 79–80, 105, 137–41, 146, 148
   church and 188, 226
political act
   Arendt's view of 61, 69–73, 78, 131, 140, 219
   technoculture and 212
political order 10, 34, 63, 67
   Christian thought and 79, 140, 223
   civil community and 144, 213
   focal community and 95
   forgiveness and 34, 71–3, 132
   nihilism and 19
   technoculture and 8, 10, 18, 49, 67, 94, 212
political realm, the political
   natality and 3, 70
   the private and 122, 141, 207, 209, 210, 212, 226, 227
   the public and 76, 79
   the social and 141, 144, 146
posthuman 1–2, 16–18, 20, 28, 112, 243
postmodern divide 81–106
privacy
   private space and 75, 93
   technology and 10, 122
private, the
   household and 64, 67, 75, 106
   the political and, *see* the political and the private
   privacy and, *see* privacy and private space
   the public and 227–9
progressivism 36, 63, 137, 168
promise, promising 34, 71; *see also* forgiveness
   uncertainty of 71–2, 133, 213, 219
providence 35–6, 50–52, 56, 109, 138–9, 168, 173
public, *see* the political and the public; the private and the public
punishment
   forgiveness and 72–5, 78, 132, 138–9
   judgment and 78–9, 117, 119–21, 124, 155

quality of life 48, 66–7, 162, 178

Rawls, John 48, 100, 145, 208
reconciliation 73
   communication and 180, 184
   forgiveness and 73–4, 133, 148, 205
   intergenerational 139–40
   promising and 131, 133
religion
   reason and 132, 138, 168
remembrance; *see also* anticipation and remembrance
   remembrance of Christ 3, 135, 179–80
repentance 3, 56, 158, 159
   Arendt's view of 34, 188
   baptism and 177–8
   confession and 126–7, 132, 147
   Eucharist and 179
   forgiveness and 133, 148, 170
   Grant's view of 116, 122
   liturgy and 107, 129, 137, 180, 224
resentment
   politics of 88, 217–18
   revenge and 210–19, 222, 224–5
   technoculture and 27
resurrection 55–6, 78–9, 110–15, 126, 129, 135, 138–9, 174–7, 179
revenge
   resentment and, *see* resentment and revenge
ritual 134, 136, 146, 224, 235–6
Robinson, Marilynne 155–8, 203–5, 239–41
Rousseau, Jean-Jacques 208
robot, robotic 17, 197–8, 204, 206, 207

sacrament 3, 97, 101, 159, 175, 179–80, 182, 201, 236
Sabbath 3, 4, 161, 176, 182–4, 188, 206, 229, 236–7
science 37, 42
   technology and 26, 30–31, 35, 40
Seabright, Paul 232
second birth 3, 65, 68, 80, 106–7, 131, 141, 146, 148, 176–7, 188, 227
self-mastery 24, 26–8, 38, 47
Smith, Adam 230–31
social, the, *see* the political and the social

social network 163, 173, 192, 196–8, 204
soteriology 55–6
space, *see* place and space
speech
　political 4, 64, 68, 70, 75–7, 79, 81, 97, 106, 219, 227
　power and 213, 220, 226, 228
　violence and 70, 97, 134, 139–40, 221, 225
story; *see also* narration
　identity formation and 134
　place and 32
　political community and 69
Strauss, Leo 38, 41
suffering 70
　alleviation of 73, 111
　Christ's 52, 55, 109, 110, 112–16, 126
　love and 39, 51
　necessity and 53
sullen, sullenness
　hyperreality and 87–8
　late modernity and 90, 93, 98, 122
　public life and 99
　resentment and 88, 211, 213, 217

technē 7, 26, 29, 31, 41
technique 11, 30, 40, 48, 158, 214, 242–3
technoculture
　alterity and 202
　authority and 132
　Christian resistance of 146–7, 176–84
　communication and 172
　community and 161, 225–6
　emergence of 7–11
　focal thing and 174–5, 188, 236
　historicism and 19–21, 105, 120, 141, 145
　hyperreality and 87
　late modernity and 2–3, 7
　moral engagement with 33, 107, 109, 129, 134, 137, 155, 158, 168
　mortality and 140
　narration and 160, 167–8, 217
　nomadic life and 4, 32, 120, 155, 159, 174, 193–5
　political ordering and 146, 208–19
　space and 163–4, 167

technological civilization 52, 54; *see also* technoculture
technological enframement 2, 31–3, 58, 66, 80, 105, 107
technological necessity 47–50
teleology 22, 55, 78, 95, 125, 128, 148, 149, 159, 160, 168, 169, 173–4, 178, 180, 210
theology 3, 51, 54, 59, 101, 109, 111, 131, 134, 139, 168
　theology of glory 52, 55, 114–16, 122
　theology of the cross 51–2, 55, 109, 122
totalitarian, totalitarianism 63, 75, 77, 94, 143, 218
trade 12, 13, 163, 230–31
tradition 22, 51, 55, 76, 81, 89, 93, 95, 124, 142, 145, 165, 175, 227, 235
transparency 196, 201–2
Turkle, Sherry 197–9, 206

Übermensch (Overman) 2, 27–9, 38, 57–8, 105
ugly 38, 44, 67, 109, 122
Umar, Yusuf 54–5

vengeance
　cycle of 72–7, 122, 131–2, 139, 148, 168
　nihilist and 27
　Overman and 27
violence
　authority and 76–7
　compassion and 73–4
　mastery and 37, 46, 106
　nihilism and 22, 27, 33, 38, 46
　the private and 64, 67
　speech and 70, 139, 225
virtual community 87–8
virtual immortality 17
virtual reality 86, 192, 242
virtual space 163–4, 166, 180, 191, 193, 195–9, 201, 204, 232–4
vita activa 61, 63, 69
vita contemplativa 61, 63

Weil, Simone 50, 51, 55, 110, 114, 199–200

will to live 57
will to power 2, 24–8, 30, 33, 38, 39, 46, 49–53, 57–8, 63, 79, 105, 112, 114, 121, 129, 138, 140, 152, 183, 187, 210, 212–13, 216, 218–19
will to will 24, 38, 54, 58, 60, 114
work 62–4
   art and 30–31
   labor and 64–7, 93, 106, 122
   leisure and 85–7, 122
   politics and 68–70, 75, 106, 140
   technology and 7, 9, 30, 80
worship 146, 170, 175, 224
   communication and 235–6
   Sabbath and 182–3
   simulated 173

Zimmerman, Michael 30–31

Lightning Source UK Ltd.
Milton Keynes UK
UKHW022057130121
377012UK00004B/30